When should I travel to get the best airfare?
Where do I go for answers to my travel questions?
What's the best and easiest way to plan and book my trip?

frommers.travelocity.com

Frommer's, the travel guide leader, has teamed up with **Travelocity.com**, the leader in online travel, to bring you an in-depth, easy-to-use resource designed to help you plan and book your trip online.

At **frommers.travelocity.com**, you'll find free online updates about your destination from the experts at Frommer's plus the outstanding travel planning and purchasing features of Travelocity.com. Travelocity.com provides reservations capabilities for 95 percent of all airline seats sold, more than 47,000 hotels, and over 50 car rental companies. In addition, Travelocity.com offers more than 2,000 exciting vacation and cruise packages. Travelocity.com puts you in complete control of your travel planning with these and other great features:

> **Expert travel guidance from Frommer's** - over 150 writers reporting from around the world!

> **Best Fare Finder** - an interactive calendar tells you when to travel to get the best airfare

> **Fare Watcher** - we'll track airfare changes to your favorite destinations

> **Dream Maps** - a mapping feature that suggests travel opportunities based on your budget

> **Shop Safe Guarantee** - 24 hours a day / 7 days a week live customer service, and more!

Whether traveling on a tight budget, looking for a quick weekend getaway, or planning the trip of a lifetime, Frommer's guides and Travelocity.com will make your travel dreams a reality. You've bought the book, now book the trip!

Also available from Hungry Minds, Inc.:

Beyond Disney: The Unofficial Guide to Universal, Sea World, and the Best of Central Florida

Inside Disney: The Incredible Story of Walt Disney World and the Man Behind the Mouse

Mini Las Vegas: The Pocket-Sized Unofficial Guide to Las Vegas

Mini-Mickey: The Pocket-Sized Unofficial Guide to Walt Disney World

The Unofficial Guide to Bed & Breakfasts in California

The Unofficial Guide to Bed & Breakfasts in New England

The Unofficial Guide to Bed & Breakfasts in the Northwest

The Unofficial Guide to Bed & Breakfasts in the Southeast

The Unofficial Guide to Branson, Missouri

The Unofficial Guide to California with Kids

The Unofficial Guide to Chicago

The Unofficial Guide to Cruises

The Unofficial Guide to Disneyland

The Unofficial Guide to Disneyland Paris

The Unofficial Guide to Florida with Kids

The Unofficial Guide to the Great Smoky and Blue Ridge Region

The Unofficial Guide to Golf Vacations in the Eastern U.S.

The Unofficial Guide to Hawaii

The Unofficial Guide to Las Vegas

The Unofficial Guide to London

The Unofficial Guide to Miami and the Keys

The Unofficial Guide to the Mid-Atlantic with Kids

The Unofficial Guide to New England and New York with Kids

The Unofficial Guide to New Orleans

The Unofficial Guide to New York City

The Unofficial Guide to Paris

The Unofficial Guide to San Francisco

The Unofficial Guide to Skiing in the West

The Unofficial Guide to the Southeast with Kids

The Unofficial Guide to Walt Disney World

The Unofficial Guide to Walt Disney World for Grown-Ups

The Unofficial Guide to Walt Disney World with Kids

The Unofficial Guide to Washington, D.C.

The Unofficial Guide to the World's Best Diving Vacations

U the nofficial Guide® to New Orleans

3rd Edition

Eve Zibart
with Bob Sehlinger

Hungry Minds™

Best-Selling Books • Digital Downloads • e-Books • Answer Networks • e-Newsletters
Branded Web Sites • e-Learning

New York, NY ◆ Cleveland, OH ◆ Indianapolis, IN

Please note that price fluctuate in the course of time, and travel information changes under the impact of many factors that influence the travel industry. We therefore suggest that you write or call ahead for confirmation when making your travel plans. Every effort has been made to ensure the accuracy of information throughout this book and the contents of this publication are believed correct at the time of printing. Nevertheless, the publishers cannot accept responsibility for errors or omissions or for changes in details given in this guide or for the consequences of any reliance on the information provided by the same. Assessments of attractions and so forth are based upon the author's own experience and therefore, descriptions given in this guide necessarily contain an element of subjective opinion, which may not reflect the publisher's opinion or dictate a reader's own experience on another occasion. Readers are invited to write to the publisher with ideas, comments, and suggestions for future editions

Your safety is important to us, so we encourage you to stay alert and be aware of your surroundings. Keep a close eye on cameras, purses, and wallets, all favorite targets of thieves and pickpockets.

Published by Hungry Minds, Inc.
909 Third Avenue
New York, New York 10022

Produced by Menasha Ridge Press

ISBN 0-7645-6214-2

ISSN 1096-5211

Manufactured in the United States of America

10 9 8 7 6 5 4 3 2

Third edition

Contents

List of Illustrations

About the Authors

Eve Zibart is a native of Nashville who began her career as a reporter at age 17 at *The Tennessean* (Nashville). She moved to Washington and *The Washington Post* in 1977 and has served as critic, editor and columnist at various times for "Style," "Weekend," "TV," "Metro," and "Magazine" sections. For the past decade, she has roamed Washington's restaurants, carryouts, bars, and nightclubs, with the occasional foray into museums and legitimate theater. In addition to her *Post* columns, Eve has written or co-written eight books and regularly appears in a variety of lifestyle magazines. Despite God's repeated physical admonishments, Eve continues to play a variety of sports, split her own firewood and haul rocks into what she hopes will become a Japanese garden within her lifetime.

Bob Sehlinger is the creator of the *Unofficial Guide* series and author of more than two dozen travel guides.

Chris Rose is a columnist for the *New Orleans Times-Picayune,* covering events and personalities in and around the city. He is also the New Orleans correspondent for *People* magazine. He has contributed to *Playboy, Smoke,* the *Gavin Report,* and various other publications. He has a young wife, Kelly, and a younger child, Kate, yet his competent pool skills are testimony to a lingering fascination with the intriguing nightlife of the town he calls home.

Tom Fitzmorris is New Orleans' leading restaurant critic. He was born on Mardi Gras and has never left New Orleans for more than three weeks at a time. Tom's passion for eating began with his mother's classic Creole cooking and grows in intensity even now. Writing about restaurants is the focus of Tom's journalistic career. He published his first restaurant review in 1972 and has written one at least weekly ever since. But he's best known for "The Food Show," a two-hour daily talk show on WSMB radio that has entertained and informed listeners since 1988. He started *The New Orleans MENU,* a review of New Orleans dining, in 1977. The Internet version of *MENU, The New Orleans Menu Daily,* began in 1997. Tom is married to the best mother in the world, Mary Ann Connell Fitzmorris. They have a son, Jude, and a daughter, Mary Leigh, and live in the countryside north of New Orleans with a dog, six cats, and several hundred bats. Some terrific, meaty bolete mushrooms grow there.

Acknowledgments

Scores of New Orleanians were gracious enough to talk about their city, both on and off the record, and I thank them all, especially Lea Sinclair and Diane Genre.

Everybody needs a place to hang out: Thanks to Jeanine, Julie and Kim (we won't forget the *real* Old Absinthe), Tiffany, Michael, Mark, Viva, the International House, St. James, and Char Thian from the Ritz-Carlton.

Very special thanks to tour guide and amateur historian Noah Robert for more good stories than I could fit in; to Grace Rogers for taking on the chauffeuring duty; and to Tom Fitzmorris, Chris "Jr. Nightlife" Rose and F. Lynne Bachleda for their contributions.

As always, thanks to Bob, Molly, Gabbie, Carolyn, and Annie for pushing forward and reading behind.

My waistline thanks (more or less) Simone Rathlé, Alexandra Stafford and Raymond Rathlé; JoAnn Clevenger and Chris Brown; and—always and everywhere—Margi Smith and Joe Hemingway, the best dinner companions any traveler could have. A dozen cities and counting . . .

—*Eve Zibart*

Let the Good Times Roll

A fine spring evening in Jackson Square. As the sun gradually lowers, the shadows of St. Louis Cathedral and the Cabildo stretch across the flagstones, brushing the tables of the tarot readers; young couples with souvenir hurricane cups stand around a man playing saxophone, its case open in front of him.

And there it is, the mystique of New Orleans in a single vignette: empire, religion, music, voodoo, and alcohol. *Laissez les bons temps rouler* —let the good times roll.

And yet there are some who say that what passes for "good times" is rolling too long and too strong these days. There is a battle raging for the soul of New Orleans, most visibly in and around the French Quarter; and while it is not a contest between good and evil, at least not in the classical sense, it will in the next few years determine whether the character of this unique city is lost, restored, or permanently altered.

That the character of the Vieux Carré has already changed is clear from a few hours' acquaintance. An odd confluence of factors—renovation of some older houses into upscale condominiums and the gradual decline of others; a much-publicized increase in street crime and heavy investment by outside commercial interests into redevelopment, frequently uprooting smaller local firms—has reduced the number of the French Quarter's permanent residents from about 15,000 a generation ago to fewer than 3,300 today. And of those, a dispiriting percentage are derelicts, street kids, and drunks, all looking for handouts and all with their vanished ambitions etched in their faces.

A high tide of cheap-souvenir and T-shirt shops has swamped Bourbon Street, and glossy, private club–style strip joints, several bankrolled from out of town, are squeezing out the older, more authentic burlesque houses. At the same time, the number of bars offering heavily amplified rock and blues music, their doors open and competing for volume dominance, makes the retreat of jazz and Dixieland more obvious. Sit-down bars that specialized in classic New Orleans cocktails such as hurricanes and Sazeracs, touristy though they may have seemed before, now appear almost quaintly sophisticated in the face of carryout frozen margarita and daiquiri counters with their crayon-colored mixes spinning in laundromat-like rows.

Yes, souvenir shops are brighter than bars, but they certainly have less character. Sure, live blues is great, but it's more Texan than Louisianan. Mardi Gras, once the most elegant and elaborate of festivities, has become the world's largest frat party, its traditions degraded, its legends distorted, and its principal actors, the Grand Krewes, overshadowed by the mobs of drinking and disrobing "spectators." Several of the oldest and most prestigious krewes have withdrawn from the celebration, and travel agents say as many residents flee New Orleans during Carnival as tourists come in.

Altogether, New Orleans is in danger of becoming a parody of itself, a mini-Epcot or Busch Gardens' Old Country simulacrum. The posters and prints feature wrought-iron fences, but the real courtyards are gated and locked tight. Steamboats play recorded music intentionally out of tune— "old-fashioned" in the hokiest sense. Self-appointed tour guides mix all their legends together: the statue in St. Anthony's Garden behind St. Louis Cathedral, memorializing French sailors who volunteered as nurses during a yellow fever epidemic, has even been explained as "the Mardi Gras Jesus" because the statue's outstretched hands are supposedly reaching for throws! And now life imitates, well, imitation: a 100-acre theme park called Jazzland is under construction only a few miles out of town.

And yet for all the tawdriness and commercialization, one cannot help falling under the city's spell. It is a foreign country within American borders, not merely a multilingual hodgepodge like Miami or New York, but a true Creole society blended through centuries. It is Old South in style, New South in ambition. It has a natural beauty that refutes even the most frivolous of franchised structures, a tradition of craftsmanship and even luxury that demands aesthetic scrutiny and surrender, and a flair for almost exquisite silliness—like those Jackson Square psychics with their Pier 1 Imports turbans—that keeps all New Orleanians young. Fine arts, fashionable cuisine, voodoo, vampires, and Mardi Gras. It's all muddled up, sometimes enchanting, sometimes infuriating.

We hope to help you find the real New Orleans, the old and gracious one, that is just now in the shadow of the Big Too-Easy. We want to open your heart, not your wallet. We think you should leave Bourbon Street behind and visit City Park, one of the finest and most wide-ranging public facilities in the United States. We want you to see Longue Vue House as well as St. Louis Cemetery. We'd like you to admire not only the townhouses of Royal Street and the mansions of St. Charles but the warehouses and row houses of the Arts District— the combined Greenwich Village and TriBeCa of New Orleans. We hope you'll walk Chartres Street in the evening shade, watch the mighty Mississippi churn contemptuously past the man-made barriers, and smell the chicory, whiskey, and pungent swamp water all mixed together the way Andy Jackson and Jean Lafitte might have the night before the great battle.

So get ready, get set, go. *Laissez les bons temps rouler!*

About This Guide

HOW COME "UNOFFICIAL"?

Most guides to New Orleans tout the well-known sights, promote the local restaurants and hotels indiscriminately, and leave out a lot of good stuff. This one is different.

Instead of pandering to the tourist industry, we'll tell you if the food is bad at a well-known restaurant, we'll complain loudly about high prices, and we'll guide you away from the crowds and traffic for a break now and then.

Visiting New Orleans requires wily strategies not unlike those used in the sacking of Troy. We've sent in a team of evaluators who toured each site, ate in the city's best restaurants, performed critical evaluations of its hotels, and visited New Orleans' wide variety of nightclubs. If a museum is boring, or standing in line for two hours to view a famous attraction is a waste of time, we say so—and, in the process, hopefully make your visit more fun, efficient, and economical.

CREATING A GUIDEBOOK

We got into the guidebook business because we were unhappy with the way travel guides make the reader work to get any usable information. Wouldn't it be nice, we thought, if we were to make guides that are easy to use?

Most guidebooks are compilations of lists. This is true regardless of whether the information is presented in list form or artfully distributed through pages of prose. There is insufficient detail in a list, and prose can present tedious helpings of nonessential or marginally useful information. Not enough wheat, so to speak, for nourishment in one instance, and too much chaff in the other. Either way, these types of guides provide little more than departure points from which readers initiate their own quests.

Many guides are readable and well researched, but they tend to be difficult to use. To select a hotel, for example, a reader must study several pages of descriptions with only the boldface hotel names breaking up large blocks of text. Because each description essentially deals with the same variables, it is difficult to recall what was said concerning a particular hotel.

Readers generally must work through all the write-ups before beginning to narrow their choices. The presentation of restaurants, nightclubs, and attractions is similar except that even more reading is usually required. To use such a guide is to undertake an exhaustive research process that requires examining nearly as many options and possibilities as starting from scratch. Recommendations, if any, lack depth and conviction. These guides compound rather than solve problems by failing to narrow travelers' choices down to a thoughtfully considered, well-distilled, and manageable few.

How Unofficial Guides Are Different

Readers care about the authors' opinions. The authors, after all, are supposed to know what they are talking about. This, coupled with the fact that the traveler wants quick answers (as opposed to endless alternatives), dictates that authors should be explicit, prescriptive, and above all, direct. The authors of the *Unofficial Guide* try to do just that. They spell out alternatives and recommend specific courses of action. They simplify complicated destinations and attractions and allow the traveler to feel in control in the most unfamiliar environments. The objective of the *Unofficial Guide* authors is not to give the most information or all of the information, but to offer the most useful information.

An *Unofficial Guide* is a critical reference work; it focuses on a travel destination that appears to be especially complex. Our authors and research team are completely independent from the attractions, restaurants, and hotels we describe. *The Unofficial Guide to New Orleans* is designed for individuals and families traveling for the fun of it, as well as for business travelers and conventioneers, especially those visiting the Crescent City for the first time. The guide is directed at value-conscious, consumer-oriented adults who seek a cost-effective, though not Spartan, travel style.

Special Features

The *Unofficial Guide* offers the following special features:

- Friendly introductions to New Orleans' most fascinating neighborhoods and districts.
- "Best of" listings giving our well-qualified opinions on things ranging from raw oysters to blackened snapper, 4-star hotels to 12-story views.
- Listings that are keyed to your interests, so you can pick and choose.
- Advice to sight-seers on how to avoid the worst of the crowds, and advice to business travelers on how to avoid traffic and excessive costs.

- Recommendations for lesser-known sights that are away from the French Quarter, but are no less worthwhile.

- A zone system and maps to make it easy to find places you want to go to and avoid places you don't.

- Expert advice on avoiding New Orleans' notorious street crime.

- A hotel chart that helps you narrow down your choices fast, according to your needs.

- Shorter listings that include only those restaurants, clubs, and hotels we think are worth considering.

- A table of contents and detailed index to help you find things fast.

- Insider advice on the French Quarter, Mardi Gras, Jazz Fest, best times of day (or night) to go places, and our secret weapon—New Orleans' streetcar system.

What you won't get:

- Long, useless lists where everything looks the same.

- Information that gets you to your destination at the worst possible time.

- Information without advice on how to use it.

How This Guide Was Researched and Written

Although many guidebooks have been written about New Orleans, very few have been evaluative. Some guides come close to regurgitating the hotels' and tourist office's own promotional material. In preparing this work, nothing was taken for granted. Each hotel, restaurant, shop, and attraction was visited by a team of trained observers who conducted detailed evaluations and rated each according to formal criteria. Team members conducted interviews with tourists of all ages to determine what they enjoyed most and least during their New Orleans visit.

While our observers are independent and impartial, they do not claim to have special expertise. Like you, they visited New Orleans as tourists or business travelers, noting their satisfaction or dissatisfaction.

The primary difference between the average tourist and the trained evaluator is the evaluator's skills in organization, preparation, and observation. The trained evaluator is responsible for much more than simply observing and cataloging. Observer teams use detailed checklists to analyze hotel rooms, restaurants, nightclubs, and attractions. Finally, evaluator ratings and observations are integrated with tourist reactions and the opinions of patrons for a comprehensive quality profile of each feature and service.

In compiling this guide, we recognize that a tourist's age, background, and interests will strongly influence his or her taste in New Orleans' wide array of attractions and will account for a preference for one sight or museum over another. Our sole objective is to provide the reader with sufficient description, critical evaluation, and pertinent data to make knowledgeable decisions according to individual tastes.

LETTERS, COMMENTS, AND QUESTIONS FROM READERS

We expect to learn from our mistakes, as well as from the input of our readers, and to improve with each new book and edition. Many of those who use the *Unofficial Guides* write to us asking questions, making comments, or sharing their own discoveries or lessons learned in New Orleans. We appreciate all such input, both positive and critical, and encourage our readers to continue writing. Readers' comments and observations will be frequently incorporated in revised editions of the *Unofficial Guide,* and will contribute immeasurably to its improvement.

How to Write the Authors:

Eve and Bob
The Unofficial Guide to New Orleans
P.O. Box 43673
Birmingham, AL 35243

When you write, be sure to put your return address on your letter as well as on the envelope—sometimes envelopes and letters get separated. And remember, our work takes us out of the office for long periods of time, so forgive us if our response is delayed.

Reader Survey

At the back of the guide you will find a short questionnaire that you can use to express opinions about your New Orleans visit. Clip the questionnaire out along the dotted line and mail it to the above address.

"Inside" New Orleans for Outsiders

It's a funny thing about New Orleans travel guides: most of them tell you too much, and a few tell you too little. That's because New Orleans is such a complex city, so ornate and enveloping and layered with history and happenstance, that it's hard to stop acquiring good stories and passing them on.

But statistics show that the majority of visitors to New Orleans stay only three or four days—and frequently that even includes spending part of the time in seminars or conventions. How much can you squeeze into a long weekend? How much do you want to see? Walking tours of the French Quarter and Garden District often point to buildings with obscure claims to fame and with only partial facades to their name (and no admission offered in any case). Walking tours of the farther reaches are often redundant; even the keenest architecture critic will probably lose heart trying to cover the third or fourth neighborhood in 48 hours. Some tour books either stint on shopping or endorse every dealer in town; some forget any fine arts or theater productions at all, as if Bourbon Street bars were the sole form of nightlife available in the city. Some are too uncritical, some too "insider." Some have all the right stuff, but are poorly organized; some are easy to read, but boring.

So, hard as it is to limit this book, we have—sort of. We have tried to make the do-it-yourself walking tours short enough that they won't exhaust you, but full enough of sights and stories to give you the city's true flavor. (And if you want to do more, we'll tell you how.) We've tried to take things easy, but we don't forgive exploitation or boost unworthy distractions. If it isn't fun, informative, or accurate, we don't want you to go. If there's a better alternative, we want you to know. We don't make purely philosophical judgments—some people believe in the supernatural, some don't—but we do try to evaluate in a dispassionate fashion what you get for your money. We hope to keep the quality of your visit high, and the irritation quotient low.

We've also divided the attractions up in various ways, often overlapping, so you can pick out the ones you'd most enjoy: In "Planning Your Visit," we suggested attractions by type—family style, musical, festive, spooky, and so on. The neighborhood profiles in Part One are more strictly geographical descriptions to help you get your bearings and focus your interests, while the zone maps are designed to help you with the logistics of arranging accommodations and sight-seeing. More elaborate walking tours are laid out for you in "Sight-Seeing and Tours," and particular museums and exhibits in each zone are explored in more detail and rated for interest by age group in the chapter entitled "New Orleans' Attractions."

For those who don't wish to do-it-themselves at all, we have listed a number of commercial and customized tours tailored to almost any interest, also in "Sight-Seeing and Tours."

In addition, even granting that your time will be tight, we have included a list of opportunities to exercise or play. That's partly because we at the *Unofficial Guides* try to keep up with our workouts when we're on the road, and also because you may be visiting old friends, old teammates, and tennis players. Beyond that, although you may not think you'll want to make time for a run or ride, experience has taught us that sight-seeing and shopping can be exhausting, make you stiff, make you long for the outdoors—and New Orleans has some of the prettiest outdoors you'll ever see.

Finally, for visitors lucky enough to have more than a couple of days to spend, or who are returning for a second or third go-round, we have sketched out a few excursions outside the city.

Please do remember that prices and hours change constantly. We have listed the most up-to-date information we can get, but it never hurts to double-check times in particular (if prices of attractions change, it is generally not by much). And although usually a day or so is all the advance notice you need to get into any attraction in New Orleans, if your party is large, you might try calling ahead.

How Information Is Organized: By Subject and by Geographic Zones

In order to give you fast access to information about the best of New Orleans, we've organized the material in several formats.

Hotels   Since most people visiting New Orleans stay in one hotel for the duration of their trip, we have summarized our coverage of hotels in charts, maps, ratings, and rankings that allow you to focus quickly your decision-making process. We do not go on page after page, describing lobbies and rooms which, in the final analysis, sound much the same. Instead, we concentrate on the specific variables that differentiate one hotel from another: location, size, room quality, services, amenities, and cost.

Entertainment and Nightlife   Visitors frequently try several different clubs or nightspots during their stay. Because clubs and nightspots, like restaurants, are usually selected spontaneously after arriving in New Orleans, we believe detailed descriptions are warranted. The best nightspots and lounges in New Orleans are profiled by category under Nightlife (see pages 168–201).

Restaurants   We provide plenty of detail when it comes to restaurants. Since you will probably eat a dozen or more restaurant meals during your stay, and since not even you can predict what you might be in the mood for on Saturday night, we provide detailed profiles of the best restaurants in and around New Orleans (see pages 304–377).

Geographic Zones   Once you've decided where you're going, getting there becomes the issue. To help you do that, we have divided the city into geographic zones:

Zone 1   French Quarter

Zone 2   Central Business District

Zone 3   Uptown below Napoleon

Zone 4   Uptown above Napoleon

Zone 5   Downtown/St. Bernard

Zone 6   Mid-City/Gentilly

Zone 7   Lakeview/West End/Bucktown

Zone 8   New Orleans East

Zone 9   Metairie below Causeway

Zone 10 Metairie above Causeway/Kenner/Jefferson Highway

Zone 11 West Bank

Zone 12 North Shore

All profiles of hotels, restaurants, and nightspots include zone numbers. If you are staying at the Royal Orleans, for example, and are interested in Creole restaurants within walking distance, scanning the restaurant profiles for restaurants in Zone 1 (the French Quarter) will provide you with the best choices.

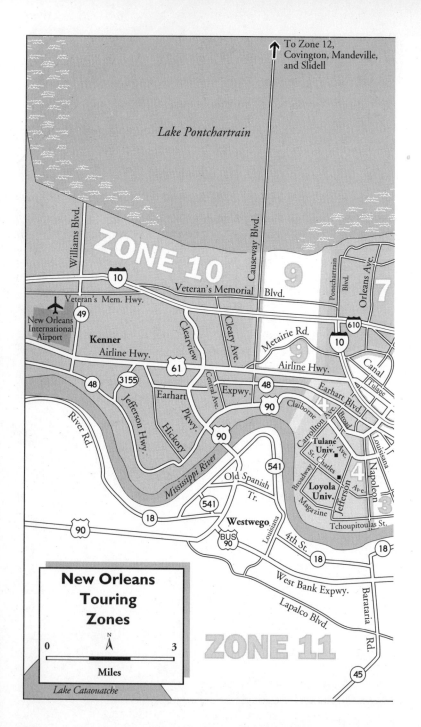

To Zone 12,
Covington, Mandeville,
and Slidell

Lake Pontchartrain

ZONE 10

Veteran's Memorial Blvd.

Veteran's Mem. Hwy.

New Orleans
International
Airport

Kenner
Airline Hwy.

Williams Blvd.

Clearview

Cleary Ave.

Causeway Blvd.

Metairie Rd.

Pontchartrain Blvd.

Orleans Ave.

Airline Hwy.

Canal

Tulane

Earhart Blvd.

Jefferson Hwy.

River Rd.

Mississippi River

Earhart Expwy.

Central Ave.

Hickory

Pkwy.

Claiborne

Carrollton Ave.

Broad

Louisiana

**Tulane
Univ.**

St. Charles Ave.

Broadway

**Loyola
Univ.**

Magazine

Jefferson Ave.

Napoleon Ave.

Old Spanish Tr.

Westwego

Louisiana

4th St.

Tchoupitoulas St.

West Bank Expwy.

Lapalco Blvd.

Barataria Rd.

ZONE 11

**New Orleans
Touring
Zones**

N

0   3

Miles

Lake Cataouatche

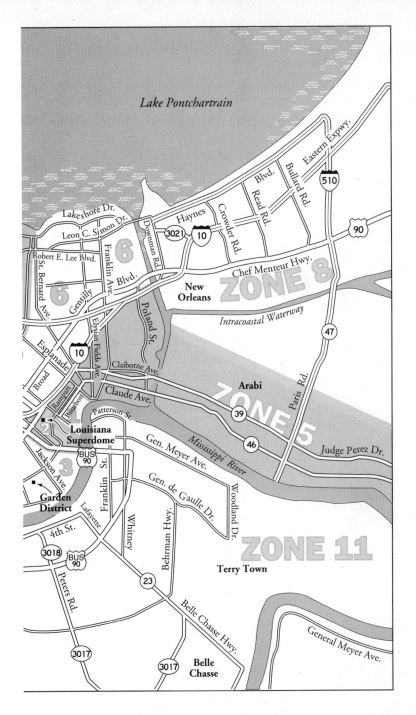

Lake Pontchartrain

Eastern Expwy.

510

Bullard Rd.

Read Rd.

Blvd.

90

Lakeshore Dr.

Leon C. Simon Dr.

Haynes

Crowder Rd.

3021

10

Downman Rd.

Robert E. Lee Blvd.

6

Franklin Ave.

St. Bernard Ave.

6

Gentilly

Blvd.

Poland St.

New
Orleans

Chef Menteur Hwy.

ZONE 8

Intracoastal Waterway

47

Esplanade

10

Elysian Fields Ave.

Claiborne Ave.

Broad

Claude Ave.

Arabi

Paris Rd.

Judge Perez Dr.

Rampart

Bourbon

Patterson St.

ZONE 5

39

46

Louisiana
Superdome

BUS
90

Gen. Meyer Ave.

Mississippi River

Jackson Ave

3

Franklin St.

Garden
District

Lafayette

Gen. de Gaulle Dr.

Woodland Dr.

ZONE 11

4th St.

Whitney

Behrman Hwy.

3018

BUS
90

Terry Town

Peters Rd.

23

General Meyer Ave.

3017

Belle Chasse Hwy.

3017

Belle
Chasse

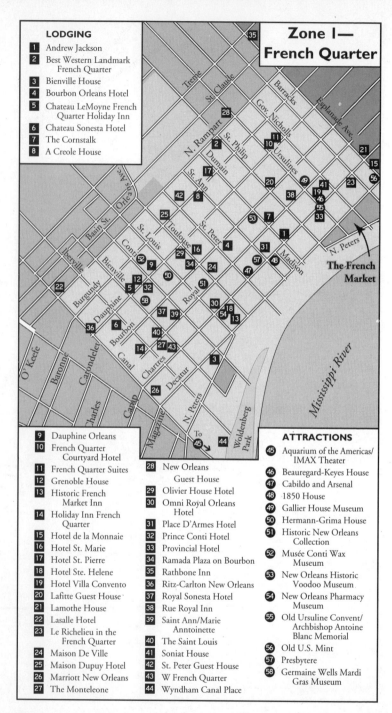

LODGING

1 Andrew Jackson
2 Best Western Landmark
   French Quarter
3 Bienville House
4 Bourbon Orleans Hotel
5 Chateau LeMoyne French
   Quarter Holiday Inn
6 Chateau Sonesta Hotel
7 The Cornstalk
8 A Creole House

Zone 1—
French Quarter

9 Dauphine Orleans
10 French Quarter
   Courtyard Hotel
11 French Quarter Suites
12 Grenoble House
13 Historic French
   Market Inn
14 Holiday Inn French
   Quarter
15 Hotel de la Monnaie
16 Hotel St. Marie
17 Hotel St. Pierre
18 Hotel Ste. Helene
19 Hotel Villa Convento
20 Lafitte Guest House
21 Lamothe House
22 Lasalle Hotel
23 Le Richelieu in the
   French Quarter
24 Maison De Ville
25 Maison Dupuy Hotel
26 Marriott New Orleans
27 The Monteleone

28 New Orleans
   Guest House
29 Olivier House Hotel
30 Omni Royal Orleans
   Hotel
31 Place D'Armes Hotel
32 Prince Conti Hotel
33 Provincial Hotel
34 Ramada Plaza on Bourbon
35 Rathbone Inn
36 Ritz-Carlton New Orleans
37 Royal Sonesta Hotel
38 Rue Royal Inn
39 Saint Ann/Marie
   Anntoinette
40 The Saint Louis
41 Soniat House
42 St. Peter Guest House
43 W French Quarter
44 Wyndham Canal Place

ATTRACTIONS

45 Aquarium of the Americas/
   IMAX Theater
46 Beauregard-Keyes House
47 Cabildo and Arsenal
48 1850 House
49 Gallier House Museum
50 Hermann-Grima House
51 Historic New Orleans
   Collection
52 Musée Conti Wax
   Museum
53 New Orleans Historic
   Voodoo Museum
54 New Orleans Pharmacy
   Museum
55 Old Ursuline Convent/
   Archbishop Antoine
   Blanc Memorial
56 Old U.S. Mint
57 Presbytere
58 Germaine Wells Mardi
   Gras Museum

The French
Market

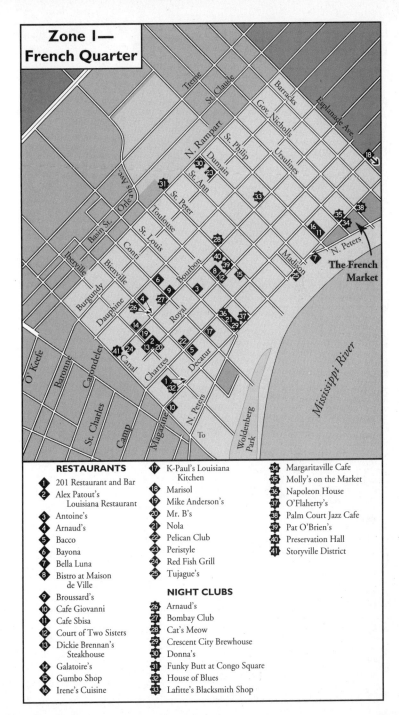

Zone 1— French Quarter

The French Market

Mississippi River

Woldenberg Park

RESTAURANTS

1. 201 Restaurant and Bar
2. Alex Patout's Louisiana Restaurant
3. Antoine's
4. Arnaud's
5. Bacco
6. Bayona
7. Bella Luna
8. Bistro at Maison de Ville
9. Broussard's
10. Cafe Giovanni
11. Cafe Sbisa
12. Court of Two Sisters
13. Dickie Brennan's Steakhouse
14. Galatoire's
15. Gumbo Shop
16. Irene's Cuisine
17. K-Paul's Louisiana Kitchen
18. Marisol
19. Mike Anderson's
20. Mr. B's
21. Nola
22. Pelican Club
23. Peristyle
24. Red Fish Grill
25. Tujague's

NIGHT CLUBS

26. Arnaud's
27. Bombay Club
28. Cat's Meow
29. Crescent City Brewhouse
30. Donna's
31. Funky Butt at Congo Square
32. House of Blues
33. Lafitte's Blacksmith Shop
34. Margaritaville Cafe
35. Molly's on the Market
36. Napoleon House
37. O'Flaherty's
38. Palm Court Jazz Cafe
39. Pat O'Brien's
40. Preservation Hall
41. Storyville District

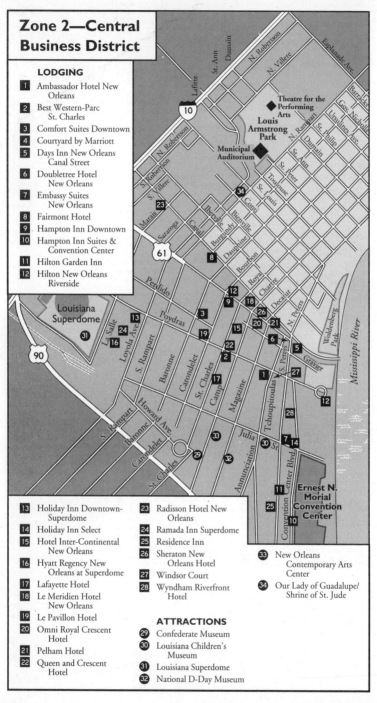

Zone 2—Central Business District

LODGING

1. Ambassador Hotel New Orleans
2. Best Western-Parc St. Charles
3. Comfort Suites Downtown
4. Courtyard by Marriott
5. Days Inn New Orleans Canal Street
6. Doubletree Hotel New Orleans
7. Embassy Suites New Orleans
8. Fairmont Hotel
9. Hampton Inn Downtown
10. Hampton Inn Suites & Convention Center
11. Hilton Garden Inn
12. Hilton New Orleans Riverside

13. Holiday Inn Downtown-Superdome
14. Holiday Inn Select
15. Hotel Inter-Continental New Orleans
16. Hyatt Regency New Orleans at Superdome
17. Lafayette Hotel
18. Le Meridien Hotel New Orleans
19. Le Pavillon Hotel
20. Omni Royal Crescent Hotel
21. Pelham Hotel
22. Queen and Crescent Hotel

23. Radisson Hotel New Orleans
24. Ramada Inn Superdome
25. Residence Inn
26. Sheraton New Orleans Hotel
27. Windsor Court
28. Wyndham Riverfront Hotel

ATTRACTIONS

29. Confederate Museum
30. Louisiana Children's Museum
31. Louisiana Superdome
32. National D-Day Museum
33. New Orleans Contemporary Arts Center
34. Our Lady of Guadalupe/ Shrine of St. Jude

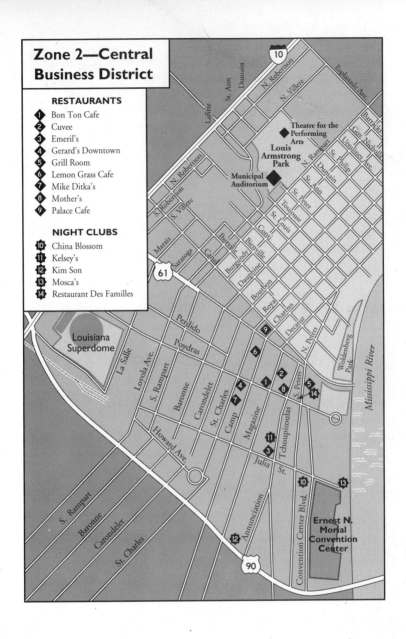

Zone 2—Central Business District

RESTAURANTS
1. Bon Ton Cafe
2. Cuvee
3. Emeril's
4. Gerard's Downtown
5. Grill Room
6. Lemon Grass Cafe
7. Mike Ditka's
8. Mother's
9. Palace Cafe

NIGHT CLUBS
10. China Blossom
11. Kelsey's
12. Kim Son
13. Mosca's
14. Restaurant Des Familles

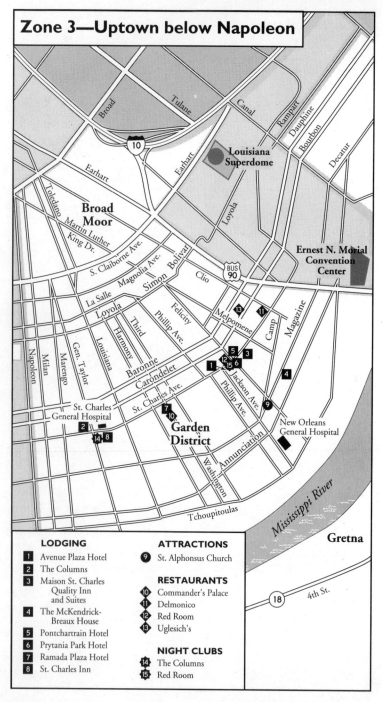

Zone 3—Uptown below Napoleon

LODGING

1. Avenue Plaza Hotel
2. The Columns
3. Maison St. Charles Quality Inn and Suites
4. The McKendrick-Breaux House
5. Pontchartrain Hotel
6. Prytania Park Hotel
7. Ramada Plaza Hotel
8. St. Charles Inn

ATTRACTIONS

9. St. Alphonsus Church

RESTAURANTS

10. Commander's Palace
11. Delmonico
12. Red Room
13. Uglesich's

NIGHT CLUBS

14. The Columns
15. Red Room

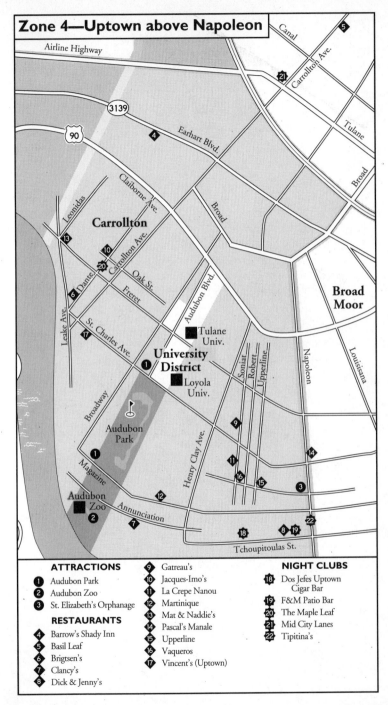

Zone 4—Uptown above Napoleon

Canal

Airline Highway

3139

90

Earhart Blvd.

Claiborne Ave.

Leonidas

Carrollton

Carrollton Ave.

Dante

Oak St.

Freret

Leake Ave.

St. Charles Ave.

Broadway

Magazine

University District

Tulane Univ.

Loyola Univ.

Audubon Blvd.

Broad

Carrollton Ave.

Tulane

Broad

Broad Moor

Soniat

Robert

Upperline

Napoleon

Louisiana

Henry Clay Ave.

Audubon Park

Audubon Zoo

Annunciation

Tchoupitoulas St.

ATTRACTIONS

1 Audubon Park
2 Audubon Zoo
3 St. Elizabeth's Orphanage

RESTAURANTS

4 Barrow's Shady Inn
5 Basil Leaf
6 Brigtsen's
7 Clancy's
8 Dick & Jenny's

9 Gatreau's
10 Jacques-Imo's
11 La Crepe Nanou
12 Martinique
13 Mat & Naddie's
14 Pascal's Manale
15 Upperline
16 Vaqueros
17 Vincent's (Uptown)

NIGHT CLUBS

18 Dos Jefes Uptown Cigar Bar
19 F&M Patio Bar
20 The Maple Leaf
21 Mid City Lanes
22 Tipitina's

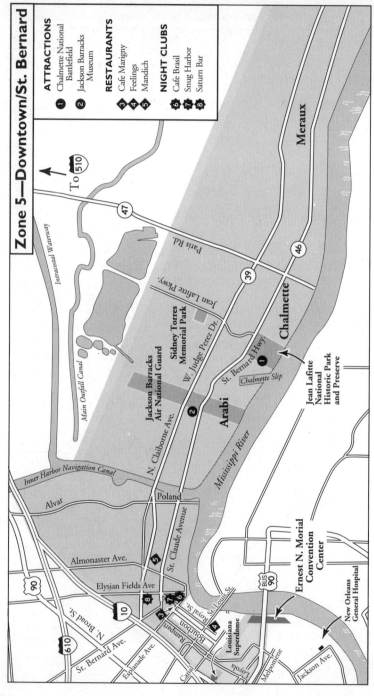

Zone 5—Downtown/St. Bernard

ATTRACTIONS
1. Chalmette National Battlefield
2. Jackson Barracks Museum

RESTAURANTS
3. Cafe Marigny
4. Feelings
5. Mandich

NIGHT CLUBS
6. Cafe Brasil
7. Snug Harbor
8. Saturn Bar

To [510]

Intracoastal Waterway

Main Outfall Canal

Inner Harbor Navigation Canal

Jackson Barracks Air National Guard

N. Claiborne Ave.

Sidney Torres Memorial Park

W. Judge Perez Dr.

Jean Lafitte Pkwy.

Paris Rd.

Meraux

Chalmette

St. Bernard Hwy.

Chalmette Slip

Jean Lafitte National Historic Park and Preserve

Arabi

Mississippi River

Poland

Alvar

Almonaster Ave.

St. Claude Avenue

Elysian Fields Ave

N. Broad St.

St. Bernard Ave.

Esplanade Ave.

Rampart

Bourbon

Royal St.

St. Louis St.

Canal

Loyola

Louisiana Superdome

Ernest N. Morial Convention Center

New Orleans General Hospital

Melpomene

Jackson Ave.

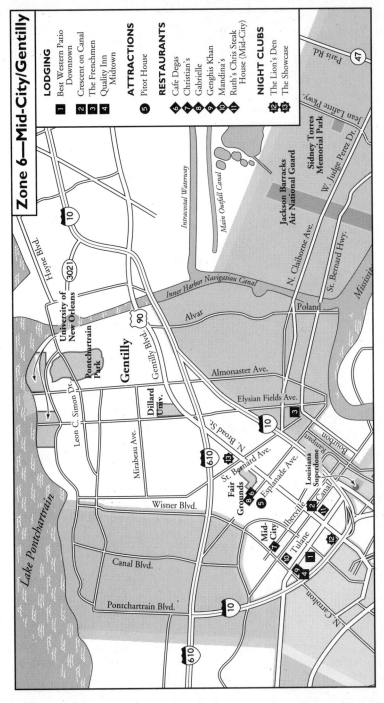

Zone 6—Mid-City/Gentilly

LODGING
1. Best Western Patio Downtown
2. Crescent on Canal
3. The Frenchmen
4. Quality Inn Midtown

ATTRACTIONS
5. Pitot House

RESTAURANTS
6. Cafe Degas
7. Christian's
8. Gabrielle
9. Genghis Khan
10. Mandina's
11. Ruth's Chris Steak House (Mid-City)

NIGHT CLUBS
12. The Lion's Den
13. The Showcase

19

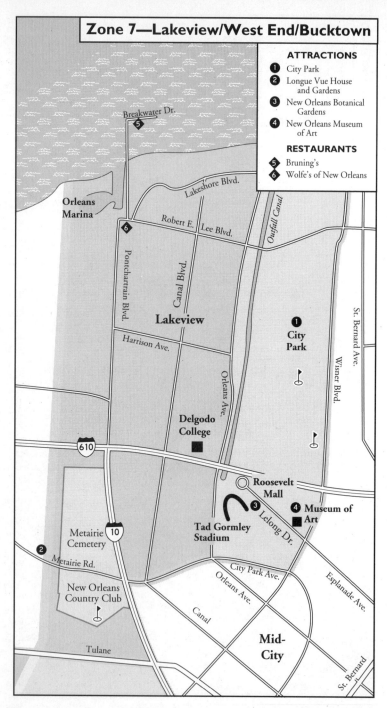

Zone 7—Lakeview/West End/Bucktown

ATTRACTIONS
1. City Park
2. Longue Vue House and Gardens
3. New Orleans Botanical Gardens
4. New Orleans Museum of Art

RESTAURANTS
5. Bruning's
6. Wolfe's of New Orleans

Breakwater Dr.

Orleans Marina

Lakeshore Blvd.

Robert E. Lee Blvd.

Outfall Canal

Pontchartrain Blvd.

Canal Blvd.

Lakeview

Harrison Ave.

St. Bernard Ave.

City Park

Wisner Blvd.

Orleans Ave.

Delgodo College

610

Roosevelt Mall

Tad Gormley Stadium

Lelong Dr.

Museum of Art

Metairie Cemetery

10

Metairie Rd.

New Orleans Country Club

City Park Ave.

Orleans Ave.

Esplanade Ave.

Canal

Tulane

Mid-City

St. Bernard

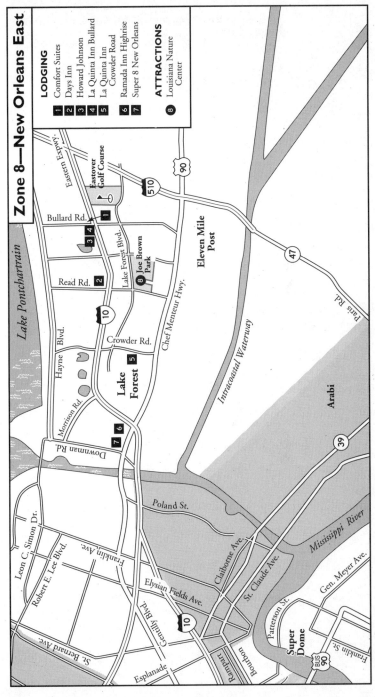

Zone 8—New Orleans East

LODGING

1. Comfort Suites
2. Days Inn
3. Howard Johnson
4. La Quinta Inn Bullard
5. La Quinta Inn Crowder Road
6. Ramada Inn Highrise
7. Super 8 New Orleans

ATTRACTIONS

8. Louisiana Nature Center

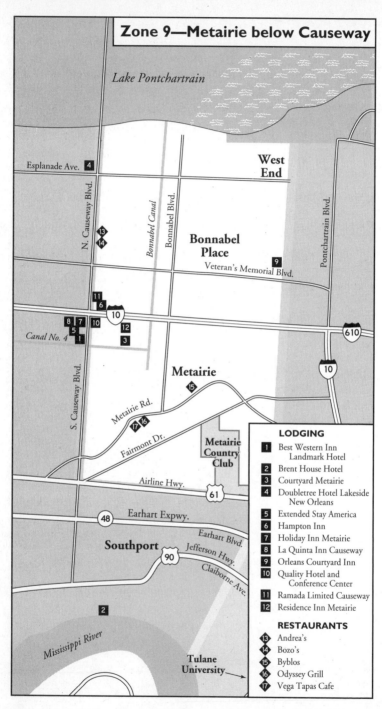

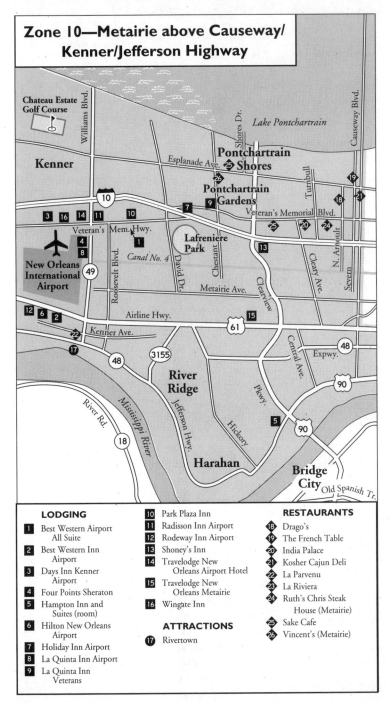

Zone 10—Metairie above Causeway/ Kenner/Jefferson Highway

Chateau Estate
Golf Course

Williams Blvd.

Lake Pontchartrain

Shores Dr.

Causeway Blvd.

Pontchartrain
Esplanade Ave. 25 **Shores**

Kenner

26

Pontchartrain
Gardens

Turnbull

19

18 21

10

3 16 14 11 10 7 9

Veteran's Memorial Blvd.

N. Arnoult

20 24

Veteran's Mem. Hwy. 1

4
8

Lafreniere
Park

25

Roosevelt Blvd.

Canal No. 4

David Dr.

Chestant

13

Cleary Ave.

Seven

New Orleans
International
Airport

49

Metairie Ave.

Clearview

12 6 2

Airline Hwy.

61

15

22 Kenner Ave.

17

48 3155

River
Ridge

Central Ave.

48

Expwy.

90

Pkwy.

River Rd.

Mississippi River

18

Jefferson Hwy.

Hickory

5

90

90

Harahan

Bridge
City Old Spanish Tr.

LODGING

1 Best Western Airport
   All Suite
2 Best Western Inn
   Airport
3 Days Inn Kenner
   Airport
4 Four Points Sheraton
5 Hampton Inn and
   Suites (room)
6 Hilton New Orleans
   Airport
7 Holiday Inn Airport
8 La Quinta Inn Airport
9 La Quinta Inn
   Veterans

10 Park Plaza Inn
11 Radisson Inn Airport
12 Rodeway Inn Airport
13 Shoney's Inn
14 Travelodge New
   Orleans Airport Hotel
15 Travelodge New
   Orleans Metairie
16 Wingate Inn

ATTRACTIONS
17 Rivertown

RESTAURANTS

18 Drago's
19 The French Table
20 India Palace
21 Kosher Cajun Deli
22 La Parvenu
23 La Riviera
24 Ruth's Chris Steak
   House (Metairie)
25 Sake Cafe
26 Vincent's (Metairie)

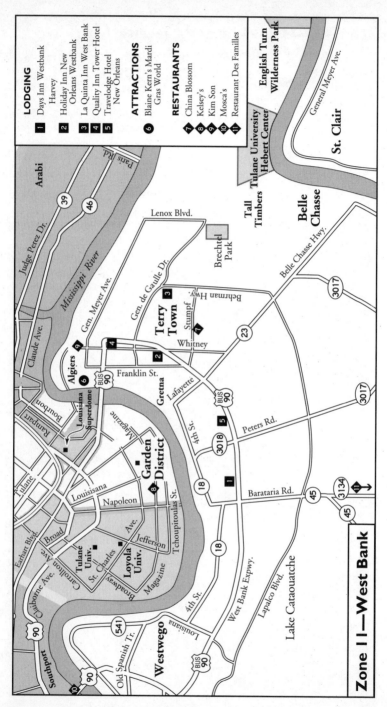

LODGING

1. Days Inn Westbank Harvey
2. Holiday Inn New Orleans Westbank
3. La Quinta Inn West Bank
4. Quality Inn Tower Hotel
5. Travelodge Hotel New Orleans

ATTRACTIONS

6. Blaine Kern's Mardi Gras World

RESTAURANTS

7. China Blossom
8. Kelsey's
9. Kim Son
10. Mosca's
11. Restaurant Des Familles

Zone 11—West Bank

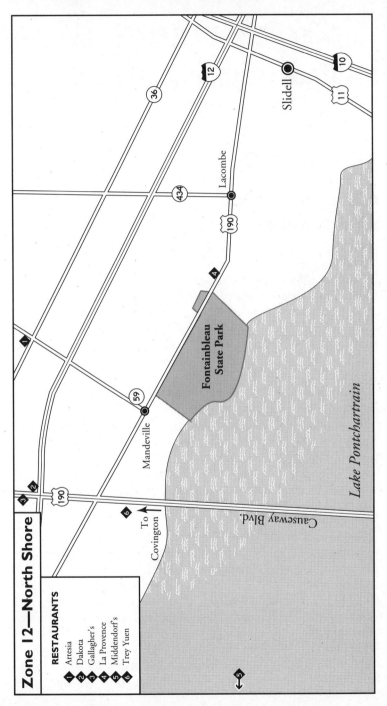

Zone 12—North Shore

RESTAURANTS

1 Artesia
2 Dakota
3 Gallagher's
4 La Provence
5 Middendorf's
6 Trey Yuen

Fontainbleau State Park

Lake Pontchartrain

Causeway Blvd.

Slidell

Lacombe

Mandeville

To Covington

Part One

Understanding the City

A Too-Short History of a Fascinating Place

New Orleans exercises a strange fascination over the rest of the country, and for good reasons. It's foreign territory at heart. It has flown three national flags—four if you count the Confederate States of America—and changed hands a couple more times than that. Like several other southern cities, it was "occupied" by then-hostile Union forces, had to repulse periodic Indian raids, and might briefly have flown a British flag as well if the Battle of Chalmette had turned out differently. (And legend aside, it might easily have done so.) Andy Jackson notwithstanding, New Orleans's legal system is still based upon the Napoleonic code.

New Orleans lives an unnatural, enchanted life, an island dug out of the swamp some yards lower than the river that embraces it, tethered to the world by bridges, ferries, and causeways. Its proximity to the swamps exposed it to almost yearly epidemics; in the course of just over 100 years, between 1795 and 1905, an estimated 100,000 lives were lost to yellow fever, malaria, or cholera. The city has been flattened by hurricanes and nearly erased by floods. And despite all that water around it, it has been destroyed twice by fire too—catastrophes that wiped out almost the entire first century of construction.

New Orleans has been identified with both the most sophisticated Creole culture and good ol' boy corruption; it has produced a rich ethnic melting pot and the most virulent racism. Oil drillers rescued it in the first half of the twentieth century, and international petroleum prices nearly strangled it in the second half. Mardi Gras is the world's most famous frat party, yet when New Orleans threw a World's Fair to celebrate itself, it nearly went bankrupt.

Somehow, as low as New Orleans gets—as much as ten feet below sea level in some places—it never quite goes under. Like that Ol' Man River that surrounds it, like those famous good times, it just keeps rollin' along.

THE FRENCH FLAG

Louisiana stood at the center of imperial rivalries right from the beginning. Columbus had claimed the New World for Spain, but the other seagoing nations also pursued colonial territory and (as they believed) Asian trade. In 1534, Cartier sailed down the St. Lawrence waterways from Canada into the northeast. Only a few years later, Hernando de Soto established settlements along the southeastern coast and actually reached the Mississippi River, but the Spanish attention was distracted by the conquest of Mexico and the expansion into the American Southwest and northern South America.

In the 1670s, while the British were planting Union Jacks up and down the Atlantic Coast from Maine to the Carolinas, Rene Cavelier, Sieur de la Salle, set out from Canada with the intention of following the Illinois River all the way to the mouth of the Mississippi River in the Gulf of Mexico and, in 1682, claimed for France all the land drained by the Mississipppi. He named the land Louisiana in honor of his sovereign lord King Louis XIV, the Sun King. Spain launched a huge manhunt in an attempt to intercept Rene Cavelier (when they finally reached his settlement, mutineers had already murdered him), but by the turn of the century, other Frenchmen had established settlements all over Louisiana and what is now the state of Mississippi.

In 1699, the Sieur de Bienville planted a huge cross at the bend of the Mississippi River, and 20 years later his brother, the Sieur d'Iberville, stood looking out over the Mississippi where it connected to Lake Pontchartrain through Bayou St. John and ordered the construction of his "city." He named it La Nouvelle Orleans in honor of Phillipe, Duc d'Orleans, who was then the Regent of France.

Marshy, mosquito-infested, and oppressively hot, New Orleans became the subject of a real-estate scam that might have inspired the Florida land boom of the 1920s. Posters and supposed "eyewitness" tales of the gold-rich territories—most promulgated by an unscrupulous Scottish crony of the regent's with the ironic name of John Law—lured thousands of French optimists and opportunists to the crude settlement, where they had little choice but to build the city they had been told already existed. Life in the settlement was so meager that in 1727, 88 women convicts were released from prison on the condition they accompany the Ursuline nuns to New Orleans as mail-order brides.

These were not the only unaristocratic imports: In fact, there were probably far more exiles, common soldiers, petty thieves, intractable slaves, and indentured servants than blue-bloods, and fewer "casket girls"— the respectable but impoverished girls who also came out as wards of the

Ursuline Sisters with their few belongings packed in small trunks—than street women. (It should be remembered, however, that life in Paris was very hard, and that many young girls fell or were sold into prostitution as a last resort, so that their records should perhaps not be held against them. They worked pitifully hard for their "freedom" in New Orleans, in any case.)

The city was laid out with the streets in a grid around a central square that faced the river—the Place d'Armes, now Jackson Square. "Vieux Carré" means Old Square, and it almost was square: it extended from the Mississippi River to Rampart Street, which was once literally a rampart or wall, and from Esplanade Avenue to Iberville. (It's generally said to extend to Canal Street, but Canal Street was originally intended to be just that, a canal dividing the French Quarter from the American sector in what is now the Central Business District.) Gradually the settlement grew, and merchants, traders, and practical farmers, as well as more restless aristocrats, came to Louisiana to stay. With them came the beginning of a caste system—aristocrats, merchants, farmers, and servants—that became a hallmark of Creole society.

THE SPANISH FLAG

In the 1760s, two other groups arrived, one in extremity and one in force. The first were the Acadians—the Cajuns—whom the British forced to leave their homes in Nova Scotia, and who settled in the bayou country west of New Orleans. Though most New Orleanians looked down on the Acadians whom they considered countrified (to say the least) and speaking an "uncultured" dialect, the Cajuns were French nationals driven into exile by France's enemy, Britain, and so they were accepted.

The other new arrivals were anything but welcome: the Spanish. To their dismay, the ethnically proud New Orleanians discovered that King Louis XV had secretly surrendered the Louisiana Territory to his Spanish cousin Charles III (some writers say it was used to pay off huge gambling debts). The residents violently resisted the Spanish takeover and succeeded in routing the first commissioner sent from Madrid. But in 1769, a more determined mercenary with the intriguing name of Don Alexander O'Reilly, or "Bloody Reilly," arrived with an armada of 24 warships and 2,000 soldiers. He executed several of the most prominent rebels and made swift work of the insurrection. The Arsenal and Cabildo were erected on the square ("cabildo" is actually the term for governing body), and the French and Spanish aristocrats began inviting each other to dinner.

By the time the American colonies declared independence from Britain, New Orleans was an important Spanish outpost, which made the entrance of the Spanish on either side potentially decisive. Finally, Oliver Pollack, a New Orleans native who had become a member of the Continental Congress, persuaded the then-governor of New Orleans, Bernardo de Galvez, to send a convoy of 20 supply ships to New York to aid the American revolutionaries. Great Britain then declared war on Spain, and de Galvez proceeded to roll over the British colonies along the Gulf of Mexico. Consequently, although Lafayette and the French are usually remembered as the key European allies of the American forces, the Spanish also played an essential role.

THREE FLAGS IN FORTY YEARS

Unsettled as New Orleans' first 60 years had been, the next 40 or so were just as dramatic.

The city was devastated by two great fires, the first in 1788 and the second, which came before the community had rebuilt, in 1794. Only a couple of buildings remain from before that time: the Old Ursuline Convent, whose age is undisputed; and Madame John's Legacy, which is the subject of some debate. Determined to prevent a third disaster, the Spanish promulgated new building codes: All roofs had to be tiled, houses were to be made of brick or plaster rather than wood, high walls had to separate gardens so one fire wouldn't spread from house to house, and alleys were eliminated to prevent a bellows effect that might feed a blaze. So what is considered classical French Quarter architecture, including arches, rear courtyards, and the famous ornamental wrought iron of the balconies and fences, is actually Spanish.

Meanwhile, the city's merchants and shippers continued to prosper. The city was not only a major exchange point between the eastern and midwest markets, but it also controlled much of the European-American import and export trade. New Orleans' strategic position, both for trade and defense, made it highly attractive to the new government of the United States, and a source of great regret to the French government. The city remained solidly French at heart, with a royalist cast of mind—another wave of French aristocrats had fled the Revolution in 1789—and so when Napoleon set out to establish his own French Empire, New Orleans became a spoil of war. In 1800, by yet another secret treaty, Spain ceded the Louisiana Territory back to France.

Napoleon became a romantic idol to the colonists, who proudly named many streets (Marengo, Milan) after his battle victories. But when things began to turn sour for him, Napoleon decided to cash in the American colonies to finance his European campaigns. When President Thomas Jefferson offered to buy the port of New Orleans, Napoleon surprised him by offering to sell the entire Louisiana Territory for the sum of $15 million. The sale was officially transacted in the Cabildo on December 20, 1803. Louisiana became a U.S. territory, and in 1812 it was granted statehood, a fact commemorated in the arrival of the first steamboat, the *New Orleans*.

Despite Napoleon's apparent betrayal, in 1820 loyal New Orleans Creoles plotted to rescue the deposed emperor from his prison on St. Helena (see the story of Napoleon House, page 236), but he died before it could be attempted. His death mask, however, was delivered to his followers and is still on display at the Cabildo.

The purchase of Louisiana by the United States inspired thousands of Americans—and not-yet-Americans, recent immigrants still looking to make their home there—to ride, raft, barge, stage, and even walk to the thriving port. In the first seven years, the population of New Orleans more than tripled, from 8,000 to 25,000. A huge non-Creole community sprang up just upriver of the Vieux Carré, near the older sugar plantations and sometimes on top of them, and out into what is now the Garden District. The new arrivals were not exactly welcomed by the more-civilized-than-thou New Orleanians. The Scotch-Irish, who had already settled along the Carolina and Virginia mountains, were a new and particularly rough presence among the old Creole families; they took the word "riffing," Gaelic for "rowing," and contemptuously referred to all the laboring men and hard-scrabble farmers who poled their way down the Mississippi as "riff raff."

A huge drainage canal emptying into the river was marked out along the upriver edge of the French Quarter, ostensibly as part of the construction of the booming city, but also to serve as an emotional if not actual barrier between the French Quarter, now also known as the First Municipality, and the American quadrant, officially the Second Municipality. In response to this subtle but elegant slight, the Americans laid out their sector, called Faubourg Ste. Marie, as a sort of mirror image of the Vieux Carré, with Lafayette Square (a seemingly polite tribute, but subtly claiming the marquis for the Americans) as a Place d'Armes; St. Patrick's as a rival to St. Louis Cathedral; and Gallier Hall, which was the official City Hall until the 1950s, in place of the old Cabildo. Each had its own mayor and council, each its own regulations. The city was not officially united until 1852.

As it happened, the canal was never built; and for a time, although it was referred to as the "neutral ground," the swath was the site of repeated brawls between Creole residents and brash, aggrandizing newcomers. Eventually a grand boulevard, divided by a great median, was paved through the strip instead and was dubbed Canal Street. Even so, it remained the acknowledged border between the two communities, and ever since, the New Orleans term for a median strip is the neutral ground.

"THE WHITES OF THEIR EYES"

The winning of the Battle of New Orleans has become such a touchstone of American pride that it has inspired hit songs (Johnny Horton's "Battle of New Orleans") and Hollywood epics (*The Buccaneer,* with Charlton Heston as Andrew Jackson and Yul Brynner as Jean Lafitte). The legend is glorious and shining—overnight excavations, secret meetings, Redcoats coming ghostlike through the fog to the banshee wailing of bagpipes, and Jackson shouting, "Don't shoot until you see the whites of their eyes!"

As is frequently the case with warfare, the truth is a little muddier. It is true, however, that the ruthless and lucky Jackson lost only 13 men while killing 2,000 British Army soldiers. It's probably true that without the combined efforts of 5,000 American, Creole, black, and Indian volunteers—not to mention the heavy arms and ammunition donated by Lafitte from his store of plunder—Jackson's Tennessee soldiers would have had a much harder time. And considering how intensely most Native Americans hated Jackson, who had commanded many brutal campaigns against the Creek and Choctaw tribes, their participation was even more remarkable.

The great irony is that the war was already over. The Treaty of Ghent had been signed a fortnight earlier. However, the campaign and victory served to unite the previously rancorous Creole and American communities and to establish New Orleans, distinctive as it might be, as an all-American city.

FREE BLACKS, SLAVES, AND MULATTOS

The presence of African and Caribbean blacks, both free and slave, in New Orleans can be documented as far back as the early clearing of the French Quarter neighborhood. In 1721, only a couple of years after the city's founding, there were 300 slaves for only 470 Europeans, and a "code noir" was enacted in 1724 as a way of regulating the slave trade.

Free blacks, people "of color" (meaning of mixed blood in almost any proportion), and slaves made up a substantial proportion of the population; the free blacks of New Orleans outnumbered those of any other Southern city. In fact, by 1803 there were exactly as many blacks and mixed-blood residents as whites: 4,000 of each, with 1,300 (40%) of the blacks being free. By the beginning of the Civil War, there were an estimated 30,000 free blacks in New Orleans.

An elaborate caste system emerged, in which the mulattos assumed social rank according to the amount of white (Creole) blood in their veins. Mulattos were half black, half white; quadroons were one-quarter white (meaning one white grandparent); and octaroons were one-eighth white. Women of mixed blood were considered exceedingly handsome, and though the Creole aristocrats would never have dreamed of marrying a black woman, it was considered a mark of wealth and good taste—another bit of conspicuous consumption—to have a well-spoken, elegantly dressed black or mixed-blood mistress. Many of these women became heads of the Creoles' city homes, running second establishments, in effect, and if they were really lucky, might be freed at their master's death. If not, at least their children might be recognized as illegitimate offspring and left some money.

This was such a widely recognized custom that the Creoles might even formally court these women, making their mothers or owners semi-official offers that included property settlements, allowances, etc. So the annual Quadroon Balls became notorious tableaux of young "available" beauties, something between an auction and a debutante ball. Many of them were held in the Orleans Ballroom, a grandiose hall built in 1817 and now a special-events site within the Bourbon Orleans Hotel.

As time went on, the *gens de couleur libre*—literally "free men of color"—developed their own quite sophisticated culture; the sons of Creole aristocrats were often given first-class education befitting their (fathers') status, and some were even sent to Europe, where such colonial cross-breeding was commonplace. Alexandre Dumas, the author and playwright, was mulatto, and by some accounts Napoleon's Josephine, from the island of Martinique, had some mixed-blood ancestors as well. Both free and slave blacks were allowed to congregate in Congo Square, near North Rampart and Orleans streets in what is now Louis Armstrong Park; as many as 2,000 gathered in this one-time Choctaw meeting place on Sundays to sing, dance, trade, eat, fight, and perhaps practice a little voodoo until the "curfew," a cannon in the Place d'Armes, sounded. (In tribute, the first New Orleans Jazz and Heritage Festival in 1969 was held in Congo Square.)

In the years just before the Civil War, New Orleans was the largest slave market in the nation. Blacks, even well-to-do mulattos and freemen, remained mere residents rather than citizens; blacks were not granted the vote until 1868, during Reconstruction and despite a campaign of terror by the Ku Klux Klan. They were effectively disenfranchised again in 1898 through a legislative maneuver requiring stringent proof of literacy. The vote was returned only in 1965, and although African-Americans make up more than half of the city's population, the first black mayor, Ernest Morial, was not elected until 1978. (His son Marc became mayor in 1994 and was re-elected in 1998.) Carnival krewes were not integrated until 1991, and some krewes boycotted or even withdrew from Mardi Gras when that happened.

THE WAR BETWEEN THE STATES AND RECONSTRUCTION

The port of New Orleans practically floated on money in the decades after the Treaty of Ghent. Steamboats were in their prime; at the peak, there were some 11,000 plying the waters of the Mississippi; some of the luxury paddle wheelers, the "show boats," had capacities of 600 and served 500 for dinner. It was, so to speak, the beginning of New Orleans' tourism industry. Cotton, tobacco, and the slave trade fueled the economy. By 1840 New Orleans was the second-busiest port in the nation, after New York, and had a population of more than 100,000. The Irish Famine of 1841 sparked another flood of immigrants, who settled northwest of the American sector in what gradually became known as the Irish Channel; a large number of Germans also moved in. Unfortunately, their arrivals were offset by the yellow-fever epidemic of 1853, which killed 11,000 people and incapacitated another 40,000, thus becoming the most deadly epidemic in the nation's history.

But in 1861, with the secession of the Confederate States, Louisiana changed flags for the fourth time—and with the taking of New Orleans by Union forces under Admiral David Farragut in 1862, flew its sixth.

The Union occupation (as New Orleanians saw it, although officially it ceased to be an "occupation" after 1865) lasted 15 years. New Orleans fell so early that its three-year occupation by "enemy troops" is the longest unfriendly occupation of any city in the United States, and amnesty was not granted Confederate officers until 1872. Reconstruction was a period of tremendous unrest in the entire region.

In the final two decades of the nineteenth century, as the reviving port began to bring new industry and pleasure seekers into the city, what might be called the Bourbon Street culture made its first bow. By 1880 there were almost 800 saloons operating in New Orleans, along with about 80 gambling parlors and even more bordellos, which, though officially banned, had never been prosecuted or even regulated. New Orleans was starting to develop a reputation as a party town, a reputation that many people resisted and resented.

In 1897, an alderman named Sidney Story proposed that all these activities be restricted to a red-light district along Basin Street adjoining the French Quarter. The business of vice prospered almost virtuously in what was quickly dubbed "Storyville." The fanciest bordellos boasted not only elegant decor, sophisticated refreshments, and fine entertainment (these "sporting palaces" were where many of the great jazz improvisors got their start), but also well-dressed and willing ladies whose names, addresses, and race mix were listed in "blue books" that parodied social registers. One of the few surviving blue books is in the Old U.S. Mint Museum, along with several beautiful stained-glass windows from a bordello.

THE TWENTIETH CENTURY

The century began promisingly: oil was discovered in Louisiana, and the new dredging and refining industry pumped new money into the regional economy (and pollutants into the water). But a second potential money-maker, jazz, which had struck its first ragtime notes just before the turn of the century, was turned out: the Storyville neighborhood, the bordello area and center of the burgeoning "jass" movement, was closed and virtually bulldozed off the face of the earth. "King" Oliver, Jelly Roll Morton, and other prominent musicians moved north to New York and Chicago, launching successful careers and a nationwide craze.

Some New Orleanians might have felt that the Great War was being fought at home. A massive hurricane struck the city in 1915, devastating the economy and widening the division between the well-to-do and the subsistence farmers; and although a cure for the dreaded yellow fever had been discovered in the early years of the century, the great influenza epidemic of 1918 killed at least 35,000 residents. In 1927 one of the worst floods in history flattened the city, ushering the Depression into the state even before it struck the rest of the nation. (Such natural disasters continue to harass Louisiana: hurricanes Betsy in 1965 and Camille in 1969 caused billions of dollars' worth of damage, and periodic floods have caused even more damage.)

Louisiana would have remained a virtual feudal society had it not been for the anti-establishment revolution of Huey Long, the "Kingfish"—a populist, demagogue, and drunk, who became governor in 1928 and bullied, bludgeoned, and blackmailed the state legislature into expanding public education, roads, and hospitals. Within a year he had been indicted on bribery charges, but was not convicted and instead was elected U.S. Senator. He began as a vocal New Deal supporter, but soon developed a populism that bordered on socialism and alarmed even the most liberal of Washingtonians. In 1935, on a trip home, he was assassinated, but the Long arm of their family law stretched on: his brother Earl was a two-time governor, and his son Russell served in the U.S. Senate from 1948 until 1986.

The growth of industry, particularly oil and natural gas, has been a boon to the state economy, if not the ecology. By 1980 there were more than 40 countries maintaining consular offices in New Orleans, an indication of the power of a trade port that accommodated more than 5,000 international vessels every year. But in 1984 the massive World's Fair Exposition, set up along three wharves with an eye toward the rejuvenation of the Warehouse District, ran heavily into debt and, combined with the collapse in world oil prices, came perilously close to bankrupting the city. What resulted was symbolic: the harder industries turned to the softer tourism industry for partnership. The wharf areas that were renovated for the World's Fair are now the site of the Riverwalk Marketplace and the vast and expanding Convention Center, which brings in more than a million people a year by itself. The luxury hotels and burgeoning Warehouse/Arts District owe their existence primarily to the face-lift connected to the fair. And the legalization of gambling has brought in some money to the state (although the on-again, off-again construction of the massive Harrah's casino near the foot of Canal Street bankrupted many smaller subcontractors along the way).

Nowadays the Mississippi riverfront is a microcosm of the city's spirit (for good or ill), combining franchised entertainment, name-brand boutiques and music clubs, huge international tankers and simulated steamboats, "real" Civil War coffee with chicory, reinvented Cajun cuisine, eighteenth-century voodoo, and twentieth-century vampires. They *laissez les bons temps rouler,* all right; they just make sure it's your money roll that's good-timing.

Parishes, Neighborhoods, and Districts

It might surprise those who think that "old" New Orleans is limited to the Vieux Carré and the Garden District, but metropolitan New Orleans has 16 National Historic Districts, including Tremé and Faubourg Marigny as well as the Warehouse/Arts District and the often-denigrated Ninth Ward.

These are all within Orleans Parish, the central portion of greater New Orleans. If you look at the map, Orleans Parish is roughly defined by the U-shaped bowl of the Mississippi River—the eponymous "crescent"—and lines running more or less north to Lake Pontchartrain. Many of these neighborhoods were originally laid out along fairly regular street grids, easily negotiated by newcomers, but because of the snaking of the Mississippi, the overall pattern of the center city now resembles a spider's web: sets of parallel streets occasionally are "pieced out" or head off at wider angles, and a few great, long, curving avenues, such as St. Charles, Claiborne, and Magazine, follow the curve of the river. It takes a little getting used to.

New Orleans also incorporates Jefferson Parish to the west beyond Audubon Park, and St. Bernard Parish downriver to the east. ("Parish" is no longer a religious jurisdiction, but the equivalent of a county.)

Only a few of New Orleans' neighborhoods are of real interest to tourists, but a quick overview of them, and how we have arranged them into zones, may help you plan your trip. These are the same zones we have used to cluster special attractions, restaurants, nightlife, entertainment, and hotels.

THE FRENCH QUARTER (ZONE 1)

Although Vieux Carré literally means "Old Square," the French Quarter is, of course, not perfectly square, as it rides a hump of Mississippi sidesaddle. And because it's tilted, it's actually closer to the shape of a diamond. (Ironically, considering the Creoles' long rivalry with their American governors, the Quarter is a fair mirror image of Washington, D.C., only in miniature.) Nevertheless, it's the easiest neighborhood to grasp logistically, because the streets do proceed in a perpendicular grid, most of them one way in alternating directions.

The boundaries are Canal Street to the southwest, North Rampart Street to the northwest, Esplanade Avenue on the northeast, and the concave line of the Mississippi to the southeast. (The legal border on the southwest is Iberville Street, but we have used Canal Street as the border throughout this book.) If you look at the neighborhood square-on, with Rampart running across the top of the grid, Jackson Square and Artillery Park are in the center at the bottom, like a stem.

This is tourist central, the neighborhood of Bourbon Street and all-night beignets, St. Louis Cathedral, Preservation Hall, and Pat O'Brien's hurricanes. It includes the oldest architectural examples in the city, the most inexhaustible souvenir vendors, and the finest antique shops, plus a handful of franchised star-power hangouts à la Planet Hollywood. The French Quarter is something of a year-round party, justly famous for strip joints and street drinking. It has also developed a second kind of "street life" in recent years, with some of the longtime street musicians giving way to groups of punk-styled teenagers and young adults, panhandlers, and vagrants; so you may want to be less freestyle with your partying. There are still full-time residents here, but in general they have withdrawn to the quieter edges of the neighborhood.

For a full description, see the walking tour of the French Quarter in Part Eleven: "Sight-Seeing and Tours."

CENTRAL BUSINESS DISTRICT (ZONE 2)

The Central Business District, generally shortened to the CBD, is a cleaver-shaped area adjoining the French Quarter on the southwest side of Canal Street and also bordering it on the northwest side of North Rampart. Zone 2 also includes two historic neighborhoods: the Warehouse/Arts District and the historic Tremé neighborhood, which itself is incorporated in the Warehouse/Arts District. On our map, the zone is defined by South Claiborne Avenue/Interstate 10 on the northwest side, Business 90/Pontchartrain Expressway on the southwest, and the Mississippi on the east, with a jag from Canal Street across Rampart to Esplanade. This is also the beginning of "uptown" New Orleans, that is, upriver from Canal Street, as opposed to "downtown."

The CBD includes the Ernest N. Morial Convention Center, the Louisiana Superdome, Riverwalk Marketplace, the World Trade Center, and City Hall. In the beginning this neighborhood was known as Faubourg Ste. Marie, and was the site of some early sugar plantations. However, when the Americans flooded in after the Louisiana Purchase, they chopped up the old plantations and began settling on the "other" side of Canal Street. Though it was begun long after unification, the U.S. Customs House on Canal Street sits as a sort of hinge between the two neighborhoods. The heart of the CBD is Lafayette Square, the Americans' answer to Jackson Square just as St. Patrick's Cathedral was their version of St. Louis.

Tremé is one of the old Creole neighborhoods, part of the plantation of Claude Tremé that was bought by the city for residential development in the early nineteenth century. (The reputation of the same Claude Tremé was somewhat elevated when St. Claude Avenue was named after him.) Tremé is where the famous Storyville red-light district was established, now the site of a disgracefully decrepit housing project. Tremé is also the area where you'll find Louis Armstrong Park, the Theatre for the Performing Arts, and the famous Congo Square, home of jazz; St. Louis Cemetery (Nos. 1 and 2); and Our Lady of Guadalupe Chapel.

The Warehouse/Arts District, on the other hand, is a fairly recent concept. The huge old storehouses, light industrial hangars, and factories on the streets south of Lafayette Square and west of the Convention Center originally had easy access to the docks. Many had been abandoned or allowed to fall into disrepair in the 1960s and 1970s, and the neighborhood was ripe for redevelopment. But when plans were made to transform the dock area for the World's Fair, artists and performers began moving in, turning them into lofts, studios, and display galleries. Now it's a trendy area, with several hot restaurants, hotels, and museums and more coming in around Lee Circle. A strong campaign is being mounted to preserve and restore the buildings rather than raze them.

And in a peculiar turnabout, the trendiness of the Warehouse/Arts District is one of the factors that has encouraged the revitalization of Canal Street not merely as a shopping strip but as a haven for high-profile hotels, including the Hotel Meridien, the Orient Express-owned Windsor Court, the Ritz-Carlton, constructed behind the facade of the old Maison Blanche department store, and one of two W hotels in the neighborhood. Even the old streetcar rails are being restored down the middle of Canal Street. (Unfortunately, much of the development near the foot of Canal was slowed by the ongoing financial travails of the huge Harrah's Casino.)

For more information, see the walking tours of both the CBD and Warehouse/Arts District in "Sight-Seeing and Tours."

UPTOWN BELOW NAPOLEON (ZONE 3)

This is the area of the Garden District, New Orleans' second most famous neighborhood, the upper-class residential portion of the old "American sector," and visually as well as historically a world away from the French Quarter. Originally there were some Creole plantation homes here, but after the turn of the nineteenth century, as Americans moved in above Canal Street, this became incorporated as the City of Lafayette (hence Lafayette Cemetery at its heart). It was annexed into New Orleans in 1852.

Although real estate promoters and area residents constantly stretch the description, the true Garden District is generally considered to fall between St. Charles Avenue and Magazine Street, Jackson Avenue on the northeast and Louisiana Avenue on the west.

However, for our purposes, Zone 3 is a somewhat larger, skirt-shaped wedge stretching from the Pontchartrain Expressway on the northeast, South Claiborne/Route 90 on the northwest, Napoleon Avenue to the west, and the river curving along the east and south.

Although the area's streets occasionally shift a little as the Mississippi curves back up, like the skirt's pleats, the Garden District is fairly gridlike within its borders and a fine residential neighborhood for exploring (see the walking tour of this area as well). Although Magazine Street had become somewhat run down, its ongoing revitalization has made it a popular shopping area (see Part Ten: "Shopping" for more information).

UPTOWN ABOVE NAPOLEON (ZONE 4)

This area, along with the Garden District, is most often what is meant by the general phrase "uptown." Its northwest border, Monticello Avenue, which strikes off from the rim of the river's "cup," marks the line between Orleans and Jefferson parishes, so in one sense the area is at the far end of the Crescent City. (Some residents of the Metairie and Kenner suburbs would say that New Orleans' older families seem to think so, too.)

The area is also called University, sort of shorthand for the "university neighborhood," because of the adjoining campuses of Loyola and Tulane universities. It is split virtually down the middle by the St. Charles Avenue streetcar, which makes it, like the Garden District, easily accessible from the French Quarter or hotel district. Its most famous landmark is Audubon Park, which stretches from the universities right to the spot where the Mississippi River turns back north, with a fine view of both banks.

At the northwest edge of the area is the neighborhood called Riverbend, which is sort of Uptown's own counter-French Quarter, with boutiques and art galleries, bookstores, and a booming restaurant scene. See the Shopping chapter for more information.

For the purposes of this book, Zone 4 is defined by Napoleon Avenue on the east, the Mississippi River on the south and west, Monticello up to Highway 61 (Old Airline Highway) on the north, and I-10 to the north and northeast.

DOWNTOWN/ST. BERNARD (ZONE 5)

This area, which adjoins the French Quarter's east side, has suffered a great deal more than the French Quarter from the vicissitudes of time and industrial development, but it contains many fine old houses, the eccentric

St. Roch Cemetery, Chalmette Battlefield and Jackson Barracks, and the Old U.S. Mint Museum. Zone 5 is defined by Esplanade Avenue on the west, I-10 to the Industrial Canal on the north, the Back Levee and Florida Avenue on the east, and the river on the south.

It actually includes parts of two parishes, since the neighborhood of Faubourg Marigny, which faces the French Quarter across Esplanade Avenue, is part of Orleans Parish; the rest is St. Bernard Parish. In fact, St. Claude Avenue becomes St. Bernard Highway at the parish line, and leads down along the Mississippi to the city of St. Bernard, where you can visit the Isleño Center and the Ducros Museum. This is also, you should note, the Ninth Ward, which is the way locals refer to it in terms of crime (see the section "How to Avoid Crime" in "Arriving and Getting Oriented").

But it has great beauty, still: Blanche DuBois's famous directions, "They told me to take a streetcar named Desire, transfer to one called Cemeteries, ride six blocks and get off at Elysian Fields," owes most of its charm to streets in Faubourg Marigny, although to be truthful, the routes wouldn't intersect. Faubourg Marigny is named for one of the greatest charmers and also greatest wastrels in New Orleans lore, Bernard Xavier Phillipe de Marigny de Mandeville, who gambled away an immense fortune and gradually sold off his vast holdings to developers. In 1807 he subdivided his own plantation ("faubourg" means something like suburb or cluster development), and it became the second-oldest neighborhood in the city; and it was he who named Elysian Fields Avenue. (He also gave the name Rue d'Amour, the Street of Love, to what is now the far more truculent Rampart Street.) These days, the western part of Faubourg Marigny, from the edge of the French Quarter past Washington Square to Elysian Fields, is a mixed but lively neighborhood of artists, gays, hip straights, musicians, and young couples working to renovate the rambling old homes, something like the downtown Riverbend, but funkier and dicier.

MID-CITY/GENTILLY (ZONE 6)

This is a fat-topped Santa's boot of a zone. Its cuff is the lakefront, which runs from the inner harbor canal on the east to I-10, follows the interstate southeast along the calf, until it makes a sharp right at the heel of the boot and runs back up the sole toward the northwest; the toe is at City Park Avenue, and the shin goes up Wisner Boulevard to Lake Pontchartrain. Within this zone are the Fairgrounds, where the Jazz and Heritage Fest is held; the University of New Orleans and Kiefer Lakefront Arena; and Bayou St. John, the original passage the French took moving in from Lake Pontchartrain toward the Mississippi (and a Native American route long before that). And the stretch of Esplanade Avenue near the Fairgrounds and bayou, known as Esplanade Ridge, makes for a nice mini-walking tour.

LAKEVIEW/WEST END/BUCKTOWN (ZONE 7)

This zone is a sort of bridge between Mid-City and Metairie, borrowing a little from each. From Lake Pontchartrain, it follows Wisner Boulevard down to City Park on the east; takes City Park Avenue west to I-10 and zigs down to Highway 61; and turns back up along the Jefferson Parish line, the 17th Street Canal, and Chickasaw Street to the lake.

Within this zone are lovely City Park (which includes the New Orleans Museum of Art, Botanical Gardens, etc.), Longue Vue House and Gardens, and Lake Lawn Metairie Cemetery. At the edge of Pontchartrain, along Lakeshore Drive, what is now developed was mostly fishing camps and speakeasies, gambling dens and partyhouses. Now it's a much fancier version, with fine yacht clubs, the West End Park, and Lakeshore Drive Park, a five-mile-long promenade (stretching into Zone 8) that includes the New Canal Lighthouse (a Coast Guard rescue center not open to the public) and the Mardi Gras Fountain.

NEW ORLEANS EAST (ZONE 8)

This zone runs west from the Inner Harbor Canal to the St. Bernard Parish line, above the Back Levee and Florida Avenue on the south. It's dominated by bayous, lakes, and marshland and includes New Orleans Lakefront Airport and the Louisiana Nature Center.

METAIRIE BELOW CAUSEWAY (ZONE 9)

If this sounds like a strange location, remember that in New Orleans, "below" and "above" are derived from the flow of the Mississippi, and that Causeway is local shorthand for Causeway Boulevard, not the Pontchartrain Causeway it runs off; so to be below Causeway in this case means on the east side of the highway, not beneath a bridge. Zone 9 is a rectangular section bordered by Causeway on the west, Highway 61/Old Airport Highway on the south, the Jefferson/Orleans parish line, the Metairie Outfall Canal and Chicasaw on the east, and the lake on the north.

Both Zone 9 and Zone 10 are suburbs with multi-ethnic populations, so there are lots of up-and-coming or locals-only restaurants here, though it's best to go with friends from town if possible.

METAIRIE ABOVE CAUSEWAY/KENNER/JEFFERSON HIGHWAY (ZONE 10)

This booming suburban area lies just beyond the university neighborhood, bounded by Causeway Boulevard and a zigzag of Highway 61 and the Jefferson Parish line on the east, the Mississippi on the south, the Jefferson/Orleans parish line on the west, and Lake Pontchartrain on the north. Within Zone 10 are New Orleans International Airport (and so quite a number of less expensive hotels) and the Rivertown museum complex.

WEST BANK (ZONE 11)

The apparently contradictory name—from most of New Orleans, this appears to be the *East* Bank, not to mention south!—comes from the fact that the Mississippi makes another of its huge loops east of the city, and these towns all lie west of that portion of the river. Among these are Algiers, Gretna, Harvey, Terrytown, and Marerro. Although Algiers is slowly being regentrified, and there are walking tours of the area designed to raise its profile, it is still not an area that offers much to the tourist, with the exception of the Canal Street Ferry landing and Blaine Kern's Mardi Gras World (see "Attractions"). Like its namesake, Algiers is regarded as foreign territory—there wasn't even a bridge from the city to Algiers until 1958—but the major ethnic presence there is now Vietnamese, not North African.

Golf fans may also find themselves on the west bank, since several of the golf courses are across the river (see "Exercise and Recreation"). If you go down to English Turn Wilderness Park or to English Turn country club, where the PGA tournament is held, you can see two other huge curves of the Mississippi River.

NORTH SHORE (ZONE 12)

This is literally the north shore of Lake Pontchartrain, a zone that includes Slidell, Mandeville, Covington, Folsom, and other areas. Few tourists will get to this side of the lake unless they are looking for the Joyce Wildlife Management Area and Global Wildlife Center (see the "Swamp Tours" section of "Sight-Seeing and Tours" on page 225), or perhaps are lured by some of the restaurants there. The Joyce area is actually crossed by Interstate 55 and Highway 51, if you happen to be able to drive into New Orleans using that route. However, if you are part of a packaged tour, you may wind up at the factory outlet stores in Slidell. This is Tammany Parish, a pretty and mostly quiet area.

The Fictional City

There are many wonderful histories and cultural studies of New Orleans, but for some reason, fiction always seems to convey more of the atmosphere and is more fun to take along on a vacation. Some of my personal favorites (not all currently in print, but widely available in secondhand stores and libraries) include the following.

Anne Rice's books about the Vampire Lestat, the Mayfair Witches, and Lasher, etc., all have New Orleans settings, of course; but far more gripping is her historical novel, *The Feast of All Saints,* about the free people of color and their culture in the years leading up to the Civil War. And if you enjoy the old-fashioned style of murder mysteries, John Dickson Carr's *Papa La-Bas,* set amid the era of Marie Laveau and the Quadroon Balls, is as good as a voodoo tour of the French Quarter.

The posthumously published black-humor masterpiece *A Confederacy of Dunces,* by John Kennedy Toole, contains some of the best dialect and Bourbon Street camp of all time. Ellen Gilchrist's interrelated short stories of Garden District life in "Victory over Japan" and "In the Land of Dreamy Dreams," and the contemporary crime novels of James Lee Burke and his Cajun hero Dave Robichaux, are quite different, but all first rate.

If you can find the books of George Washington Cable, you will love his late nineteenth-century stories of Creole romance and adventure. (One of his stories inspired the name of Madame John's Legacy, a historic house in the French Quarter.) The same is true of the novels of Frances Parkinson Keyes, notably *Dinner at Antoine's, Steamboat Gothic* (set at San Francisco Plantation), and *Madame Castel's Lodger,* about the house she and Beauregard both lived in. (See a description of this house, now a museum, in Part Twelve: "New Orleans Attractions.")

Walker Percy might be the city's foremost "serious" novelist, edging out William Faulkner by dint of long residence (Faulkner only stayed a few years). Percy had an almost unequaled sense of the minute degrees of social distinction, coming as he did from one of the area's most prominent clans. Most of his novels, among them *The Moviegoer* and *Love among the Ruins,* are set in the New Orleans area. Faulkner's novel *Pylon* and several of his short stories have New Orleans backgrounds. So do Tennessee Williams' *A Streetcar Named Desire, The Rose Tattoo,* and *Suddenly Last Summer,* among others. The residences of Williams, Faulkner, and several others are pointed out in the walking tour of the French Quarter described in Part Eleven: "Sight-Seeing and Tours."

In recent years, Kate Chopin's works, particularly *The Awakening,* one of the first great feminist novels of the late nineteenth century (and set in New Orleans), have been rediscovered, and deservedly so. William Sidney Porter, better known as O. Henry, lived in New Orleans for a little while before the turn of the century, and some of his stories, including "Cherchez la Femme," are set in the city. In fact, local legend has it that he borrowed his famous pseudonym from a popular bartender, whose services were routinely summoned by a call of "Oh, Henry!" The city also makes several cameo appearances in Mark Twain's *Life on the Mississippi,* the sketches he wrote about piloting a steamboat.

Finally, if you'd like to raise a toast to your favorite writer, O. Henry fans should head to Tujague's (823 Decatur Street). For almost everyone else—Hearn, Twain, Walt Whitman, William Makepeace Thackeray, and even Oscar Wilde—go to the Old Absinthe House at 240 Bourbon Street. Ask for a Sazerac.

Part Two

Planning Your Visit to New Orleans

When to Go

PICK YOUR PARTY

Meteorologically speaking, most residents consider that New Orleans really has only two seasons: summer—a sticky, sweltering Southern classic prone to afternoon showers and dramatic sunsets that lasts roughly from May 1 to October 1; and a long, cool, and almost identically damp fall-into-spring that rarely dips to the freezing point.

But in terms of tourism, New Orleans has gradually developed four major holiday "seasons": Carnival (or, as most people think of it, Mardi Gras), which falls somewhere between February 3 and March 9; the New Orleans Jazz and Heritage Festival, from the last weekend of April through the first weekend of May; Halloween, which is booming in the Anne Rice era; and Creole Christmas, a lower-key but increasingly popular group of events spread throughout December and lasting through New Year's Eve and the Sugar Bowl. And that doesn't even count the occasional Super Bowl or the dozens of other festivals and celebrations around the city.

If you plan to come during the four big holidays, there are a few things you ought to consider. First, the fun is only nominally free. Don't be surprised if you have to pay premium rates for hotel rooms and airline seats, especially around Mardi Gras and Jazz Fest, *if* you can get them. That's another thing to know: you'd better get a hotel reservation immediately, because most of the events are sold out well in advance, and some people make reservations for Mardi Gras more than a year ahead. Mardi Gras can fall on any Tuesday between February 3 and March 9. It falls on February 12 in 2002, March 4 in 2003, February 24 in 2004, and February 8 in 2005. (The festival moves because it is fixed 46 days before Easter, which is itself fixed by the lunar schedule, falling on the first Sunday after the first full moon after the equinox.) You might seriously consider staying in the suburbs to avoid the almost 24-hour noise; or at least try to get something in the Garden District or Warehouse/Arts District, where you can enjoy the traditional decorations without the full French Quarter hedonism.

A third factor is that the sheer size of the crowd may begin to sour on you after a while. Many restaurants and bars simply pack up the tables during Mardi Gras and settle for making money on the itinerant drinkers; restaurants that maintain their poise may refuse to make reservations or require you to leave a deposit or credit card number in case you fail to show up. (And realize again that with such a crowd, getting around town is really tricky.) Rest rooms quickly overload, and overloaded drinkers may settle for the street. An increasing number of nicer restaurants, especially along parade routes, are opting to close entirely during the last week of Carnival.

If you're coming in a Super Bowl year, you'll have the same problem with overcrowding: even football fans without game tickets flock to the city, either in hopes of scalping seats or just to enjoy the televised hoopla. But if you can't resist these most famous events, read the special information on each in "New Orleans's Major Festivals," which starts on page 62.

If you have more general interests or want to take the family, pick a less frenetic time to go: Between Easter and the Jazz Fest, usually in early May, is very quiet, and you can enjoy the French Quarter Festival, a miniature and more local Jazz and Heritage Festival not yet too crowded; September and early October are warm and usually fine; in March you can enjoy another underestimated attraction—the astonishing, high-spirited Tennessee Williams Festival. Even winter can be nice if you like a brisk walk, and there are certainly no crowds in the museums. If you're traveling on business, of course, you may not have much of a choice.

The good news is that except during the big festivals, you will rarely have to stand in line, except for a table. There are so many distractions in New Orleans that only a couple of attractions (the ticket booth at the Aquarium of the Americas and IMAX theater, perhaps) collect much of a queue. And you can usually avoid that by going early or buying tickets a day in advance.

WEATHER OR NOT . . .

If you aren't used to Southern summers, you may find your visit to New Orleans a sticky experience. (You'll see T-shirts all over the French Quarter that read, "It's not the heat, it's the stupidity," which gives you some idea how tired the natives are of hearing tourists complain.) Thunderstorms are almost a daily occurrence in June, July, and August, but they provide only temporary relief. The epidemics of yellow fever, malaria, and cholera that used to strike from the swamp are a thing of the past, but the social and

New Orleans's Average Temperatures and Precipitation			
	Average High	**Average Low**	**Average Rainfall**
January	69	43	4.97"
February	65	45	5.23"
March	71	52	4.73"
April	79	59	4.50"
May	85	65	5.07"
June	90	71	4.63"
July	91	74	6.73"
August	90	73	6.02"
September	87	70	5.87"
October	79	59	2.66"
November	70	50	4.06"
December	64	45	5.27"

performance calendars still tend to duck the extremes of summer, and so should you, when the sun is highest. If you skim the calendar of special events, you'll see they drop off in summertime, because even in early May, during the Jazz and Heritage Festival, temperatures can hit 100°.

On the other hand, compared to most places the climate is pretty mild. Snow is a rare and festive occurrence, and the average low temperature, even in January, is 43. (The average high is 69, which should also give you an idea of how much the mercury can swing from midnight to mid-afternoon.) So you can easily consider an off-peak vacation.

There is one more fact to remember about late summer and early fall: hurricanes. These are extremely rare, and generally there is plenty of warning from local authorities. However, just in case you have to deal with some temporary disaccommodation because of bad weather, it's a good idea to have any essential medication on hand and perhaps to pack a small flashlight. If you're going to sign up for one of those haunting expeditions, you'll want it anyway.

Gathering Information

Brochures, historical background, and up-to-date schedules are available from the **New Orleans Metropolitan Convention and Visitors Bureau** (1520 Sugar Bowl Drive, New Orleans, LA 70112-1259, (800) 672-6124 or (504) 566-5003). For information targeted to African-American visitors, contact the **Greater New Orleans Multicultural Tourism Network** at (800) 725-5652. Gay and lesbian visitors may want to contact the **New**

Orleans Gay and Lesbian Community Center at (504) 945-1103. Jewish visitors can call the **Jewish Community Center** at (504) 897-0143. Incidentally, the area code for the entire New Orleans metro area is 504; that should be assumed for all phone numbers in this guide unless otherwise noted.

USING THE INTERNET

The advent of the Internet and its immense popularity have brought about many changes in the way we seek out everyday information. Travel information is one of the most popular and useful areas of publishing and access on the Internet. In just a few short years we have gone from getting most of our travel information from printed books or magazines and our favorite travel agent to a time where we can book entire vacations online. But as wonderful as this sounds, there are pitfalls. It's no small task figuring out how to find the information you need and understanding the tricks that make navigating the Internet easy. Finally, even as an accomplished Internet user, you may be surprised to find that your most valuable travel resource is still your tried-and-true travel agent.

You may have heard that travel providers like to sell directly to consumers on the Internet in order to avoid paying commissions to travel agents, and that the commission savings are passed along to the buyer. While there is some truth in this, discounts (online or anywhere else) have much more to do with time perishability of travel products than with commissions. An empty seat on an airliner, for example, cannot be sold once the plane has left the gate. As the point of perishability approaches, the travel provider (hotel, airline, cruise line, etc.) begins cutting deals to fill its rooms, cabins, and seats. Websites provide a cheap, quick, and efficient way for travel sellers to make these deals known to the public. You should understand, however, that the same deals are usually also communicated to travel agents.

We like the Internet as a method of window-shopping for travel, for scouting deals, and for obtaining information. We do not believe that the Internet is necessarily the best or cheapest way of purchasing travel or that it can be substituted for the services of a good travel agent. The people who get the most out of the Internet are those who work in cooperation with their travel agent, using it as a tool to help their agent help them. First, almost any deal you locate online can be purchased through a travel agent, and second, the more business you give your travel agent, the harder your agent will work for you. It's all about relationships.

It is a bit convoluted to write about the interactive travel experience on paper without the benefit of the very medium we are discussing. We urge you to use your computer or to find a friend with a computer and Internet connection in order to get the most out of these guidelines. We guarantee that you will discover some wonderful things along the way, many things in all likelihood that even we haven't seen. Each person's experience on the Internet is unique, and you'll find many compelling distractions along the way. But bring your patience, because it can take some time getting used to Internet, and it is not perfect. Once you know your way around even slightly you will save a lot of time, and occasionally, some money. When you find resources that you like, bookmark them in your browser. The more you use them the more efficient you will become.

NEW ORLEANS ON THE INTERNET

Searching the Internet for New Orleans information is like navigating an immense maze in search of a very small piece of cheese. There are quite a few New Orleans web pages that offer information, advertisements, and services. To be sure, there is a lot of information available on the Internet, but if you do not use specific addresses, you may have to wade through list after list until you find the addresses you need. Once you have them, finding information can also be time consuming.

Here are some addresses we found helpful:

- www.neworleans.com is maintained by the New Orleans Publishing Group and contains advertisements, travel coupons, a hotel booking service, and articles on various subjects. Business people researching New Orleans will find useful articles on banking, industry, and trade.

- www.neworleansonline.com is a fun web page that is maintained by a group called the New Orleans Marketing Corporation. Subjects found on this page include music, history, people, and dining. On the practical side, you can search by amenity for a hotel room or check out the calendar of events.

- www.nawlins.com is an extensive web page maintained by the New Orleans Convention and Visitors Bureau. Although this page contains helpful information for leisure travelers, meeting and convention planners will find it particularly useful.

- www.nola.com is maintained by the New Orleans *Times-Picayune* and offers information on news, events, entertainment, and festivals. It also offers a five-day weather forecast and a chat forum.

MAJOR TRAVEL AND RESERVATION SITES

The travel and booking sites are some of the most useful sites on the Internet today. They allow you to designate your destinations and preferences and then immediately check on a variety of available flights, cruises, tours, hotels, and rental cars. If you see something you like, you can purchase the ticket online. Each service has its own unique interface and design, and you may find one easier to use than another, depending on the kind of travel you do.

You should fill out a travel profile in each site you try; it is what allows you to indicate your preferences, such as favorite airline, aisle seat, or cheapest fare. Most of these sites allow you to register to receive an e-mail notification when a great fare or special deal comes up for your favorite destinations. Websites always have the latest information on any fare wars that might be happening. Just like any bargain, if you see a good price you should try to make a decision about it as soon as possible, because if you take too much time it could easily be gone when you come back.

Although there are great deals to be found on the Internet, remember that each travel provider's site is nothing more than an electronic media billboard. Be prepared for all of the hype, purple prose, and exaggeration you would find in any other kind of advertisement. Also be aware that filling out a profile will potentially make you a target for all of the provider's promotional messages. If you like to receive a lot of e-mail, fine. Otherwise, be selective.

When a deal comes along that you like, do not assume that it is the best you can do. Check the websites of direct competitors as well as deals in newspapers that target the travel provider's primary geographic market. Los Angeles, for example, is a primary market for most Las Vegas casinos, and you can often find deals in the Sunday travel section of the *Los Angeles Times* that equal or beat what you find on the Internet. When you have narrowed your possibilities, bring your travel agent into the loop and give him or her an opportunity to improve on any deals you have found.

There's a fair amount of cross-pollination in websites, with some companies sharing information and features. Some have travel content along with booking features (Travelocity and ITN), and others offer a variety of vacation packages along with the comprehensive booking information (www.previewvacations.com). But even if you just need a flight from San Francisco to Los Angeles, with the cheapest fare, at the most convenient time, and don't need the other travel information, you can bookmark the page of the site that allows you to set up an itinerary or go directly to it.

If you make a reservation online, remember that it's just like making reservations on the phone or through your travel agent. Make sure that you are aware of any restrictions or refund policies that the sites or the related companies have in place. If you make a reservation with an airline through a website, you can generally assume that this airline's policies apply. If you are purchasing a vacation package or something else from one of the vacation sites, be sure to visit the policies or disclaimer sections of the site so you understand what will happen if you need to change or cancel your plans. Always check this before you submit your order.

You may have read some of the news stories about the security of doing transactions over the Internet and presenting your credit card online. Much progress has been made in this area in the past year, and you'll find that most, if not all, of these sites allow you to enter through a secure server, which simply means that they are taking extra steps to protect your personal information. As the online transaction businesses grow, the technology will only get better. In reality, there have been very few problems with completing transactions online, but if you prefer, most sites will give you the option to call a toll-free number to make your purchase.

SOME RESERVATION SITES TO CHECK OUT

Listed below are some sites we find particularly useful. We are not listing all the reservation sites with booking capabilities—just the main ones as of this writing. New sites are launched every month.

www.travelocity.com	www.sabre.com
www.itn.com	www.expedia.com
www.previewvacations.com	www.outtahere.com
www.reservations.com	www.trip.com

The Airlines

Most of the airlines have sites these days, and they can be quite useful if you like to stick to one carrier. These sites will include flight schedules, information about frequent-flier clubs, policies, and specials. One of the best things about airline-specific sites is the information on fare specials and last-minute discounts. There are often excellent deals available. Sometimes the deals are so good you want to look for a reason to go.

If you just want the best fare or the most convenient itinerary, then looking only at one airline's schedule will not give the full picture. You should also be aware that there are certain airlines, generally those that offer extra-discounted fares most of the time, that are not part of the major reservation systems. So if you want to fly on these airlines you either have to call them directly, use your travel agent, or go to their websites. At the time of this writing, Southwest Airlines is one of the airlines not participating in the main reservations systems.

Hotels and Rental Cars

Most of the travel sites listed above also have connections to hotel and rental-car booking services, and they work in much the same way as making airline reservations. On the airlines' sites you will find that airlines generally have a relationship with one or two car-rental companies and will put you in touch with them for reservations. And like the airlines, the rental-car companies have their own sites, but that means if you want to comparison shop you have to go to multiple sites.

THE TRAVEL AND LOCAL INFORMATION RESOURCES

The most dynamic places to find all kinds of travel information are the unique travel websites that present information in a totally new way. There are also many sites presented by some of the big players in the Internet business that are designed to provide detailed information about particular cities—not only travel information, but also information on the government, schools, movies, shopping, services, and transportation. These sites can be very useful as you prepare to leave for your destination or, if you are lucky enough to have a computer with you, after you arrive. One of the best all-around resources for finding information on just about any place in the world is Excite's City.Net (**www.city.net** or through **www.excite.com**). While it presents some information directly on its site, City.Net is primarily a resource of other travel providers on the Internet. Almost all of these sites have direct links or partnerships with the reservations sites listed above.

At this point most major cities' newspapers have websites, and they are often excellent sources of local information. You may also want to check with your regional AAA office to see if they have a website. For example, AAA of Northern California, Nevada, and Utah has an excellent website that contains information about the auto club's road services and their extensive travel planning services. It is a great resource.

Listed below are some of our favorite travel and local-information resource sites:

www.city.net	www.citysearch.com
www.gorp.com	www.digitalcity.com
www.csaa.com	www.sfgate.com
www.nytimes.com	www.latimes.com
www.washingtonpost.com	www.tribune.com

SEARCH ENGINES AND DIRECTORIES

One of the best ways to make your time on the Internet the most useful and fun is to learn how to use one or more search engines. The most popular, and arguably the best, include Yahoo! (**www.yahoo.com**), Excite (**www.excite.com**), Lycos (**www.lycos.com**), Infoseek (**www.infoseek.com**), and Alta Vista (**www.altavista.com**), which is also the search engine that is used in Yahoo! along with their directories. The "directories" in Yahoo! and the "channels" in Excite, for example, are lists of sites that are already organized into categories and can be very useful. But if you don't see what you want in these directories, read on.

If you can, we suggest that you take an hour or two and just experiment. Input the same search topic in each and compare the results. For example: Alaskan Cruises. You will get different results from each site (sometimes slightly different, sometimes totally different), but each should give you some useful sites. These are essential tools if you can describe what you are looking for but have no idea where to find it, or if you have looked in the better-known travel sites and have not seen the information you want. There is usually a tutorial or "help" area on the search-engine site that will show you how to get the most out of that particular service. All of these services figure importantly in having a good Internet experience. You will probably find a favorite service and use it frequently.

Before you take your trip you should take a few minutes and visit a few other sites. One is Amazon.com (**www.amazon.com**). Its bookstore contains millions of titles you can order, so if you want to know more about the history, culture, or sights in the region you will be visiting, Amazon is a terrific resource. When it comes time to pack, you can go to the Weather Channel online (**www.weather.com**) and see a forecast, precipitation map, the business travelers' forecast with airport delays, and much more. It is even better than their cable channel because you don't have to wait until your area comes on the air—you can just go directly to it.

All of these services will only get better with time and improved technology. While the amount spent on online booking of travel is only a tiny fraction of what is spent today, the predicted growth rate of these businesses is nothing short of phenomenal. So go online and try booking a trip today.

Special Considerations

WHAT TO PACK

Perhaps a little sadly, this once most elegant of societies has become extremely informal. You probably won't see a black tie or tuxedo outside of a wedding party unless you are fortunate enough to be invited to a serious social event. Even an old, established restaurant such as Galatoire's requires only a jacket (after 5 p.m. and all day Sunday) but not a tie, and most others only "recommend" a jacket.

Shorts and polo shirts are everywhere, night or day, and a sundress or reasonably neat pair of khakis will make you look downright respectable. A rainproof top of some sort, a lightweight jacket, and a sweater, even a sweatshirt, may be all you'll need in the summer, and remember that you will probably be going in and out of air conditioning as well as rain. Something along the lines of a trenchcoat with zip-in lining or a wool walking coat with a sweater will usually do in winter. (Fur coats are not a moral issue in New Orleans, but are rarely necessary, and the constant bustle of people carrying glasses and food around on the streets might make it a risk unless you plan to spend most of the time in nicer hotels and restaurants.)

Frankly, the two most important things to consider when packing are comfortable shoes (this is a culture of asphalt, concrete, and flagstone streets) and skirts or pants with expandable waistlines. Even if you don't think you're going to eat much, the scent of food constantly fills the air, and the Café du Monde by Jackson Square is still making those beignets—fried doughnuts dusted with powdered sugar, three for a buck—24 hours a day. Second, there is no other city in which the food is so rich and full of fat, cholesterol, and calories as this, and even if you don't eat more than usual, you may temporarily feel the effects. (Add a third item to your packing list—Alka Seltzer.) If you don't want to pack "fat day" clothes, you'd better pack your running shoes, too.

And finally, this city has developed a crime problem (see "How to Avoid Crime" on page 146), so there is no good reason to walk around flashing expensive jewelry. Leave it at home and stick to the Mardi Gras beads.

PLAYING HOST

If you are coming in with a family or business group and are in charge of arranging some sort of party or reception, there are plenty of restaurants, music clubs (check out the Voodoo Garden at House of Blues or the private room at Lucky Cheng's), steamboats, and hotels with private rooms. But there are also a few less ordinary places to throw a party, if you really want to make an impression. Within City Park, for example, the New Orleans Botanical Garden has the 9,000-square-foot **Pavilion of the Two Sisters** (488-2896), and **Storyland** and **Carousel Gardens** (483-9381) can be reserved after hours. The carousel provides on-site catering as well. The **Contemporary Arts Center** (523-1216) and the **Louisiana Children's Museum** (523-1357), both within easy walking distance of the Convention Center, have spaces for rent. Blaine Kern's **Mardi Gras World** in Algiers lets guests try on the parade masks (361-7821). The restored third-floor "Appartement de l'Empereur" at the Napoleon House can be reserved as well, and even though Bonaparte himself never came here, the atmosphere is quite imperial.

But here's another idea that might enliven either a purely social event, such as a family reunion or wedding, or provide an unusual "spouses' function" during a business convention: playing chef for a day.

The only thing more famous than Mardi Gras is probably New Orleans' restaurants, and devotees of Cajun and Creole cuisine can not only indulge in it, but also apprentice to it, at least temporarily. There are several cooking schools in New Orleans, most associated with local celebrity chefs, that offer classes during which visitors can either actively participate or simply watch and taste, depending on their ambitions.

The most traditional and least expensive of the schools is the **New Orleans School of Cooking** at 524 St. Louis Street, 525-2665. Monday through Saturday, it offers three-hour Cajun/Creole cooking classes for $25; this covers the class-cooked lunch (something like jambalaya and bananas Foster) and a Dixie beer. Groups of 25 or more can arrange a private demonstration.

The **Culinary Institute of New Orleans** is in the Garden District (2100 St. Charles Avenue, 525-CHEFS), where former G&E Courtyard chef Mark Uddo is one of the instructors. Classes are actually run out of the Chef's Table restaurant, and visitors can choose from a three-hour guest lecture with meals or four-hour hands-on classes for which day chefs get to wear chef's jackets and toques. Classes, which can be either classic New Orleans–style or not, as you desire (but which go beyond gumbo to oysters Rockefeller and veal with grits, even if you do go native), are made by appointment; larger groups of up to 300 can be accommodated with advance notice—another convention blockbuster.

Most recently, Chef Horst Pfeifer of **Bella Luna** restaurant in the French Market (914 N. Peters Street, 529-1583), which despite its name is as much Creole-Southwestern fusion as Italian, has expanded what were only small, rare classes to regular demonstration lunches. Pfeifer's classes include a trip to his herb garden on the grounds of the historic Ursuline convent and are held in his own home across the street from the convent. He also does large convention classes for groups of up to 100 at the restaurant.

EXCHANGING VOWS

Carried away by the romance of it all? Want to make it permanent? There is a three-day waiting period between getting a license and being married, but the judge has the option of waiving it, so your weekend could turn pretty spectacular. And he may even waive the requirement for your birth certificate if you seem sober enough. Contact the Marriage Clerk at 568-5182, 8 a.m.–4 p.m. weekdays.

NEW ORLEANS FOR FAMILIES

Of course, New Orleans is most famous as a sort of adults' playground, but if you're considering a family vacation here, don't worry: for all the round-the-clock bars and burlesque houses, New Orleans is full of family-style attractions, both in and out of the French Quarter. And since these are year-round, you can avoid the special-event crowds altogether. Just remember that warnings about dehydration in the city's heat go double for children.

Within the Vieux Carré is the entire **French Market, Jackson Square** with all its balloon twisters, clowns, and mule-drawn carriages that, while somewhat undependable as far as historic detail is concerned, are very entertaining. The **Musée Conti Wax Museum** is a perennial favorite, as is the free **Canal Street ferry** ride across the Mississippi. There are several doll and toy museum-stores that may attract some children, as well as **Le Petit Soldier store** and, for some, the **Pharmacy Museum.** By far the most fantastic collection of antique dolls belongs to author Anne Rice: you can see them at the former **St. Elizabeth's Orphanage** in the Garden District. Kids who play dress-up will love the Carnival exhibit at the **Old U.S. Mint,** with its Aladdin's cave of crowns and pins. (And you should check the schedule of **Le Petit Théâtre du Vieux Carré,** which sometimes has children's productions.)

The state-of-the-art **Louisiana Children's Museum** is in the Warehouse/ Arts District. At the edge of the riverwalk area is the **Aquarium of the Americas,** from which you can take a boat directly to **Audubon Zoo** in the Garden District. (The Zoo is also accessible from the St. Charles streetcar, which is another family possibility.)

City Park in Mid-City has an antique carousel, miniature rideable trains, a toy museum, the Storyland playground designed around Mother Goose characters, plus botanical gardens and a riding stable. Beyond that, in eastern New Orleans, is the **Louisiana Nature Center,** which has a planetarium, hands-on exhibits, and 86 acres of forest trails.

East of the city on the way to Chalmette National Battlefield, site of the Battle of New Orleans, is a remarkable military museum at the **Jackson Barracks** that will almost certainly transfix any normally bloody-minded kid. **The Confederate Museum,** while more specific and semi-hagiographic, is close to the new D-Day Museum and the Louisiana Children's Museum.

Near the airport is a treasure trove for families, a complex of attractions called **Rivertown** that includes an observatory and planetarium, Mardi Gras and toy-train museums, the New Orleans Saints Hall of Fame, a Native American–living museum within the Louisiana Wildlife Museum, and the Children's Castle, where puppet and magic shows are staged. There is also a repertory theater there.

And if you're interested in swamp and bayou life, you can either sign up for one of the several swamp tours or cruises or take a short drive to the **Barataria Preserve**—Jean Lafitte's old stronghold and now a 20,000-acre park with a Park Service visitors center, trails, and boardwalks that wind among the cypress swamps and freshwater branches. Even wilder, spend the night at the **Global Wildlife Center** near Folsom and go nose-to-nose with a giraffe (see Chapter Eleven: "Sight-Seeing and Tours").

If you bring the kids along for the convention but have to get a little work time in, contact **Accents on Arrangements** (524-1227) to hook up with children's tours; or the day care/field trip–oriented **Conference Child Care Service** (248-9457), which is a member of the Greater New Orleans Multicultural Tourism Network.

TIPS FOR INTERNATIONAL TRAVELERS

Visitors from Western Europe, the United Kingdom, Japan, or New Zealand who stay in the United States fewer than 90 days need only a valid passport, not a visa, and a round-trip or return ticket. Canadian citizens can get by only with proof of residence. Citizens of other countries must have a passport (good for at least six months beyond the projected end of the visit) and a tourist visa as well, available from any U.S. consulate. Contact consular officials for application forms; some airlines and travel agents may also have forms available.

If you are taking prescription drugs containing narcotics or requiring injection by syringe, be sure to get a doctor's signed prescription and instructions. Also check with the local consulate to see whether travelers from your country are currently required to have any inoculations; there are no set requirements to enter the United States, but if there has been any sort of epidemic in your homeland, there may be temporary restrictions.

If you arrive by air, be prepared to spend as much as two hours entering the country and getting through Customs. Canadians and Mexicans crossing the borders either by car or by train will find a much quicker and easier system. Every adult traveler may bring in, duty-free, up to 1 liter of wine or hard liquor; 200 cigarettes, 100 non-Cuban cigars, or 3 pounds of loose tobacco; and $100 worth of gifts, as well as up to $10,000 in U.S. currency or its equivalent in foreign currency. No food or plants may be brought in. For information on sales tax refunds, see Chapter Ten: "Shopping."

Credit cards are by far the most common form of payment in New Orleans, especially American Express, Visa (also known as BarclayCard in Britain) and MasterCard (Access in Britain, Eurocard in Western Europe, or Chargex in Canada). Other popular cards include Diners Club, Discover, and Carte Blanche. Travelers checks will be accepted at most hotels and restaurants if they are in American dollars; other currencies should be taken to a bank or foreign exchange and turned into dollar figures (the Mutual of Omaha office offers this service and wires funds in or out).

The dollar is the basic unit of monetary exchange, and the entire system is decimal. The smaller sums are represented by coins. One hundred cents (or pennies, as the 1-cent coin is known) equal one dollar; 5 cents is a nickel (20 nickels to a dollar); 10 cents is called a dime (10 dimes to a dollar); and the 25-cent coin is called a quarter (4 to a dollar). The dollar coin is the only one that is not perfectly round, but octagonal, so it's easily identified. Beginning with one dollar, money is in currency bills (there are both one-dollar coins and bills). Bills come in $1, $5, $10, $20, $50, $100, $500, and so on, although you are unlikely to want to carry $1,000 or more. Stick to $20s for taxicabs and such; drivers rarely can make change for anything larger.

If you need any additional assistance, there is an Immigration Service desk at the airport (467-1713). For language assistance, try the AT&T language line at (800) 874-9426.

And throughout the United States, if you have a medical, police, or fire emergency, dial 911, even on a pay telephone, and an ambulance or police cruiser will be dispatched to help you.

TIPS FOR THE DISABLED

Visitors who use walking aids should be warned: only the larger museums and the newer shopping areas can be counted on to be wheelchair accessible. Many individual stores and smaller collections are housed in what were once private homes with stairs, and even those at sidewalk level are unlikely to have wider aisles or specially equipped bathrooms. The restaurants that we profile later in the book all have a disabled access rating, but you need to call any other eatery or store in advance. Similarly, you need to call any stores you're interested in. Antique stores in particular tend to be tightly packed and with shelving at all levels.

FOR THE NOSE THAT KNOWS

If you are allergy sensitive, watch out for spring. As for smoking, it is prohibited in any public building, on the streetcars, and in taxis. Restaurants with more than 50 seats have to have a nonsmoking section, but that's not practical in a smaller restaurant; bars welcome smokers.

A Calendar of Special Events

These are New Orleans' major celebrations and their approximate dates (specific ones where possible). Remember, if the event requires tickets, it's best to try to arrange them before leaving home; otherwise you may find yourself paying extra or being locked out entirely. Please note that many festivals, especially in the summer, move around from year to year, and that some close down or are replaced by others; so if you are interested, contact organizers as soon as possible.

In addition to the contacts listed below, **TicketMaster** (522-5555) may be able to supply tickets to particular events, although there will be an additional handling charge.

JANUARY

Sugar Bowl   One of the three major collegiate alliance bowls, held New Year's Day. For information on tickets and festivities, contact organizers at 1500 Sugar Bowl Drive, New Orleans, LA 70112, or call 525-8573. Sugar Bowl tickets can be purchased through TicketMaster, or by calling (877) 99-SUGAR. Associated with the football classic are other sporting events, including flag football, tennis, races, and basketball.

Super Bowl (to be held again in New Orleans in 2002)   Apart from the football showdown itself, events include a celebrity golf tournament, a huge public meet-the-players party, and a "theme park" of football games at the convention center. Contact the Convention and Visitors Bureau, 1520 Sugar Bowl Drive, New Orleans, LA 70112, or call 566-5005.

Twelfth Night   January 6, or the Feast of Epiphany, when the Three Wise Men reportedly reached Bethlehem, also marks the beginning of Carnival season in New Orleans; contact the Convention and Visitors Bureau.

The Anniversary of the Battle of New Orleans   Early January. The actual date is January 8, and the special mass is held on that day (see the profile of St. Ursuline's Convent in "New Orleans Attractions"). However, the reenactment of the battle, with Redcoats, cannons, and encampment demonstrations, varies slightly around that. Call Chalmette National Park at 281-0510.

FEBRUARY

NCAA Baseball   For tickets and times contact the Superdome Ticket Office, P.O. Box 50488, New Orleans, LA 70150, or call 587-3663.

MARCH

Louisiana Black Heritage Festival   Early March. A two-day celebration, with exhibits and concerts set up along Riverwalk, Audubon Park, and the Louisiana State Museum buildings. Contact the festival at 6500 Magazine Street, New Orleans, LA 70118, or 861-2537.

Mardi Gras   February 12 in 2002, March 4 in 2003, February 24 in 2004, February 8 in 2005, and February 28 in 2006. Contact the Convention and Visitors Bureau and ask for the latest schedules. The day before, now called Lundi Gras or "Fat Monday," is also an organized event; contact Riverwalk, 1 Poydras Street, New Orleans, LA 70130, or call 522-1555.

St. Patrick's Day   Mid-March. The actual date is March 17, but the parade dates vary. For information on the French Quarter celebration, contact Molly's Pub at the Market, 1107 Decatur Street, New Orleans, LA 70116, or call 525-5169.

St. Joseph's Day   Mid-March. The Italian equivalent of St. Patrick's Day salutes Jesus's adoptive father and officially falls on March 19. But like St. Paddy's, the celebrations spread out a little. The gift of the feast is fava beans, which the saint is believed to have showered upon the starving of Sicily. Contact the American Italian Renaissance Foundation at 522-7294.

Spring Fiesta   Mid-March. A five-day celebration, dating back to the 1930s, featuring tours of historic homes, courtyard receptions, and plantation tours, culminating in a grand parade down River Road with costumed figures from history riding in horse-drawn carriages. Arias pour out over the French Quarter in honor of such past stars as Adelina Patti and Jenny Lind. Tickets are $20 for city tours, $50 for the plantation tours. Contact organizers at 826 St. Ann Street, New Orleans, LA 70112, or call 581-1367.

Tennessee Williams New Orleans Literary Festival Third week of March to early April. This five-day event features seminars, dramatic readings (often featuring Hollywood and Broadway celebrities), theatrical productions, walking tours of the French Quarter, and the popular Stella & Stanley Shouting Competition in Jackson Square. Contact the Tennessee Williams/New Orleans Literary Festival, 5500 Prytania Street, Suite 217, New Orleans, LA 70115, call 581-1144, or go to their website at www.tennesseewilliams.net.

April

French Quarter Festival Mid-April. This is something of an apology to area residents, and performers, for the fact that the Jazz and Heritage Festival has gotten so large and so national. Throughout the Quarter, free concerts are performed on 11 separate stages, and there are patio tours, fireworks, and second-lining brass parades. On Sunday, the whole of Jackson Square becomes a huge jazz brunch, thanks to the efforts of several dozen Cajun and Creole restaurants. Contact the French Quarter Festival office at 100 Conti Street, New Orleans, LA 70130, or call 522-5730.

Crescent City Classic Mid-April. An international field runs this scenic 10K race from Jackson Square to Audubon Park. Write the CCC at 8200 Hampson Street, Suite 217, New Orleans, LA 70118, or call 861-8686.

New Orleans Jazz and Heritage Festival Last weekend in April through the first weekend in May. See details above, or contact Jazz Fest, P.O. Box 53407, New Orleans, LA 70153, or call 522-4786.

May

Zoo-To-Do Early May. The fundraiser for Audubon Zoo is one of the most profitable events in the country and includes food, decorations, and special performances. Call 565-3020, ext. 602.

Compaq Classic of New Orleans Early May. This PGA tournament sports a million-dollar purse and is held at the English Turn Golf & Country Club in Metairie. Contact Beth Bares, 110 Veteran's Blvd. #170, New Orleans, LA 70148, or call 831-4653.

Greek Festival Late May. All those streets around Lee Circle didn't get to be named for the Muses for no reason. Enjoy folk dancing, Greek food, music, and crafts. The $3 fee enters you in a drawing for a trip to Greece. Contact festival organizers at Holy Trinity Cathedral, 1200 Robert E. Lee Boulevard, New Orleans, LA 70122, or call 282-0259.

JUNE

The Great French Market Tomato Festival   Around the first of June. Cooking demonstrations, tastings, and music along the French Market promenade. Contact organizers at P.O. Box 51749, New Orleans, LA 70151, or call 522-2621.

Reggae Riddums Festival   Mid-June. City Park hosts a weekend of international performers of reggae, calypso, and soca, surrounded by booths selling food and African-American crafts. Contact Ernest Kelly, P.O. Box 6156, New Orleans, LA 70174, or call (504) 367-1313.

New Orleans Food & Wine Experience   Mid–late June. The premier taste-of-the-town event distributes goodies from more than 40 restaurants and 150 wineries. Contact organizers at P.O. Box 70514, New Orleans, LA 70172, or call 529-WINE.

JULY

Go Fourth on the River   July 4. Independence Day celebrations include street performances, shopping specials, discounts to riverfront attractions, concerts, parades, and fireworks. Contact the French Quarter Festival office.

Essence Music Festival   Early July. A half million people hear four days of soul, jazzy R&B, and blues in the Superdome, along with seminars, crafts, and a book fair. Contact the Visitor's Bureau for more information.

AUGUST

White Linen Night   Early August. Warehouse/Arts District galleries mount simultaneous openings with performing arts along Julia Street. Contact the Contemporary Arts Center, 900 Camp Street, New Orleans, LA 70130, or call 523-1216.

OCTOBER

Jazz Awareness Month   Throughout October. Concerts, many of them free, lectures, and family events. Contact the Louisiana Jazz Federation at 522-3154.

Octoberfest   Weekends throughout the month. Venues and restaurants around town set out German food and drink; watch for polka lessons. Call 522-8014.

Art for Art's Sake   The new season kicks off with gallery openings up and down Julia, Magazine, and Royal streets. Contact the Contemporary Arts Center, 900 Camp Street, New Orleans, LA 70130, or call 523-1216.

Swamp Festival Early to mid-October. Sponsored by the Audubon Institute and held at the zoo over two weekends, this offers close encounters with indigenous animals, a taste of Cajun food, and music and crafts. Contact the Audubon Institute, 6500 Magazine Street, New Orleans, LA 70118, or call 861-2537.

New Orleans Film & Video Festival Mid-October. Regional and world premieres of films and screenings of award-winners; the main screenings are at Canal Street Cinemas. Call 523-3818.

Jeff Fest Mid-October. This onetime family picnic is now an annual community event with 30 bands and plenty of food in Metairie's Lafreniere Park. Contact organizers at 3816 Haring Road, Metairie, LA 70006, or call 888-2900.

Boo at the Zoo End of October. Annual Halloween extravaganza at Audubon Zoo with special children's entertainment, a "ghost train," and a haunted house. Contact the Audubon Institute, 6500 Magazine Street, New Orleans, LA 70118, or call 861-2537.

NOVEMBER

Racing Season at the Fairgrounds Late November to early January. The country's third-oldest racetrack still hosts thoroughbred races Thursday through Monday during the holiday season—opening day is Thanksgiving. For reservations call (800) 262-7893 within Louisiana, or 944-5515.

Celebration in the Oaks Late November to early January. City Park kicks off the holiday season with a display of 750,000 lights, music, seasonal foods, and special events. Contact City Park, #1 Palm Drive, New Orleans, LA 70124, or call 482-4888.

Bayou Classic Late November. One of collegiate football's long-standing rivalries. Grambling and Southern University wind up the season at the Superdome; P.O. Box 50488, New Orleans, LA 70150, or call 587-3663.

DECEMBER

New Orleans Christmas Throughout the month. See "Creole Christmas" on page 76, for details.

New Year's Eve December 31. Jackson Square may not be as big as Times Square, but it holds a heck of a street party, complete with countdown and, yes, a lighted ball that drops from the top of Jax Brewery. Contact the Convention and Visitors Bureau, 1520 Sugar Bowl Drive, New Orleans, LA 70112, or call 566-5005.

Part Three

New Orleans's Major Festivals

Mardi Gras Mania

You could write a book about Mardi Gras, and many people have. The big picture, you already know: it's a loud, public, and highly indulgent series of parades, "second-line" dancing (that refers to the parasol-wielding high-steppers who traditionally formed a second line behind the brass band, and who gradually acquire a civilian train like a comet attracting cosmic detritus), and formal masques and balls. There's partying in the streets, in the bars, in the restaurants, in the courtyards, in the parks, in the alleys—no wonder most French Quarter residents rent their homes out for the week and flee uptown, or even out of town. There's little sleep to be had, with more than a million visitors—an estimated two million in 1999—packed elbow to armpit and mug to go-cup. Tourism officials estimate that Mardi Gras spending has reached a billion dollars a year.

But in recent years, the ever-increasing incidents of public inebriation, fighting, nudity, petty (and occasionally greater) crime, and general vagrancy have for many people irretrievably tarnished the event; some of the oldest and most respected societies have pulled out entirely. Some, it must be pointed out, have pulled out with less plausible excuses: After the City Council ruled in 1991 that the all-white krewes had to integrate their parades, two of the three oldest parading krewes, the venerable Comus and Momus, chose to stop parading rather than integrate. They were followed the next year by Proteus, the fourth-oldest parading krewe, though it returned to active duty in 2000. They now maintain their balls strictly as private parties. A recent Rex float, florid with flames and demons, was titled "Momus in Hades," a tribute to one of the most famous parades in Mardi Gras history, the 1877 "Hades, a Dream of Momus," which managed to insult nearly every politician at the state or national level; however, some city residents took it as a poke from Rex to its less amenable rival. (It would have been more appropriate than they knew: Although it's not often mentioned, white supremacists and anti-federalist groups often used Mardi Gras parades, and costume masks, as a cover for rallies and sometimes riots during Reconstruction. Some, including the Mystick Krewe of Comus, were at times virtual fronts for such groups.)

The pleading for beads and other *lagniappes* (pronounced lan-yap) and the traditional cries of "Throw me somethin', mister," have degenerated to the point where members of even the highest-profile krewes knowingly twirl their fanciest prizes and demand that women bare their breasts to earn the treasure. Grown-ups (we use the phrase ironically) now far out-perform the most spoiled and insatiable small children by stealing beads tossed to others, concealing the size of their trove, and even snatching stuffed animals and toys. Wearing the biggest and showiest beads is now a sort of measure of either testosterone or nubility, depending on the wearer. It's no wonder that the locals tend to avoid Bourbon Street and enjoy smaller parties in the suburbs; or they pick and choose their events.

But tarnished or not, no city, except perhaps for Rio de Janeiro, is so closely associated with Carnival as New Orleans. In fact, it almost seems as if the city's destiny was to be the biggest Mardi Gras party town in the world: On March 3, 1699, when the Sieur d'Iberville (brother of the Sieur de Bienville) camped on the Mississippi River, the day *was* Mardi Gras, and that was what he named the site—Mardi Gras Point. Hedging a little bit, perhaps, the city declared the 1999 Carnival season the 300th anniversary celebration. Nevertheless, it is clear that there were some rudimentary carryings-on in the area—Mobile had a Boeuf Gras, a "fatted calf" club, even before the city of New Orleans formally existed—almost from the very beginning, so observing Mardi Gras in the Crescent City is one of those things a lot of people feel they ought to do at least once. If you want to immerse yourself in the spirit, we can try at least to make it a little easier on you.

Mardi Gras, for those who think it means "bottoms up," actually translates as "Fat Tuesday"; it's so called because it's the last day before Lent, when observant Catholics were supposed to give up meat-eating (and, ideally, various other fleshly pleasures). The weeks between Twelfth Night and Lent are called "Carnival," from the Latin for "farewell to meat," although the festival season certainly involves plenty of feasting—stocking up, so to speak. Although many people refer to the entire Carnival season as Mardi Gras, that title rightfully applies to only the one day, and using the term wrongly is one way to brand yourself a really green outsider. The day after Fat Tuesday is Ash Wednesday, the beginning of the sober Lenten season, which continues until Easter. In other words, Tuesday is supposed to be the last day to enjoy oneself for nearly seven weeks. Hence it became an occasion for overindulgence, followed by extreme penitence, beginning smack on the mark with midnight mass. Nowadays most people settle for the indulgences and watch the tape replay of Ash Wednesday services on television later. In fact, St. Louis Cathedral doesn't even hold midnight mass at the end of Mardi Gras any more because of the unruly crowds.

Mardi Gras is also a legal holiday in Louisiana, so get your banking done on Monday. (But be sure to check the calendar there, too; in 1999, for example, the Monday before Mardi Gras coincided with the federal holiday Presidents' Day, so there was no banking from Friday to Wednesday, and no postal service from Saturday to Wednesday. It was also Valentine's Day on Sunday, and the end of spring break for a lot of college students; so now you know how they wound up with two million people in the streets.)

Mardi Gras has a long and suitably flamboyant history in New Orleans. The French colonists celebrated Mardi Gras, or more generally, Twelfth Night, in some form for nearly 50 years, but when the city was turned over to the Spanish empire, which adhered to a much more rigorous and ascetic form of Catholicism, the governor banned the festivities—and the anti-Catholic Americans who took over after the Louisiana Purchase weren't favorably inclined toward such Papist displays, either. In fact, there was nearly a serious dust-up over whether the music played at Carnival season was to be in English or in French. However, there was always at least some private partying to keep the spirit alive. By 1823 the balls were legal again, and within a few years the street parties took hold; the first walking parades were organized in 1837. As in modern times, the crowds kept swelling; a parade of mounted "Bedouins" was a huge public success in 1852, but by 1855, newspaper reports, focusing on the violence of the rabble and the drunkenness of some participants (ahem), called for an end to the celebrations.

Instead, a group of aristocratic Creoles formed the first secret krewe, the Mystick Krewe of Comus, to give the mayhem some form. It was Comus that designed the first great classical tableaux and theme parade floats and debuted them in early 1857. The Twelfth Night club first selected a queen and threw trinkets soon after the Civil War (during which, due to the occupation, all celebrations were cancelled); the Krewe of Rex designed the first "doubloon" in 1884. That same year, incidentally, Comus picked its first queen, Mildred Lee, daughter of the "sainted" Robert E. Lee—payback for those four years, perhaps. The theme song, the rather sappy "If Ever I Cease to Love," was a signature song of New York vaudeville star Lydia Thompson, who was performing in New Orleans in 1872. The lovesick Grand Duke Alexis of Russia followed her south, and in his honor every krewe played the number in its parade (except Momus, which fortunately had thrown its inaugural parade on New Year's Eve). Now it's not so common, but Rex and his court still begin their ball with it.

The first "electric parade" was in 1889, when the appropriately named Krewe of Electra wired the headdresses of more than 125 paraders. The first black organization, the Original Illinois Club, was founded in 1895; the first all-woman krewe, Les Mysterieuses, followed suit the next year and held a formal ball, though the first all-woman parade, by the Krewe of Venus, wasn't launched until 1941. (It has since disbanded.) The gay Krewe of Petronius threw its first ball in 1962; there are now four gay krewes. Mardi Gras has survived wars (though the only times it has been cancelled were during the Civil War and World Wars I and II), Prohibition (only Rex paraded in 1920), fires, blizzards, monsoons, epidemics (most of it was lost to yellow fever in 1879), racial tensions (with losses, as mentioned), and hurricanes (1965's Betsy chewed up a chunk of several krewes).

The major parades include dozens of floats, punctuated by marching bands and mounted police, and may require the talents of 2,000 or 3,000 people. Mardi Gras expert Arthur Hardy, who has been publishing the semi-official guide to Mardi Gras for more than 20 years, has calculated that the parades of Endymion, Bacchus, and Orpheus, which are held the three nights leading up to Mardi Gras, among themselves account for 3,750 members, 110 floats, 90 marching bands, and 375 units.

Most of the krewes (the only correct spelling for Mardi Gras "crews") have names and themes taken from classical mythology: Aphrodite, Pegasus, Mercury, Ulysses, Saturn, Rhea, Argus, Atlas, Atreus, Helios, Orion, Poseidon, Pan, Hermes, Zeus, Juno, Diana, Hercules, Venus, Midas, Mithras, Isis, Iris, Thor, and Thoth ("tote," as it's pronounced locally) have all had their own krewes, although not all survive or parade. Most members are masked, and many never even reveal their membership, especially those who belong to charitable clubs.

Although the strict secrecy has eased a little, some krewes still keep parade themes and rulers quiet until the last minute. The captain of the krewe, who is actually the executive officer, is a permanent position, but the king, queen, and court change from year to year. Rex, considered the real King of Carnival, is never publicly identified until the night before. The "dictator" or the Krewe d'Etat, which was formed only in 1996 and is trying to return the parades to their original political and satirical tone, is never publicly identified. Depending on the krewe, the royals may either be mature members of the business/social communities, or up-and-comers, with queens and ladies drawn from the debutante circle. In the older social families, there may be more than one generation of kings and queens, and several lesser lights.

Bacchus, on the other hand, is most celebrity-conscious and regularly crowns actors of, let us say, obvious appetites, such as John Goodman and James Belushi, and the verbally voracious Larry King. The Krewe of Orpheus, named after the musician so eloquent he persuaded Pluto to release his dead wife (although she slipped away again), was founded in 1994 by Harry Connick Jr. as the first "super krewe" with male and female members, and its parade on Saturday night is considered one of the modern highlights. Over the years, celebrities as wide-ranging as the Beach Boys, Dolly Parton, Stevie Wonder, Whoopi Goldberg, Bob Hope, Britney Spears, and Jackie Gleason have been lured to the throne of Parade floats.

In its heyday, and even up until fairly recently, Creole Carnival season was a much more elegant affair, with fancy dress and masquerade balls, elaborate trinkets, and lagniappes, a word meaning something like "a little extra" and applied to any small gift or token, even a nibble or free drink. Nowadays, yelling "Throw me somethin', mister" may get you beads, candy, bikini pants, or almost anything—if you can wrest it away from the next guy, or the girl on his shoulders. (The familiar purple, green, and gold colors represent justice, faith, and power, and you may need all three to survive.) Even now, being a krewe member is fairly expensive; it costs more than $3,000 to ride with Krewe of America.

Obviously, you need not be a New Orleans resident to participate—the Southern Trial Lawyers Association annually schedules its convention in New Orleans to coincide with Mardi Gras so that members may parade with the Bards of Bohemia—but the most traditional dances are still sponsored by old-line krewes, and their parties are still by closely guarded invitation only, many of them doubling as the debutante balls of their members' daughters. They often get to sit in special boxes along the parade routes and be saluted by their loyal following on the floats, and some actually ride and toss themselves.

Even if somehow you do get invited to a traditional krewe ball, remember that you are not a member and can only sit in the spectator seats and enjoy the show. (The only exception is a woman guest issued a "call-out card"; she will sit with the other called women until the dancing begins and her escort calls her out.) And it is quite a show: the last year's court will be presented, and the costumes displayed in tableaux. The ball of the Krewe of Rex, for example, which is probably the most intently traditional, follows so rigid a line that the stories in the *Times-Picayune* are reprinted almost word for word every year—sort of an inside joke:

It begins about 6 p.m. the day before Mardi Gras (Lundi Gras or "Fat Monday") with Rex's being ferried downriver (in the 19th century it was a paddleboat; these days, he's transported by Coast Guard cutter) to land at Spanish Plaza at the foot of Canal Street. There he is greeted by the King of Zulu. Rex reads a proclamation declaring the advent of festivities— a little late, but then he is the official King of Carnival—fireworks ensue, and he and his retainers head for their ball, usually held at a downtown hotel or the convention center. The captain announces the arrival of the court, in order of precedence; the court dances the first dance and then everybody gets to join in. Around 9 p.m., however, a messenger from the Krewe of Comus is announced; he invites Rex and his Queen to visit the Comus court (usually in the neighboring ballroom), and Rex and company head over for another presentation to the King of Comus, who, unlike Rex, is never unmasked.

Some outsiders may find all this pompous circumstance a little strange, especially in contrast to the other parties in the street. (Among the better-natured spoof parades is the annual Mystic Krewe of Barkus parade, a fundraiser for the LSPCA that has chosen such themes as "Lifestyles of the Bitch and Famous" and "Jurassic Bark.") However, there are many newer and more liberal krewes that throw more public and less tradition-bound "supper dances," and you may be able to get tickets to some of those. Orpheus and Tucks, for example, sell party tickets through TicketMaster. You can even join a krewe and ride for a few hundred bucks. Get a copy of Arthur Hardy's annual *Mardi Gras Guide* magazine for more information. It will probably be all over town when you get there, but you would be smart to have one in advance, because it includes maps, schedules, tips, gossip, features, and even the occasional coupon. Write to P.O. Box 19500, New Orleans, LA 70005, call (504) 838-6111, or write to him via his email address: mardihardy@aol.com.

Carnival season in New Orleans traditionally begins with the Krewe of Twelfth Night ball held on Twelfth Night or Epiphany (January 6), but the pace gradually picks up: The last 10 or 12 days of Carnival is high parade season—nearly 70 parades in the 4 metropolitan parishes—when at almost any moment police sirens announce the imminent arrival of a marching band, motorcycle drill team, or horseback troupe, stilt-walking clowns, acrobats, balloon-twisters, and professional and amateur dancing girls. Although these are rarely as elaborate or as lengthy as those in the final few days, they are often just as entertaining and not nearly so crowded. The French Quarter in particular erupts into walking parades of ordinary celebrants that form behind bands and second-liners. One of the sweetest is a parade of elementary-school children, with a tiny king who sometimes loses his crown as his mule-drawn carriage turns a corner. (For ideas on renting or buying costumes, see the section "Mardi Gras and Music" on page 228, or look in Part Ten: "Shopping in New Orleans".)

And since any real business pretty much comes to a halt after lunch on Friday, the city has instituted a more recent celebration on Lundi Gras which is actually one of the best things about Carnival these days, involving a whole day of music, two stages' worth, on the riverfront and in front of the Aquarium of the Americas; followed by the landing of Rex and the fireworks on the Spanish Plaza, a free public masquerade ball and the lavish one-two parades of the Bards of Bohemia (all professional entertainers, including the fire-swallower who was married to his assistant on the float as they passed City Hall) and the celebrity-laden Orpheus.

Though the most famous parades use St. Charles Avenue and Canal Street, not all the parades do: Various routes go uptown, downtown, or into the suburbs, and some guidebooks have maps and information. (The French Quarter is no longer used for the big parades except in a few cases, and only for a couple of blocks.) The *Times-Picayune* publishes a daily list of routes and times of parades—along with anecdotes, full-color photographs, ball-queen presentations, and literally pages of trivia—throughout the Carnival season.

Mardi Gras day more or less officially kicks off with one of the real highlights, the Zulu Social Aid and Pleasure Club parade. The role of Zulu is a key one, because it brings up some racial issues still not very smoothly settled in New Orleans, as we've mentioned elsewhere. The Zulu parade dates from early in this century, when a black resident named William Storey parodied the elaborately crowned Rex by strutting behind his float wearing an old lard can on his head and calling himself "King Zulu." Gradually, however, the Zulus' plucky sense of humor, their no-holds-barred self- *and* social parody, and their very serious accomplishments (like the best of the old krewes, Zulu is made up of respected professionals and community activists) have given it a rare prestige in that often narrow-minded city. Nowadays the Zulu's gilded coconut shells are among the most coveted throws, and it is an even greater honor, especially for a white resident, to be invited to participate. Of course, they have to wear blackface and a grass skirt; but then even the black members and the king himself do the minstrel-show makeup thing.

And finally, in 1999, at "the last Mardi Gras of the millennium" as they said inaccurately but grandly, Rex not only accepted King Zulu's greeting at the river, but also exchanged greetings, king to king. It was a subtle shift, but one obvious to everyone in the crowd, and it may have been the most important event of the entire festival. It was also the 50th anniversary of the year that Louis Armstrong rode as King Zulu, and that was frequently alluded to as one of Fat Tuesday's greatest moments. (Armstrong's wife returned as queen in 1973.)

So the parade of Zulu, which leads straight into Rex, is a touchstone event of the day—the inaugural event, in fact. It begins at 8:30 a.m. (theoretically), and heads off toward downtown as the various "walking clubs" are promenading about town to set the tone. These range from the Half-Fast

Walking Club, founded by legendary jazz clarinetist Pete Fountain, that walks the traditional Canal and St. Charles route; to more daringly clad entertainers of Bourbon Street's bars and strip joints; to the fantastically beaded and befeathered black "Indians" of Kenner and Metairie, such as the revered Wild Tchoupitoulas tribe, whose chiefs are required to sew their costumes themselves and indulge in great competitions of face, style, and song. The highly competitive Bourbon Street Awards, the gay costume competition that gathers around the intersection of St. Ann and Burgundy streets outside the Rawhide Bar, warms up around midday, as less formal processions are forming all over town.

The most elaborately "classical" float, the crown-shaped vessel of Rex, King of Carnival, takes off at 10 a.m. and arrives at Gallier Hall around midday, preceded by a cohort of gold-helmeted lieutenants and white horses. Atop one of Rex's floats is a papier-mâché fatted ox, or "boeuf gras," reminding you of that meatless future. The parade route goes across St. Charles Avenue starting as far back as Napoleon Street, so if you can find a place along St. Charles, you can see everything without being swamped by the Bourbon Street brawlers. There are limited bleachers put up, but the public tickets generally go on sale right after Christmas; contact the Metropolitan Convention and Visitors Bureau. (The Hotel Inter-Continental at 444 St. Charles is among those setting up grandstand seats and selling them in a package with buffet meals; call 525-5566.)

Don't worry about running dry; to accommodate early parade-goers, many bars open at 8 a.m., and, of course, the convenience stores along the parade routes do a continual carry-out business as well. But remember, Fat Tuesday ends on Ash Wednesday, and like Cinderella's coach, it turns into a pumpkin exactly at midnight. This is the one and only time that "time" is definitely called in New Orleans, so be prepared. The police, led by the many mounted officers who warm up for duty by parading during the day, "sweep" the French Quarter in a maneuver that is as invariably part of the next day's newspaper photo spread as Miss America jumping in the surf off Atlantic City the morning after the pageant.

In the meantime, try to pace yourself. Consider the paucity of rest rooms; most hotels issue colored wristbands to make sure only paying guests get in, and no bar or restaurant is going to welcome you if you don't plan to purchase anything. The city does place some portable toilets around the parade routes, near the music stages along the riverfront, but they quickly become overloaded, and many people, especially the younger guys, are reluctant to go so far from their parade-side stations to use them. Unfortunately, since a lot of people will lose either patience or control, you'll have to be careful where you walk, much less sit, especially in the Quarter.

However, if you do some careful scouting early in the day, you may see a fairly new Mardi Gras phenomenon: pay-per-visit portapotty parks. A few clever entrepreneurs have taken to renting toilets, setting them up in strategic locations, and charging for their use. A couple of years ago, a guy put up 28 of them near Bourbon Street and Iberville, and clients paid $1 per visit during the day and $2 after 6, or bought an all-day pass for $10. In return, a host stayed on duty to maintain order, keep the johns as clean as possible, and spray them with air freshener. The next year, several more porto-parks appeared, including one right on Canal Street. Some restaurants and shops also put signs up advertising toilet privileges for $2 or $3 a trip, but the quality control leaves a lot more to be desired.

To be quite frank, the best way to enjoy Mardi Gras is to pick a couple of days, immerse yourself in the party spirit and be gone by the time Fat Tuesday gets into high gear. You could come for Friday and Saturday, see the Endymion and Bacchus parades, among others, and get your fill of beads and friendly strangers while the bloom is still on the rose. (Traditionally, many local residents pull out on Sunday morning.) Or even come in as the first wave of hotel guests goes, spend Sunday and Monday, getting the most out of Lundi Gras, and take the early Tuesday flights out. The detritus starts to build up pretty heavily by Monday—in 1999 streetcleaners, sweeping up right behind the police, gathered up an estimated 932 tons of garbage and that's just in New Orleans alone, not counting the neighboring parishes.

But if you want to see the real thing, here are some tips on how to have fun and look like a native. If you're going to be within tossing distance at a night parade—that is, either in a stand with fairly good access or staked out right behind the barricades—you should also have a handful of quarters in your pocket to throw to the torch bearers, called *flambeaux*. They are reminders of the men who carried real flaming-pitch torches (these are naphtha) for the Krewe of Comus, which was the first to figure out how to turn parading into a nighttime spectacle. Really experienced flambeaux carriers not only twirl these heavy torches; they can spot the glint of coin from yards away. They have to—although this traditional tribute goes back a long way, few non-natives know about it, and so despite the huge popularity of Mardi Gras, the cut of flambeaux carriers has been getting pretty short in recent years. So if you feel like looking for dollar coins to toss, they'd be grateful.

In terms of food supplies, it's smart to bring your own. Aside from a couple of vendor trucks offering steam-table Thai or Chinese, you'll probably have to settle for a hot dog or pizza. (This is along the parade route; there will be more of those turkey leg and jambalaya concessionaires along the river.) Plastic containers are a lot safer than glass or metal, but since so many people will be buying alcohol as the day goes on, you'll be surrounded by both eventually, so real shoes are a good idea, too. And you should bring a lot of water or soda, because you will be dehydrated, and the mark-ups at quick-stops are steep.

Veteran parade-goers also take along duffle bags or shopping totes to put their goodies in. You can only put so many beads over your shoulders—you will find that the cumulative weight is pretty surprising—and come the next parade, or the next morning, it starts all over again. According to "Mardi Gras Man" Hardy again, just those same three parades, Endymion, Bacchus and Orpheus, toss more than 1.5 million plastic cups, 2.5 million doubloons, and around 25 million beads. And they aren't even the only krewes parading at a time. So you might as well be picky; hold on to the good ones, and let the cheapies go to the kids.

(One of the perennial mysteries of Ash Wednesday is not a spiritual but a material one: What do you do with all those trinkets? Do you ship them home? Throw them out? Try to sell them to a bead merchant for the next year? Good luck. Personally, I suggest donating them to a shelter, a hospital children's ward, or the like. You could decorate your Christmas tree with them, but you'll still have to store them for eight months. Trust me, a few strands will do you.)

Another thing that comes in handy if you're serious about being really close to the action is goggles of the sort used in racquetball, especially for children whose reflexes may not be as quick. A slung rope of beads is like an Argentine bolo, and pretty dangerous. There are likely to be incoming missiles from several angles at once; and as the parades get more elaborate and the crowds get rowdier, you are almost certain to get a few bruises. It may come as a rude surprise, but the 50-year-old tourist trying to revive his career as a Lothario can be just as much of a toss hog as any teenager. Worse, in fact. And now that beads are bigger and heavier, and the float riders start showing off by slinging out huge handfuls of them at a time, you can occasionally take quite a shot. Even large cheap sunglasses might help, if you can keep them on.

Don't carry a lot of cash and put it someplace other than your pocket. Leave your car well out of the neighborhood if possible; many streets are closed off, and parking regulations are vigorously enforced. If you inadvertently drive into a parade route, it can cost you a cool $100.

First-time Mardi Gras celebrants, many of whom have never been to New Orleans at all, frequently come anticipating dinner at the famous restaurants of the French Quarter. Be sure to make your reservations well in advance, because a fair number of the trendiest ones will be closed Tuesday or even for several days beforehand because the closing-off of parade routes makes it so hard for their patrons to get in and out that it's not worth staying open. Some give up the sit-down dishes in favor of sandwiches and salads. Others that are located in hotels, such as the Windsor Grill in the Windsor Court, are open only to hotel guests who can show their identification bands. So do some advance work. And if you get the little doll in your slice of the tricolor King Cake, you have to throw the next party.

Here's another piece of logic that often fails to dawn on outsiders: Since so many of the parade routes include St. Charles Avenue and Canal Street, the streetcar doesn't run on Fat Tuesday, and not for huge parts of the days and nights beforehand. (The parade routes are not only marked off by portable fences, they are actively patrolled by police officers, who are reluctant to let civilians cross the road and are sometimes downright truculent about the available options.) Similarly, since many of the parades wind up down at the convention center or major hotels where the krewe balls are held, the Riverfront Line is blocked off. So quaint as they are, and handy as it may seem, this is one time you're not going to be able to use public transportation. Cabs are going to have a hard time negotiating the area as well, so the best thing is to have a coherent plan and be ready to walk it.

And you should also realize that these parades are long, long affairs, several hours' worth—sometimes all day. For one thing, you have to beat the band. Unless you have a grandstand ticket (and to some extent, even if you do, because they are only for sections, not specific seats), you need to stake out a position along the parade route a couple of hours early. Many people who want prime territory spend all night or show up at the literal crack of dawn toting sofas, stepladders, and lawn chairs. So if, for example, you decide to view Zulu and Rex from further uptown, and Zulu is scheduled to start off at 8:30 a.m., you need to be down on the street by 6:30 or 7 a.m., if not sooner.

Then, even if Zulu does get off on time, it will be 10:30 or 11 a.m. before it turns the corner of St. Charles onto Canal (so you need to be in position by 8:30 or 9 a.m., and then expect to have to hold your ground against invaders). Each parade takes a couple of hours to pass, followed immediately by Rex, followed by the dozen of Elks club trucks, followed by the Crescent City Trucks, which are huge semis honking and wheezing, still all bearing dozens of bead-tossers and breast-beggars, followed by the Krewe of America . . . and sometimes the police barricades never open in between. So if you stake out your position at 8 a.m., it may be 6 p.m. before you can cross the parade without going a very, very long way out of your way. Especially if you're downtown, you need to be sure which side of Canal—in the Quarter or out—you want to spend most the day. If you want to see the costume parades and balcony parties on Bourbon Street, plan to cross Canal before 9:30 a.m., catch a bit of Zulu, and cut away.

The same goes at night; if you enjoy the Lundi Gras festival at Spanish Plaza, which generally lasts until around 7:30 p.m., then get into position for Bards of Bohemia, you may be there until after midnight waiting for

Orpheus to finish up. So make sure you consider the map in advance. (It's midnight: do you know where your hotel is?)

If you want to come to Mardi Gras and bring your kids, but don't necessarily want to take them to the parades with you (or don't think they need to get their first lessons in anatomy along Bourbon Street), there are a fair number of activities for them in addition to those mentioned earlier in "New Orleans for Families"; check the *Times-Picayune*. Several of the hotels provide kids' carnivals or parties, and the Louisiana Children's Museum offers special in-house parades, mask-making classes, and so on.

You could opt for seeing the parades in Metairie or Kenner: these are much more family-style events, and the "Indian" walking parades are famously rousing, with good music and flamboyant costumes of a huge and feathered sort particularly attractive to kids. You could go out to the fairgrounds racetrack and see an afternoon of races; in 1999, jockey Julie Kron won her 350th race on Mardi Gras and turned back flips for the crowd.

Or you could skirt the entire issue: there is a rather different but fascinating Cajun Mardi Gras celebration in Lafayette, Louisiana, about 3 hours from the city; see "Cajun Country Festivals" at the end of this chapter.

Jazz and Heritage Fest

The New Orleans Jazz and Heritage Festival spans a 10-day period in late April and early May. It's usually called Jazz Fest for short, and in fact the first festival, organized over a quarter century ago by the same folks who brought you the Newport Jazz Festival, featured such stars as Duke Ellington, Mahalia Jackson, and Al Hirt. Now, however, the folk, gumbo, zydeco, Latin, R&B, swamp rock, brass, bounce (brass crossed with rap), ragtime-revival, bluegrass, gospel, and even klezmer performers far outnumber the jazz traditionalists; it's estimated that close to 5,000 musicians show up.

Long a favorite of lower-key visitors, in recent years it has come to rival Carnival in its crowds and extravagance (although not yet in its sheer overindulgence). The main stages, a dozen of them, are erected at the Fair Grounds near City Park, with the biggest performance stage right in the racetrack infield and tents all around the 25-acre site. The music is big-time but wide-ranging: veterans include the Neville Brothers, the Marsalis brothers (and sometimes patriarch Ellis as well), Irma Thomas, Gladys Knight, Wilson Pickett, the Indigo Girls, the Dave Matthews Band, Walter "Wolfman" Washington, Raful Neal, Kenny Neal, the Radiators, Buck-wheat Zydeco, Joan Baez, and Van Morrison. You just wander around until something grabs your fancy. There are related concerts at clubs and venues all around the city, some even on the water, and the streets are full.

Meanwhile, parts of the Fair Grounds are spread out with scores of food concessions—not the usual fast-food junk, but gumbo, fried alligator, red beans and rice, jambalaya, crabs, oysters, po-boys, and even roast pig. Jewelry, hand-crafted furniture, finer hand-crafted instruments, decoys, beadwork, and baskets make for some of the most worthwhile souvenirs the city has to offer.

The Fair Grounds are in a constant state of ferment from 11 a.m. to 11 p.m.; tickets are $14 in advance or $18 at the gate (kids tickets are $1.50 in advance, $2 at the gate). Nighttime concerts, with tickets ranging up to $30, are held at various locations, although if you cock an ear toward the nicer hotel lounges and jazz clubs, you may pick up a free jam or two.

If you have a choice, go for the second part of the festival—on Sunday morning, New Orleans's most famous falsetto, Aaron Neville, usually steps up with the famous Zion Harmonizers at the gospel show.

Note that this festival frequently falls during one of the first real heat waves, so be sure to pack sunglasses, sunblock, water, and a hat or at least a bandanna. And forget driving there; either take public transportation or a cab. Or hoof it.

For more information, contact the **Jazz and Heritage Festival** office at P.O. Box 53407, New Orleans, LA 70153, or call (504) 522-4786. The festival also has a web site: www.nojazzfest.com. *Off Beat* magazine puts out a comprehensive guide to the festival every year, although after the fact, but check their website for hints: www.offBEAT.com. You can also buy advance tickets through **TicketMaster:** (800) 488-5252 or (504) 522-5555.

Incidentally, if you're more interested in Cajun, Indian, and island music, consider the **Festival Internationale de Louisiane** in Lafayette at the end of April, which takes over a five-block piece of downtown and draws about 100,000 fans. For more information call (318) 232-8086 or go to www.festivalinternationale.com.

Halloween

Real Anne Rice fans probably already know about the **Memnoch Ball,** a.k.a. the Vampire Lestat Extravaganza. It is held in the former chapel at St. Elizabeth's Orphanage, which figures heavily in *Memnoch the Devil* and which she bought and renovated as her company's offices. The orphanage, now open to tourists (see Part Twelve: "New Orleans Attractions"), hosts Rice's hundreds of antique dolls, odd antiques (Nipper the RCA dog, for example), and Hollywood monster characters, as well as the coffin she sometimes uses for grand entrances. More recently, Rice has purchased the Happy Hour Theatre, a former cinema at the corner of Magazine and St.

Andrew's streets, which she is considering turning into a Cafe Lestat restaurant with elaborate black statuary and effects; it is possible that the Memnoch Ball will be held there, instead.

To find out how you can get a ticket to the Memnoch Ball, contact the **Vampire Lestat Fan Club** at Box 58277, New Orleans, LA 70158-8277; or surf Rice's comprehensive Internet site (www.annerice.com).

If you want to dress for the occasion in ultra-Lestat mode, there are plenty of stores that will frill you and thrill you to the utmost. One of the most luxuriantly decadent is **Armed and Dangerous** (529 Dumaine Street, 568-1100). It stocks wonderful velvet coats in which you can pass either as Louis the vampire or Louis XIV, with ruffled shirts to match, swords to swash and wide belts to buckles, plus all the gauntlets, ornaments, and daggers to match—even the fanciest neo-romantic crosses, if you dare.

But you don't have to be invited to the coven ball to enjoy Halloween in New Orleans. In fact, if you have any love for dressing up and acting out, this is one of the most wonderful times to be in the city. It's as flamboyant as Mardi Gras, but with far more wit, sheer theatricality (as opposed to theatrical classicism), and fun—and not nearly so much puking and public urination. The weather is apt to be warmer, and the restaurants stay open. And, since the event has become a great draw for gay costumers and drag queens, any display of breasts is at least scientifically interesting. Drag bars have a long illustrious history in New Orleans, going back at least a century and probably longer. And in addition to the fine professional drags in the Quarter and over in Faubourg-Marigny, you are apt to be serenaded, fondled, and generally scooped up by a raft of, as they used to say of Emma Peel, herself an obvious favorite of the gay crowd here, "talented amateurs." Informal parades and smartly turned-out paraders are showered with beads and coins from the galleries just as they are during Mardi Gras. Altogether, it's a great affair, unless you're uptight about who's tight in those tights.

There are costume parties all over the French Quarter, a huge one at the Convention Center (an annual fundraiser for New Orleans regional AIDS groups; call 945-4000 or 821-2601 for more information), a midnight **"Witches' Run"** (not so much to offset all that trick-or-treating as an excuse to run in costume), and for kids, the **Boo at the Zoo** festival (see calendar on page 61). Contact the **Metropolitan Convention and Visitors Bureau,** 1520 Sugar Bowl Drive, New Orleans, LA 70112, or call 566-5005.

Of course, between Lestat and Marie Laveau, you can make a Halloween holiday of your own any time; see the sections on "Walking on the Dark Side" and "The Great Hereafter" in Part Eleven: "Sight-Seeing and Tours."

Creole Christmas

This is the sort of tourism-industry creation that still seems a little packaged—in fact, some brochures refer to it as "New Orleans Christmas" or "Christmas, New Orleans style" because, although old Creole society supplied the inspiration for many of the events, visitors tend to lump Cajun and Creole culture together. (If you're confused yourself, see "A Too-Short History of a Fascinating Place" in Part One.)

Gradually, however, New Orleans Christmas has developed some fine moments. Starting at Thanksgiving, City Park's old live oaks are hung with thousands of lights in the shapes of fleur-de-lis, harps, and stars, and you can ride the miniature trains or even hire a carriage. Many fine older homes are decorated in the old style and lit up at night. Plenty of holiday events are free—special walking tours and concerts, parades (with Papa Noel himself heading up the second line), brass bands, museum exhibits, house tours, tree lightings, cooking and ornament-making workshops for kids, cooking exhibitions, and candlelight caroling in Jackson Square—and perfect for a family vacation. The whole French quarter is lit up, and street performers, jugglers, and dancers fill the parks. Midnight mass in St. Louis Cathedral is lovely, even if you aren't Catholic, with carols, candles, wonderful stained glass, and so on. There are almost nightly gospel concerts as well, either in St. Louis Cathedral or historic St. Mary's on Chartres. (There are also menorah lights and Kwanzaa activities and other cultural celebrations.)

Many hotels, both chain and independent, offer special low "Papa Noel" or "Creole Christmas" rates, while restaurants of the quality of Arnaud's, Brennan's, Galatoire's, Boussard's, Upperline Cafe, and Commander's Palace set out "Reveillon" menus adapted from old Creole celebrations which usually include champagne or eggnog and perhaps a little *lagniappe*. ("Reveillon" means "awakening," because the great Creole houses used to celebrate the holiday with a huge dinner after attending midnight mass on Christmas Eve.) Costumed impersonators from New Orleans history (Baroness Pontalba, Lola Montez, Andrew Jackson, Edgar Degas, Buffalo Bill Cody, and so on) walk the street to talk with passers-by.

Probably the most famous Christmas display in town outside City Park, and one that's nearly as elaborate although not as restrained, is at the Metairie home of entrepreneur Al Copeland, founder of the Popeye's and Copeland's restaurant chains. Just follow the line of cars taking Veterans Highway to Transcontinental Avenue, turn right, then left onto Folse, and go two blocks. You can't miss it.

At 7 p.m. on Christmas Eve, scores of huge bonfires are set up and down the Mississippi around the plantations (by some estimates 100 of them in 50 miles) and across the river from the city on the West Bank of

Algiers. Homes in the country are all decked out, which makes this a really good time to plan your plantation tour. For more about New Orleans Christmas, plus a second booklet of caroling schedules, lightings, fireworks, and so on, as well as discount coupons on shopping, dining, and attractions, call (800) 474-7621.

Of course, major party town that it is, New Orleans doesn't really surrender the Christmas season until New Year's Eve, which is another wild, woolly, loud, and lively night on the town, culminating with a giant crowd singing "Auld Lange Syne" in Jackson Square. New Year's Eve also coincides with the collegiate football championship Sugar Bowl, held in the Superdome. Just as for Mardi Gras, you need to make your hotel reservations early; however, you may be able to sneak in a good airfare by waiting to come until, say, December 27 or 28 and staying over until after New Year's Day.

Or you could stay through until Twelfth Night on January 6, when the first Carnival krewe kicks off the pre-Mardi Gras season . . . or even January 8, for the annual celebration of Jackson's victory at the Battle of New Orleans . . .

Cajun Country Festivals

There is more and more interest in Cajun culture—just notice what sort of music all those souvenir shops are blaring out onto Bourbon Street these days. What's called "Cajun Mardi Gras" in Lafayette, Louisiana, about three hours west of New Orleans, is a much more family-style festival than the Bourbon Street blowout. There the festival's sovereigns are King Gabriel and Queen Evangeline, from Longfellow's epic story of the Cajun diaspora (see "A Too-Short History of a Fascinating Place" on page 26), and several of the events are geared specifically to children. And unlike the Rex ball, the final party is open to the public (though you should still tie that black tie). You can also participate in some even older, country-style events, such as house-to-house partying. For information contact the **Lafayette Parish Convention and Visitors Commission,** P.O. Box 52066, Lafayette, LA 70505, or call (800) 346-1958.

Around the third week of September, Lafayette is the site of a multi-theme celebration, the Festivals Acadiens, spotlighting Cajun traditions and history. The best-known part is the Festival de Musique Acadienne, now more than 20 years old and drawing 50,000 fans of two-step, zydeco, and traditional Cajun-French music. Set up alongside the music stages is the Bayou Food Festival, a mouthwatering abundance of smothered quail, oysters en brochette, boudin sausages, and other Cajun specialties, prepared by area restaurants. The Louisiana Native Crafts Festival spotlights traditional methods and native materials: duck decoy carving, caning, basket weaving, quilting, pottery-making, jewelry, and even alligator skinning. Artists over 60 have their own seniors circuit, so to speak, the RSVP (Retired Senior Volunteer Program) Fair, where you get the tall tales along with the traditional crafts.

You can find Cajun tradition (and likely, some smaller festival or other) any time you visit Lafayette.

There are also Mardi Gras celebrations along the Mississippi Gulf Coast, notably in Biloxi and Gulfport. Contact the Mississippi Gulf Coast Convention and Visitors Bureau at P.O. Box 6128, Gulfport, MS 39506-6128; call (888) 467-4853; or go to www.gulfcoast.org.

Part Four

New Orleans Lodging

Deciding Where to Stay

New Orleans, you must understand, has an almost palpable feel. History here is cumulative, and from the French to the Spanish to the Confederacy to the present, every sailor, gambler, barmaid, and merchant has left something for you to savor. When you are in New Orleans, you know without being told that you are someplace very different. In fact, it's not so much a place to be as a place to know. Even as a first-time tourist, your heart aches to know this city intimately, to be part of its exotic rhythms and steaminess. The city never, never leaves your consciousness. You wear it and breathe it at the same time, all of it, and hundreds of years of blues in the night, chicory coffee, and sweat on the docks become part of your reality.

This reality is sustained by the river, the humidity, the narrow streets, and even by the city's grittiness and poverty. And it is reflected by its small, quirky hotels and inns. Some of the most delightful, interesting, and intimate hotels in America can be found in New Orleans. Ditto for guest houses and bed-and-breakfasts. Zoning and historic preservation ordinances, particularly in the French Quarter, have limited the construction of modern high-rise hotels and stimulated the evolution of an eclectic mix of medium- and small-sized properties, many of which are proprietorships. In an age of standardization and cookie-cutter chain hotels, these smaller hotels, distinguished by cozy courtyards, shuttered windows, balconies, and wrought-iron trim, offer guests a truly unique lodging experience.

Hotels in New Orleans are concentrated in the French Quarter and along Canal Street between Claiborne Avenue and the river. Most of the larger, modern chain hotels are situated near the convention center at the river end of Canal Street. Smaller hotels, inns, and guest houses are sprinkled liberally around the French Quarter and along St. Charles Avenue west of Lee Circle. Historically, there have been relatively few hotels located in other parts of town. Although today there are some hotels near the airport and along I-10 east of the city, hotels outside of the downtown/French Quarter area are relatively scarce.

Because New Orleans thrives on tourism, weekday hotel rates are often lower than weekend rates (the opposite of most cities where business travel rules). If you would like to visit during any holidays other than Mardi Gras or Jazz Fest, make your reservations six months or more in advance. For Mardi Gras (late February to early March) you need to plan nine months to one year ahaead, and for the New Orleans Jazz and Heritage Festival (late April to early May), give yourself at least ten months.

While we would not dissuade you from experiencing Mardi Gras, be advised that the city is pretty much turned upside down. Hotels are jammed, prices are jacked up, parking is impossible, and the streets are full of staggering drunks. In the French Quarter many bars and restaurants dispatch their furniture and fixtures to warehouses to make room for the throng of wall-to-wall people. While Mardi Gras is a hell of a good party, it essentially deprives visitors of experiencing "the real" New Orleans.

If you happen to be attending one of the big conventions, book early and use some of the tips listed below to get a discounted room rate. To assist you in timing your visit, we have included a convention and trade-show calendar in Part Five: "Visiting New Orleans on Business."

Some Considerations

1. When choosing your New Orleans lodging, make sure your hotel is situated in a location convenient to your recreation or business needs, and that it is in a safe and comfortable area.

2. New Orleans hotels generally offer lower-quality rooms than those in most cities profiled by the *Unofficial Guides*. A meager 21% of the hotels in New Orleans merit a quality rating of four stars or higher. Compare this with Chicago, where 36% of the hotels are rated four stars and higher, Washington, D.C., where 37% of the hotels are four stars or higher, and San Francisco, which boasts 40% of its hotels as four- and five-star properties. Need we mention New York City's impressive 84%? As a consequence of the generally lower-quality standard, newer chain hotels have not had to invest in superior rooms in order to be competitive.

   Surprisingly, New Orleans is not home to a single five-star hotel. Two of the nicest hotels in New Orleans, the **Windsor Court** and the **Omni Royal Crescent,** are older properties that have found ways to cram insane amounts of luxurious amenities into shoebox-sized rooms. These hotels rely as much on their dignified reputations as on their guest-room quality to attract guests. Although extremely nice, their rooms lack the square footage to be called "luxurious" by any standard. One hotel that satisfies all requirements of space and opulence has finally made its way into the French Quarter. The **Ritz-Carlton** on the French-Quarter side of Canal Street, which opened its doors in October 2000, has set a new standard for New Orleans expectations.

New Orleans is full of old hotels, some well maintained, some not. Many are situated in ancient buildings, with guest rooms in varying states of renovation and dilapidation. Lobbies of the nicer hotels are characteristically decorated in gaudy antique gilt, with Old World sculptures and crystal chandeliers. Along similar lines, you are likely to find more antique and antique-replica furniture in New Orleans hotel rooms than in most any other U.S. tourist destination. Four-poster rice beds are a particular favorite.

And it's gonna cost you. In general, New Orleans hotels are pricey. But good deals can be found, and upon inspection, a pattern emerges. With a handful of exceptions, the hotels that offer the best values are found outside the French Quarter. And within the French Quarter, those hotels found on or within one block of Bourbon Street are often outrageously expensive. So, as is often the case with urban hotels, the address of the hotel is the deciding factor in the room price.

For example, the most expensive hotel in New Orleans, the **Best Western Inn** on Bourbon, is located right in the middle of the Bourbon Street action. Although the Best Western Inn on Bourbon offers only a three-star room, it is continually booked due to location.

Before making any reservations, find out when the guest rooms in your prospective hotel were last renovated. Request that the hotel send you its promotional brochure. Ask if brochure photos of guest rooms are accurate and current.

3. If you plan to take a car, inquire about the parking situation. Some hotels offer no parking at all, some charge dearly for parking, and some offer free parking. Check the Hotel Information Chart at the end of this chapter for availability and prices.

4. If you are not a city dweller, or perhaps are a light sleeper, try to book a hotel on a quieter side street. In the French Quarter, avoid hotels on Bourbon Street. If you book a Central Business District or Canal Street hotel, ask for a room off the street and high up.

5. When you plan your budget, remember that New Orleans' hotel tax is 11%.

6. The ratings and rankings in this chapter are based solely on room quality and value. To determine if a particular hotel has room service, a pool, or other services and amenities, see the alphabetical Hotel Information Chart beginning on page 100.

Getting a Good Deal on a Room

Value Season

New Orleans' value season generally starts the first weekend in July (it seems New Orleans is not a popular Fourth destination) and ends on the first weekend in September.

Special Weekday Rates

Although well-located New Orleans hotels are tough for the budget-conscious, it's not impossible to get a good deal, at least relatively speaking. For starters, many French Quarter hotels that cater to tourists offer special weekday discount rates that range from 5 to 25% below weekend rates. You can find out about weekday specials by calling individual hotels or by consulting your travel agent.

Getting Corporate Rates

Many hotels offer discounted corporate rates (5–12% off rack). Usually you do not need to work for a large company or have a special relationship with the hotel to obtain these rates. Simply call the hotel of your choice and ask for their corporate rates. Many hotels will guarantee you the discounted rate on the phone when you make your reservation. Others may make the rate conditional on your providing some sort of bona fides, for instance a fax on your company's letterhead requesting the rate, or a company credit card or business card on check-in. Generally, the screening is not rigorous.

Half-Price Programs

The larger discounts on rooms (35–60%), in New Orleans or anywhere else, are available through half-price hotel programs, often called travel clubs. Program operators contract with an individual hotel to provide rooms at deep discounts, usually 50% off rack rate, on a "space available" basis. Space available generally means that you can reserve a room at the discounted rate whenever the hotel expects to be at less than 80% occupancy. A little calendar sleuthing to help you avoid Mardi Gras, Jazz Fest, special events, and city-wide conventions will increase your chances of choosing a time when the discounts are available.

Most half-price programs charge an annual membership fee or directory subscription charge of $25 to $125. Once enrolled, you are mailed a membership card and a directory that lists participating hotels. Examining the directory, you will notice immediately that there are many restrictions and exceptions. Some hotels, for instance, "black out" certain dates or times of year. Others may offer the discount only on certain days of the week, or require you to stay a certain number of nights. Still others may offer a much smaller discount than 50% off the rack rate.

Programs specialize in domestic travel, international travel, or both. More established operators offer members between 1,000 and 4,000 hotels to choose from in the United States. All of the programs have a heavy concentration of hotels in California and Florida, and most have a very limited selection of participating properties in New York City or Boston. Offerings in other cities and regions of the United States vary considerably. The programs with the largest selections of New Orleans hotels are Encore, ITC-50, Great American Traveler, and Entertainment Publications. Each of these programs lists between 9 and 30 hotels in the greater New Orleans area.

Encore	(800) 444-9800
ITC-50	(800) 987-6216
Great American Traveler	(800) 833-0123
Entertainment Publications	(800) 445-4137
	www.entertainment.com

One problem with half-price programs is that not all hotels offer a full 50% discount. Another slippery problem is the base rate against which the discount is applied. Some hotels figure the discount on an exaggerated rack rate that nobody would ever have to pay. A few participating hotels may deduct the discount from a supposed "superior" or "upgraded" room rate, even though the room you get is the hotel's standard accommodation. Though hard to pin down, the majority of participating properties base discounts on the rate published in the *Hotel & Travel Index* (a quarterly reference work used by travel agents) and work within the spirit of their agreement with the program operator. As a rule, if you travel several times a year, your room-rate savings will easily compensate you for program-membership fees.

A noteworthy addendum: deeply discounted rooms through half-price programs are not commissionable to travel agents. In practical terms this means that you must make your own inquiry calls and reservations. If you travel frequently, however, and run a lot of business through your travel agent, he or she will probably do your legwork, lack of commission notwithstanding.

PREFERRED RATES

If you cannot book the hotel of your choice through a half-price program, you and your travel agent may have to search for a lesser discount, often called a preferred rate. A preferred rate could be a discount made available to travel agents to stimulate their booking activity, or a discount initiated to attract a certain class of traveler. Most preferred rates are promoted through travel industry publications and are often accessible only through an agent.

We recommend sounding out your travel agent about possible deals. Be aware, however, that the rates shown on travel agents' computerized reservations systems are not always the lowest rates obtainable. Zero in on a couple of hotels that fill your needs in terms of location and quality of accommodations, and then have your travel agent call the hotel for the latest rates and specials. Hotel reps are almost always more responsive to travel agents because travel agents represent a source of additional business. There are certain specials that hotel reps will disclose only to travel agents. Travel agents also come in handy when the hotel you want is supposedly booked. A personal appeal from your agent to the hotel's director of sales and marketing will get you a room more than 50% of the time.

WHOLESALERS, CONSOLIDATORS, AND RESERVATION SERVICES

If you do not want to join a program or buy a discount directory, you can take advantage of the services of a wholesaler or consolidator. Wholesalers and consolidators buy rooms, or options on rooms (room blocks), from hotels at a low, negotiated rate. They then resell the rooms at a profit through travel agents or tour operators, or directly to the public. Most wholesalers and consolidators have a provision for returning unsold rooms to participating hotels, but are not inclined to do so. The wholesaler's or consolidator's relationship with any hotel is predicated on volume. If they return rooms unsold, the hotel may not make as many rooms available to them the next time around. Thus wholesalers and consolidators often offer rooms at bargain rates, anywhere from 15–50% off rack, occasionally sacrificing their profit margins in the process, to avoid returning the rooms to the hotel unsold.

When wholesalers and consolidators deal directly with the public, they frequently represent themselves as "reservation services." When you call, you can ask for a rate quote for a particular hotel or, alternatively, ask for their best available deal in the area you prefer to stay. If there is a maximum amount you are willing to pay, say so. Chances are the service will find something that will work for you, even if they have to shave a dollar or two off their own profit. Following is a list of several services that sell rooms in New Orleans:

Hotel Reservations Network	(800) 964-6835
	www.hoteldiscount.com
Room Finders USA	(800) 473-7829
(headquartered in New Orleans)	www.turbotrip.com
RMC Travel	(800) 245-5738
Accommodations Express	(800) 444-7666

The discount available (if any) from a reservation service depends on whether the service functions as a consolidator or a wholesaler. Consolidators are strictly sales agents who do not own or control the room inventory they are trying to sell. Discounts offered by consolidators are determined by the hotels with rooms to fill. Consolidator discounts vary enormously depending on how desperate the hotel is to unload the rooms. When you deal with a room reservation service that operates as a consolidator, you pay for your room as usual when you check out of the hotel.

Wholesalers have longstanding contracts with hotels that allow the wholesaler to purchase rooms at an established deep discount. Some wholesalers hold purchase options on blocks of rooms, while others actually pay for rooms and own the inventory. Because a wholesaler controls the room inventory, it can offer whatever discount it pleases, consistent with current demand. In practice, most wholesaler reservation-service discounts fall in the 10–40% range. When you reserve a room with a reservation service that operates as a wholesaler, you must usually pay in advance with your credit card for your entire stay. The service then sends you a written confirmation and usually a voucher (indicating prepayment) for you to present at the hotel.

Our experience has been that the reservation services are more useful in finding rooms when availability is scarce than in obtaining deep discounts. Calling the hotels ourselves, we were often able to beat the reservation services' rates when rooms were generally available. When the city was booked, however, and we could not find a room by calling the hotels ourselves, the reservation services could almost always get us a room at a fair price.

How to Evaluate a Travel Package

Hundreds of New Orleans package vacations are offered to the public each year. Packages should be a win/win proposition for both the buyer and the seller. The buyer has to make only one phone call and deal with a single salesperson to set up the whole vacation: transportation, rental car, lodging, meals, attraction admissions, and even golf and tennis. The seller, likewise, has to deal with the buyer only once, eliminating the need for separate sales, confirmations, and billing. In addition to streamlining sales, processing, and administration, some packagers also buy airfares in bulk on contract like a broker playing the commodities market. Buying a large number of airfares in advance allows the packager to buy them at a significant savings from posted fares. The same practice is also applied to hotel rooms. Because selling vacation packages is an efficient way of doing business, and because the packager can often buy individual package components (airfare, lodging, etc.) in bulk at discount, savings in operating expenses realized by the seller are sometimes passed on to the buyer so that, in addition to convenience, the package is also an exceptional value. In any event, that is the way it is supposed to work.

All too often, in practice, the seller cashes in on discounts and passes none on to the buyer. In some instances, packages are loaded with extras that cost the packager next to nothing, but inflate the retail price sky-high. Predictibaly, the savings to be passed along to customers do not materialize.

When considering a package, choose one that includes features you are sure to use; whether you use all the features or not, you will most certainly pay for them. Second, if cost is of greater concern than convenience, make a few phone calls and see what the package would cost if you booked its individual components (airfare, rental car, lodging, etc.) on your own. If the package price is less than the a la carte cost, the package is a good deal. If the costs are about the same, the package is probably worth buying just for the convenience.

If your package includes a choice of rental car or airport transfers (transportation to and from the airport), take the transfers if you plan to spend most of your time in the French Quarter or the Central Business District. If you want to run around town or go on excursions outside the city, take the car. If you take the car, be sure to ask if the package includes free parking at your hotel.

The following tour operators specialize in vacation packages to New Orleans. Book directly or through your travel agent.

Destination Management	(800) 366-8882
Hotarz Vacations	(800) 535-2732
Travel New Orleans	(800) 535-8747

Tour operators, of course, prefer to sell you a whole vacation package. When business is slow, however, they will often agree to sell you just the lodging component of the package, usually at a nicely discounted rate.

Hotel-Sponsored Packages

In addition to tour operators, packages are frequently offered by hotels. Usually "land only" (i.e., no airfare included), the hotel packages are sometimes exceptional deals. New Orleans hotels (especially those that are larger and closest to the Convention Center) seem to have good package deals that include room upgrades, special services (e.q. concierge, dry cleaning, etc.) and some meals for those in town for multiple nights over large convention weekends. Many packages are specialized, offering plantation tours, jazz tours, or the like, while others are offered only at certain times of the year, such as "Papa Noel" deals during the December holiday season. Promotion of hotel specials tends to be limited to the hotel's primary markets, which for most properties is Louisiana, Texas, Alabama, Florida, Mississippi, Georgia, Arkansas, and Tennessee. If you live in other parts of the country, you can take advantage of the packages but probably will not see them advertised in your local newspaper. An important point regarding hotel specials is that the hotel reservationists do not usually inform you of existing specials or offer them to you. In other words, *you have to ask.*

HELPING YOUR TRAVEL AGENT HELP YOU

When you call your travel agent, ask if he or she has been to New Orleans. If the answer is no, be prepared to give your travel agent some direction. Do not accept any recommendations at face value. Check out the location and rates of any suggested hotel and make certain that the hotel is suited to your itinerary.

Because some travel agents are unfamiliar with New Orleans, they may try to plug you into a tour operator's preset package. This essentially allows the travel agent to set up your whole trip with a single phone call and still collect an 8–10% commission. The problem with this scenario is that most agents will place 90% of their New Orleans business with only one or two wholesalers or tour operators. In other words, it's the line of least resistance for them, and not much choice for you.

Travel agents will often use wholesalers who run packages in conjunction with airlines, like Delta's Dream Vacations or American's Fly-Away Vacations. Because of the wholesaler's exclusive relationship with the carrier, these trips are very easy for travel agents to book. However, they will probably be more expensive than a package offered by a high-volume wholesaler who works with a number of airlines in a primary New Orleans market.

To help your travel agent get you the best possible deal, do the following:

1. Determine where you want to stay in New Orleans, and if possible choose a specific hotel. This can be accomplished by reviewing the hotel information provided in this guide, and by writing or calling hotels that interest you.

2. Check out the hotel deals and package vacations advertised in the Sunday travel sections of the *Atlanta Journal-Constitution, New Orleans Times-Picayune,* or *Dallas Morning News* newspapers.

Often you will be able to find deals that beat the socks off anything offered in your local paper. See if you can find specials that fit your plans and include a hotel you like.

3. Call the hotels or tour operators whose ads you have collected. Ask any questions you have concerning their packages, but do not book your trip with them directly.

4. Tell your travel agent about the deals you find and ask if he or she can get you something better. The deals in the paper will serve as a benchmark against which to compare alternatives proposed by your travel agent.

5. Choose from the options that you and your travel agent uncover. No matter which option you select, have your travel agent book it. Even if you go with one of the packages in the newspaper, it will probably be commissionable (at no additional cost to you) and will provide the agent some return on the time invested on your behalf. Also, as a travel professional, your agent should be able to verify the quality and integrity of the deal.

IF YOU MAKE YOUR OWN RESERVATION

As you poke around trying to find a good deal, there are several things you should know. First, always call the specific hotel rather than the hotel chain's national 800 number. Quite often, the reservationists at the national 800 number are unaware of local specials. Always ask about specials before you inquire about corporate rates. Do not be reluctant to bargain. If you are buying a hotel's weekday package, for example, and want to extend your stay into the following weekend, you can often obtain at least the corporate rate for the extra days. Do your bargaining, however, before you check in, preferably when you make your reservations.

Hotels and Motels: Rated and Ranked
WHAT'S IN A ROOM?

Except for cleanliness, state of repair, and decor, most travelers do not pay much attention to hotel rooms. There is, of course, a discernible standard of quality and luxury that differentiates Motel 6 from Holiday Inn, Holiday Inn from Marriott, and so on. In general, however, hotel guests fail to appreciate the fact that some rooms are better engineered than others.

Contrary to what you might suppose, designing a hotel room is (or should be) much more complex than picking a bedspread to match the carpet and drapes. Making the room usable to its occupants is an art, a planning discipline that combines both form and function.

Decor and taste are important, certainly. No one wants to spend several days in a room whose decor is dated, garish, or even ugly. But beyond the decor, several variables determine how livable a hotel room is. In New Orleans, for example, we have seen some beautifully appointed rooms that are simply not well designed for human habitation. The next time you stay in a hotel, pay attention to the details and design elements of your room. Even more than decor, these will make you feel comfortable and at home.

It takes the *Unofficial Guide* researchers quite a while to inspect a hotel room. Here are a few of the things we check that you may want to start paying attention to:

Room Size   While some smaller rooms are cozy and well designed, a large and uncluttered room is generally preferable, especially for a stay of more than three days.

Temperature Control, Ventilation, and Odor   The guest should be able to control the temperature of the room. The best system, because it's so quiet, is central heating and air conditioning, controlled by the room's own thermostat. The next best system is a room module heater and air conditioner, preferably controlled by an automatic thermostat, but usually by manually operated button controls. The worst system is central heating and air without any sort of room thermostat or guest control.

The vast majority of hotel rooms have windows or balcony doors that have been permanently sealed. Though there are some legitimate safety and liability issues involved, we prefer windows and balcony doors that can be opened to admit fresh air. Hotel rooms should be odor and smoke free, and not feel stuffy or damp.

Room Security   Better rooms have locks that require a plastic card instead of the traditional lock and key. Card and slot systems allow the hotel, essentially, to change the combination or entry code of the lock with each new guest. A burglar who has somehow acquired a conventional room key can afford to wait until the situation is right before using the key to gain access. Not so with a card and slot system. Though larger hotels and hotel chains with lock and key systems usually rotate their locks once each year, they remain vulnerable to hotel thieves much of the time. Many smaller or independent properties rarely rotate their locks.

In addition to the entry lock system, the door should have a deadbolt, and preferably a chain that can be locked from the inside. A chain by itself is not sufficient. Doors should also have a peephole. Windows and balcony doors, if any, should have secure locks.

Safety   Every room should have a fire or smoke alarm, clear fire instructions, and preferably a sprinkler system. Bathtubs should have a nonskid surface, and shower stalls should have doors that either open outward or slide side-to-side. Bathroom electrical outlets should be high on the wall and not too close to the sink. Balconies should have sturdy, high rails.

Noise   Most travelers have been kept awake by the television, partying, or amorous activities of people in the next room, or by traffic on the street outside. Better hotels are designed with noise control in mind. Wall and ceiling construction are substantial, effectively screening routine noise. Carpets and drapes, in addition to being decorative, also absorb and muffle sounds. Mattresses mounted on stable platforms or sturdy bed frames do not squeak, even when challenged by the most acrobatic lovers. Televisions enclosed in cabinets, and with volume governors, rarely disturb guests in adjacent rooms.

In better hotels, the air conditioning and heating system is well maintained and operates without noise or vibration. Likewise, plumbing is quiet and positioned away from the sleeping area. Doors to the hall, and to adjoining rooms, are thick and well fitted to better block out noise.

If you are easily disturbed by noise, ask for a room on a higher floor, off main thoroughfares, and away from elevators and ice and vending machines.

Darkness Control   Ever been in a hotel room where the curtains would not quite meet in the middle? Thick, lined curtains that close completely in the center and extend beyond the edges of the window or door frame are required. In a well-planned room, the curtains, shades, or blinds should almost totally block light at any time of day.

Lighting   Poor lighting is an extremely common problem in American hotel rooms. The lighting is usually adequate for dressing, relaxing, or watching television, but not for reading or working. Lighting needs to be bright over tables and desks, and beside couches or easy chairs. Since so many people read in bed, there should be a separate light for each person. A room with two queen beds should have individual lights for four people. Better bedside reading lights illuminate a small area, so if one person wants to sleep and another to read, the sleeper will not be bothered by the light. The worst situation by far is a single lamp on a table between beds. In each bed, only the person next to the lamp will have sufficient light to read. This deficiency is often compounded by weak light bulbs.

In addition, closet areas should be well-lit, and there should be a switch near the door that turns on room lights when you enter. A seldom seen but desirable feature is a bedside console that allows a guest to control all or most lights in the room from bed.

Furnishings   At bare minimum, the bed(s) must be firm. Pillows should be made with nonallergic fillers and, in addition to the sheets and spread, a blanket should be provided. Bedclothes should be laundered with fabric softener and changed daily. Better hotels usually provide extra blankets and pillows in the room or on request, and sometimes use a second topsheet between the blanket and spread.

There should be a dresser large enough to hold clothes for two people during a five-day stay. A small table with two chairs, or a desk with a chair, should be provided. The room should be equipped with a luggage rack and a three-quarter- to full-length mirror.

The television should be color and cable-connected; ideally, it should have a volume governor and remote control. It should be mounted on a swivel base, and preferably enclosed in a cabinet. Local channels should be posted on the set and a local TV program guide should be supplied. The telephone should be touchtone, conveniently situated for bedside use, and should have, on or near it, easy-to-understand dialing instructions and a rate card. Local telephone directories should be provided. Better hotels install phones in the bathroom and equip room phones with long cords.

Well-designed hotel rooms usually have a plush armchair or a sleeper sofa for lounging and reading. Better headboards are padded for comfortable reading in bed, and there should be a nightstand or table on each side of the bed(s). Nice extras in any hotel room include a small refrigerator, a digital alarm clock, and a coffeemaker.

Bathroom   Two sinks are better than one, and you cannot have too much counter space. A sink outside the bath is a great convenience when one person bathes as another dresses. Sinks should have drains with stoppers.

Better bathrooms have both a tub and shower with a nonslip bottom. Tub and shower controls should be easy to operate. Adjustable shower heads are preferred. The bath needs to be well lit and should have an exhaust fan and a guest-controlled bathroom heater. Towels and washcloths should be large, soft, and fluffy, and generously supplied. There should be an electrical outlet for each sink, conveniently and safely placed.

Complimentary shampoo, conditioner, and lotion are a plus, as are robes and bathmats. Better hotels supply bathrooms with tissues and extra toilet paper. Luxurious baths feature a phone, a hair dryer, sometimes a small television, or even a jacuzzi.

Vending   Complimentary ice and a drink machine should be located on each floor. Welcome additions include a snack machine and a sundries (combs, toothpaste) machine. The latter are seldom found in large hotels that have restaurants and shops.

ROOM RATINGS

To distinguish properties according to relative quality, tastefulness, state of repair, cleanliness, and size of standard rooms, we have grouped the hotels and motels into classifications denoted by stars. Star ratings in this guide apply to New Orleans area properties only, and do not necessarily corre-spond to ratings awarded by Mobil, AAA, or other travel critics. Because stars carry little weight when awarded in the absence of commonly recog-nized standards of comparison, we have linked our ratings to expected lev-els of quality established by specific American hotel corporations.

Star ratings apply to room quality only, and describe the property's stan-dard accommodations. For most hotels and motels a "standard accommo-dation" is a hotel room with either one king bed or two queen beds. In an all-suite property, the standard accommodation is either a one- or two-room suite. In addition to standard accommodations, many hotels offer luxury rooms and special suites that are not rated in this guide. Star ratings for rooms are assigned without regard to whether a property has restau-rant(s), recreational facilities, entertainment, or other extras.

In addition to stars (which delineate broad categories), we also employ a numerical rating system. Our rating scale is 0–100, with 100 as the best possible rating, and zero (0) as the worst. Numerical ratings are presented to show the difference we perceive between one property and another. Rooms at the Hotel de la Monnaie, Grenoble House, and Dauphine Orleans are all rated as three and a half stars (★★★½). In the supplemental numerical ratings, the Hotel de la Monnaie is rated an 82, the Grenoble House is rated an 81, and Dauphine Olreans is rated a 77. This means that within the three-and-a-half-star category, the Hotel de la Monnaie and Grenoble House are comparable, and both have slightly nicer rooms than Dauphine Orleans.

The location column identifies the New Orleans zone where you will find a particular property.

How the Hotels Compare

Cost estimates are based on the hotel's published rack rates for standard rooms. Each "$" represents $40. Thus a cost symbol of "$$$" means a room (or suite) at that hotel will cost about $120 a night.

Below is a hit parade of the nicest rooms in town. We've focused strictly on room quality, and excluded any consideration of location, services, recreation, or amenities. In some instances, a one- or two-room suite can be had for the same price or less than that of a hotel room.

If you use subsequent editions of this guide, you will notice that many of the ratings and rankings change. In addition to the inclusion of new prop-erties, these changes also consider guest-room renovations or improved maintenance and housekeeping. A failure to maintain guest rooms properly or a lapse in housekeeping standards can affect negatively the ratings.

Finally, before you begin to shop for a hotel, take a look at this letter we received from a couple in Hot Springs, Arkansas:

We cancelled our room reservations to follow the advice in your book [and reserved a hotel room highly ranked by the Unofficial Guide*]. We wanted inexpensive, but clean and cheerful. We got inexpensive, but [also] dirty, grim, and depressing. I really felt disappointed in your advice and the room. It was the pits. That was the one real piece of information I needed from your book! The room spoiled the holiday for me aside from our touring.*

Needless to say, this letter was as unsettling to us as the bad room was to our reader. Our integrity as travel journalists, after all, is based on the quality of the information we provide our readers. Even with the best of intentions and the most conscientious research, however, we cannot inspect every room in every hotel. What we do, in statistical terms, is take a sample: We check out several rooms selected at random in each hotel and base our ratings and rankings on those rooms. The inspections are conducted anonymously and without the knowledge of the management. Although unusual, it is certainly possible that the rooms we randomly inspect are not representative of the majority of rooms at a particular hotel. Another possibility is that the rooms we inspect in a given hotel are representative, but that by bad luck a reader is assigned a room that is inferior. When we rechecked the hotel our reader disliked, we discovered our rating was correctly representative, but that he and his wife had unfortunately been assigned to one of a small number of threadbare rooms scheduled for renovation.

The key to avoiding disappointment is to snoop around in advance. We recommend that you ask for a photo of a hotel's standard guest room before you book, or at least get a copy of the hotel's promotional brochure. Be forewarned, however, that some hotel chains use the same guest room photo in their promotional literature for all hotels in the chain; a specific guest room may not resemble the brochure photo. When you or your travel agent call, ask how old the property is and when your guest room was last renovated. If you arrive and are assigned a room inferior to that which you had been led to expect, demand to be moved to another room.

How the Hotels Compare

Hotel	Zone	Room Quality Rating	Room Star Rating	Cost ($=$40)
Ritz-Carlton New Orleans	1	95	★★★★½	$$$$$$+
Windsor Court	2	94	★★★★½	$$$$$+
Omni Royal Crescent Hotel	2	90	★★★★½	$$$$–
Wyndham Canal Place	1	90	★★★★½	$$$$–
Omni Royal Orleans Hotel	1	89	★★★★	$$$$–
Royal Sonesta Hotel	1	89	★★★★	$$$$$–
Ambassador Hotel New Orleans	2	88	★★★★	$$$–
Hampton Inn Suites & Convention Center	2	88	★★★★	$$$$–
Le Pavillon Hotel	2	88	★★★★	$$$$$$–
McKendrick-Breaux House	3	88	★★★★	$$$+
Pelham Hotel	2	88	★★★★	$$$$$
Residence Inn	2	88	★★★★	$$$$–
Residence Inn Metairie	9	88	★★★★	$$$$–
Fairmont Hotel	2	86	★★★★	$$$$$$$$–
Hilton New Orleans Riverside	2	86	★★★★	$$$$–
Le Meridien Hotel New Orleans	2	86	★★★★	$$$$$$–
Maison Dupuy Hotel	1	86	★★★★	$$+
Hilton Garden Inn	2	85	★★★★	$$$$–
Sheraton New Orleans Hotel	2	85	★★★★	$$$$–
Maison De Ville	1	84	★★★★	$$$$$–
Queen and Crescent Hotel	2	84	★★★★	$$$–
Wyndham Riverfront Hotel	2	84	★★★★	$$$+
Chateau Sonesta Hotel	1	83	★★★★	$$$$$$–
Doubletree Hotel Lakeside New Orleans	9	83	★★★★	$$$$$+
Hotel Inter-Continental New Orleans	2	83	★★★★	$$$$$+
Hyatt Regency New Orleans at Superdome	2	83	★★★★	$$$$–
Embassy Suites New Orleans	2	82	★★★½	$$$–
Holiday Inn Select	2	82	★★★½	$$$$
Hotel de la Monnaie	1	82	★★★½	$$$$–
The Monteleone	1	82	★★★½	$$$$$–

		Room Quality	Room Star	Cost
Hotel	Zone	Rating	Rating	($=$40)
Courtyard by Marriott	2	81	★★★½	$$$$
Grenoble House	1	81	★★★½	$$$$–
Bienville House	1	80	★★★½	$$$–
Holiday Inn Downtown-Superdome	2	80	★★★½	$$$$+
Marriott New Orleans	1	80	★★★½	$$$+
Pontchartrain Hotel	3	80	★★★½	$$$
Prince Conti Hotel	1	80	★★★½	$$$–
Soniat House	1	80	★★★½	$$$$+
W French Quarter	1	80	★★★½	$$$$+
Avenue Plaza Hotel	3	79	★★★½	$$$–
The Cornstalk	1	79	★★★½	$$$–
Hotel Ste. Helene	1	79	★★★½	$$$+
Hilton New Orleans Airport	10	78	★★★½	$$$$–
Holiday Inn French Quarter	1	78	★★★½	$$$$–
Lafayette Hotel	2	78	★★★½	$$$$$–
Rathbone Inn	1	78	★★★½	$$–
Dauphine Orleans	1	77	★★★½	$$$–
Provincial Hotel	1	77	★★★½	$$$–
Best Western Airport All Suite	10	76	★★★½	$$$–
Brent House Hotel	9	75	★★★½	$$+
Hampton Inn Downtown	2	75	★★★½	$$$$–
Place D'Armes Hotel	1	75	★★★½	$$$–
Doubletree Hotel New Orleans	2	74	★★★	$$$$$$
Extended Stay America	9	74	★★★	$$$+
Olivier House Hotel	1	74	★★★	$$$+
Ramada Plaza on Bourbon	1	74	★★★	$$$$$+
The Saint Louis	1	74	★★★	$$$–
Comfort Suites	8	73	★★★	$$$–
Holiday Inn Airport	10	73	★★★	$$$+
Hotel St. Marie	1	73	★★★	$$$
Bourbon Orleans Hotel	1	72	★★★	$$+
Courtyard Metairie	9	72	★★★	$$$–
Four Points Sheraton	10	72	★★★	$$$$–
New Orleans Guest House	1	72	★★★	$$+
Ramada Plaza Hotel	3	72	★★★	$$$$–

How the Hotels Compare (continued)

Hotel	Zone	Room Quality Rating	Room Star Rating	Cost ($=$40)
Wingate Inn	10	72	★★★	$$$+
Ramada Limited Causeway	9	71	★★★	$$−
Best Western Inn Landmark Hotel	9	70	★★★	$$$$$−
Chateau LeMoyne French Quarter Holiday Inn	1	70	★★★	$$$$−
Historic French Market Inn	1	70	★★★	$$$$+
Lafitte Guest House	1	70	★★★	$$$$$−
Radisson Hotel New Orleans	2	70	★★★	$$$$$+
Radisson Inn Airport	10	70	★★★	$$$+
Ramada Inn Superdome	2	70	★★★	$$$−
Best Western Patio Downtown	6	69	★★★	$$$−
French Quarter Suites	1	69	★★★	$$$+
Le Richelieu in the French Quarter	1	69	★★★	$$$+
Crescent on Canal	6	68	★★★	$$$$
Hampton Inn and Suites (suite)	10	68	★★★	$$$$−
Prytania Park Hotel	3	68	★★★	$$$+
St. Peter Guest House	1	68	★★★	$$+
The Columns	3	67	★★★	$$$+
Hampton Inn	9	67	★★★	$$+
Holiday Inn Metairie	9	66	★★★	$$$−
Hotel Villa Convento	1	66	★★★	$$$−
Holiday Inn New Orleans Westbank	11	65	★★★	$$+
Maison St. Charles Quality Inn and Suites	3	65	★★★	$$$−
Best Western-Parc St. Charles	2	64	★★½	$$$$$$+
Comfort Suites Downtown	2	64	★★½	$$$+
La Quinta Inn Crowder Road	8	64	★★½	$$+
Best Western Landmark French Quarter	1	6 3	★★½	$$$$−
La Quinta Inn Airport	10	63	★★½	$$−
Quality Hotel and Conference Center	9	63	★★½	$$+
Saint Ann/Marie Anntoinette	1	63	★★½	$$$−

How the Hotels Compare *(continued)*

Hotel	Zone	Room Quality Rating	Room Star Rating	Cost ($=$40)
Best Western Inn Airport	10	62	★★½	$$$–
French Quarter Courtyard Hotel	1	62	★★½	$$$–
Rue Royal Inn	1	62	★★½	$$$+
Hampton Inn and Suites (room)	10	61	★★½	$$$–
La Quinta Inn Bullard	8	61	★★½	$$–
La Quinta Inn Veterans	10	61	★★½	$$–
Andrew Jackson	1	60	★★½	$$+
The Frenchmen	6	60	★★½	$$$
La Quinta Inn West Bank	11	60	★★½	$$
Quality Inn Midtown	6	60	★★½	$$$–
Quality Inn Tower Hotel	11	60	★★½	$$–
Orleans Courtyard Inn	9	59	★★½	$$–
St. Charles Inn	3	59	★★½	$$–
La Quinta Inn Causeway	9	58	★★½	$$–
Lasalle Hotel	1	58	★★½	$$–
Shoney's Inn	10	58	★★½	$$–
Super 8 New Orleans	8	58	★★½	$$–
Travelodge New Orleans Airport Hotel	10	58	★★½	$$–
Rodeway Inn Airport	10	56	★★½	$$–
Days Inn Westbank Harvey	11	55	★★	$+
Lamothe House	1	55	★★	$$+
Park Plaza Inn	10	55	★★	$$–
Days Inn New Orleans Canal Street	2	54	★★	$$+
Days Inn	8	52	★★	$$+
Ramada Inn Highrise	8	52	★★	$$–
Days Inn Kenner Airport	10	50	★★	$+
Hotel St. Pierre	1	50	★★	$$$–
A Creole House	1	49	★★	$$+
Travelodge Hotel New Orleans	11	49	★★	$$
Travelodge New Orleans Metairie	10	47	★★	$+
Howard Johnson	8	41	★½	$$–

THE TOP 30 BEST DEALS IN NEW ORLEANS

Having listed the nicest rooms in town, let's reorder the list to rank the best combinations of quality and value in a room. As before, the rankings are made without consideration of location or the availability of restaurant(s), recreational facilities, entertainment, and/or amenities. Once again, each lodging property is awarded a value rating on a 0–100 scale. The higher the rating, the better the value.

A reader recently complained to us that he had booked one of our top-ranked rooms in terms of value and had been very disappointed in the room. We noticed that the room the reader occupied had a quality rating of ★★½. We would remind you that the value ratings are intended to give you some sense of value received for dollars spent. A ★★½ room at $30 may have the same value rating as a ★★★★ room at $85, but that does not mean the rooms will be of comparable quality. Regardless of whether it's a good deal or not, a ★★½ room is still a ★★½ room.

Listed below are the best room buys for the money, regardless of location or star classification, based on averaged rack rates. Note that sometimes a suite can cost less than a hotel room.

The Top 30 Best Deals in New Orleans				
Hotel	Zone	Room Quality Rating	Room Star Rating	Cost ($=$40)
1. Maison Dupuy Hotel	1	86	★★★★	$$+
2. Rathbone Inn	1	78	★★★½	$$–
3. Queen and Crescent Hotel	2	84	★★★★	$$$–
4. Ambassador Hotel New Orleans	2	88	★★★★	$$$–
5. Brent House Hotel	9	75	★★★½	$$+
6. McKendrick-Breaux House	3	88	★★★★	$$$+
7. Bienville House	1	80	★★★½	$$$–
8. Wyndham Canal Place	1	90	★★★★½	$$$$–
9. Ramada Limited Causeway	9	71	★★★	$$–
10. Omni Royal Crescent Hotel	2	90	★★★★½	$$$$–
11. Wyndham Riverfront Hotel	2	84	★★★★	$$$+
12. Prince Conti Hotel	1	80	★★★½	$$$–
13. The Cornstalk	1	79	★★★½	$$$–
14. Embassy Suites New Orleans	2	82	★★★½	$$$–
15. Avenue Plaza Hotel	3	79	★★★½	$$$–

The Top 30 Best Deals in New Orleans *(continued)*

Hotel	Zone	Room Quality Rating	Room Star Rating	Cost ($=$40)
16. Best Western Airport All Suite	10	76	★★★½	$$$–
17. Hampton Inn Suites & Convention Center	2	88	★★★★	$$$$–
18. Place D'Armes Hotel	1	75	★★★½	$$$–
19. Dauphine Orleans	1	77	★★★½	$$$–
20. Provincial Hotel	1	77	★★★½	$$$–
21. Sheraton New Orleans Hotel	2	85	★★★★	$$$$–
22. Shoney's Inn	10	58	★★½	$$–
23. New Orleans Guest House	1	72	★★★	$$+
24. Hilton New Orleans Riverside	2	86	★★★★	$$$$–
25. Residence Inn	2	88	★★★★	$$$$–
26. Residence Inn Metairie	9	88	★★★★	$$$$–
27. Pontchartrain Hotel	3	80	★★★½	$$$
28. Super 8 New Orleans	8	58	★★½	$$–
29. Omni Royal Orleans Hotel	1	89	★★★★	$$$$–
30. Hyatt Regency New Orleans at Superdome	2	83	★★★★	$$$$–

Hotel	Quality	Star Rating	Zone	Address
Ambassador Hotel New Orleans	88	★★★★	2	535 Tchoupitoulas Street New Orleans, LA 70130
Andrew Jackson	60	★★½	1	919 Royal Street New Orleans, LA 70116
Avenue Plaza Hotel	79	★★★½	3	2111 Street Charles Avenue New Orleans, LA 70130
Best Western Airport All Suite	76	★★★½	10	2438 Veterans Memorial Blvd. Kenner, LA 70062
Best Western Inn Airport	62	★★½	10	1021 Airline Drive Kenner, LA 70062
Best Western Inn Landmark Hotel	70	★★★	9	2601 Severn Avenue Metairie, LA 70002
Best Western Landmark French Quarter	63	★★½	1	920 N. Rampart Street New Orleans, LA 70116
Best Western Patio Downtown	69	★★★	6	2820 Tulane Avenue New Orleans, LA 70119
Best Western- Parc Street Charles	64	★★½	2	500 Street Charles Avenue New Orleans, LA 70130
Bienville House	80	★★★½	1	320 Decatur Street New Orleans, LA 70130
Bourbon Orleans Hotel	72	★★★	1	717 Orleans Street New Orleans, LA 70116
Brent House Hotel	75	★★★½	9	1512 Jefferson Highway Jefferson, LA 70121
Chateau LeMoyne French Quarter Holiday Inn	70	★★★	1	301 Rue Dauphine New Orleans, LA 70112
Chateau Sonesta Hotel	83	★★★★	1	800 Iberville Street New Orleans, LA 70112
The Columns	67	★★★	3	3811 Street Charles Avenue New Orleans, LA 70115
Comfort Suites	73	★★★	8	7051 Bullard Avenue New Orleans, LA 70128
Comfort Suites Downtown	64	★★½	2	346 Baronne Street New Orleans, LA 70112
The Cornstalk	79	★★★½	1	915 Royal Street New Orleans, LA 70113
Courtyard by Marriott	81	★★★½	2	124 Street Charles Avenue New Orleans, LA 70130

Phone	Fax	Reservations	Rack Rate	No. of Rooms
(504) 527-5271	(504) 527-5270	(888) 527-5271	$$$	75
(504) 561-5881	(504) 596-6769	(800) 654-0224	$$+	22
(504) 566-1212	(504) 525-6899	(800) 535-9575	$$$–	250
(504) 469-2800	(504) 469-2800	(800) 528-1234	$$$–	78
(504) 464-1644	(504) 469-1193	(800) 333-8278	$$$–	168
(504) 888-9500	(504) 885-8474	(800) 277-7575	$$$$$–	342
(504) 524-3333	(504) 522-8044	(800) 535-7862	$$$$–	100
(504) 822-0200	(504) 822-2328	(800) 270-6955	$$$–	76
(504) 522-9000	(888) 211-3448	(888) 211-3447	$$$$$$+	255
(504) 529-2345	(504) 525-6079	(800) 535-7836	$$$–	82
(504) 523-2222	(504) 525-8166	(800) 521-5338	$$$+	211
(504) 835-5411	(504) 842-4160	(800) 535-3986	$$+	158
(504) 581-1303	(504) 523-5709	(800) 447-2830	$$$$	171
(504) 586-0800	(504) 586-1987	(800) 788-3782	$$$$$$	250
(504) 899-9308	(504) 899-8170	(800) 445-9308	$$$+	19
(504) 244-1414	(504) 240-1414	(800) 228-5150	$$$–	65
(504) 524-1140	(504) 523-4444	(800) 524-1140	$$$+	102
(504) 523-1515	(504) 522-5558	NA	$$$	14
(504) 581-9005	(504) 581-6224	(800) 654-3990	$$$$	140

Hotel	Pool	Sauna	Room Service
Ambassador Hotel New Orleans	N	N	Y
Andrew Jackson	N	N	N
Avenue Plaza Hotel	Y	Y	N
Best Western Airport All Suite	Y	Y	N
Best Western Inn Airport	Y	N	Y
Best Western Inn Landmark Hotel	Y	Y	Y
Best Western Landmark French Quarter	Y	N	Y
Best Western Patio Downtown	Y	N	N
Best Western-Parc Street Charles	Y	N	N
Bienville House	Y	N	N
Bourbon Orleans Hotel	Y	N	Y
Brent House Hotel	Y	Y	Y
Chateau LeMoyne French Quarter Holiday Inn	Y	N	Y
Chateau Sonesta Hotel	Y	N	Y
The Columns	N	N	N
Comfort Suites	Y	N	N
Comfort Suites Downtown	N	Y	N
The Cornstalk	N	N	N
Courtyard by Marriott	N	N	N

Parking	TV	VCR	Free Breakfast	Exercise Facilities
18	Y	N	Continental	N
No lot	Y	N	Continental	N
16	Y	N	N	Y
None	Y	N	Continental	N
None	Y	N	N	Y
None	Y	N	N	Y
10	Y	N	N	N
None	Y	N	Continental	N
17	Y	N	Continental	Y
15	Y	N	Continental	Off site
24	Y	N	N	Off site
None	Y	N	N	Y
18	Y	N	N	N
19	Y	N	N	Y
No lot	N	N	Full	N
None	Y	N	Continental	Off site
16	Y	N	Continental	Y
15	Y	N	In-room continental	N
16	Y	N	N	Y

Hotel	Quality	Star Rating	Zone	Address
Courtyard Metairie	72	★★★	9	2 Galleria Blvd. Metairie, LA 70001
A Creole House	49	★★	1	1013 St. Ann Street New Orleans, LA 70116
Crescent on Canal	68	★★★	6	1732 Canal Street New Orleans, LA 70112
Dauphine Orleans	77	★★★½	1	415 Dauphine Street New Orleans, LA 70112
Days Inn	52	★★	8	5801 Read Road New Orleans, LA 70127
Days Inn Kenner Airport	50	★★	10	1300 Veterans Memorial Blvd. Kenner, LA 70065
Days Inn New Orleans Canal Street	54	★★	2	1630 Canal Street New Orleans, LA 70112
Days Inn Westbank Harvey	55	★★	11	3750 Westbank Expressway Gretna, LA 70058
Doubletree Hotel Lakeside New Orleans	83	★★★★	9	3838 N. Causeway Blvd. Metairie, LA 70002
Doubletree Hotel New Orleans	74	★★★	2	300 Canal Street New Orleans, LA 70130
Embassy Suites New Orleans	82	★★★½	2	315 Julia Street New Orleans, LA 70130
Extended Stay America	74	★★★	9	3300 I-10 & Causeway Blvd. Metairie, LA 70001
Fairmont Hotel	86	★★★★	2	123 Baronne Street, University I New Orleans, LA 70112
Four Points Sheraton	72	★★★	10	6401 Veterans Memorial Blvd. Metairie, LA 70003
French Quarter Courtyard Hotel	62	★★½	1	1101 N. Rampart Street New Orleans, LA 70116
French Quarter Suites	69	★★★	1	1119 N. Rampart Street New Orleans, LA 70116
The Frenchmen	60	★★½	6	417 Frenchmen Street New Orleans, LA 70116
Grenoble House	81	★★★½	1	329 Dauphine Street New Orleans, LA 70112
Hampton Inn	67	★★★	9	2730 N. Causeway Blvd. Metairie, LA 70002

Phone	Fax	Reservations	Rack Rate	No. of Rooms
(504) 838-3800	(504) 838-7050	(800) 654-3990	$$$–	153
(504) 524-8076	(504) 581-3277	(800) 535-7858	$$+	19
(504) 558-0201	(504) 529-1609	(800) 236-6119	$$$$	1036
(504) 586-1800	(504) 586-1409	(800) 521-7111	$$$–	112
(504) 241-2500	(504) 245-8340	(800) 331-6935	$$+	143
(504) 469-2531	(504) 468-4269	(800) 325-2525	$+	312
(504) 586-0110	(504) 581-2253	(800) 232-3297	$$+	216
(504) 348-1262	(504) 348-0624	(800) 221-2222	$+	106
(504) 836-5253	(504) 846-4562	(800) 222-TREE	$$$$$+	210
(504) 581-1300	(504) 522-4100	(800) 222-8733	$$$$$$	367
(504) 525-1993	(504) 525-3437	(800) 362-2779	$$$–	316
(504) 837-5599	(504) 837-5009	(800) 326-5651	$$$+	102
(504) 529-7111	(504) 529-4764	(800) 441-1414	$$$$$$$$–	750
(504) 885-5700	(504) 888-5815	(800) HOLIDAY	$$$$	220
(504) 522-7333	(504) 522-3908	(800) 290-4233	$$$–	51
(504) 524-7725	(504) 522-9716	(800) 457-2253	$$$+	17
(504) 948-2166	(504) 948-2258	(800) 831-1781	$$$	25
(504) 522-1331	(504) 524-4968	(800) 722-1834	$$$$	17
(504) 831-7676	(504) 831-7478	(800) HAMPTON	$$+	111

Hotel	Pool	Sauna	Room Service
Courtyard Metairie	Y	Y	N
A Creole House	N	N	N
Crescent on Canal	N	N	N
Dauphine Orleans	Y	N	N
Days Inn	Y	N	N
Days Inn Kenner Airport	Y	N	N
Days Inn New Orleans Canal Street	Y	N	N
Days Inn Westbank Harvey	Y	N	N
Doubletree Hotel Lakeside New Orleans	Y	Y	Some
Doubletree Hotel New Orleans	Y	N	Some
Embassy Suites New Orleans	Y	Y	Y
Extended Stay America	N	N	N
Fairmont Hotel	Y	N	Y
Four Points Sheraton	Y	N	Y
French Quarter Courtyard Hotel	Y	N	N
French Quarter Suites	Y	Y	N
The Frenchmen	Y	Y	N
Grenoble House	Y	Y	N
Hampton Inn	Y	N	N

Parking	TV	VCR	Free Breakfast	Exercise Facilities
None	Y	N	N	Y
16	Y	N	Continental	N
17	Y	N	Continental	N
12	Y	N	Continental	Y
None	Y	N	N	N
None	Y	N	N	N
12	Y	N	N	N
None	Y	N	Continental	N
10	Y	N	N	Y
16	Y	N	N	Y
18	Y	N	Full	Y
None	Y	N	N	N
19	Y	N	N	Y
None	Y	N	N	Y
15	Y	N	Y	N
15	Y	N	Continental	N
No lot	Y	N	Continental	N
No lot	Y	N	Y	N
None	Y	N	Continental	Y

Hotel	Quality	Star Rating	Zone	Address
Hampton Inn and Suites (room)	61	★★½	10	5150 Mounes Street Harahan, LA 70123
Hampton Inn and Suites (suite)	68	★★★	10	5150 Mounes Street Harahan, LA 70123
Hampton Inn Downtown	75	★★★½	2	226 Carondelet Street New Orleans, LA 70130
Hampton Inn Suites & Convention Center	88	★★★★	2	1201 Convention Center Blvd. New Orleans, LA 70130
Hilton Garden Inn	85	★★★★	2	1001 S. Peters Street New Orleans, LA 70130
Hilton New Orleans Riverside	86	★★★★	2	Poydras at Mississippi River New Orleans, LA 70140
Hilton New Orleans Airport	78	★★★½	10	901 Airline Highway Kenner, LA 70062
Historic French Market Inn	70	★★★	1	501 Decatur Street New Orleans, LA 70130
Holiday Inn Airport	73	★★★	10	2929 Williams Blvd. Kenner, LA 70062
Holiday Inn Downtown-Superdome	80	★★★½	2	330 Loyola Avenue New Orleans, LA 70112
Holiday Inn French Quarter	78	★★★½	1	124 Royal Street New Orleans, LA 70130
Holiday Inn Metairie	66	★★★	9	3400 S. I-10 Service Road Metairie, LA 70001
Holiday Inn New Orleans Westbank	65	★★★	11	100 Westbank Expressway Gretna, LA 70053
Holiday Inn Select	82	★★★½	2	881 Convention Center Blvd. New Orleans, LA 70130
Hotel de la Monnaie	82	★★★½	1	405 Esplanade Avenue New Orleans, LA 70116
Hotel Inter-Continental New Orleans	83	★★★★	2	444 Street Charles Avenue New Orleans, LA 70130
Hotel Street Marie	73	★★★	1	827 Toulouse Street New Orleans, LA 70112
Hotel Street Pierre	50	★★	1	911 Burgundy Street New Orleans, LA 70116
Hotel Ste. Helene	79	★★★½	1	508 Rue Chartres New Orleans, LA 70130

Phone	Fax	Reservations	Rack Rate	No. of Rooms
(504) 733-5646	(504) 733-5609	(800) HAMPTON	$$$–	128
(504) 733-5646	(504) 733-5609	(800) HAMPTON	$$$$–	128
(504) 529-9990	(504) 529-9996	(800) 292-0653	$$$$	186
(504) 566-9990	(504) 566-9997	(800) 292-0653	$$$$–	288
(504) 525-0044	(504) 525-0035	(800) HILTONS	$$$$$–	286
(504) 584-3999	(504) 584-3979	(800) HILTONS	$$$$–	1600
(504) 469-5000	(504) 465-1101	(800) 872-5914	$$$$–	317
(504) 561-5621	(888) 211-3448	(888) 211-3447	$$$$+	68
(504) 467-5611	(504) 469-4915	(800) HOLIDAY	$$$+	303
(504) 581-1600	(504) 586-0833	(800) 535-7830	$$$$+	300
(504) 529-7211	(504) 522-7930	(800) 447-2830	$$$$	252
(504) 833-8201	(504) 838-6829	(800) HOLIDAY	$$$–	194
(504) 366-2361	(504) 362-5814	(800) HOLIDAY	$$+	307
(504) 524-1881	(504) 528-1005	(800) 535-7830	$$$$	170
(504) 947-0009	(504) 945-6841	NA	$$$$–	53
(504) 525-5566	(504) 523-7310	(800) 327-0200	$$$$$+	481
(504) 561-8951	(504) 571-2802	(800) 366-2743	$$$	100
(504) 524-4401	(504) 524-6800	(800) 225-4040	$$$–	72
(504) 522-5014	(504) 523-7140	(800) 348-3888	$$$+	26

Hotel	Pool	Sauna	Room Service
Hampton Inn and Suites (room)	Y	N	N
Hampton Inn and Suites (suite)	Y	N	N
Hampton Inn Downtown	N	N	N
Hampton Inn Suites & Convention Center	Y	N	N
Hilton Garden Inn	Y	Y	Some
Hilton New Orleans Riverside	Y	Y	Y
Hilton New Orleans Airport	Y	Y	Y
Historic French Market Inn	Y	N	Y
Holiday Inn Airport	Y	Y	Some
Holiday Inn Downtown-Superdome	Y	N	Y
Holiday Inn French Quarter	Y	N	Y
Holiday Inn Metairie	Y	Y	Y
Holiday Inn New Orleans Westbank	Y	N	Some
Holiday Inn Select	N	N	Y
Hotel de la Monnaie	Y	N	N
Hotel Inter-Continental New Orleans	Y	N	Y
Hotel Street Marie	Y	N	Y
Hotel Street Pierre	Y	N	N
Hotel Ste. Helene	Y	N	N

Parking	TV	VCR	Free Breakfast	Exercise Facilities
None	Y	N	Continental	Off site
None	Y	N	Continental	Off site
17	Y	N	Continental	Y
16	Y	N	Continental	Y
18	Y	N	N	Y
20	Y	N	N	Y
None	Y	N	N	Y
15	Y	N	Y	N
None	Y	Y	N	Y
20	Y	N	N	Y
19	Y	N	N	Y
N	Y	N	N	Y
None	Y	N	N	Y
18	Y	N	N	Y
None	Y	N	N	Y
25	Y	N	N	Y
15	Y	N	N	N
None	Y	N	Continental	N
12	Y	N	Continental	N

Hotel	Quality	Star Rating	Zone	Address
Hotel Villa Convento	66	★★★	1	616 Ursulines Street New Orleans, LA 70116
Howard Johnson	41	★½	8	4200 Old Gentilly Road New Orleans, LA 70126
Hyatt Regency New Orleans at Superdome	83	★★★★	2	500 Poydras Plaza New Orleans, LA 70113
La Quinta Inn Airport	63	★★½	10	2610 Williams Blvd. Kenner, LA 70062
La Quinta Inn Bullard	61	★★½	8	12001 I-10 Service Road New Orleans, LA 70128
La Quinta Inn Causeway	58	★★½	9	3100 I-10 Service Road Metairie, LA 70001
La Quinta Inn Crowder Road	64	★★½	8	8400 I-10 Service Road New Orleans, LA 70127
La Quinta Inn Veterans	61	★★½	10	5900 Veterans Memorial Blvd. Metairie, LA 70003
La Quinta Inn West Bank	60	★★½	11	50 Terry Parkway Gretna, LA 70056
Lafayette Hotel	78	★★★½	2	600 St. Charles Avenue New Orleans, LA 70130
Lafitte Guest House	70	★★★	1	1003 Bourbon Street New Orleans, LA 70116
Lamothe House	55	★★	1	621 Esplanade Avenue New Orleans, LA 70116
Lasalle Hotel	58	★★½	1	1113 Canal Street New Orleans, LA 70112
Le Meridien Hotel New Orleans	86	★★★★	2	614 Canal Street New Orleans, LA 70130
Le Pavillon Hotel	88	★★★★	2	833 Poydras Street New Orleans, LA 70112
Le Richelieu in the French Quarter	69	★★★	1	1234 Chartres Street New Orleans, LA 70116
Maison De Ville	84	★★★★	1	727 Rue Toulouse New Orleans, LA 70130
Maison Dupuy Hotel	86	★★★★	1	1001 Rue Toulouse New Orleans, LA 70112
Maison St. Charles Quality Inn and Suites	65	★★★	3	1319 St. Charles Avenue New Orleans, LA 70130

Phone	Fax	Reservations	Rack Rate	No. of Rooms
(504) 522-1793	(504) 524-1902	(800) 887-2817	$$$–	25
(504) 944-0151	(504) 945-3053	(800) 446-4656	$$–	96
(504) 561-1234	(504) 587-4141	(800) 233-1234	$$$$–	1184
(504) 466-1401	(504) 466-0319	(800) 531-5900	$$	187
(504) 246-3003	(504) 242-5539	(800) 531-5900	$$	130
(504) 835-8511	(504) 837-3383	(800) 531-5900	$$	101
(504) 246-5800	(504) 242-5091	(800) 531-5900	$$+	105
(504) 456-0003	(504) 885-0863	(800) 531-5900	$$–	153
(504) 368-5600	(504) 362-7430	(800) 531-5900	$$	154
(504) 524-4441	(504) 523-7327	(800) 733-4754	$$$$$–	44
(504) 581-2678	(504) 581-2678	(800) 331-7971	$$$$$–	14
(504) 947-1161	(504) 943-6536	(800) 367-5858	$$+	20
(504) 523-5831	(504) 525-2531	(800) 521-9450	$$–	60
(504) 525-6500	(504) 586-1543	(800) 543-4300	$$$$$$–	494
(504) 581-3111	(504) 586-1543	(800) 535-9095	$$$$$$	222
(504) 529-2492	(504) 524-8179	(800) 535-9653	$$$+	88
(504) 561-5858	(504) 528-9939	(800) 634-1600	$$$$$$–	23
(504) 586-8000	(504) 525-5334	(800) 535-9177	$$+	198
(504) 522-0187	(504) 529-4379	(800) 831-1783	$$$	130

Hotel	Pool	Sauna	Room Service
Hotel Villa Convento	N	N	N
Howard Johnson	Y	N	N
Hyatt Regency New Orleans at Superdome	Y	N	Y
La Quinta Inn Airport	Y	N	N
La Quinta Inn Bullard	Y	N	N
La Quinta Inn Causeway	Y	N	N
La Quinta Inn Crowder Road	Y	N	N
La Quinta Inn Veterans	Y	N	N
La Quinta Inn West Bank	Y	N	N
Lafayette Hotel	N	N	Y
Lafitte Guest House	N	N	N
Lamothe House	Y	Y	N
Lasalle Hotel	N	N	N
Le Meridien Hotel New Orleans	Y	Y	Y
Le Pavillon Hotel	Y	N	Y
Le Richelieu in the French Quarter	Y	N	Y
Maison De Ville	Y	N	Y
Maison Dupuy Hotel	Y	Y	Y
Maison St. Charles Quality Inn and Suites	Y	Y	N

Parking	TV	VCR	Free Breakfast	Exercise Facilities
6	Y	N	Continental	N
None	Y	Y	Continental	N
19	Y	N	N	Y
None	Y	N	Continental	Y
None	Y	N	Continental	N
None	Y	N	Continental	N
None	Y	N	Continental	Off site
None	Y	N	Continental	N
None	Y	N	Continental	N
15	Y	Y	N	N
10	Y	Most	In room continental	N
None	Y	N	Continental	N
8	Y	N	Continental	N
19	Y	N	N	Y
22	Y	N	N	Y
N	Y	N	N	N
18	N	Y	Continental	Off site
13	Y	Y	N	Y
10	Y	N	N	N

Hotel	Quality	Star Rating	Zone	Address
Marriott New Orleans	80	★★★½	1	555 Canal Street New Orleans, LA 70140
The McKendrick-Breaux House	88	★★★★	3	1474 Magazine Street New Orleans, LA 70130
The Monteleone	82	★★★½	1	214 Rue Royal New Orleans, LA 70130
New Orleans Guest House	72	★★★	1	1118 Ursulines Street New Orleans, LA 70116
Olivier House Hotel	74	★★★	1	828 Toulouse Street New Orleans, LA 70112
Omni Royal Crescent Hotel	90	★★★★½	2	535 Gravier Street New Orleans, LA 70130
Omni Royal Orleans Hotel	89	★★★★	1	621 St. Louis Street New Orleans, LA 70140
Orleans Courtyard Inn	59	★★½	9	3800 Hessmer Avenue Metairie, LA 70002
Park Plaza Inn	55	★★	10	2125 Veterans Memorial Blvd. Kenner, LA 70062
Pelham Hotel	88	★★★★	2	444 Common Street New Orleans, LA 70130
Place D'Armes Hotel	75	★★★½	1	625 St. Ann Street New Orleans, LA 70116
Pontchartrain Hotel	80	★★★½	3	2031 St. Charles Avenue New Orleans, LA 70140
Prince Conti Hotel	80	★★★½	1	830 Conti Street New Orleans, LA 70112
Provincial Hotel	77	★★★½	1	1024 Rue Chartres New Orleans, LA 70116
Prytania Park Hotel	68	★★★	3	1525 Prytania Street New Orleans, LA 70130
Quality Hotel and Conference Center	63	★★½	9	2261 N. Causeway Blvd. Metairie, LA 70001
Quality Inn Midtown	60	★★½	6	3900 Tulane Avenue New Orleans, LA 70113
Quality Inn Tower Hotel	60	★★½	11	100 Westbank Expressway Gretna, LA 70053
Queen and Crescent Hotel	84	★★★★	2	344 Camp Street New Orleans, LA 70130

Phone	Fax	Reservations	Rack Rate	No. of Rooms
(504) 581-1000	(504) 523-6755	(800) 654-3990	$$$+	1290
(504) 586-1700	(504) 522-7138	(888) 570-1700	$$$+	8
(504) 523-3341	(504) 528-1019	(800) 535-9595	$$$$$$–	600
(504) 566-1177	NA	(800) 562-1177	$$+	14
(504) 525-8456	(504) 529-2006	NA	$$$+	40
(504) 527-0006	(504) 523-0806	(800) 843-6664	$$$$–	98
(504) 529-5333	(504) 529-7089	(800) 843-6664	$$$$–	346
(504) 455-6110	(504) 455-0940	(800) 258-2514	$$–	52
(504) 464-6464	(504) 464-7532	(800) (504) 7275	$$–	128
(504) 522-4444	(504) 539-9010	(888) 211-3447	$$$$$	60
(504) 524-4531	(504) 571-2803	(800) 366-2743	$$$–	80
(504) 524-0581	(504) 529-1165	(800) 777-6193	$$$	104
(504) 529-4172	(504) 581-3802	(800) 366-2743	$$$–	50
(504) 581-4995	(504) 581-1018	(888) 594-5271	$$$–	100
(504) 524-0427	(504) 522-2977	(888) 209-9002	$$$+	62
(504) 833-8211	(504) 828-5476	(800) 228-5151	$$+	204
(504) 486-5541	(504) 488-7440	(800) 827-5543	$$$	105
(504) 366-8531	(504) 362-9502	(800) 654-2000	$$	177
(504) 587-9700	(504) 587-9701	(800) 975-6652	$$$–	129

Hotel	Pool	Sauna	Room Service
Marriott New Orleans	Y	Y	Y
The McKendrick-Breaux House	N	N	N
The Monteleone	Y	N	Y
New Orleans Guest House	N	N	N
Olivier House Hotel	Y	N	N
Omni Royal Crescent Hotel	Y	N	Y
Omni Royal Orleans Hotel	Y	N	Y
Orleans Courtyard Inn	Y	N	N
Park Plaza Inn	Y	N	Y
Pelham Hotel	N	N	Y
Place D'Armes Hotel	Y	N	N
Pontchartrain Hotel	N	N	Y
Prince Conti Hotel	N	N	Y
Provincial Hotel	Y	N	Y
Prytania Park Hotel	N	N	N
Quality Hotel and Conference Center	Y	Y	Y
Quality Inn Midtown	Y	Y	Y
Quality Inn Tower Hotel	Y	N	N
Queen and Crescent Hotel	N	N	N

Parking	TV	VCR	Free Breakfast	Exercise Facilities
19	Y	N	N	Y
None	Y	N	Continental	N
15	Y	N	N	Y
N	Y	N	Full	N
N	Y	N	N	N
17	Y	N	N	Y
19	Y	N	N	Y
None	Y	N	Continental	Y
None	Y	N	Continental	Y
18	Y	N	N	N
15	Y	N	Continental	N
13	Y	Y	Full	Off site/Fee
15	Y	N	N	N
11	Y	N	N	N
10	Y	N	Continental	N
None	Y	N	N	Y
None	Y	N	N	N
None	Y	N	N	N
18	Y	N	Continental	Y

Hotel	Quality	Star Rating	Zone	Address
Radisson Hotel New Orleans	70	★★★	2	1500 Canal Street New Orleans, LA 70112
Radisson Inn Airport	70	★★★	10	2150 Veterans Memorial Blvd. Kenner, LA 70062
Ramada Inn Highrise	52	★★	8	6324 Chef Menteur Highway New Orleans, LA 70126
Ramada Inn Superdome	70	★★★	2	1315 Gravier Street New Orleans, LA 70112
Ramada Limited Causeway	71	★★★	9	2713 N. Causeway Blvd. Metairie, LA 70002
Ramada Plaza Hotel	72	★★★	3	2203 St. Charles Avenue New Orleans, LA 70140
Ramada Plaza on Bourbon	74	★★★	1	541 Bourbon Street New Orleans, LA 70130
Rathbone Inn	78	★★★½	1	1227 Esplanade Avenue New Orleans, LA 70116
Residence Inn	88	★★★★	2	345 St. Joseph Street New Orleans, LA 70130
Residence Inn Metairie	88	★★★★	9	3 Galleria Blvd. Metairie, LA 70001
Ritz-Carlton New Orleans	95	★★★★½	1	921 Canal Street New Orleans, LA 70112
Rodeway Inn Airport	56	★★½	10	851 Airline Highway Kenner, LA 70062
Royal Sonesta Hotel	89	★★★★	1	300 Bourbon Street New Orleans, LA 70140
Rue Royal Inn	62	★★½	1	1006 Royal Street New Orleans, LA 70116
Saint Ann/ Marie Anntoinette	63	★★½	1	717 Rue Conti New Orleans, LA 70130
The Saint Louis	74	★★★	1	730 Bienville Street New Orleans, LA 70130
Sheraton New Orleans Hotel	85	★★★★	2	500 Canal Street New Orleans, LA 70130
Shoney's Inn	58	★★½	10	2421 Clearview Parkway Metairie, LA 70001
Soniat House	80	★★★½	1	1133 Chartres Street New Orleans, LA 70116

Phone	Fax	Reservations	Rack Rate	No. of Rooms
(504) 522-4500	(504) 525-2644	(800) 333-3333	$$$$$+	759
(504) 467-3111	(504) 469-4634	(800) 333-3333	$$$+	244
(504) 241-2900	(504) 241-5697	(800) 228-2828	$$	204
(504) 586-0100	(504) 586-0100	(800) 535-9141	$$$–	157
(504) 835-4141	(504) 833-6942	(800) 228-3838	$$–	128
(504) 566-1200	(504) 581-1352	(800) 443-4675	$$$$–	132
(504) 524-7611	(504) 568-9427	(800) 535-7891	$$$$$+	186
(504) 947-2100	(504) 947-7454	(800) 947-2101	$$	15
(504) 522-1300	(504) 522-6060	(800) 654-3990	$$$$–	213
(504) 832-0888	(504) 832-4916	(800) 654-3990	$$$$–	120
(504) 524-1331	(504) 524-7675	(800) 241-3333	$$$$$$+	452
(504) 467-1391	(504) 466-9148	(800) 228-2000	$$–	98
(504) 586-0300	(504) 586-0335	(800) SONESTA	$$$$$–	500
(504) 524-3900	(504) 558-0566	(800) 776-3901	$$$+	17
(504) 525-2300	(504) 524-8925	(800) 535-9111	$$$–	65
(504) 581-7300	(504) 524-8925	(800) 535-9111	$$$–	71
(504) 525-2500	(504) 595-5550	(888) 396-6364	$$$$–	1127
(504) 456-9081	(504) 455-6287	(800) 222-2222	$$–	145
(504) 522-0570	(504) 522-7208	(800) 544-8808	$$$$+	24

Hotel	Pool	Sauna	Room Service
Radisson Hotel New Orleans	Y	N	Y
Radisson Inn Airport	Y	N	Y
Ramada Inn Highrise	Y	N	Y
Ramada Inn Superdome	Y	N	N
Ramada Limited Causeway	Y	N	N
Ramada Plaza Hotel	N	N	Y
Ramada Plaza on Bourbon	Y	N	Y
Rathbone Inn	N	Y	N
Residence Inn	Y	N	N
Residence Inn Metairie	Y	Y	N
Ritz-Carlton New Orleans	Y	Y	Y
Rodeway Inn Airport	Y	N	N
Royal Sonesta Hotel	Y	N	Y
Rue Royal Inn	N	N	N
Saint Ann/Marie Anntoinette	Y	N	Y
The Saint Louis	N	N	Y
Sheraton New Orleans Hotel	Y	Y	Y
Shoney's Inn	Y	N	N
Soniat House	N	N	N

Parking	TV	VCR	Free Breakfast	Exercise Facilities
None	Y	N	Corp. only	Y
None	Y	N	Some	Y
None	Y	N	N	N
No lot	Y	N	N	N
None	Y	N	Continental	Y
15	Y	N	N	N
16	Y	N	N	Y
N	Y	N	Continental	N
15	Y	N	Continental	Y
None	Y	N	Continental	Y
25	Y	Y	N	Y
None	Y	N	Continental	N
19	Y	N	Continental	Y
15	Y	N	Continental	N
17	Y	N	N	N
17	Y	N	N	N
24	Y	N	N	Y
None	Y	N	Continental	N
19	Y	Y	N	N

Hotel	Quality	Star Rating	Zone	Address
St. Charles Inn	59	★★½	3	3636 St. Charles Avenue New Orleans, LA 70115
St. Peter Guest House House	68	★★★	1	1005 St. Peter Street New Orleans, LA 70116
Super 8 New Orleans	58	★★½	8	6322 Chef Menteur Highway New Orleans, LA 70126
Travelodge Hotel New Orleans	49	★★	11	2200 Westbank Expressway Gretna, LA 70058
Travelodge New Orleans Airport Hotel	58	★★½	10	2240 Veterans Memorial Blvd Kenner, LA 70062
Travelodge New Orleans Metairie	47	★★	10	5733 Airline Highway Metairie, LA 70003
W French Quarter	80	★★★½	1	316 Chartres Street New Orleans, LA 70130
Windsor Court	94	★★★★½	2	300 Gravier Street New Orleans, LA 70130
Wingate Inn	72	★★★	10	1501 Veterans Memorial Blvd Kenner, LA 70062
Wyndham Canal Place	90	★★★★½	1	100 Rue Iberville New Orleans, LA 70130
Wyndham Riverfront Hotel	84	★★★★	2	701 Convention Center Blvd. New Orleans, LA 70130

Phone	Fax	Reservations	Rack Rate	No. of Rooms
(504) 899-8888	(504) 899-8892	(800) 489-9908	$$–	40
(504) 524-9232	(504) 523-5198	(800) 535-7815	$$+	23
(504) 241-5650	(504) 241-2178	(800) 800-8000	$$–	96
(504) 366-5311	(504) 368-2774	(800) 578-7878	$$	212
(504) 469-7341	(504) 469-7922	(800) 578-7878	$$–	196
(504) 733-1550	(504) 734-1554	(800) 578-7878	$+	80
(504) 581-1200	(504) 522-3208	(800) 448-4927	$$$$+	100
(504) 523-6000	(504) 596-4513	(800) 262-2662	$$$$$+	324
(504) 305-1501	(504) 305-1500	(800) 228-1000	$$$+	102
(504) 566-7006	(504) 553-5120	(800) 228-3000	$$$$	438
(504) 524-8200	(504) 524-0600	(800) WYNDHAM	$$$+	202

Hotel	Pool	Sauna	Room Service
St. Charles Inn	N	N	N
St. Peter Guest House	N	N	N
Super 8 New Orleans	Y	N	N
Travelodge Hotel New Orleans	Y	N	Y
Travelodge New Orleans Airport Hotel	Y	Y	Y
Travelodge New Orleans Metairie	Y	N	N
W French Quarter	Y	N	Y
Windsor Court	Y	Y	Y
Wingate Inn	N	Y	N
Wyndham Canal Place	Y	N	Y
Wyndham Riverfront Hotel	N	N	Y

Parking	TV	VCR	Free Breakfast	Exercise Facilities
None	Y	N	Continental	N
16	Y	N	Continental	N
None	Y	N	Continental	N
None	Y	N	Continental	N
None	Y	N	N	N
None	Y	N	N	N
24	Y	Y	N	N
18	Y	Y	N	Y
None	Y	N	Continental	Y
25	Y	N	N	Y
18	Y	N	N	Y

Part Five

Visiting New Orleans on Business

New Orleans Lodging for Business Travelers

The primary hotel considerations for business travelers are affordability and proximity to the site or area where you will transact your business. Identify the zone(s) where your business will take you, and then use the hotel chart to cross-reference the hotels located in that area. Once you have developed a short list of possible hotels that are conveniently located, fit your budget, and offer the standard of accommodations you require, you (or your travel agent) can make use of the cost-saving suggestions discussed in the previous part to obtain the lowest rate.

LODGING CONVENIENT TO MORIAL CONVENTION CENTER

If you are attending a meeting or trade show at **Morial Convention Center,** the most convenient lodging is in the Central Business District or in the French Quarter. Closest to the convention center are the **Hampton Inn and Suites** and the **Hilton Garden Inn** directly across the street, and the **Residence Inn** on St. Joseph. Next are the **Embassy Suites, the Holiday Inn Select** and **the Wyndham Riverfront Hotel.** The hotels on Canal Street and those in the western side of the French Quarter are also within decent proximity. Two Vieux Carré shuttle bus routes combine with the Riverfront Streetcar to make commuting from the French Quarter to the convention center easy. It takes about 10–12 minutes to walk from the exhibit halls to the river end of Canal Street and about 5–12 minutes more to reach hotels in the upper Quarter (between St. Peter and Canal streets). Parking is available at the convention center, but it is expensive and not all that convenient. We recommend that you leave your car at home and use shuttles, streetcars, or cabs.

Commuting to Morial Convention Center from the suburbs or the airports during rush hour should be avoided, if possible. If you want a room near the convention center, book early—very early. If you need a room at the last minute, try a wholesaler or reservation service, or one of the strategies listed below.

CONVENTION RATES: HOW THEY WORK AND HOW TO DO BETTER

If you are attending a major convention or trade show, the meeting's sponsoring organization probably has negotiated convention rates with a number of hotels. Under this arrangement, hotels agree to block a certain number of rooms at an agreed-upon price for conventioneers. Sometimes, as in the case of a small meeting, only one hotel is involved. In the event of a large convention at Morial Convention Center, however, a high percentage of Central Business District and larger French Quarter hotels will participate in the room block.

Because the convention sponsor brings a lot of business to the city and reserves a large number of rooms, it usually can negotiate a volume discount on the room rate, a rate that should be substantially below rack rate. The bottom line, however, is that some conventions and trade shows have more bargaining clout and negotiating skill than others. Hence, your convention sponsor may or may not be able to obtain the lowest possible rate.

Once a convention or trade-show sponsor has completed negotiations with participating hotels, it will send its attendees a housing list that includes all the hotels serving the convention, along with the special convention rate for each. When you receive the housing list, you can compare the convention rates with the rates obtainable using the strategies listed below. If the negotiated convention rate doesn't sound like a good deal, you can try to reserve a room using a half-price club, a consolidator, a reservations service, or a tour operator. Remember, however, that many of the deep discounts are available only when the hotel expects to be at less than 80% occupancy, a condition that rarely prevails when a big convention comes to town.

Strategies for Beating Convention Rates

There are several tactics for getting around convention rates:

1. Reserve early. Most big conventions and trade shows announce meeting sites one to three years in advance. Get your reservation booked as far in advance as possible using a half-price club. If you book well ahead of the time the convention sponsor sends out the housing list, chances are good that the hotel will accept your reservation.

2. Compare your convention's housing list with the list of hotels presented in this guide. You may be able to find a suitable hotel that is not on the housing list.

3. Use a local reservations service, a wholesaler, or a room consolidator. This is also a good strategy to employ if you need to make reservations at the last minute. Local reservations services, wholesalers, and consolidators almost always control some rooms, even in the midst of a huge convention or trade show.

The Ernest N. Morial Convention Center

The **Morial Convention Center** is located at 900 Convention Center Boulevard, New Orleans, LA 70130. The phone number is 582-3000, and the fax is 582-3088.

The Morial Convention Center includes 1.1 million square feet of contiguous exhibit space under one roof since its Phase III expansion was completed in early 1999. All this muscle backs up to and stretches out along the bank of the Mississippi. The front of the Center runs along South Front Street, also called Convention Center Boulevard, reached easily from Interstate 10 by the Tchoupitoulas/St. Peter exit. For pedestrians attending an event at the Convention Center, the battle is won after you've found the front door. For many attendees coming from the Canal Street major hotels and the French Quarter lodgings, the way in is simply not clear from a distance, nor is it distinctly marked once you come to it. The primary entrance is on Convention Center Boulevard, but the doors are actually perpendicular to the street, not parallel to the facade. The entrance is not marked by a plaza, flags, sculpture, or a fountain—nothing really shouts, "Enter Here!"

This only poses a problem on that first critical day of registration when many people still feel disoriented. The best advice is to head for the Riverwalk Marketplace shopping center, which is highly visible on the Mississippi at Canal, Poydras, and Julia streets. As you face it (and the River), go to your right and have faith that the door will appear. It is a low-key ramp

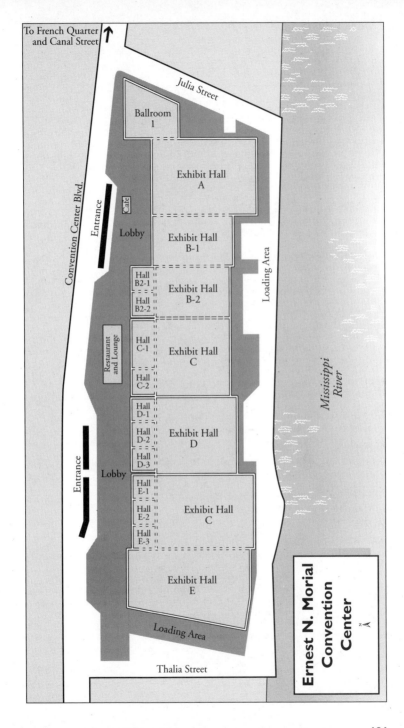

To French Quarter
and Canal Street

Julia Street

Ballroom
1

Exhibit Hall
A

Convention Center Blvd.

Entrance

Café

Lobby

Exhibit Hall
B-1

Hall
B2-1

Hall
B2-2

Exhibit Hall
B-2

Loading Area

Restaurant
and Lounge

Hall
C-1

Hall
C-2

Exhibit Hall
C

Hall
D-1

Hall
D-2

Hall
D-3

Exhibit Hall
D

Entrance

Lobby

Hall
E-1

Hall
E-2

Hall
E-3

Exhibit Hall
C

Exhibit Hall
E

Loading Area

Thalia Street

Mississippi River

Ernest N. Morial
Convention
Center

N

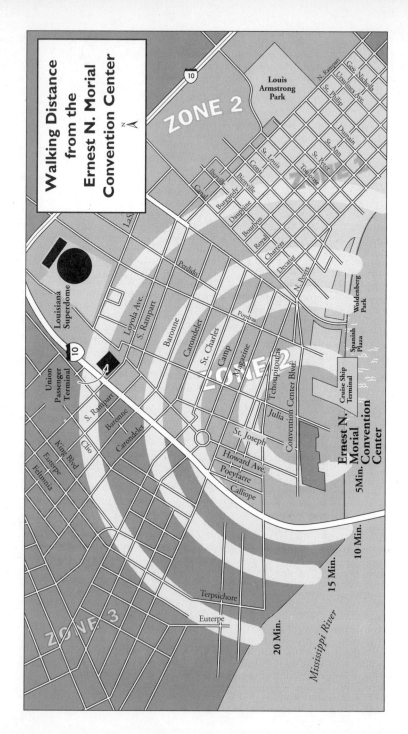

leading to a series of glass doors. Once you're inside, the facility is very well marked. The exhibit halls are alphabetically labeled, with "A" nearest the main entrance.

If the original architect missed the downbeat, the Convention Center administration does its best to set the right tempo. Clear, handsome promotional literature is readily available by calling the marketing and sales department office. The publication details the floor plans of the facility, including the capacities of the various spaces. There are 55 spaces for highway vans and 13 freight drive-in entrances. The same brochure specifies the dimensions of these entrances, the floor load capacity (350 lbs./ sq. ft.) and a host of other details needed by exhibitors. The facility is nonunion.

Another handy piece to help you get around is "Walking Tours of the Warehouse District & Lafayette Square: Art, History & Architecture," produced by the Downtown Development District in cooperation with the Warehouse District Arts Association. (Ask the Convention Center or the Chamber of Commerce for it. You can also find it in hotel lobby racks.) The Convention Center borders this district, and this brochure lists museums and institutions, galleries, landmarks, hotels, cafes and restaurants, and the St. Charles streetcar route, all within walking distance of the Center.

GETTING FOOD

The food in the Center is definitely above average, and the promo literature makes much of their prize-winning chef, Leon West, who supervises the production of two kitchens, each of which can produce 20,000 meals in a 24-hour period. In the 400-seat Atrium/Restaurant Lounge you can order Cajun and Creole favorites. There are conventional concession/ refreshment areas located off each exhibit hall floor. Prices are not as high as they could be, but no bargains can be found either.

If you can break free, there are several good restaurants within a 10–15-minute walk. A terrific, delicious value is at **Taqueria Corona,** 857 Fulton, where an outstanding Mexican lunch can be yours for about $5. They also serve dinner later in the day (they're closed in the mid-afternoon). **True Brew Coffee,** 200 Julia Street, can make the vegetarians happy; they also have a pastrami and pepper-cheese sandwich. Some sidewalk seating is available, and they have a bar. The **Red Bike Cafe,** 746 Tchoupitoulas, specializes in bakery goods and vegetarian delights. **Ernst Cafe,** 600 South Peters, offers plate lunches and sandwiches. Business people needing a quieter atmosphere can dine at the **Sugar House Restaurant** inside the

Embassy Suite Hotel at 315 Julia Street. The muffuletta joints across the street from the Convention Center are another quick option. There are also many choices, some featuring local cuisine on short order, at the **Bon Fête Food Court** inside the Riverwalk Marketplace next door to the Convention Center.

Part Six

Arriving and Getting Oriented

Coming into the City

Nothing spoils a vacation quicker than a traffic jam, a missed connection, or a too-long walk with luggage—the sorts of misadventures that often are overlooked in the excitement of planning a trip. New Orleans happily abandons its claim to mystery when it comes to making tourists comfortable: It's well supplied with public transportation; the airport is new and efficient but not impersonal or intimidating; and once you sling a little lingo, you can get directions from anyone. Just take a few minutes to get organized before you cut loose.

BY PLANE

New Orleans Moisant International Airport (464-0831) is located about ten miles west of New Orleans, in Kenner. At four feet above sea level, it's a frequent source of jokes about "high-flying" airstrips and so on, but it is relatively high and dry, at least compared to the surrounding area—and if you fly in, watching the complex gradually take shape from the swampland around it, you'll see why that's important.

The airport is fully wheelchair accessible, and the telephone banks in each concourse have TDD phones as well. Ticket counters are in the center on the upper level, with the four concourses at the ends, and information counters, concessions, and gift stands scattered about. A full-service Whitney National Bank, 24-hour automated-teller machines, and a post office are in the main central hall. There is a **Traveler's Aid Booth** (464-3522) in the east end of the lobby, as well as general information desks on both ends. The **Mutual of Omaha Business Service Center** (465-9647) office and an American Express traveler's check machine are in the west lobby.

Transportation and baggage claim are downstairs, with additional ATMs; there are elevators at each end. The airport-shuttle desk downstairs (465-9780) is staffed around the clock.

New Orleans is served by more than a dozen airlines. American, Northwest/KLM, USAirways, and USAir Express all use Concourse A. Some American Airlines flights also go into the larger Concourse B, along with Continental, Continental Express, Southwest, and TWA. Aeromexico, Aviateca, LACSA, TACA, and United Air Lines all use Concourse C, and Delta uses Concourse D.

Incidentally, the rest rooms in the airport are very nice. The toilets are automatically sanitized with each flush, and motorized seat covers slip over the seats at the push of a button. All faucets are touch-free as well, operated by electric eyes.

Getting to the City from the Airport

To get from the airport to the city, you may take the **Airport Shuttle** (592-0555) for $10 per person; the van, which operates around the clock, will take you directly to the hotel. If you want to have the shuttle pick you up and take you back to the airport, call 24 hours in advance with your flight-departure information, and they will schedule a pickup.

Taxi fare from the airport is currently $21 for one or two passengers, with rates ranging up to $40 for five. You can either pick one up off the line or contact **United Cabs** in advance (at (800) 323-3303 or 522-9711) and arrange to have a driver waiting for no additional charge. (Never accept an offer for a cab or limo made by a stranger in the terminal or baggage claim. At best, you will be significantly overcharged for the ride. At worst, you may be abducted.) A limo can be ordered from the airport shuttle service, or a luxury-class stretch limo can be hired from **Olde Quarter Livery** (944-3332): $50 for four or $65 for the full six-passenger model and uniformed chauffeur—great for honeymooners. Other limousine services include **London Livery** (831-0700), **Carey Bonomolo** (523-5466), and **A Touch of Class** (522-7565). Rates from the airport to Downtown/French Quarter range from about $80–107 (plus 15–20% for driver) for a six-passenger limo. *Hint:* If you want a showy chauffeur during any of the special events in town (i.e., Super Bowl or Mardi Gras), better call in early.

A **Louisiana Transit** (818-1077 or www.gcwl.com/jet) express bus to the Central Business District puts you within a few blocks' walking distance of many of the newer hotels along Canal Street; it costs only $1.50, which may be the best choice if you are not lugging tons of baggage. The bus leaves the airport every 20 minutes or so, but it is available only between 6 a.m. and 6:30 p.m. The terminus is on Tulane Avenue between Elks Place and South Saratoga Street.

There are also regular **Regional Transit Authority** buses that may serve your route; call RTA at 248-3900 for exact times. (For more on RTA passes, see "Public Transportation" on page 154.)

The rent-a-car counters are in the lower level of the airport: **Hertz,** (800) 654-3131; **Avis,** (800) 331-1212; **Sears,** (800) 527-0770; **Budget,** (800) 527-0700; **National,** (800) 227-7368; and **Dollar,** (800) 800-4000 are all on site and also have second offices downtown, if for some reason you don't want to return the car to the airport. **Alamo,** (800) 327-9633 has an airport lot only. From the rental-car lots, signs will direct you onto Interstate 10 to the city (be sure to read "By Car" below).

For Private Planes

There is a small private airstrip for those who fly or charter their own aircraft. New Orleans Lakefront Airport, on the south side of Lake Pontchartrain, also has some rentals; call 243-4010, or Radan 241-9400, for more information.

BY CAR

New Orleans is connected to the interstate highway system by Interstate 10, which goes pretty much right through the city east and west, with a few tricky spots. One thing to remember is that I-10 makes an unusual V-dip toward the French Quarter and Central Business District (CBD), while I-610 sails straight across the mid-city region and dumps you back out on I-10 at the east end of town; it won't get you where you want to go, and it is a rush-hour trap of the first order. The other thing to know is that there is no marked French Quarter exit off I-10; it's marked Vieux Carré, Exit 235A. (If your hotel is along Canal Street in the CBD, take the Poydras Street exit.) Signage is not particularly good here in any case, and turn signal indicators seem to be a lost art, so be careful.

If you are driving in from the east along I-10, there is a Visitors Information Center at the Paris Road exit where you can pick up brochures, maps, discount coupons, and coffee, and make last-minute hotel reservations, if necessary.

East-west US 61 is Airline Highway, the older route from Kenner into the city, and becomes Tulane Avenue heading to the CBD near the French Quarter. US 90, also called the Old Spanish Trail, makes a squiggly circle around the river, curving around uptown and the West Bank before scooting back south and west toward New Iberia and Lafayette. (US 90 is the scenic route to Cajun country, but you can take I-10 nearly to Lafayette and on to Baton Rouge.)

Interstate 12 runs east-west as well, but along the north shore of Lake Pontchartrain, as if putting a lid on the bowl of I-10. From I-12 you can take either I-59 or I-56 south. The 24-mile-long Lake Pontchartrain Causeway (toll road) is the world's longest over-water bridge, and it's a beautiful drive; sometimes you can see nothing but sky and water, and sometimes even glimpses of the skyline or sailboat fleets. The causeway comes straight south and joins I-10, US 61/Airline Highway, US 90/Claiborne Avenue, and so on. Interstate 59 (north-south) intersects I-10 east of the city; I-56 from Jackson, Mississippi, joins I-10 west of the city.

BY BUS OR TRAIN

Greyhound Bus Lines coaches (call (800) 231-2222) roll into Union Terminal at Loyola and Howard Avenues at the edge of the Central Business District not far from the Superdome. Ticket counters are open 24 hours.

Union Terminal is also the **Amtrak** station (call (800) 872-7245, or 524-7571) with connections to New York/Washington, Miami, Los Angeles, and Chicago. Ticket counters are open 24 hours (check for senior-citizen discounts and special fares). There is a taxi stop outside the terminal, of course.

WHERE TO FIND TOURIST INFORMATION IN NEW ORLEANS

You can get an amazing amount of material and background from the **New Orleans Metropolitan Convention and Visitors Bureau** (1520 Sugar Bowl Drive, New Orleans, LA 70112-1259; 566-5011), which also operates information centers within each terminal of the New Orleans Moisant International Airport. For specialized information, contact the **Greater New Orleans Multicultural Tourism Network** (523-5652). In the French Quarter itself, there is a combined **Louisiana state welcome office** and **NOMCVB info center** right on Jackson Square in the Pontalba Apartments (529 St. Ann Street, 566-5011) that has hundreds of brochures on attractions and tours and street maps. And the visitors bureau also distributes these brochures on a motorized cart that stops during the day at such gathering spots as Union Terminal, Aquarium of the Americas, Spanish Plaza, the Louisiana Children's Museum, and the 600 block of Canal Street.

If you have trouble, contact the **Traveler's Aid Society** (525-8726) or stop by the booth in the east lobby of the airport.

Once you are in town, the main source of information on special events, sports, arts, and tours is the *Times-Picayune,* which has an entertainment calendar every day and a special pull-out section on Fridays, called "Lagniappe," devoted to recreation and family fun. Among the free magazines you'll see around town and in hotel and restaurant lobbies are *Offbeat,* which covers the local music and nightlife scene (you can peruse it in advance at www.

nola.com), *Gambit, Arrive,* and *Where. Ambush* magazine (www.ambush mag.com) and *Impact Gulf South News* are gay-and-lesbian publications. Or check in bookstores for *New Orleans Magazine* and the black-oriented monthly *New Orleans Tribune.*

Getting Oriented

New Orleans geography is confusing (even for locals), because it conflicts with our notion of U.S. geography and our basic sense of north/south orientation. Louisiana is shaped like an L. New Orleans is at the bottom of the L on the east end and is sandwiched between Lake Pontchartrain to the north and the Mississippi River to the south. Most folks picture the Mississippi River as flowing due south and emptying into the Gulf of Mexico. While this is correct, generally speaking, the river happens to snake along in west-to-east fashion as it passes New Orleans, not veering south again until after Chalmette, where the battle of New Orleans was fought in the War of 1812. To the surprise of many, the mouth of the Mississippi River is actually more than five hours south of New Orleans by boat.

If you spend time in New Orleans, the presence of the lake and the river are inescapable. As you begin to explore, you will discover that much of the city is tucked into one long bend of the river and that many of the streets and highways follow the curve of that bend. The curve in question, when viewed in the customary north/south orientation, is shaped like the smile of a happy face. Although suburbs and industrial areas parallel the river both east and west of the smile (and also across the river—south of the smile), the areas of the city most interesting to visitors are located within the curve. This curve, or smile as we put it, is why New Orleans is called The Crescent City.

The oldest part of the city, the French Quarter or Vieux Carré, is situated at the right (east) corner of the smile, while the University District, with Tulane and Loyola Universities, is located at the left (west) corner. Moving from the right corner toward the bottom of the smile, you will leave the French Quarter, cross Canal Street, and enter the Warehouse/Arts and Central Business Districts. The Central Business District is New Orleans' *real* downtown. The warehouses line the river and serve the city's bustling port.

If you look at a map of downtown, you will notice that all the streets emanating from the French Quarter change names after they cross Canal Street. Royal Street in the French Quarter becomes St. Charles Avenue in the business district and parallels the river like a mustache above the smile. On St. Charles, you can drive or take the St. Charles streetcar around the curve of the smile to visit some of New Orleans' most interesting neighborhoods. As you work down the smile to the bicuspids and incisors, you will encounter the Irish Channel, the Garden District, and finally, the University District, including Audubon Park (described in Part Eleven, "Sight-Seeing and Tours.")

If you are driving in New Orleans, picture holding a fan upside-down over the happy face. Position the fan so that the handle points north toward the lake and the curved spread of the fan aligns with the bend in the river (the smile). Tchoupitoulas Street runs at the edge of the fan along the river. A few blocks inland is St. Charles, paralleling both Tchoupitoulas and the river. Farther away from the river toward the handle is Claiborne Avenue, following the same crescent-shaped route. The sides of the fan angling up to the handle are Esplanade on the right (east) and Carrollton on the left (west). The handle of the fan extends to the lake and includes City Park. Tourists, convention-goers, and most business visitors spend the vast majority of their time within the area of the fan.

Just outside the fan to the west is Metairie, where you can access the Lake Pontchartrain Causeway. Farther west is Kenner and the airport. To the northeast is Elysian Fields and Gentilly, where you will find Dillard and Southern Universities, the University of New Orleans, and Pontchartrain Park. To the southeast along the river is the Chalmette Battlefield, Jean Lafitte National Historic Park, and Pakenham Oaks.

FINDING YOUR WAY AROUND THE FRENCH QUARTER

While orientation in the greater New Orleans area tends to be confusing, finding your way around the French Quarter is a cinch. The French Quarter is rectangular and arranged in a grid, like Midtown Manhattan. The river forms one long side of the rectangle, and Rampart Street forms the other. The short sides of the rectangle are Canal Street, New Orleans's main downtown thoroughfare, and Esplanade Avenue.

The longer streets, which parallel the river, are the French Quarter's primary commercial, traffic, and pedestrian arteries. Moving from the river inland, these streets are Decatur, Chartres, Royal, Bourbon, Dauphine, Burgundy, and finally, Rampart. The more commercially developed blocks toward Canal Street are traditionally known as the Upper Quarter, while the quieter, more residential blocks toward Esplanade are called the Lower Quarter.

As recently as 30 years ago, upper Decatur, next to the river, was the domain of visiting sailors and home of the fabled Jax Brewery. Lower Decatur then, as now, was home to the French Market. With the closing of the brewery and the advent of the Riverwalk promenade, Decatur was effectively sanitized and turned into a souvenir shopping mall and restaurant venue. St. Louis Cathedral and Jackson Square face Decatur, and most of the modern tourist development is between Jackson Square and Canal Street. Moving down Decatur toward Esplanade is a rejuvenated French Market, the timeless Café du Monde, and the Central Grocery, with its signature muffuletta Italian sandwich.

Heading away from the river, you'll come to Chartres, with its galleries, restaurants, cozy taverns, and small hotels. Chartres, perhaps more than any other French Quarter street, has maintained its historic identity. Commerce rules here, as elsewhere, but it's softer, less crass, and much more respectful of its heritage.

Royal, the next street over, has always been the patrician of the Quarter's main thoroughfares. Lined with antique and art galleries, as well as some of the city's most famous restaurants, hotels, and architecture, Royal Street is the prestige address of the Vieux Carré.

One block walking takes you from the grand and sophisticated to the carnal and crass: you have arrived on Bourbon Street. While Bourbon Street has always appealed to more primitive instincts, it did so within the worn, steamy context of its colorful past. But today, Bourbon Street is a parody of itself, a plastic corporate version of the honky-tonks, burlesque shows, and diners that molded its image. Between the T-shirt shops, trendy bars, and modern, upscale strip clubs, you can still find a few survivors from Bourbon Street's halcyon days, but they are an endangered species.

Burgundy and Dauphine, the two streets between Bourbon and the boundary of the French Quarter at Rampart Street, were once primarily residential. During the past two decades, however, homes have made way for small hotels, shops, and restaurants. Burgundy and Dauphine, while less architecturally compelling than Royal or Chartres, are nonetheless quite lovely. Quieter and less commercial than the streets between Bourbon and the river, Burgundy and Dauphine provide a glimpse of what the Quarter was like when it was still a thriving neighborhood.

Rampart Street, like Canal and Esplanade, is essentially a border street: broad, heavily trafficked, and very different from the streets within the French Quarter. Twelve streets run from Rampart to Decatur, intersecting the main commercial thoroughfares discussed above and completing the grid.

St. Peter and St. Ann Streets bisect the Vieux Carré halfway between Canal and Esplanade. St. Peter, especially the block between Bourbon and Royal, is regarded by many as the "heart of the Quarter." Most of the tourist and commercial activity in the French Quarter occurs toward Canal Street, and from Bourbon Street down to the river. Except for lower Decatur and the French Market, the Esplanade half of the Vieux Carré remains residential, albeit with an increasing number of proprietary hotels and guest houses.

Things the Natives Already Know
NEW ORLEANS CUSTOMS AND PROTOCOL

New Orleans is a city that prides itself on Southern hospitality, and most residents and business owners have learned to be very patient with tourists. They need to be. And so may you.

To be blunt about it, for all the mutterings about crime you will hear from locals (see "How to Avoid Crime and Keep Safe in Public Places," below), it's almost certain that the biggest problem you'll run into in New Orleans is other tourists, particularly on Bourbon Street. Women will have to be prepared for a few juvenile remarks from the inebriated and the eternally self-deluded (amazing how attractive some people seem to consider themselves). There is a vital gay community here, and gay and lesbian visitors are welcome, but as always, there may be a few ill-mannered heteros to ignore. And a few visitors may be taken aback by the number of extravagantly dressed punksters on the streets, with their Technicolor spiked hair and heavy leathers. Longtime locals seem to find them a little scary, but they don't seem particularly interested in bothering anyone so far as we can tell. And there are more panhandlers than there used to be, though most of them will spin you a tale rather than just accost you.

Otherwise, just go by what you might call the flip side of the Golden Rule: Do nothing unto others that would be embarrassing if done unto you.

Incidentally, sections of the French Quarter—specifically parts of Bourbon Street, Royal, and some areas around Jackson Square—are often closed to cars, encouraging pedestrian traffic. And many intersections have stop signs in both directions (these are one-way streets, remember). But don't let that lead you into dropping your guard on other streets. Just be aware of where you are, or you may find yourself stepping in front of a moving vehicle.

TALKING THE TALK

Ironically, for a city with so many obvious European influences, New Orleans talks with a very American accent. (So American, in fact, that a lot of "dese guys," especially the ones with roots in the Irish Channel and Metairie, sound as if they just disembarked from Brooklyn or New Jersey, because they come from the same river roustabout stock.)

What that means for outsiders is that local names can be wildly confusing—not to mention the name of the city itself. Much has been written about how to say it (and to be fair, there isn't an easy answer), but what it is *not,* is Nawlins, in two syllables, or Noo OrLEENS in three or New Or-Lee-Uns in four. It's something in between: Noo-AW-lins, or, in what's left of the Creole dialect, New-YAW-yuns, with the first two syllables blending together, sort of two-and-a-half beats. Unfortunately, Orleans Street *is* pronounced Or-LEENS, and so is Orleans Parish.

Then comes the Vieux Carré (View Kah-RAY), the original name for the French Quarter; it's one of the few things around that are still spoken with a French accent aside from beignets (ben-yays), Arnaud's (Ar-KNOWS), and Treme and Faubourg Marigny (Truh-may and Foh-burg Mare-in-yee), the neighborhoods adjoining the Vieux Carré. Metairie is pronounced Met-uh-ree; Pontchartrain is PAWN-cha-tren. And Marie Laveau is Mar-ee Lah-voh, Jean Lafitte is Zhawn Lah-feet, and Mardi Gras is Mar-dee Grah, of course.

Most confusing of all are the street names, which have in many cases been translated first from Spanish to French (memorialized on blue-and-white tile signs on the sides of buildings at intersections throughout the French Quarter), and then from French to fractured French, or to Italianese, or occasionally to English (for example, most people say Royal Street now, though you will still see Rue Royale on some business cards).

Burgundy is pronounced bur-GUN-dee; Conti is con-TIE; Chartres is CHAR-ters; Esplanade is es-pluh-NADE; Carondelet is kuh-ron-duh-LET (not LAY); Milan is MY-lun; and Iberville is EYE-ber-ville.

Even worse is what happened to the classic Greek names of the Muses east of the Garden District: Terpsichore is TERP-si-core; Calliope is KAL-ee-ope; Clio is KLIE-oh; Melpomene is MEL-poe-mean; and so on.

The Indian Tchoupitoulas is easier than it looks, like an old tomahawk joke on "Laugh-In": chop-it-TOOL-us.

As for the city's various nicknames—"The Big Easy," "Crescent City," or the older "Paris of America" and "The City That Care Forgot"—none is particularly popular, and you probably will never hear a resident use one.

Incidentally, although it works wonderfully in literary sense to speak of Desire, as in *A Streetcar Named Desire,* the line's destination was originally pronounced Desiré (dez-ih-RAY), a popular woman's name, and like many other ladies' names was applied to a wharf—just in case you wondered.

DRESS

In a town as hot and humid as New Orleans, only bankers, lawyers, and maitres d' regularly wear suits. That's something of an exaggeration, but not much: what it really boils down to is that self-respecting New Orleanians dress, tourists don't. Decades of Southern culture still persuade many women to wear dresses and hose, and you'll notice the docents and information ladies usually do. The minimum "dress" for women is nice earrings and long pants rather than shorts, shoes rather than athletic wear or sandals for men.

But again, this is a tourist town, and you're on vacation, so you can decide how much you care about sticking out or fitting in. Except for social occasions, you're not likely to be penalized for wearing shorts or sports clothes anywhere around town. It's just that those who do dress neatly may get better treatment or tables than those who don't.

Even at night, only a few restaurants ask men to wear a jacket, mostly the older standbys such as Antoine's and Arnaud's. But "dressy casual" is the style at most of the new celebrity spots such as Nola, Emeril's, and Mr. B's, and you may feel more comfortable in a jacket, even wearing it over a golf shirt or nice T-shirt—that is, unmarked and monotone, a la Don Johnson. The most famous exception is Galatoire's, which continues to demand jacket and tie at dinner and all day Sunday.

EATING IN RESTAURANTS

New Orleans fare may be famous, but it's not all that varied. Continental, Creole (which is very similar, but has kept more traditional, rich cream sauces than modern Continental), and Cajun styles dominate, particularly in the areas tourists are most likely to visit. And to be honest, you may find several days of such food not only filling but a trifle too rich; go slow. Most other restaurants are either new-American or Italian (or franchised).

Compared to many cities, the number of restaurants in New Orleans that do not accept reservations is fairly high. (During Mardi Gras, you may not find anybody willing to take a reservation.) Standing in line at Galatoire's, where the host is amazingly deft at juggling parties in his head, and at K-Paul's Louisiana Kitchen, where you may share your table with another party, is the stuff of legend. (K-Paul's now takes reservations for its upstairs dining room.)

As a rule, the restaurants that require reservations tend to be the same ones that require a jacket. In the same way, however, many of those would be willing to seat you, perhaps at the bar, if you are dressed at least neatly.

(A tip for dining at Antoine's: If you can make a reservation with a particular waiter, you can enter through the unmarked door just to the left of the main entrance, go down the hallway, ask for said waiter, and be seated with a little more respect and speed than if you just arrive at the "tourist" entrance. This probably means, however, that you have a friend who is a regular there—in which case you should get him to take you, anyway—or you should become a repeat customer.)

It shouldn't require saying, but having seen too many slightly overexuberant tourists trying to slip into restaurants past the queue, we will say it: Please be considerate, and stay in place. Besides, these hosts are pros; they'll catch you.

TIPPING (AND STRIPPING)

New Orleans is a service-oriented economy, and you should expect to recognize that. The going tip rate for bartenders or waiters and taxi drivers is 15–20%, although if you use them as sources of local information—which is always a good bet—add a dollar for luck. In your hotel, you should leave the maids at least $1 per day of your stay, and it really should be $2. If there is a bellman, give him $1 per suitcase, and while it isn't quite rude not to slip the doorman a buck for getting you a taxi, it never hurts. After all, it might be a longer wait next time.

As for tipping strippers, it's usually $1 in one of the older, cheaper joints, or $5 for something special (you will probably be offered a "table dance," which offers a sort of up-close-and-personal view). In the really upscale places, such as Maiden Voyage or Rick's, the going rate may be a little higher, but it's up to you. Total nudity is prohibited, so there will be some sort of G-string, skimpy bathing suit, or garter to tuck it into.

However, there are a few strip-joint no-nos you should be aware of (all common sense, but as we've said, the behavior of some tourists will astound you): Absolutely no fondling of the dancers is allowed, and you may find the dancers ready to retaliate if you try. If you visit a burlesque house (this reminder more often applies to women who are escorted by men), behave yourself; don't make faces, denigrate the dancers, or pull on your escort to get away. If you are offended by the spectacle, don't go.

NEW ORLEANS ON THE AIR

Aside from the usual babble of format rock, talk, easy-listening, and country-music stations, New Orleans is home to a few stations that really stand out for high-quality broadcasting. Tune in to what hip locals are listening to.

New Orleans's Radio Stations		
Station	**Frequency**	**Format**
WWNO	89.9 FM	National Public Radio
WWOZ	90.7 FM	Lots of music with local history
WQUE	93.3 FM	Hip-hop, soul, R&B
WEZB	97.1 FM	Conventional and mainstream Top-40 radio
WNOE	101.1 FM	New Orleans's country-music flagship
KKND	106.7 FM	Hottest alternative and modern rock
WODT	1280 AM	All-blues radio

How to Avoid Crime and Keep Safe in Public Places

CRIME IN NEW ORLEANS

From the news clips of Mardi Gras, New Orleans may seem like an X-rated Disney World, but this is real life—and it's real life in a city with big gaps in income levels and housing. That, combined with a history of police corruption, translated into a dire and long-standing crime problem from which the city has only recently begun to recover.

New Orleans was in an unfortunate contest with Washington, D.C., for that infamous title, Murder Capital of the Nation; its murder rate was five times that of New York City, and only about a third of New Orleans murders were being solved. In 1994, homicides hit a record high of 421. New Orleans's poverty level is the third worst in the country. It is legal in New Orleans to carry a concealed weapon. And since the 1980s, crack cocaine has been big bad business here, fueling tensions and gang machismo.

While the overwhelming majority of violent crimes still occurs in the poorest parts of town, around the housing projects, you cannot take for granted that you are safe even in the French Quarter. After all, that's where the rich—or at least those who appear rich by housing-project standards—are to be found.

Tourists are particularly easy marks; so are the dancers and waitstaff at bars, who earn much of their money in cash tips. During the 1996 Thanksgiving holidays, an advertising executive was raped and killed by a parking-lot attendant near the Ursuline Convent, and three of four employees of the Louisiana Pizza Kitchen in the French Market died of gunshot wounds they received during a hold up. And in May 1997, a Kentucky postal worker and father of three visiting New Orleans for a convention was shot and killed in a botched robbery as he and a companion walked through the Quarter to their hotel.

To make matters worse, the New Orleans Police Department has a long history of notorious corruption. In the last decade NOPD officers were convicted of having witnesses beaten and even executed, of robbery and murder, and of institutional extortion.

Admittedly, such reports make things sound pretty bad, and local authorities finally began to take them—and their effect on the city's reputation—seriously. The latest attempt to reform the police department began with the hiring of former D.C. deputy police chief Richard Pennington in 1994. Pennington launched a number of highly publicized police initiatives, as well as numerous anti-corruption efforts, firing or disciplining hundreds of officers, hiring hundreds more, and raising salaries and standards. A private coalition of New Orleans businesses and residents kicked in the money to hire consultants Jack Maple, former deputy commissioner of the New York Police Department, and John Linder to set up a computerized "map" of the city's highest crime spots; the same method is credited with having cut the New York murder rate in half since 1993.

Residents disagree on how effective such methods have been; in general, the perception of Pennington's success is directly proportionate to the distance people live from the French Quarter. Suburban commuters think things are much better, while French Quarter residents say they never see any police except those sitting in their cars around the Royal Street precinct station. Nevertheless, crime statistics have dropped while property values have risen. Between 1994 and last year, violent crime is down by over 60%, while the murder rate decreased by 55%. In June of 2000, New Orleans was given the City Livability Award by the United States Conference of Mayors, placing the city first among 14 other major cities. The award came as a result of police reform and crime reduction.

Still, you should be careful, as you would in any major city. The whole French Quarter is pretty safe during the day, but after dark you should stick to the more populated streets—Bourbon, Royal, Chartres, Decatur, Canal, and Dauphine; and Burgundy between Dumaine and Canal—and even then you should be wary of the outer blocks. Avoid walking alone outside the commercial areas, and be sure not to flash your personal belongings if you do. Jackson Square is a good bet at all hours, thanks to the round-the-clock crowd at the Café du Monde. Still, travel in a group or take a cab; if you aren't sure how safe an area is, ask one of the locals.

The cemeteries may seem pretty quiet, but they have become particularly dangerous to visitors wandering about; even in daylight, you should go only with a tour or at least several friends. Audubon Park and City Park are both fine and busy during the day, but again, you shouldn't be strolling through them after sunset, and you should probably avoid Armstrong Park altogether, at least until the city's elaborate plans to fix it up as a community music center and to secure it are complete. Although the St. Charles Streetcar runs 24 hours a day, it's best to use it in the wee hours only if your destination is within sight of the stop, or perhaps if you just want to take a round trip to view the great houses of the Garden District lit up.

Don't leave a lot of money or traveler's checks in your hotel room; even though the employees are probably dependable, the older, smaller buildings are not exactly inaccessible. And if you buy any valuable antiques of the sort that can be easily pawned, such as silver or gems, ask the hotel to lock them in the safe.

Unless you actually drove into the city, you will find that you don't really want a car. Wait until you're headed into the country to rent one, or just take a cab. Parking can be tough and several days' parking is quite expensive;

traffic customs carry more weight than laws in some cases. Tickets are stiff, and unless you're familiar with all the one-way roads and eccentric highway signage, you can make life harder on yourself. Besides, a parked car is another target for criminals and drunks.

The worst time, not surprisingly, is around Mardi Gras, when the throngs and lubrication invite pickpockets. In any case, if you are accosted by a thief, don't argue; try to stay calm, and hope he or she does, too.

HAVING A PLAN

Random violence and street crime are facts of life in any large city. You've got to be cautious and alert, and plan ahead. When you are out and about you must work under the assumption that you must use caution because you are on your own; if you run into trouble, it's unlikely that police or anyone else will be able to come to your rescue. You must give some advance thought to the ugly scenarios that could occur, and consider both preventive measures and an escape plan just in case.

Not being a victim of street crime is sort of a survival-of-the-fittest thing. Just as a lion stalks the weakest members of the antelope herd, muggers and thieves target the easiest victims. Simply put, no matter where you are or what you are doing, you want potential felons to think of you as a bad risk.

On the Street   For starters, you always seem less of an appealing target if you are with other people. Second, if you must be out alone, act alert, be alert, and always have at least one of your arms and hands free. Felons gravitate toward preoccupied folks, the kind found plodding along, staring at the sidewalk, with both arms encumbered by briefcases or packages. Visible jewelry (on either men or women) attracts the wrong kind of attention. Men, keep your billfolds in your front trouser or coat pocket, or in a shoulder pouch. Women, keep your purses tucked tightly under your arm; if you're wearing a coat, put it on over your shoulder-bag strap.

Here's another tip: Men can carry two wallets, including one inexpensive one, carried in your hip pocket, containing about $20 in cash and some expired credit cards. This is the one you hand over if you're accosted. Your real credit cards and the bulk of whatever cash you have should be in either a money clip or a second wallet hidden elsewhere on your person. Women can carry a fake wallet in their purse, and keep the real one in a pocket or money belt.

If You're Approached   Police will tell you that a criminal has the least amount of control over his intended victim during the few moments of initial approach. A good strategy, therefore, is to short-circuit the crime scenario as quickly as possible. If a felon starts by demanding your money, for instance, quickly take out your billfold (preferably your fake one), and hurl it in one direction while you run shouting for help in the opposite direction. The odds are greatly in your favor that the felon will prefer to collect your silent billfold rather than pursue you. If you hand over your wallet and just stand there, the felon will likely ask for your watch and jewelry next. Also, the longer you hang around, the greater your vulnerability to personal injury or rape.

Secondary Crime Scenes   Under no circumstance, police warn, should you ever allow yourself to be taken to another location—a "secondary crime scene," in police jargon. This move, they explain, provides the felon more privacy and consequently more control. A felon can rob you on the street very quickly and efficiently. If he tries to remove you to another location, whether by car or on foot, it is a certain indication that he has more in mind than robbery. Even if the felon has a gun or knife, your chances are infinitely better running away. If the felon grabs your purse, let him have it. If he grabs your coat, come out of the coat. Hanging onto your money or coat is not worth getting mugged, raped, or murdered.

Another maxim: Never believe anything a felon tells you, even if he's telling you something you desperately want to believe, for example, "I won't hurt you if you come with me." No matter how logical or benign he sounds, assume the worst. Always, always, break off contact as quickly as possible, even if that means running.

In Public Transport   When riding a bus, always take a seat as close to the driver as you can; never ride in the back. Likewise, on the streetcars, sit near the driver's or attendant's compartment. These people have telephones and can summon help in the event of trouble.

In Cabs   While it is possible to hail a cab on the street in New Orleans at night, it's best to go to one of the hotel stands or call a reliable cab company and stay inside while they dispatch a cab to your door. When your cab arrives, check the driver's certificate, which must, by law, be posted on the dashboard. Address the cabbie by his last name (Mr. Jones or whatever) or mention the number of his cab. This alerts the driver to the fact that you are going to remember him and/or his cab. Not only will this contribute to your safety, but it will also keep your cabbie from trying to run up the fare.

If you need to catch a cab at the train station or at the airport, always use the taxi queue. Taxis in the official queue are properly licensed and regulated. Never accept an offer for a cab or limo made by a stranger in the terminal or baggage claim. At best, you will be significantly overcharged for the ride. At worst, you may be abducted.

Personal Attitude

While some areas of every city are more dangerous than others, never assume that any area is completely safe. Never let down your guard. You can be the victim of a crime, and it can happen to you anywhere. If you go to a restaurant or nightspot, use valet parking or park in a well-lighted lot. A woman leaving a restaurant or club alone should never be reluctant to ask to be escorted to her car.

Never let your pride or sense of righteousness and indignation imperil your survival. It makes no difference whether you are approached by an aggressive drunk, an unbalanced street person, or an actual felon, the rule is the same: Forget your pride and break off contact as quickly as possible. Who cares whether the drunk insulted you, if everyone ends up back at the hotel safe and sound? When you wake up in the hospital with a concussion and your jaw sewn shut, it's too late to decide that the drunk's filthy remark wasn't really all that important.

Felons, druggies, some street people, and even some drunks play for keeps. They can attack with a bloodthirsty hostility and hellish abandon that is beyond the imagination of most people. Believe me, you are not in their league (nor do you want to be).

Self-Defense

In a situation where it is impossible to run, you'll need to be prepared to defend yourself. Most police officers insist that a gun or knife is not much use to the average person. More often than not, they say, the weapon will be turned against the victim. The best self-defense device for the average person is Mace. Not only is it legal in most states, it is nonlethal and easy to use.

When you shop for Mace, look for two things: it should be able to fire about eight feet, and it should have a protector cap so it won't go off by mistake in your purse or pocket. Carefully read the directions that come with your device, paying particular attention to how it should be carried and stored, and how long the active ingredients will remain potent. Wearing a rubber glove, test-fire your Mace, making sure that you fire downwind of yourself.

When you are out about town, make sure your Mace is someplace easily accessible, say, attached to your keychain. If you are a woman and you keep your Mace on a keychain, avoid the habit of dropping your keys (and the Mace) into the bowels of your purse when you leave your hotel room or your car. The Mace will not do you any good if you have to dig around in your purse for it. Keep your keys and your Mace in your hand until you have safely reached your destination.

CARJACKINGS AND HIGHWAY ROBBERY

With the recent surge in carjackings, drivers also need to take special precautions. "Keep alert when you're driving in traffic," one police official warns. "Keep your doors locked, with the windows rolled up and the air conditioning or heat on. In traffic, leave enough space in front of you so that you're not blocked in and can make a U-turn. That way, if someone approaches your car and starts beating on your windshield, you can drive off." Store your purse or briefcase under your knees when you are driving, rather than on the seat beside you.

Also be aware of other drivers bumping you from the rear or driving alongside you and gesturing that something is wrong with your car. In either case, do not stop or get out of your car. Continue on until you reach a very public and well-lighted place where you can check things out, and if necessary, get help.

RIP-OFFS AND SCAMS

A lively street scene harboring hundreds of strolling tourists is a veritable incubator for ripoffs and scams. Although pickpockets, scam artists, and tricksters work the whole French Quarter, they are particularly active on Bourbon Street, Jackson Square, Decatur, and along the Riverwalk. While some of the scams, such as the cocky teen who bets $5 he can tell you where "you got your shoes," are relatively harmless ("You got them on your feet, sucker!"), others can be costly as well as dangerous.

Pickpockets work in teams, often involving children. One person creates a distraction such as dropping coins, spilling ice cream on you, or trying to sell you something, while a second person deftly picks your pocket. In most cases your stolen wallet is instantly passed to a third team member walking past. Even if you realize immediately that your wallet has been lifted, the pickpocket will have unburdened himself of the evidence.

Because pickpockets come in all shapes and sizes, be especially wary of any encounter with a stranger. Anyone, from a six-year-old child wobbling toward you on a bicycle to a man in a nice suit asking directions, could be creating a diversion for a pickpocket. Think twice before rendering assistance and be particularly cognizant of other people in your immediate area. Don't let children touch you or allow street peddlers to get too close. Be particularly wary of people whose hands are concealed by newspapers or other items. Oh yeah, one more thing: if somebody *does* spill ice cream on you, be wary of the Good Samaritan who suddenly appears to help you clean up.

Most travelers carry more cash, credit cards, and other stuff in their wallet than they need. If you plan to walk in a busy tourist area in New Orleans or anywhere else, transfer exactly what you will need to a very small, low-profile wallet or pouch. When the *Unofficial Guide* authors are on the street, they carry one American Express card, one VISA or MasterCard, and a minimal amount of cash. Think about it: you don't need your gas credit cards if you are walking or those hometown, department-store credit cards if you are away from home.

Do not, under any circumstances, carry your wallet and valuables in a fanny pack. Thieves and pickpockets can easily snip the belt and disappear into the crowd with the entire fanny pack before you realize what's happened. As far as pockets are concerned, front pockets are safer than back or coat pockets, though, with a little extra effort, pickpockets can get at front pockets, too. The safest place to carry valuables is under your arm in a shoulder holster–style pouch. Lightweight, comfortable, and especially accessible when worn under a coat or vest, shoulder pouches are available from catalogs and at most good travel stores. Incidentally, avoid chest pouches that are suspended around your neck by a cord. Like the fanny pack, they can be removed easily by pickpockets.

MORE THINGS TO AVOID

When you do go out, walk with a minimum of two people whenever possible. If you have to walk alone, stay in well-lighted areas that have plenty of people around. Don't ask for directions from just anyone. (When in doubt, shopkeepers are a good bet.) Don't count your money in public, and carry as little cash as possible. At public phones, if you must say your calling-card number to make a long-distance call, don't say it loud enough for strangers around you to hear. And, with the exception of the Riverfront area near Jackson Square, avoid public parks after dark.

While this litany of warnings and precautions may sound grim, it's really commonsense advice that applies to visitors in any large American city. Finally, remember that millions of visitors a year still flock to New Orleans, making it one of the most-visited destinations in the United States. The overwhelming majority encounter no problems with crime during their New Orleans visit.

THE HOMELESS

If you're not from a big city or haven't visited one in a while, you're in for a shock when you come to New Orleans, where there is a fairly substantial homeless population. Though most evident along the Riverwalk, Decatur Street, and Jackson Square, you are likely to bump into them any place that's frequented by tourists.

Who Are These People?   "Most are lifelong [city] residents who are poor," according to Joan Alker, assistant director of the National Coalition for the Homeless, an advocacy group headquartered in Washington. "The people you see on the streets are primarily single men and women. A disproportionate number of them are minorities and people with disabilities—they're either mentally ill, or substance abusers, or have physical disabilities."

Are They a Threat to Visitors?   "No," Ms. Alker says. "Studies done in Washington show that homeless men have lower rates of conviction for violent crimes than the population at large. We know that murders aren't being committed by the homeless. I can't make a blanket statement, but most homeless people you see are no more likely to commit a violent crime than other people."

Should You Give the Homeless Money?   "That's a personal decision," Ms. Alker says. "But if you can't, at least try to acknowledge their existence by looking them in the eye and saying, 'No, I can't.'" While there's no way to tell if the guy with the Styrofoam cup asking for a handout is really destitute or just a con artist, no one can dispute that most of these people are what they claim to be: homeless.

Ways to Help   It's really a matter for your own conscience. We confess to being both moved and annoyed by these unfortunate people: moved by their need and annoyed that we cannot enjoy the city without running a gauntlet of begging men and women. In the final analysis, we found that it is easier on the conscience and spirit to carry an overcoat or jacket pocket full of change at all times. The cost of giving those homeless who approach you a quarter really does not add up to all that much.

There is a notion, perhaps valid in some instances, that money given to a homeless person generally goes toward the purchase of alcohol or drugs. If this bothers you excessively, carry granola bars for distribution, or, alternatively, buy some inexpensive gift coupons that can be redeemed at a McDonald's or other fast-food restaurant for coffee or a sandwich.

Those moved to get more involved in the nationwide problem of homelessness can send inquiries—or a check—to the National Coalition for the Homeless, 1612 K Street, NW, Suite 1004, Washington, D.C., 20006.

Part Seven

Getting Around New Orleans

New Orleans is a very hands-on, hospitable city. And the main neighborhood attractions, especially for tourists, are accessible by public transportation, give or take a taxi or two. But you will probably be asking for directions and addresses, and those are two of the most peculiar things about this idiosyncratic city. Names can be unrecognizable, and maps can seem upside down. In fact, in at least one case, west really is east, as you'll see below.

Public Transportation

As we pointed out earlier, you probably don't need or want a car in the city. Most of the time, whether you're in the French Quarter or any other neighborhood, you'll be walking. If you think you'll want a car, you should figure out exactly what excursions you want to take outside the city and only rent one for those days. Otherwise you'll have to worry about parking lots, parking tickets, and perhaps vandalism—not to mention being impounded. (If you are, call the **Claiborne Auto Pound** at 565–7450.) If you are staying at one of the larger hotels around Canal Street or in the suburbs, it may have parking (which may or may not be free). But most visitors will find the buses, streetcars, and taxis handy to any place they want to go.

By far the nicest way to get from one neighborhood to the other, or to rest your feet after a good promenade, is the streetcar. (Locals always used to call them "trolleys," but perhaps because of the heavy promotion the lines are getting these days, the word "streetcar" is gradually winning out. Still, you will sound less like a tourist if you refer to them as trolleys.)

There is one streetcar that runs the length of the Quarter, the **Riverfront Streetcar,** which originates near Esplanade Avenue and makes stops all the way to the Warehouse/Arts District near the Convention Center.

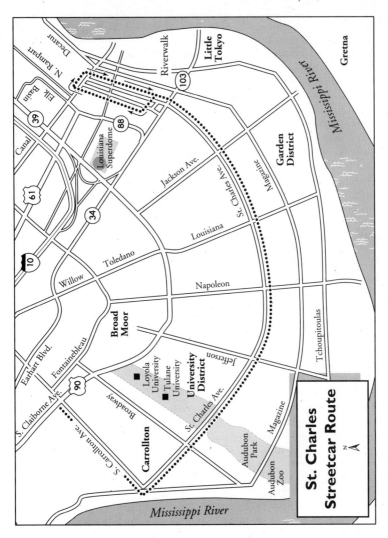

Each trip costs $1.25. The Riverfront Streetcar operates from 6 a.m. to midnight weekdays and 8 a.m. to midnight on weekends.

The more famous **St. Charles Avenue Streetcar** originates at Canal Street and runs 24 hours a day through the Garden District past Audubon Park and Riverbend. Each one-way trip is $1. But, although the St. Charles line has cars running about every 18 minutes most of the day, it runs only once an hour after midnight, so keep that in mind if you have a late dinner planned.

In a sort of historical about-face, the two lines are connected by track down the center of Canal Street. Unfortunately, since the city, in a previous face-lift, had decided the streetcar was dispensable, it had long since paved over the old Canal Street tracks, and the median had to be dug up for the tracks to be re-laid.

The **Vieux Carré Jitney** circles the French Quarter and hotel district across Dauphine and Baronne to Poydras, down Magazine to the Convention Center, and back across Chartres and Decatur—from 8 a.m. to 6 p.m. daily; it costs $1 per trip.

City bus trips are also $1; transfers are 10 cents (25 cents for express buses). But both the streetcars and the buses are operated by the Regional Transit Authority, and you can get one- or three-day VisiTour passes good for unlimited rides on any of them. A one-day pass is $4, and a three-day pass, which really saves you money, is only $8. Most hotels and information centers, and many shops, sell the RTA passes, or you can purchase them at the Grayline Tours kiosks around town. For bus routes and times, call the 24-hour RTA RideLine at 248–3900.

Taxicabs are pretty easy to find in the French Quarter, especially around hotels, but if you're out somewhere without a lift, call **White Fleet** (948-6605), **Yellow-Checker Cabs** (943-2411), or **United** (524-9606). New Orleans cabs run on meters—base charge $2.50, plus 20 cents for each one-sixth of a mile or 40 seconds, and $1 per additional passenger—but if you come during a special event, such as Jazz and Heritage Fest, there may be a base $3 charge in effect. Taxis can also usually be hired for a flat rate if a group of several people want to tour a few attractions; call the dispatcher's office and see what sort of deal you can get. Or if you happen to be picked up by one of the really friendly ones (and New Orleans cabbies can be hilariously well informed), find out if he freelances.

You can also rent a bicycle and combine touring and exercise: **Bicycle Michael's** has a variety of mountain bikes, three-speeders, and even bicycles built for two (622 Frenchmen Street, 945–9505). **French Quarter Bicycles** stocks mostly mountain bikes (522 Dumaine Street, 529–3136). Rental prices range from $4.50 an hour to $16.50 a day.

Walking the Walk

Much of New Orleans can be covered on foot, and that's a good thing, because it means you can settle for pedestrian directions such as "turn right" and "go three blocks on." What you *don't* want to get into is traditional directions—north, south, etc.—because in New Orleans, it just isn't very helpful. Because of the Mississippi River's snaking, the city somewhat resembles an open fan: although various neighborhoods have right angles within themselves, including the Garden District and the French Quarter, just about the only intersection that aligns with the compass is Napoleon Avenue and Tchoupitoulas Street.

So directions in New Orleans are given according to the biggest landmarks around: the Mississippi River and Lake Pontchartrain. Locals speak of going "toward the river" or of something's being "riverside"; an address "toward the lake" might also be "lakeside"—very roughly north. "Uptown" is above—that is, more or less west of—Canal Street, while "downtown" is said to be below, or on the French Quarter side, of Canal. That also helps tell you which is "upriver"—toward uptown—vs. "downriver." Audubon Park is upriver, as are the River Road plantations, but the French Quarter is downriver from the Garden District. Got it?

Other apparently specific directions are merely relative. South Claiborne actually goes mostly northwest, and North Claiborne swings in a curve that runs mostly east and southeast. As for the West Bank . . . it's south and east of the city, somewhere between Algiers and Gretna. The East Bank, naturally, is to the west.

Public Accommodations

The *Unofficial Guides* are starting to get a reputation for worrying about rest rooms, or rather, about your being able to find them. This is a tribute to the relatively short staying power of our founder, Bob Sehlinger, and someday we'll stop teasing him about it. But he has a good point: being uncomfortable doesn't help you enjoy a walking tour or a museum. And especially in summer, when New Orleans can be so hot, it's tempting to drink a lot. (When, while in New Orleans, is it *not* tempting to drink a lot?)

The greatest concentration of rest rooms in the French Quarter is down near the water (no pun intended, surely): Riverwalk, Jax Brewery–Millhouse Complex, Canal Place, and World Trade Center all have good, clean bathrooms, as does the French Market (two sets, in the 900 and 1200 blocks). Across from Jackson Square, there are rest rooms in Waldenburg Park. City Park and the Audubon Park tennis courts also have public rest rooms. Museums and department stores are equipped as well. Some places have pay toilets, so it's a good idea to keep some emergency change around; and where there is an attendant, it's considered polite to leave a tip, though you need leave only a quarter or so—cheap by big-city standards.

The large-hotel lobbies usually have rest rooms, although you should only take advantage of them in an emergency, and when you are reasonably well dressed. If you are really in a pinch, go to a bar and at least order a soda before you hit the john.

Part Eight

Entertainment and Nightlife

Performing Arts

Let's be up-front about this: few people head for New Orleans intending to spend a night at the theater. But that's not to say you shouldn't look around for something beyond the strip joints and jazz bars. There is no multistate performing-arts center here like New York's Lincoln Center or Washington's Kennedy Center, but there are several venues, most in the Central Business District, that book touring companies of Broadway shows, concerts, etc. Most shows will be listed in the *Times-Picayune*.

The main theatrical venue to check into is the **Saenger Performing Arts Center** (524-2490) at Rampart and Canal, a gorgeously restored Renaissance-style cinema worth visiting just for its "living sky" ceiling of drifting clouds and constellations; it books national touring companies of Broadway productions and the occasional big-name pop star. The **State Palace Theater** (522-4435) at Rampart and Basin is another old venue whose boxes and chandeliers go rather strangely with some of its non-middle-of-the-road music acts. The grand-old-style **Mahalia Jackson Theatre of the Performing Arts** (565-7470 or 565-8081), although in the somewhat questionable Louis Armstrong Park at the edge of the French Quarter, is home to the New Orleans Opera Association and the primarily imported productions of the New Orleans Ballet Association.

The **Louisiana Philharmonic Orchestra** (523-6530) performs, in a season that roughly matches the school year, at the ornately restored Beaux Arts **Orpheum Theatre**—part of the original Orpheum vaudeville circuit—on University Place just off Canal; Maxim Shostakovich, conductor of the LPO's predecessor, the bankrupt New Orleans Symphony, occasionally picks up the baton. The only Equity company in New Orleans, the **Southern Repertory Theater** (861-8163), has a small 150-seat house on the third floor of Canal Place. It's not the most professional of companies yet, but the fact that so many of its productions have local connections—plays by Tennessee Williams, Lillian Hellman, and others—makes it interesting. **Le Petit Théâtre du Vieux Carré** (522-2081) has plenty of atmosphere and a reputed phantom to boot, though its seasons aren't as ambitious as they once were.

The **Contemporary Arts Center** (523-1216) in the Warehouse/Arts District books more cutting-edge productions, which sometimes are merely artsy-for-art's-sake and more apt to draw local residents than tourists. (On the other hand, Edward Albee directed his own "Fragments" at CAC, using local actors.) The Center has two stages, so sometimes dance and theatrical performances are booked at the same time. **Le Chat Noire** (581-5812) offers an entertaining array of cabaret, spoken word, and alternative theater productions in one of the city's more stylish stage settings

Uptown, both **Loyola** and **Tulane** universities frequently offer classical or dramatic works; contact the Loyola ticket office (865-3492) or Tulane box office (865-5143).

Big-name rock and pop concerts are usually scheduled either for the **Louisiana Superdome** (call 587-3800 or TicketMaster), the more intimate **New Orleans Arena** next door (phone number same as for Superdome), or the University of New Orleans's **Kiefer Lakefront Arena,** a 10,000-seat venue near Lake Pontchartrain at UNO's east campus (280-7222).

New Orleans Nightlife

THE QUARTER

New Orleans is indeed a nightlife town. For all the city fathers' efforts to portray the Big Easy as a family-oriented destination, there's little doubt that legions of folks come here to do what they can't or won't do back home—holler in the streets and drink all night. They've come to the right place, with its relaxed laws, lusty hideaways, and rich, sultry nights. There are hundreds of bars here to cater to every conceivable appetite and mood. And it all starts in one special place—the French Quarter.

When most folks think of the French Quarter, they think Bourbon Street—with its tawdry parlors, beer-soaked juke joints, strip clubs, and drunken college kids stumbling about with go cups full of super-potent hurricanes. The street has a reputation for being the epicenter of improvisational jazz and blues, but the fact is, it never really was.

Bourbon Street is and always has been a mishmash of nightlife styles—elegant, rowdy, punky, sleazy, gay (in all senses of the term). But a majority of the city's great hangouts and, in particular, the great venues for live music, are not on Bourbon Street. The street's live music scene is largely relegated to a series of bad cover bands, karaoke clubs, and cheap trios playing to recorded drum machine accompaniment. There are, of course, exceptions, and plenty of visitors find on Bourbon Street just what they're looking for.

The **Storyville District** (125 Bourbon, 410-1000) is the most notable exception to the bad-music-on-Bourbon reality. A financial and creative teaming of the New Orleans Jazz and Heritage Festival's producers with a wing of the legendary Brennan's restaurant family gives Storyville the pull to book A-list New Orleans jazz and R&B talent all day long, throughout the week, in its two music parlors. A no-cover policy helps get folks through the door.

At the **Chris Owens Club** (500 Bourbon, 523-6400) the club's name-sake matriarch cranks out two high-energy dance shows a night, despite her rapidly advancing septuagenarianism. Whoopi Goldberg, a devout Owens fan, has been known to join Owens onstage during her frequent visits to New Orleans.

Patout's Cajun Cabin (501 Bourbon, 529-4256) offers spirited and visitor-friendly Cajun music, long on familiar favorites but often wanting a true roadhouse feel.

Oddly, the most popular and crowded spot on Bourbon is often the **Cat's Meow** (701 Bourbon, 523-2788), the city's flagship karaoke bar. The most romantic spot on Bourbon is undoubtedly **Lafitte's Blacksmith Shop** (941 Bourbon, 523-0066), which is dimly lit, heated by fire in the winter, and an ideal spot to disappear into a dark corner (by the piano bar in the back). Three of the city's major gay dance clubs are clustered on Bourbon: the **Bourbon Pub and Parade** (801 Bourbon, 529-2107), **Cafe Lafitte in Exile** (901 Bourbon, 522-8397), and the upstart **Oz** (800 Bourbon, 593-9491), a straight-friendly, anything-goes, dance-all-night kind of place.

There are a bunch of strip clubs on Bourbon Street, both elegant and sleazy. Larry Flynt's **Hustler Club** (225 Bourbon, 524-0010) and **Rick's Cabaret** (315 Bourbon, 524-4222) are two of the city's premier upscale gentlemen's clubs. During Marci Gras, *Playboy's* bunnies-for-hire take over the balcony at **Temptations** (327 Bourbon), lenging it an air of credibility.

There are literally dozens of other hangouts where beer and Jell-O shots outpace scintillating conversation. Not everyone cruising down Bourbon Street is on the make for the second coming of Buddy Bolden; in fact, many just want a good, clean place to let it hang out a bit. The **Famous Door** (339 Bourbon, 522-7626), the **Funky Pirate** (727 Bourbon, 523-1960), and **Krazy Korner** (640 Bourbon, 524-3157) book jazz, R&B, and the occasional Cajun cover band to amuse the masses who stream in.

The **Tropical Isle** (721 Bourbon, 529-4109) is a tropical-theme hang-out with lots of Jimmy Buffett sing-alongs, both from the jukebox and the bands that sit in. At Tropical Isle's original location around the corner (738 Toulouse, 525-1689) various Buffett cover bands have been pulling in a hardcore local following for more than 15 years. It's loud and late. And fun.

Johnny White's **Sports Bar** (718 Bourbon, 588-1239) is a corner dive featuring round-the-clock Mardi Gras videos for voyeurs who have come in the off season. **735 Club** (735 Bourbon, 581-6740) offers cutting-edge dance music and various Goth and glam-themed evenings

Then there's the dozen or so daiquiri specialty shops on Bourbon. And the windows that dispense with any pretense and just serve to pedestrians on the sidewalk. Add to all this the scores of taverns with courtyard hideaways for intimacy or second-story balconies offering a visual feast of the sea of stumbling, bead-mongering party animals from across the globe below, and you realize what the truth is: just about every 20 feet down the street there's another bar beckoning you inside. We are confident that you can find a giggle or two on this most lively and entertaining stretch of American roadway.

The rest of the French Quarter is also a mesh of varying styles and atmospheres, from the impressive and ornately decorated **House of Blues** (225 Decatur, 529-BLUE), where the biggest names in the music business congregate; to the affected elegance of the **Bombay Club** (830 Conti, 586-0972), where $9 martinis rule the roost; to the ultimate in barroom bizarro, the **Dungeon** (738 Toulouse, 523-5530), which opens at midnight and offers an experience not unlike the LSD sequence by Peter Fonda in **Easy Rider,** complete with black lights, Gothic decor, and heavy-metal dance tapes. To get an idea of just how late this place goes, the happy hour 3-for-1 starts at 4 a.m.

The well-known **Pat O'Brien's** (718 St. Peter, 525-4823) is said to boast the largest alcohol sales of any bar in America, but New Orleans is full of stories like that. Check out the dueling-pianos bar and the flaming water fountain in the courtyard.

Over on Rampart Street are **Donna's Bar and Grill** (800 N. Rampart, 596-6914) and the **Funky Butt at Congo Square** (714 N. Rampart, 558-0872), two venues featuring hot young brass bands from around the city, often till the wee hours.

The **Shim Sham Club** (615 Toulouse, 565-5400) is a mixed bag of jazz, country, punk, and retro music; of special note are the quarterly appearances by the Shim Shammettes, a retro burlesque troupe that stunningly recreates the mood and look of Bourbon Stret in the 1940s. Look for them in the local newspaper listings; it's a rear treat.

El Matador (504 Esplanade, 569-8361) is a hip and retro club featuring weekly flamenco shows, brass-band blowouts, and mellow jazz and swing nights featuring local rising stars Ingrid Lucia and the Flying Neu-trinos. The club, owned by the son of Hollywood director Taylor Hack-ford, is a popular hangout for edgier celebs like comic bad boy David Arquette and surrealist poet Andrei Codrescu.

O'Flaherty's (514 Toulouse, 529-1317) and **Kerry Irish Pub** (331 Decatur, 527-5954), the area's only Irish music clubs, feature live music and Guinness on tap. **Ryan's Irish Pub** (241 Decatur, 523-3500) offers no live musical fare, but is a lively, well-lit tavern and pool hall, often filling up after House of Blues concerts have ended just up the block.

You'll rarely run into the owner at **Jimmy Buffett's Margaritaville Cafe** (1104 Decatur, 592-2565), but the open-air windows along the side-walk and the good-time music—pop, blues, piano bangers, and such—make for an atmosphere that would please the boss.

Another local and international favorite is the **Napoleon House** (500 Chartres, 524-9752), a watering hole for the Quarter's literary folk, a dark and dusty corner tavern where the classical music on the stereo mixed with the clop-clop of the mule-drawn buggies outside and the many languages of the clientele make for a European nostalgia.

There are loads of neighborhood hangouts (yes, people live in the Quarter) for straight folks (notably, the 1100 block of Decatur Street) and gay (perhaps best known is the low-key **Good Friends** at 740 Dauphine, 523-9938).

The Quarter has more, so much more. Literally dozens more juke joints, pool halls, daiquiri bars, meat markets (both gay and straight), strip clubs of all varieties, video-poker hangouts, sports bars, and something you won't see anywhere else in town: the speakeasy at **Lucky Cheng's** (720 St. Louis, 529-2045), a restaurant staffed entirely by Asian drag queens.

There are so many establishments of so many colors that, at times, it seems there are as many bars in the French Quarter as there are T-shirt shops. But this is only an illusion.

THE JAZZ SCENE

Yes, jazz is everywhere. In many forms, variations, and presentations, from the cobblestones of Jackson Square to the overdressed cigar bars around town, someone somewhere is carrying on the traditions of the great mas-ters of American improvisational music.

In the French Quarter alone, the strains of horn solos pour forth, it seems, from every street corner. The music ranges from the sublime to the downright cheesy, but it's what people come to hear, and the city aims to please. For the most part, the term "jazz" in New Orleans refers to tradi-tional Dixieland, the stuff of old Satchmo and Al Hirt records. On Bour-bon Street, the **Famous Door Jazz Cafe** (339 Bourbon, 522-7626) offers Dixieland among its many afternoon and evening music shows. The

Richelieu Room at Arnaud's restaurant (corner of Bienville and Bourbon streets, 523-2847) and **The Court of Two Sisters** (613 Royal, with an entrance on Bourbon, 522-7261) offer jazz while you eat. The lobby bar of the **Royal Sonesta Hotel** (300 Bourbon, 586-0300) generally offers low-key combos in the evenings.

Across the French Quarter spectrum, there's **Preservation Hall** (726 St. Peter, 523-8939), where tourists congregate in thick lines to hear some of the great old traditional jazzmen of the city play in a dusty and dim old-time listening hall. (The thirsty beware: there are no refreshments served.)

The **Palm Court Jazz Cafe** (1202 Decatur, 525-0200) is a prime venue for traditional New Orleans jazz, and the **Crescent City Brewhouse** (527 Decatur, 522-0571) is the Quarter's only brewpub and a playground for some of the area's fresh-faced young jazz players.

Elsewhere in the Quarter, the cafes, restaurants, and pubs where you can hear native music are nearly too plentiful to mention. Just walk about. A few places of note include **Andrew Jaeger's Seafood House** (622 Conti, 522-4964), where Dr. John's old recording pal, drummer Freddy Staehle, holds court with friends. **Cafe Sbisa** (1011 Decatur, 522-5565) serves up jazz with dinner on weekends. The many cafes and public kiosks of the French Market host jazz bands nightly on the sidewalks, free for the listening from nearby benches. A great moment to remember in the city is the night you danced arm-in-arm on the curbside while a mule buggy clopped by and a saxman serenaded you in the rain. It happens all the time.

Outside the Quarter, several hotels offer jazz samplings in their lobby bars. Among these are the **Fairmont** (123 Baronne, 529-7111), the **Marriott New Orleans** (555 Canal, 581-1000), the **Hotel Inter-Continental** (444 St. Charles, 525-5566), and the **Hotel Meridien** (614 Canal, 525-6500). In the **Hilton Hotel** (2 Poydras, 561-0500), Pete Fountain, America's first prince of the clarinet, plays to full houses in the club that bears his name. (Call ahead for reservations; he's very popular with the old Johnny Carson crowd.) Down in the city's Ninth Ward, one of the area's favorite jazz traditions unfolds Thursday nights, when Kermit Ruffins, the second coming of Louis Armstrong, cooks turkey-neck stew for the patrons and plays trumpet at **Vaughan's Lounge** (4229 Dauphine, 947-5562). A little farther off the path are the **Steak Knife** restaurant (888 Harrison, 488-8981) in the Lakeview neighborhood, offering late-night weekend shows, and the **Sandbar** pub, located in the Cove student-union building at the University of New Orleans, where university students, under the tutelage of jazz granddaddy and UNO instructor Ellis Marsalis, perform for intimate and undersized crowds on Wednesday nights during the school year.

Sweet Lorriane's (1931 St. Claude, 946-9654) is a mellow jazz joint of a mature thread, the closest thing to a Cotton Club left in New Orleans. The **Tin Roof Cafe** (532 Frenchmen, 948-3100) brings traditional Dixieland into the considerably more contemporary musical environs of the Faubourg Marigny entertainment district.

Two high-quality jazz destinations in the Uptown direction are the luxurious **Red Room** (2040 St. Charles, 528-9759), a spacious dinner-and-dance hall featuring all manner of jazz, swing, Latin, and lounge music; and **Dos Jefes Uptown Cigar Bar** (5535 Tchoupitoulas, 891-8500), offering live jazz seven nights a week in a comfortable neighborhood setting with, yes, plenty of cigar accompaniment.

And, finally, for those who really want to get away from the maddening crowd, the famed Dukes of Dixieland play weekend dinner shows on the **Steamboat Natchez** (at the Toulouse Street Wharf behind the Jax Brewery, 586-8777).

WHAT ELSE IS THERE?

Indigenous Louisiana music forms other than jazz—primarily Cajun and zydeco—are among the state's great exports. In New Orleans, they are plentiful. **Mid City Lanes, Mulate's,** and **Tipitina's** are all profiled in the following section, but fiddles and accordions abound in lesser-known areas as well. **Patout's Cajun Cabin** (501 Bourbon, 529-4256) pulls crowds off the street for dancing and fun, lured by the crazy syncopated washboard rhythms. **Michaul's** (840 St. Charles, 522-5517) offers Cajun cuisine and two-stepping six nights a week in a roadhouse atmosphere.

The Four Columns (3711 Westbank Expressway, 340-4109) is a dance hall on the West Bank of the Mississippi River, in the Harvey suburb, where Cajun families gather for fais-do-dos on a frequent but irregular basis. (Check listings in the *Times-Picayune,* or call ahead.) A little farther down the road, in Crown Point, the **Bayou Barn** (Route 1 at Highway 45, 689-2663) has Sunday afternoon barbecues and dances. For the real deal in Cajun and zydeco, you need to drive about two hours west, to the Acadiana Parishes of Louisiana—Cajun Country—but that's a whole different guidebook.

The blues is the stepchild of New Orleans musical tradition: every bit as vital and necessary to the development of the city's heritage, but often overlooked as a cultural staple.

The name notwithstanding, the **House of Blues** is not actually a blues club, per se, as much as a blues museum. Its actual live musical fare covers all spectrums, from Latin to punk to funk to fusion. **Tipitina's, The Maple Leaf,** and **The Showcase** are all profiled in the following section, but there are plenty of other spots around town where you can drown your sorrows in wailing guitar riffs.

The **Canal Bus Stop** (2828 Canal, 822-2011) recalls the many soulful neighborhood clubs around town from the 1950s through the 1970s, before the street corners got scary and the bar scene started re-segregating itself. The amazing New Orleans ambassador of love, Walter "Wolfman" Washington holds court on weekends and consistently churns out some of the hottest and most genuine American soul and R&B not only in New Orleans, but anywhere.

Pampy's Tight Squeeze (200 N. Broad, 949-7970) not only has the best name in town, but it's where New Orleans mayor Marc Morial and some of his cronies sit in tight quarters and bury their deficit blues. Ernie K-Doe's **Mother-in-Law Lounge** (1500 N. Claiborne, 947-1078) is an out-of-the-way musical museum dedicated to the curious career of the R&B warrior proprietor, who scored a hit with "Mother-in-Law" in the late 1950s and milked a career out of the song for the next 40 years. This is a one-of-a-kind place. K-Doe usually plays on Sunday nights; his wife Antoinette serves complimentary beans and rice.

The Circle Bar (1032 St. Charles, 588-2616) is a late-night hangout for singers and songwriters of various stripes, from Latin to lounge. Of particular note here is the young trio Royal Fingerbowl, a homage to Tin Pan Alley sensibilities with a decidedly contemporary accent.

The blues mix with rock and pop at a legion of other clubs around town. **Jimmy's** (8200 Willow, 861-8200) and the neighboring **Carrollton Station** (8140 Willow, 865-9190) both offer local and national acts in intimate Uptown surroundings. Sunday nights at Carrollton Station sometimes finds local rock guru Peter Holsapple—keyboard player for both R.E.M. and Hootie and the Blowfish—playing silly songs and inviting friends out of the audience to join him (among them, his wife, the silky-voiced Susan Cowsill of the 1960s singing family). **The Dragon's Den** (435 Esplanade, 949-1750) and **Checkpoint Charlie** (501 Esplanade, 947-0979) on the outer fringe of the French Quarter dabble in all forms of contemporary music, from jazz to funk to folk. The Checkpoint is especially curious; it also houses a laundromat and a paperback book exchange.

Le Bon Temps Roule (4801 Magazine, 895-8117) is a boozy neighborhood pool palace with live bands in the back room one or two nights a week.

Out on River Road, past the Uptown section of the city, are two clubs located across the street from the levee, and maybe it's all the river air that makes them a little looser and less serious than everywhere else around town. **Live Bait Bar and Grill** (501 River Road, 831-3070) is literally a bait and tackle shop annex, an open roadhouse setting that also happens to be a rising player on the live-music scene. To define the genre would be impossible: smoky jazz one night, rollicking R&B the next, southern rock the next. Check your listings, and check it out.

Just up the road, the **Rivershack Tavern** (3449 River Road, 834-4938) boasts the largest tacky-ashtray collection in the world and also a roster of offbeat and always lively weekend music shows that spill out into the gravel parking lot where, on the good nights, the fog off the river touches your soul and maybe even scares you a little.

The **Acadian Brewing Company** (201 N. Carrollton, 483-3097) is one of two New Orleans brewpubs, featuring homemade suds and occasional folk- and rock-music sets. (The other brewpub, Crescent City, is featured in the following section.)

For the nonalcoholic set, the **Neutral Ground Coffee House** (5110 Daneel, 891-3381), tucked away in a residential Uptown neighborhood, is the city's foremost folk and singer/songwriter showcase, with no cover charge.

Contrary to popular belief, not every bar in New Orleans is a jazz club, or even a music club, for that matter. Conversation and the art of flirting are alive and well on the bayou, and places abound to indulge. A favorite of artists and celebrities is the deliciously offbeat and out-of-the-way **Saturn Bar** (3067 St. Claude, 949-7532), where Alec Baldwin, Sam Shepard, Robbie Robertson, and Nicolas Cage are among the many notables who have dropped in to drop out of the local scene for a night. It's dark, quiet, and full of bad art and poets who smoke too much. **Bernie's** (5243 Canal Boulevard, 488-0100) is an in-the-know trendy spot for 30- and 40-somethings who favor walk-in humidors and expensive martinis in a more suburban atmosphere to Marlboros and draft beer in the Quarter. **Amberjack's** (7306 Lakeshore, 282-6660) is a lively singles dance club on the north end of town with a comedy showcase Wednesday nights and a great view of Lake Pontchartrain.

The **Balcony Bar** (3201 Magazine, 895-1600) and the **Bulldog** (3236 Magazine, 891-1516) are anchors of the expanding yuppie nightlife scene in the arts and antiques district Uptown, both offering big beer selections and great people-watching venues.

In the Warehouse District, the **Ernst Cafe** (600 S. Peters, 525-8544) is a popular happy-hour hangout for upwardly mobiles, and is one of local hero John Goodman's many favorite spots.

A NOTE ON SAFETY

New Orleans is a city with predictable danger zones and drug-peddling neighborhoods. Some deserving bars and nightclubs have been left out of this guide because the risks involved in going to them are not worth it. Most visitors are aware of the city's high murder and robbery rates, and you should always bear these unflattering statistics in mind. Fringe areas of the French Quarter are particularly vulnerable spots for robbery. Always be aware when walking the streets, and don't hesitate to cross a street or turn around to avoid coming face to face with what appears to be an unsavory character. The risk of offending said stranger is far outweighed by ensuring your personal safety. In short, the deal is this: In the highly commercial areas of the French Quarter, feel free and safe to walk about. In all other areas, we recommend you take a cab. They're cheap and efficient.

There is a common scam on Bourbon Street that goes like this: A stranger approaches you and says, "I bet I know where you got them shoes. I know the street and the city and the state where you got them shoes." Don't take the bet. He knows: You got them shoes on your feet on Bourbon Street, in New Orleans, Louisiana.

Get it? No matter. If you take the bet, be prepared to pay up or face a bad scene on the street. Never play games on other people's playing fields. That's it for the lecture. Now go ahead, have fun.

ARNAUD'S

Beau monde hideaway
Who goes there: Lawyers, old-line locals, tourists, former Queens of
Mardi Gras, 30+

813 Bienville Street, 523-5433   French Quarter Zone 1

Cover: None
Minimum: None; jazz club $4
Mixed drinks: $3.50 and up
Wine: $5.75 and up
Beer: $3 and up
Dress: Suits, party dresses, casual
  elegance, and the occasional
  black tie

Food available: Creole, with a sophisticated twist
Disabled access: Yes
Hours: Cigar bar open 6–10:30 p.m.;
  restaurant open 11:30 a.m.–2:15
  p.m. for lunch, and 6 –9:45 p.m.
  weekdays; open till 10:15 p.m.
  Friday and Saturday

What goes on: Arnaud's is primarily known as one of the great high-end, old-line Creole restaurants of the French Quarter, often mentioned in the same breath as Antoine's, Broussard's, and Brennan's. Off to the far side of the 17-room restaurant is the old lounge, a bar filled with diners who are waiting for their tables, and those who have already polished off their pompano plates and are enjoying the rewards of classic New Orleans post-supper culture. In the midst of these restaurant patrons are locals who have just come for a drink and to revel in this beautiful cocktail chamber, where local wags and kingmakers decide who will back the next mayor of New Orleans and who will be named the next Queen of Mardi Gras—equally important decisions in these curious times.

Setting & atmosphere: "Count" Arnaud Cazenave (he had no bona fide claim to the title) opened the restaurant in an antebellum mansion in 1918, and it has been a local high-society staple ever since. With its player piano and green, upholstered men's-club motif, a small but well-stocked humidor, and the requisite white tile and period gas lamps, Arnaud's interior reminds one of a Victorial parlor. This is a great place to knock back a few martinis and argue with the ghost of Huey Long.

If you go: Seek out proprietor Archie Casberian, who serves two valuable functions. A cigar aficionado from the days before super models posed with stogies on trendy magazine covers, Casberian is the man to consult for an after-dinner smoke. He also presides over the restaurant's famous Mardi Gras museum, a series of tiny rooms that offer life-size renditions of the gowns and finery and feathers of Mardi Gras past. It's all such a long story—the New Orleans Mardi Gras and attendant mysteries, controversies, and layers of social complexity. The small but endearing exhibit poses more questions than it answers, but then that's the charm. Don't miss it.

BOMBAY CLUB

Delightfully pretentious gin joint and armchair lounge
Who goes there: 30–75, movers, shakers, pols, yuppies, buppies, second sceners, the courthouse crowd

830 Conti Street, 586-0972   French Quarter Zone 1

Cover: Festivals and major shows only
Minimum: None
Mixed drinks: $4.25–15
Wine: $5–7
Beer: $3–4.50; drinks at least $6 for festivals and major shows
Dress: The sign says "Proper attire required." Let that be your guide. Jackets for men.
Specials: When its offered, "New Orleans Networking Night" is a promotion enhanced by free drinks for women all night.
Food available: Appetizers along the lines of pâté, salmon plates, and cheese boards
Disabled access: Yes
Hours: Tuesday–Saturday, 4 p.m.– 2 a.m.; late night menu Wednesday–Saturday

What goes on: Networking, schmoozing, flirting, and general bedazzling, both physical and verbal. The Bombay is where monied but demure locals gather to chatter and booze to the soft piano strains of local and generally very talented ivory ticklers. The Bombay was the first of the city's upscale cigar and martini bars—by ten years—and still stands above the others.

Setting & atmosphere: Downright Churchillian, the Bombay has the trappings of a British men's club, which is what it was supposed to be when it opened. But there are not many Brits here, and it turns out women like it too. It is darkly paneled with rich reds amid the decor, and a variety of bar stools, booths, and sofas, in comfy living-room settings. The subtle hints at old-line decadence, the hushed conversation emanating from the booths, and the background sound of tinkling glasses make for a convivial step back in time to an era when a slew of martinis after work was considered classy, not reprehensible.

If you go: Demure, please. Remember, everyone is putting on a show, but no one wants to look like it. Play the game. Overtip. Don't sing along to the piano. Don't ogle the enhanced cleavage, and there is plenty. Overdress—go ahead, get your stones out of the hotel safe for this one. Recommended refreshments: clear liquors are the toast of the Bombay—all the great, new, triple-distilled, and overpriced gins and vodkas. Try one. Try two and take a cab. Please.

CAFÉ BRASIL

International watering hole and live-music club
Who goes there: Latins, Africans, rastas, punks, rockers, Liv Tyler,
and New Yorkers who miss the Village

2100 Chartres Street, 949-0851   Downtown/St. Bernard Zone 5

Cover: Varies, from none to $10
Minimum: None
Mixed drinks: $3 and up
Wine: $3 and up
Beer: $2.50 and up
Dress: Turtlenecks, sandals, dreads,
   tie-dyes, leather, kenta cloth,

Sex Pistols T-shirts
Food available: None
Disabled access: Yes
Hours: Varies. Generally, daily, 6
   p.m.–3 a.m., but much is left to
   the whims of club management

What goes on: Situated just a block outside the French Quarter, in the trendy Faubourg Marigny section of town, Café Brasil led the revival of this funky and decidedly hip neighborhood, now full of bistros and music clubs. Brasil is an international town hall, with many complexions, dialects, and orientations at play. The music is mellow early, a place for young lions of jazz to show their chops, then more dance oriented in the later evening, generally along the lines of funk, Latin, or reggae.

Setting & atmosphere: Wide open and neon, it looks more like New York—or perhaps Brazil—than New Orleans. The clientele spills onto the street and sidewalk nightly, creating a vibrant and colorful neighborhood atmosphere. Plenty of Harleys, tattoos, lounging dogs, and clove cigarettes to make for a funky, underground feel.

If you go: Relax and enjoy. No one here is in a hurry. Drink coffee or imported beer and soak up the international flair. So close to the French Market side of the Quarter, it's a safe walk. Also, check out the handful of other music clubs in the area—The Dragon's Den, The Dream Palace, Checkpoint Charlie's, and Snug Harbor—all listed elsewhere in this chapter. These, and the smattering of bistros on Frenchmen Street, have made the Marigny an unofficial extension of the Vieux Carré, with a considerably more local and multicultural accent.

CAT'S MEOW

Bourbon Street karaoke
Who goes there: **20–45**, suburban singles, folks who wouldn't be caught dead in a place like this back home

701 Bourbon Street, 523-2788   French Quarter Zone 1

Cover: Friday and Saturday $5 for those under 21 only
Minimum: None
Mixed drinks: $4.50–5.75
Wine: $4
Beer: $3.75
Dress: Anything goes

Specials: Happy hour 4–8 p.m. weekdays, with three-for-one drinks
Food available: None
Disabled access: Yes
Hours: Monday–Friday, 4 p.m.–4 a.m.; Saturday and Sunday, 2 p.m.–sunrise

What goes on: For reasons no one seems able to explain, this is on many nights the most crowded and raucous club on a very crowded and raucous street. It is certainly the city's premier karaoke club and has the best sound, the most selections, and a staff of professional hosts/singers to keep the night running with controlled chaos and provide at least the occasional bearable performance. If you want to participate, be prepared to wait—as you'll see, a lot of people think they belong onstage in this world, and most of them wind up here.

Setting & atmosphere: We're talking dead-center, ground-zero Bourbon Street here. People are stacked shoulder to shoulder, so you never really see the decor, other than the bright stage lights and the pink-and-green neon backdrop. If the street level proves too crowded for your taste, walk up to the balcony; Mardi Gras plays out 365 days a year on the street below. Hooting, hollering, bartering for plastic beads, and flashing are part of the nightly ritual.

If you go: Be prepared to wear some beer on your clothes. It's hot and crowded, and jostling for space and movement is inevitable. Along with tourists, the place draws younger suburban folks looking for a good drink and a few laughs. This is no place for the uptight or the overdressed.

THE COLUMNS

Part sophisticated-singles club, part debutante ball
Who goes there: Debs, old frats, old money, Uptowners, porch potatoes

3811 St. Charles Avenue, 899-9308   Uptown below Napoleon Zone 3

Cover: None
Minimum: None
Mixed drinks: $3–6.50
Wine: $2–6.50
Beer: $2.50–3.50
Dress: Polo, Ralph, post-ballroom, $75 shorts
Specials: Weekdays, happy hour 5–

7 p.m., $2 house wines
Food available: Hot-plate munchies during happy hour only
Disabled access: Yes
Hours: Monday–Thursday, 3 p.m.–midnight; Friday, 2 p.m.–2 a.m.; Saturday, 11 a.m.–2 a.m.; Sunday 11 a.m.–midnight

What goes on: From the expansive Victorian front porch, watch the streetcars run up and down the oak-lined, placidly genteel avenue—New Orleans's most famous and beautiful. Inside the rich and lusty barroom, tell your best investment stories. On some Tuesday or Wednesday nights your might find some jazz trio noodling around in the side parlor.

Setting & atmosphere: This old hotel was the setting for *Pretty Baby,* Brooke Shields' breakout film, but don't hold that against the place. It's musty and a little lopsided, but full of the charm and mystery of old-line Uptown New Orleans—eccentric, monied, and talkative. It is cozy, romantic, sultry, and on hot nights, sweaty—but in the best sense. Take the time to soak in the architectural details of the parlors off the main bar, a trove of pilasters, cornices, chandeliers, gilded frames, and Victorian mirrors and furniture.

If you go: Make no plans after The Columns: you could get stuck here for hours, imprisoned by the absolute passivity and laissez-faire of the locals who congregate to tell the stories of their gloried pasts. If this all sounds pretentious, it's not. In fact, consider the place to be one of the city's communal living rooms, where family and friends gather in sloe-gin comfort.

CRESCENT CITY BREWHOUSE

French Quarter brewpub and jazz joint
Who goes there: 25–75, tourists, home brewers

527 Decatur Street, 522-0571   French Quarter Zone 1

Cover: None	**Food available:** Full menu of pastas,
Minimum: None	seafood, steaks, gumbo, and an
Mixed drinks: $4.75+	oyster bar
Wine: $4–7	**Disabled access:** Yes
Beer: $3.95–7.25	**Hours:** Sunday–Thursday, 11 a.m.–
Dress: Suits to sandals	10 p.m.; Friday and Saturday,
Specials: Weekdays, happy hour	11 a.m.–midnight; bar sometimes
5–7 p.m., two-for-one	open later than restaurant

What goes on: This is a spacious and lively brewpub pushed right up on one of the busiest sidewalks in the Quarter. Music is usually provided by trios of wannabe young lions, cutting jazz chops. Sometimes it's a Latin combo. Either way, the band is usually background to chatter and conversation, though Wynton Marsalis did show up one night when his little brother was playing, and that pretty much shut everybody up.

Setting & atmosphere: Before your very eyes are the huge copper vats in which Red Stallion and Black Forest ales are brewed, as well as Crescent City Pilsner and a variable beer of the month. Fine brews, all. Lots of exposed and shiny wood, very clean, very modern. Tons of seats. Plenty of light. Always a friendly and energetic crowd.

If you go: Check a stool at the bar; it gives you a look at the brewing process, the band, and the sidewalk, where an endless parade of buggies, buses, skateboarders, gutter punks, waiters, and Kansans loll by. If the band doesn't impress you and you long for grander vistas, go upstairs on the balcony overlooking Decatur, where the view affords Mississippi River traffic, with its tankers, steamers, barges, and paddle wheelers.

DONNA'S

Live brass-band jazz
Who goes there: Euro jazzhounds, second liners, old hats, thrill seekers

800 N. Rampart Street, 596-6914   French Quarter Zone 1

Cover: $5
Minimum: One drink per set
Mixed drinks: $3–5.50
Wine: $3
Beer: $3
Dress: Very casual, umbrellas optional

Food available: Southern barbecue, ribs, pulled pork sandwiches, étouffée, and burgers
Disabled access: Adequate
Hours: Wednesday–Monday, 6:30 until; Tuesday, closed

What goes on: Donna Sims has built the headquarters for the city's hottest musical renaissance—brass-band jazz, the swirling and frenetic interplay of horns and percussion. This is the place for nationally touring acts like Kermit Ruffins, the Rebirth Brass Band, the Tremé Brass Band, and lesser-known yet more adventurous gangs like the Soul Rebels and Newbirth Brass bands, who mix urban shades of hip-hop with the traditional brass.

Setting & atmosphere: The bar stools, beer lights, and industrial carpet don't make much for aesthetics, but that's not why people come here. Be ready to dance and sashay or grab a space out of the way and against the wall. Locals will pull out hankies and umbrellas and act like their old Uncle Joe just died and this is his jazz funeral. Out of respect for old Uncle Joe, get off your duff and live a little. Do the funky chicken. Grab a stranger and dance. You may already have gotten this impression, but Donna's is loose on structure and form. What else can you say about a place where you have to part soloing trombonists to get to the rest rooms?

If you go: Beware: Rampart Street is the dark side of the Quarter, literally and figuratively. It is seedier and more dangerous than the spry and lively Bourbon and Decatur streets. This doesn't mean don't go there. It means take a cab to the door. If you're already nearby in the Quarter and are with a group of three or more, feel safe to hoof it, but be on maximum alert in the street. After hours, scram. All this information becomes even more pertinent when you realize Donna's takes cash only—no credit cards.

DOS JEFES UPTOWN CIGAR BAR

Cigar bar and jazz joint with a speakeasy feel
Who goes there: Locals, music students, jam-session junkies, dates, off-duty Uptown waiters

5535 Tchoupitoulas Street, 891-8500   Uptown above Napoleon   Zone 4

Cover: None	**Specials:** Happy hour 5–8 p.m.
Minimum: None	**Food available:** Limited menu of bar
Mixed drinks: $4 and up	food
Wine: $3.75 and up	**Disabled access:** None, but doorman
Beer: $2.25 and up	will help with steps
Dress: Suits to shorts; casual but	**Hours:** Every day, 5 p.m. until
clean	

What goes on: Yeah, yeah, the big American cigar craze has run its course, but realize this—the trend didn't get to New Orleans until it was playing out on the East and West coasts, so let us have our fun. Cigars aren't really the buzz here anyway; the 50 brands or so in the wall humidor are just lagniappe, a New Orleans term for something special to go with the regular fare of the place. It's a sit-and-chat jazz joint, with music seven nights a week ranging from Cadillac Red punching out old Professor Longhair and Fats Domino standards on Tuesdays, to the Thursday night bebop party, to the Sunday night gatherings of local college students cutting their chops with improv jam sessions.

Setting & atmosphere: It's got a nice speakeasy feel to it: tables pushed close together and a couch or two to sink into while the music flows over the place. There's a cozy outdoor beer garden, brightly painted and surrounded by lush flora, rendering a Caribbean feel to the place. It's a loose locale with no general rules; sometimes the crowd drowns the music, sometimes, when the personalities and compositions intertwine on one of those magic nights, the horn sessions get to some smoking levels that even Satchmo might admire, and that reminds the oft-jaded locals in the house why they live in New Orleans.

If you go: First of all, don't complain about the smoke. It's part of the program, but it shouldn't be too much of a problem since the air-filter system works pretty well. The musicians here are paid peanuts, so a fiver in the jar might be nice. This is a polite, genteel, and comfortable place to close out an evening spent at any one of the top-shelf Uptown fine-dining restaurants—the Upperline, Clancy's, Gautreau's, Martinique, or Brigtsen's.

F&M PATIO BAR

Late-night party bar
Who goes there: Uptowners, debs, post-debs, lawyers, post-grads, cops, insomniacs, John Goodman

4841 Tchoupitoulas Street, 895-6784	Uptown above Napoleon Zone 4
Cover: None	Food available: New Orleans bar
Minimum: None	food: cheese fries, quesadillas,
Mixed drinks: $3 and up	burgers, and po'boys
Wine: $3 and up	Disabled access: Adequate, but men's
Beer: $2.50 and up	rest room is inaccessible.
Dress: Parrothead chic, Saints jer-	Hours: Everyday, 5 p.m.–4 a.m. or
seys, loose ties, food stains from	later
dinner	

What goes on: This is the party after the party, the place where folks go after the Quarter, after the music, after the Carnival ball, and after their other favorite bars have closed. Nowhere do well-heeled Orleanians display more consistently and more forcefully the city's all-night colors than here, shouting lyrics to Beatles tunes on the jukebox, dancing on pool tables, and cramming four at a time into the bar's trademark photo booth. The scene plays out on many levels, from last-chance pick-up joint to a place to wind down the wee hours.

Setting & atmosphere: Truthfully, there is nothing particularly New Orleanian about the place. It's a basic fraternity house basement decor: bare cement floors, neon beer signs, pinball tables, etc. The jukebox is rich with pop classics, from Haley to Hootie. Sometimes the smell of beer is a little pungent.

If you go: It can be rowdy sometimes, and a little too collegiate for some tastes, but it's mostly a harmless place to catch up on the goings-on of Uptown locals, many of whom have cell phones, children, and 401k plans and know better than to be here at this hour. It is a party until the last gasps of dawn have surrendered to the sun, so bring your sunglasses—it can be awfully harsh walking out into the sunny glare of the industrial Tchoupitoulas Street corridor.

FUNKY BUTT AT CONGO SQUARE

Jazz, blues, and jazzy blues in a Deco setting
Who goes there: Lounge lizards, nighthawks, poets, bohos, jazzheads

714 N. Rampart Street, 558-0872   French Quarter Zone 1

Cover: None–$10
Minimum: One drink per set
Mixed drinks: $3–5
Wine: $3.50–7
Beer: $1–4
Dress: Anything goes; Gothic to
  black tie
Specials: Funky Buttjuice, a $6
concoction of secret ingredients,
  for the daring only
Food available: Gumbo, jambalaya,
  étouffée
Disabled access: Adequate; wheel-
  chair access through kitchen;
  upper level is inaccessible.
Hours: Daily, 9 p.m.–3 a.m.

What goes on: When proprietor Richard Rochester isn't giving guided tours of French Quarter haunted properties (that's another story), he is here hosting one of the hippest music clubs in town. Carved out of the classic and formerly exclusive Art Deco restaurant called Jonathan, the Funky Butt is a lively mélange of conversation and dance, seven nights a week, with the likes of piano professors Henry Butler or Jon "King" Cleary and other world-class keyboard and horn players holding court. The Funky Butt, by the way, was the name of a dance that accompanied the music of the pioneering Buddy Bolden, the city's first King of Jazz and a cornet player with chops so loud that legend tells of listeners enjoying his solos from half a mile away. We cannot, however, document this.

Setting & atmosphere: Downstairs, the lounge retains many of the Deco treasures and details from the Jonathan era—black-lacquered woods, cut-glass fixtures, and Erte prints. The jukebox is one of the great archives of New Orleans music history. Upstairs, the live-music club is dark, with a few hidden corners for discreet couples. One reviewer called the decor "a cross between a 1930s jazz crib and a brothel," and we think the description fitting.

If you go: Like its neighbor Donna's (see profile), the Funky Butt hovers on the sketchy side of the Quarter. We suggest alertness when coming and going, and a cab to do both.

HOUSE OF BLUES

National-, regional-, and local-circuit music club
Who goes there: Dan Aykroyd and friends, out-of-towners,
locals because it's the only place left to see the Neville Brothers

225 Decatur Street, 529-BLUE   French Quarter Zone 1

Cover: Varies from $5 for good local acts to $25+ for the rare appearances of heavy hitters like Jackson Brown or Bob Dylan. The back bar—where you can watch the show on live TV —is free.

Minimum: None

Mixed drinks: $4.50 and up

Wine: $4.50 and up

Beer: $3.75 and up

Dress: To fit the show. For Trisha Yearwood, boots and buckles would suit; for the Nevilles, perhaps something in unity colors. For the Gospel Brunch, dare to be different: dress nice.

Food available: Full menu of Louisiana, Cajun, and American cafe dishes

Disabled access: Yes

Hours: Tuesday–Thursday, 11 a.m.– midnight, or whenever the show ends; Saturday and Sunday, 11 a.m. –4 a.m.; Monday, 11 a.m.–sunrise; restaurant closes at 11 p.m.

What goes on: When the House of Blues opened in 1994, its New Age–friendly motto, "Help Ever, Hurt Never," was tarnished by the club's cutthroat pursuit of every major player in the local rock, blues, and jazz circles, outbidding and nearly snuffing out several local and long-established music clubs. In the ensuing years, an easy equilibrium has settled over the local industry; it's a given now that the House gets the biggest names in the business, from Eric Clapton to Mystikal. And the biggest crowds. Also, the addition of The Parish—a nightclub within a nightclub—has allowed the House to book smaller and more daring acts—jazz trios, lonesome songwriters and such—many of them well suited to the smaller and more intimate stage setting of this cozy second-story ballroom.

Setting & atmosphere: This is a New York club in a small town; the goon-sized bouncers with headsets and ear phones, quite frankly, scare the hell out of some locals, who prefer to hang out at a place where they can park within three or four blocks of the front door. On the positive side, HOB has amassed an awesome collection of Southern folk art, which hangs everywhere, including the rest rooms. Take the time to look at these colorful treasures from Louisiana, Mississippi, and Alabama.

If you go: First and foremost, never mess with the bouncers. There are stories. Second, be ready to pay the price—both monetarily and in comfort. There is not enough seating available, and what there is seems always reserved for visiting celebrities who hinted to management that they were coming, but never showed up. This leaves the great seats empty on the most crowded nights and adds to the generally antagonistic relationship between the club and longtime local music fans who have lived by a first come, first served basis for decades. But these ill-wishing locals realize that the House of Blues will succeed, even thrive, on one-time customers or those who will put up with the club's icy treatment because it's the only place to catch the great national tours. And the Nevilles.

THE HOWLIN' WOLF

Live regional, alternative, progressive country, and folk music
Who goes there: **Rockers, cow punks, musicians**

828 S. Peters Street, 523-2551   Central Business District Zone 2

Cover: Varies with act, roughly $0–30
Minimum: None
Mixed drinks: $3.50 and up
Wine: $3.50 and up
Beer: $3 and up
Dress: Rock-club casual

Food available: None
Disabled access: Yes
Hours: 9 p.m. until the show ends
(anywhere from midnight to 8 a.m.)

What goes on: The Wolf is the musicians' music club; half the house on any night may be the city's rock fraternity checking out the latest acts on the local alternative, rockabilly, or singer/songwriter circuit. The Wolf also draws an eclectic array of lesser-known but established national acts—anybody from country-crooning Iris Dement to jazz poet John Sinclair to surf-guitar guru Dick Dale. This is where up-and-coming bands play before the House of Blues gets wind of who they are and books them on the next tour.

Setting & atmosphere: A roomy two-level music hall decorated with old movie-set signs, the Wolf is dimly lit but very clean. The clientele is respectful of the music, so don't be surprised to find the pool-table light extinguished before the performance; many acoustic acts will request your attention. It's a mix of listening and dancing crowds; feel free to do either. If you need to be off your feet for the evening, get there early, as available bar stools and raised tables are rare.

If you go: The Wolf operates on a time-honored rock tradition—the music begins when the music begins, and ends when it ends. The newspaper will no doubt list a performance at 10:00, and this raises a strategic riddle: do you go on time and end up cooling your heels for an hour while band members drift in, or do you arrive late and risk missing the rare prompt performer? Our advice: go on time, get a table, and if the show is late, chill out to the great sound system and a cold Abita draft.

LAFITTE'S BLACKSMITH SHOP

Romantic hideaway and piano lounge
Who goes there: Couples, romantics, Quarter rats, pirates

941 Bourbon Street, 523-0066   French Quarter Zone 1

Cover: None
Minimum: One drink (not strictly
  enforced)
Mixed drinks: $3.75 and up
Wine: $3.50
Beer: $3.50 and up

Dress: Casual
Food available: None
Disabled access: Yes, but access to the
  rest rooms is hindered by a step;
  staff members are glad to help.
Hours: Daily, noon–3 a.m. or later

What goes on: Located in one of the oldest buildings in the city, Lafitte's is said to be America's oldest bar, but that's another one of those oft-repeated stories... What we do know is that the building actually belonged to the famed privateer Jean Lafitte—or one of his colleagues—and was used for the storage of loot pilfered from ships in Barataria Bay and the Gulf of Mexico. Somewhere along the line, many years after Lafitte disappeared into the Confederate mist, the building became one of the city's most beloved bars.

Setting & atmosphere: Other than a single bulb behind the bar, the only light in here is provided by candles and, during cool seasons, the fireplace. It is dark, damp, and lusty inside, made of old brick, stone, crumbling mortar, and exposed beams. In the back cove, local piano-bar aficionados gather around the keys and sing along to time-honored classics every night except Wednesday. There's an overgrown and musty courtyard on the side for those who truly want to disappear.

If you go: This is an ideal spot to get to know that special someone you met at the planning seminar earlier in the day at the Marriott conference center. Lafitte's is a port of calm on Bourbon Street's sea of bedlam, so if the racket is getting to you but you still want to be a part of the night scene, pull in here for a couple of hours. The closed quarters and slow and easy pace of the staff and clientele beg for intimacy.

THE LION'S DEN

The place Irma Thomas calls home
Who goes there: European youngsters and American oldies,
the neighborhood, music historians

2655 Gravier Street, 822-4693   Mid-City/Gentilly Zone 6

Cover: $15 only on nights with live entertainment; call ahead
Minimum: None
Mixed drinks: $4 and up
Wine: $4 and up
Beer: $4 and up
Dress: Old striped suits with open collars, fedoras, rhinestones, big earrings
Food available: Varies (see below)
Disabled access: Yes, but rest rooms may be an issue
Hours: Varies, generally 3 or 4 p.m. until

What goes on: Irma Thomas, the Soul Queen of New Orleans, hit the Billboard charts in 1964 with "Wish Someone Would Care," followed by "It's Raining," and "Breakaway," putting her alongside Fats Domino, Ernie K-Doe, and Frogman Henry as the ambassadors of New Orleans R&B over the next two decades. She and her band, the Professionals, play here about one weekend every month or two, and always during peak tourist events like Mardi Gras, Jazz Fest, and the Sugar and Super Bowls. It is a quintessential New Orleans music showcase, full of horns, heartache, love lost and found, and plenty of soul.

Setting & atmosphere: During a Jazz Fest gig in the late 1980s, Thomas promised the festival crowd that if they came to see her husband's new nightclub that night, she would feed them. They filled the house; she filled their bellies. Now it's a tradition. If her mood and schedule allow it, Thomas will brew up some gumbo, fish stew, or red beans for the audience on performance nights. The decor is urban lounge, very 1970s.

If you go: Be advised: Thomas and the Professionals are the only live act at The Lion's Den. Since they tour internationally, their local gigs are irregularly scheduled. Call ahead or look in Friday's *Times-Picayune* entertainment section. And one caution: The Lion's Den is on an out-of-the-way side street in the Bail Bond district. We don't know what the Bail Bond district looks like in your hometown, but ours ain't pretty. Take a cab.

LOA

Swinging singles meet the Hip Hop Nation
Who goes there: 21–75, suburban voyeurs, downtown lawyers, rap stars, buppies and the ghost of Marie Laveau

221 Camp Street, 553-9550   Central Business District Zone 2

Cover: None
Minimum: None
Mixed Drinks: $4.50 and up
Wine: $5.50
Beer: $4 and up
Dress: Suits, loose ties, and the occa-

sional casual elegance
Specials: None
Food Available: No
Disabled access: Yes
Hours: Monday–Saturday, 11–2 a.m.; Sunday, closed.

What goes on: Loa is a trendy hotel bar in a trendy hotel, a watering hole for the suit-and-seersucker set after the factory whistle blows, and a busy singles hangout by nightfall. Thrown into this mix is the fact that the hotel in question, the International House, has emerged as ground zero for high-end African American travelers, therefore the joint attracts more than its share of bold-face names—particularly rap and R&B stars, former pro athletes and the occasional TV star.

Setting & atmosphere: The place is small but the turnover is steady; most folks seem to stop by Loa on their way to or from someplace else. (Though it doesn't matter if the crowd surges; the hotel lobby can easily accommodate.) The décor is muted pales and off whites, lit almost entirely by votive candles at night. High windows along two walls lend Loa its big-city, downtown feel. It could be Manhattan, really, but it has a warm feel to it.

If you go: Dress sharply and be prepared to wait a few minutes if the crowd numbers in the dozens. And one more thing: Loa is a word from the voodoo dictionary that means the pantheon of the gods. Don't be surprised if you walk in on an impromptu voodoo ceremony; they're held now and then to keep the spirits clean. Just so you know.

LUCY'S RETIRED SURFER'S BAR

Singles sidewalk hangout
Who goes there: **25–45, suits, debs, hot shots, climbers, condo-dwellers**

701 Tchoupitoulas Street, 523-8995   Central Business District Zone 2

Cover: None

Minimum: None

Mixed drinks: $3.50 and up

Wine: $3.50

Beer: $3 and up

Dress: Loose ties, Hawaii Five-O, Banana Republic

Specials: Monday happy hour 4–7

p.m., drinks $1.50–2.50

Food available: A full California/Mex-American menu

Disabled access: Yes

Hours: Monday, happy hour, 4 p.m.–7 p.m.; Tuesday–Saturday, 11 a.m.–2 a.m.; Sunday, closed

What goes on: Big on happy hour and weekend nights, Lucy's fills to capacity with young banker and lawyer types from the neighboring Central Business District and with the rising number of yuppie Warehouse District inhabitants escaping from the confines of their nearby cubicle condos. Though everyone seems to know everyone else here, a well-timed compliment on a tie or nail color may open doors for strangers in the crowd.

Setting & atmosphere: Sidewalk chic; even in the heat of summer, the crowd at Lucy's flows into the street, making for a super-casual block-party environment. The interior is exposed brick with hints of South Pacific blues and greens. Generally patrons stand three or four deep at the bar, but there are booths and a back room for stretching out.

If you go: The scene at Lucy's is somewhat interchangeable with a smaller, funkier, less hustling, and more intimate tavern across the street, Vic's Kangaroo Cafe, a Down Under joint serving up imported drafts, Aussie meat pies, and live blues bands on weekends. This is a late-night watering hole for the black-and-white-clad waiters and waitresses of the many chic bistros of the Warehouse District. Vic's also has the last and only Asteroids video game that we have found in the city, if that matters.

THE MAPLE LEAF

Live regional music

Who goes there: Dancers, poets, chessmen, Uptowners, celebrities escaping the fuss

---

8316 Oak Street, 866-9359   Uptown above Napoleon Zone 4

Cover: Varies with act, generally $5–10; higher for jazz festival

Minimum: None

Mixed drinks: $3.50 and up

Wine: $3 and up

Beer: $2.50 and up

Dress: Bowling shirts, sundresses, jeans, bandannas

Food available: None

Disabled access: Yes

Hours: Sunday–Thursday, 3 p.m.–2 a.m.; Friday and Saturday, 3 p.m. –3 a.m.

What goes on: Dancing and drinking nightly, with a broad range of local and regional musical offerings: poetry on Sunday afternoons, Cajun and zydeco on Thursdays, and blends of the blues, Latin, and funk the rest of the week. Shows get rolling around 10:30 p.m. The Tuesday-night brass-band jam, hosted by the Rebirth Brass Band, is a weekly microcosmic Mardi Gras. Packed with locals and visitors alike, the frenetic three-hour sessions literally pulse with energy and serious second-line spirit. At 2 a.m. you'll look around and wonder just what kinds of jobs all these dancing people have, but until then just enjoy being a guest at the city's most rollicking weekly house party. Go see this.

Setting & atmosphere: One of the great old survivors of the local music scene, The Maple Leaf long ago ditched its courtyard laundromat—a local favorite—but retains all the other aspects of its funky Uptown charm: the pressed tin ceiling; the skinny yet inviting dance floor; the overgrown and candle-lit patio; the reliable musical palette; and the loveable, unemployable intellectuals who plop on bar stools every afternoon and bet on TV's "Jeopardy"—and always score better than anyone on the show.

If you go: Be ready for one of New Orleans's favorite contact sports, two-stepping. The Leaf's dance floor is famously narrow, and when the likes of Rockin' Jake or Jumpin' Johnny's Blues Party open the throttle, it gets a little bouncy. If you get bumped, get out of the way or bump back. No whining. Also, the Leaf is two short blocks off the streetcar line Uptown. Take the St. Charles line there, then take a cab home.

MARGARITAVILLE CAFE

French Quarter music club
Who goes there: Tourists, Parrotheads, afternoon souvenir shoppers on
rum break

1104 Decatur Street, 592-2565   French Quarter Zone 1

Cover: Only on mainstage and
during festivals
Minimum: None
Mixed drinks: Margaritas start at
 $4.25
Wine: $4.50 and up
Beer: $3.75 and up
Dress: Bermudas, sandals, and
Hawaiian shirts
Specials: None
Food available: Gulf coast cookin'
 with a late-night menu until 10:30
 p.m.
Disabled access: Yes
Hours: 11 a.m.–midnight or so,
 every day

What goes on: As the name might imply, Margaritaville is part of pop-music icon and Gulf Coast favorite son Jimmy Buffett's considerable business empire. He's not quite a mogul of his cousin Warren's caliber, but the Margarita Man's publishing, music, real-estate, and retail accomplishments are impressive. The proprietor comes around occasionally, as New Orleans is among his preferred ports of call, but his appearances on stage are always unannounced, yet jammed with loyal fans—the famous Parrotheads—who communicate on these matters via the Internet. Mostly, though, the musical fare is top-of-the-line New Orleans R&B, from lunchtime 'til the wee hours, with several sets of music throughout the day performed by varying solo artists, duos, and full bands. Hoodoo guitar slinger Coco Robicheaux is a favorite here, playing late-afternoon sets of down-and-dirty Delta blues with a touch of local gris-gris thrown in for kicks, and 9th Ward country crooner Mike West is creating a whole new genre of hillbilly Cajun music here. You really should hear it.

Setting & atmosphere: It has Buffett's personality: laid back, tropical, lazily seductive. It's a carefully contrived Key West/Caribbean setting that doesn't offend. Set along the busy lower Decatur Street sidewalk, home to edgy boutiques and vintage-clothing stores, there's lots of roomy seating in both the back and front bars, and plenty of exposure to the busy and eclectic street traffic. The decor is a biography of Buffett's career.

If you go: No rules, really. It's a prime spot to waste away again in Margaritaville, slurping the plenitude of fancy tequila- and rum-based specialties of many hues and flavors, served in those towering, frou-frou cocktail glasses for which these kinds of places are known. Since you're here, you might as well stock up on the multitude of colorful Buffett-inspired and island-related gifts, T-shirts, and various paraphernalia. You can pass many hours here and wonder where the day went.

THE MERMAID LOUNGE

Live performance art, lounge music, and the general rants and raves of music-minded if sometimes unsavory misfits
Who goes there: 25–45, Goths, rockers, the Paisley Parade, human tattoos, poseurs, the Lounge Nation

1100 Constance Avenue, 524-4747   Central Business District: Zone 2

Cover: $2–10
Minimum: None
Mixed drinks: $3–4
Wine: $3
Beer: $3.50–4
Dress: Glitter, gloss, Elton John as Pinball Wizard, black tie, whatever. Go ahead, try to be noticed.

Specials: $1.50 Schaefer beers
Food available: The consortium of 30- and 40-something partners likes to host impromptu cookouts, buffets, and barbecues, but when it happens is up to whimsy.
Disabled access: Poor
Hours: 9:30 p.m. until

What goes on: When the Mermaid opened in 1994, it gave a nightclub presence to a varied and overlooked array of Louisiana artists: Glyn Styler, the local angst-ridden crooner and champion of lounge lizards; the Hackberry Ramblers, an octogenarian Cajun swing band; C.C. Adcock, a guitar-blazing swamp-pop incarnation; and Quintron, a local curiosity who locks himself in a room offstage and raises racket out of old electric organs. The club also books the more daring and unknown acts out of towns like Austin, Atlanta, and New York City. The Mermaid has become the epicenter of the alternative nightclub scene, wonderfully bizarre and calculatingly offbeat.

Setting & atmosphere: The bar hosts rotating art shows and could be hanging anything from neon art to ersatz porn on any given weekend. There is no describing how casual this place can be, so full of attitude and European cigarettes. The crowd generally spills out onto the sidewalk for impromptu street scenes among the Harleys and 1972 Impalas. Its reclusive location and costumed clientele often give it the feeling of being on the set of a Mad Max movie.

If you go: Take a cab, not because it's so dangerous, but because the Mermaid is the hardest club in the city to find, tucked away under an interstate ramp at the end of a one-way street. Just hope the cab driver can find it.

MID CITY LANES

Rock 'n Bowl
Who goes there: Bowlers, rockers, two-steppers, Zydecajuns, Ashley Judd, The Rolling Stones (just to watch, not play)

4133 S. Carrollton Avenue, 482-3133	Uptown above Napoleon Zone 4

Cover: $5–15
Minimum: None
Mixed drinks: $3.50–5
Wine: $3
Beer: $1.50–4.50
Dress: Zydeco Festival T-shirts, shorts, bandannas, bowling shoes
Food available: New Orleans bar

food: cheese fries, shrimp po'boys, buffalo wings
Disabled access: No
Hours: For bowling, seven days a week, open at noon. For music, Tuesday–Saturday, noon–10 p.m. or later

What goes on: Bizarre story. Johnny Blancher, a down-on-his-luck crawfish broker, makes a pilgrimage in the late 1980s to Medjogore, the Jugoslavian village where the Virgin Mary is said to appear to the Catholic faithful. He asks for a sign, something to dig his family out of debt. Back home, he is approached about the sale of an old bowling alley. The sellers—the Knights of Columbus! He figures that's the sign he was waiting for. He buys this charming but crooked alley above a strip shopping center, starts booking bands, and in short time, is running the happiest and most interesting bar in the city. It's a hotbed of zydeco music Wednesday and Thursday nights. On weekends, the playlist is pumped-up R&B, soul, and more zydeco. It's loud, lively, fun, frenetic, and, quite frankly, the best bar in America. Do not miss it. If you don't go anywhere else in New Orleans, go here.

Setting & atmosphere: It's a place lost in time, a bowling alley where you still keep score in pencil. There's plenty of dancing room, and plenty of places to get off your feet. Tom Cruise's rental shoes hang alongside portraits of Elvis and the Virgin Mary. Let's just say there's nothing like this where you come from. On Saturday nights and during peak seasons, Blancher opens up a dance hall underneath the alley, called Bowl Me Under (get it?) and books more zydeco. On big nights, he'll book four bands from around southwest Louisiana.

If you go: Look for Blancher—he's the guy in the pink bowling shirt doing the funky chicken. He'll get you a lane or teach you how to two-step, whatever you want. Don't be intimidated by the local dancers; they're real good and they know it. Fake it, stumble over your feet, give it a whirl—no one will laugh at you. We recommend going early and locking in a lane for the night. The ten bucks an hour is worth it. Once you have zydeco-stomped to Nathan and the Zydeco Cha-Chas in bowling shoes, you will never be the same. Also, the place is a celebrity magnet; everyone making movies in town drops by. Also, when Jon "King" Cleary is on the bill, don't be surprised if Bonnie Raitt shows up to play with him. They're pals.

MOLLY'S ON THE MARKET

French Quarter watering hole, media hangout
Who goes there: The press, their sources, pols, tattoos, locals, former professional athletes, video-poker junkies, gutter punks

1107 Decatur Street, 525-5169   French Quarter Zone 1

Cover: None	Specials: Frozen Irish coffee, bloody
Minimum: None	mary, $3
Mixed drinks: $2.75–5	Food available: A full Chinese menu
Wine: $2.50	from restaurant behind bar
Beer: $2.50–3.75	Disabled access: Yes
Dress: Suits to grunge	Hours: Daily, 10 a.m.–6 a.m.

What goes on: Local and visiting media have established Molly's as a news bureau of sorts, where rookies and old pros trade stories and shooters. On Thursday nights there's usually a celebrity bartender from the worlds of journalism, sports, or politics, and a complimentary cocktail for members of the working press. The rest of the week offers a general mix of French Quarter regulars: tourists, a few local drunks, a skinhead or two, and often a pretty good political argument at one of the raised tables.

Setting & atmosphere: Nothing fancy. A pub atmosphere with a long bar down one side and a few tables with bar stools up the other. The walls are crammed with press clippings about the place, from *Esquire* to *Le Monde* to the local *Times-Picayune*. The jukebox plays mostly rock, oldies, and New Orleans music. The open-air window on the sidewalk makes for quality people-watching on this busy nightlife stretch of the Quarter.

If you go: Keep an open mind about the eclecticism of the Quarter and its many thirsty denizens. Don't fear the skinhead bartenders; they won't bite. Remember, they're somebody's kids, too.

MULATE'S

Cajun dance and dinner hall
Who goes there: Bus tours, Kansans, local two-steppers, folks too short
on time to drive to Lafayette

201 Julia Street, 522–1492   Central Business District Zone 2

Cover: None
Minimum: One drink
Mixed drinks: $3.25–5
Wine: $3.75 and up
Beer: $3.25 and up
Dress: Last year's Festivals Acadiens
  T-shirt, bermudas, cotton
Food available: Full-service Cajun
restaurant—blackened catfish,
gumbo, couscous, crawfish salad
Disabled access: Yes
Hours: Daily, 11 a.m.–11 p.m.
  Music: Monday–Thursday,
  7–10:30 p.m.; Friday–Sunday,
  7–11 p.m.

What goes on: The first Mulate's opened nearly 30 years ago in the little
town of Breaux Bridge, Louisiana, and along with New Orleans chef Paul
Prudhomme and the famed bayou band Beausoleil, it helped put Cajun
culture on the forefront of the American pop-culture landscape. The recipe
was simple: good, hot Cajun food and nightly dancing. The Breaux Bridge
location's remarkable success in sales and patronage has been duplicated in
Baton Rouge and at this New Orleans location. Mulate's takes great care to
book the best available Cajun musicians, importing them nightly from
southwest Louisiana.

Setting & atmosphere: There's no way anyone can reproduce the old-
time Cajun dance halls of Acadiana here in the city, but Mulate's nearly
pulls it off. It's huge, and they've tried their best to give it a country feel,
with attention to faux-rustic detail and artwork by some of Cajun Country's notable painters like George Rodrigue—he of Blue Dog fame—and
Francis Pavy, "the zydeco painter."

If you go: Lose your fear and dance. There are enough locals on hand to
show you how to two-step, Cajun style. It is more fun than it looks, and it
looks very fun. Caveat: Cajun dancing is a contact sport—be tolerant of
the occasional butt-bounce from the couple next to you. And never, ever
be afraid to ask a stranger to dance in a place like this. That's why strangers
come here.

NAPOLEON HOUSE

French Quarter institution
Who goes there: Writers, intellectuals, tourists, yuppies, bar flies, and storytellers

500 Chartres Street, 524-9752   French Quarter Zone 1

Cover: None
Minimum: None
Mixed drinks: $3.50 and up
Wine: $3 and up
Beer: $2.50 and up
Dress: Whatever you're wearing
Food available: Salads, jambalaya, po'-
boys, and the best muffulettas in town
Disabled access: Yes
Hours: Monday–Thursday, 11 a.m.–midnight; Friday and Saturday, 11 a.m.–1 a.m.; Sunday, 11 a.m.–7 p.m.

What goes on: Nothing, and that's the joy. It's a place to sit and think, or sometimes just sit. The building was secured in the nineteenth century to be the great Emperor Bonaparte's residence in exile after his defeat at Waterloo, but he died before ever making it to the States. Now it's just a French Quarter corner bar, albeit a classic, where locals and visitors alike gather to cool their heels.

Setting & atmosphere: Sublime. The building is hundreds of years old, dark, with fading paint and chipped plaster. And a variety of Napoleon renderings. The stereo—a turntable!—spins classical and opera recordings. It is sultry, romantic, and intimate. The staff is indifferent at best, surly at worst.

If you go: There is no better way to beat the city heat than to duck into any of the dark tavern or patio corners and sip a Pimm's Cup, a New Orleans standard made of ginger-spiced gin, lemonade, and 7-Up, with a slice of cucumber. Totally refreshing. If you're on a fast track, stay away—conversation is the currency of the club and few here are in a hurry, including the waiters.

O'FLAHERTY'S

Live Irish music club and entertainment complex
Who goes there: 30–75, beer drinkers, dart players, tourists, neo-folkies,
trivia buffs, and sing-along lovers

---

514 Toulouse Street, 529–1317   French Quarter Zone 1

Cover: Thursday–Sunday only, $3–5
Minimum: One drink per set in music
  club
Mixed drinks: $1.75 and up
Wine: $2–4
Beer: $1.50–3.75

Dress: Casual
Food available: Shepherd's pie, Irish
  stew, and such
Disabled access: Yes
Hours: Daily, noon–3 a.m.; music
  starts at 7:30 p.m.

What goes on: Plenty. One room holds the lively music club, which features local, national, and international Celtic performers seven nights a week. Another room is a traditional Irish pub with darts on the wall, slow-rolling Guinness on tap, and traditional dancing on Saturday nights. There's also a sultry courtyard in the back for lounging about, and a gift shop selling not only souvenirs but Irish groceries as well. O'Flaherty's is also a gathering point for European soccer fans; there's almost always a match on the tube.

Setting & atmosphere: A grand old eighteenth-century building and courtyard, with traditional exposed-brick French Quarter comfort and a hint of Old World decadence. Added attractions are the four ghosts said to inhabit the premises, from spurned lovers to old generals. They live upstairs. For more on that, ask proprietor Danny O'Flaherty to fill you in.

If you go: The folks are friendly here, but won't hesitate to remind you to be respectful of the music. If you want to sing the chorus, fine. If you want to chatter, head for the pub. For the trivia-minded, the pub hosts congenial three-person contests on Sunday nights from March to October, with loads of gifts and giveaways. While prizes are Irish—mugs and glasses, beer, travel prints, and such—the questions cover all bases, from world history to quantum physics to college sports.

PALM COURT JAZZ CAFE

Jazz bar and restaurant
Who goes there: 35–75, jazz pilgrims, hipsters, Europeans

1204 Decatur Street, 525-0200   French Quarter Zone 1

Cover: $5 for table seat; free to lean on the bar	Dress: Casual to casually elegant
Minimum: None	Food available: Traditional Creole and international cuisine
Mixed drinks: $4–6	Disabled access: Yes
Wine: $3.50–6	Hours: Wednesday–Sunday, 7–
Beer: $3.50	11 p.m.

What goes on: George Buck gave his wife, Nina, a birthday present back in the 1980s, something she always wanted—a jazz club. Now Nina Buck runs the classiest traditional jazz joint in town, while upstairs, George presides over the industry's largest independent jazz record distributorship. This club is where Danny Barker, Pud Brown, and Louis Nelson finished their careers, and where their legacy plays on five nights a week from the likes of rising jazz masters Lucien Barbarin, Gregg Stafford, and Lionel Ferbos.

Setting & atmosphere: With its expansive tile-floored layout, mahogany bar, Steinway piano, and overhead lamps, the Palm Court suggests Roaring 1920s decor. It's a wide-open place with plenty of seats and a comfortable bar to lean on. Nina Buck sets the tone for the night; if she breaks out her umbrella and handkerchief for a second line, fall in behind. Between sets, there's plenty of history in the paintings, photographs, and record albums displayed throughout the hall. The records—that's right, vinyl!—are for sale.

If you go: Make a night of it. The food is good, and the shows are top-class performances by the old generals and young lions of New Orleans tradjazz. Every night at Palm Court is a celebration of the city's vibrant musical history.

PAT O'BRIEN'S

International tourist mecca
Who goes there: Tourists—all of them, visiting football fans, suburban 20-somethings seeking French Quarter thrills

718 St. Peter Street, 525-4823   French Quarter Zone I

Cover: None	Dress: Anything goes
Minimum: None	Specials: None
Mixed drinks: $3.50 and up; Hurricanes start at $5.50	Food available: In adjacent Courtyard restaurant until 2 a.m.
Wine: $3.50 and up	Disabled access: Yes
Beer: $3 and up	Hours: 10 a.m.–4 a.m.

What goes on: Purported to rack up the highest alcohol sales of any bar in America, Pat O's is a big rollicking adult fun house where folks from around the world come to drink the trademark Hurricanes—four ounces of rum mixed with red fruit juice and served in a souvenir glass that most people get too buzzed to remember to take home with them.

Setting & atmosphere: Pat O's is a three-in-one venue. Down the carriageway and to the left is a standard saloon with a loud juke box and a handful of locals hanging out among the tourists. To the right is the duel piano bar, a tribute to the kind of New Orleans portrayed in Elvis Presley's *King Creole*. Through the afternoon and evening, two big-haired, painted, and leggy dames with attitude crank out tons of barrelhouse fun, from holiday tunes to famous American standards to contemporary pop hits. It's loud in here, and the huge collection of steins hanging from the ceiling give it a German-beer-garden sort of atmosphere. The place draws big visiting crowds during football weekends in the fall, and the fans who've followed their teams to town for games against Tulane, LSU, or the Saints get absolutely wild with joy that the piano players know their beloved alma mater's fight song—and they always know. The third venue is the lush and gigantic courtyard in the back, a big draw for bachelor parties and roving gangs of conventioneers who slurp Hurricanes and talk too loud. A beautiful water fountain with a natural-gas flame burning inside the water spray is a trick to see. Night-blooming vines lend a sweet Southern smell to the place in summer and fall.

If you go: Don't wear your nice shoes; it's pretty sticky. It's also really touristy, but necessarily so. It's fun and you should experience it, if only once. However, watch the Hurricane intake if you've got appointments in the morning. More than a few folks who consider themselves tavern veterans back home go down for the count after an exuberant evening of John Denver sing-alongs here.

PRESERVATION HALL

Old-time jazz hall
Who goes there: Tourists—all of them

726 St. Peter Street, 522-2841   French Quarter Zone 1

Cover: $5	Dress: Casual
Minimum: None	Food available: None
Mixed drinks: Drinks are prohibited	Disabled access: Yes
Wine: None	Hours: Daily, 8 p.m.–midnight,
Beer: None	music at 8:30 p.m.

What goes on: Although the building—and the musicians—appears to have been standing here since the dawn of jazz, the place actually opened in 1961. Since that time, it has become synonymous with the great tradition of New Orleans Dixieland jazz, and deservedly so, for the musicians are top notch. The club hosts changing bands and musicians nightly, and also puts together national and world tours of musicians under the name Preservation Hall Jazz Band. Everyone who was anyone during the past 30 years has been associated with this place, including Danny and Blue Lu Barker, Kid Thomas, Tuba Fats, and the Olympia Brass Band.

Setting & atmosphere: Comfort is not a premium here. It's a small room with very limited seating—just a few benches. Overflow sits on the floor and stands around the walls on the side and in back. The band's enthroned on chairs in the front, looking every bit like a 50-year-old postcard.

If you go: Be prepared to invest time in this one; lines can be long. The hall does not serve refreshments of any kind, and there is no smoking. We suggest a cocktail sipped from one of the city's famed go-cups while you wait in line. This is one of those must-see deals in guidebooks and travel stories, and apparently readers take the recommendation seriously. The show is only about 40 minutes long; then you're quickly ushered out to make room for next crowd in. But we've never heard people complain about the brevity—perhaps because they were getting thirsty toward the end.

RED ROOM

Swanky dinner and dance club
Who goes there: The beau monde, models, suits, bold-faced names, junior partners, Rhonda Shear

2040 St. Charles Avenue, 528-9759   Uptown below Napoleon Zone 3

Cover: $5–15
Minimum: None
Mixed drinks: $5 and up
Wine: $6 and up
Beer: $3 and up
Dress: Sharp. No jeans allowed.
Specials: Wednesday–Saturday

late-night DJ; Friday and Saturday
hip-hop
Food available: Elegant continental
menu in dining rooms
Disabled access: Yes
Hours: Bar open 7 p.m. until

What goes on: Dinner and dancing. Cocktails and cell phones. Flirtatious eyes lingering over $9 martinis. This is the It Bar in town, a super trendy, gotta-go-to dance palace for New Orleans's serious see-and-be-seen crowd. It's the Big Easy's salute to the Big Apple's Rainbow Room—romantic notions of tango, salsa, and swing delivered by some of the city's great jazz and Latin ensembles. It's become the city's main draw for visiting and hometown celebrities: Harry Connick Jr. likes to sit in with house trumpeter Jeremy Davenport; Britney Spears and Dennis Rodman hit the joint just about every time they're in town; actresses Sela Ward and Ashley Judd are fans. On the right kind of night—when the music is simmering and the couples are swaying and the clinking of champagne glasses sounds like Christmas bells—it can feel like New York or Paris in the late 1930s. On a bad night—when the locals drown out the sax solos with investment success stories—it's just a nattily dressed meat market.

Setting & atmosphere: In the early 1980s, a consortium of businessmen bought the restaurant on the deuxieme etage of the Eiffel Tower in Paris, packed it up, and brought it to New Orleans in 11,000 pieces. No foolin'. The broad and airy restaurant was reconstructed on the city's premiere St. Charles Avenue, on the streetcar line, but bad business decisions and cost overruns made it one of the city's most embarrassing structures for the more than ten years it remained dark. Finally, in 1997, entrepreneurs Jonn and Peggy Spradlin stepped in and drenched the place in 13 different shades of red—the carpet, the drapes, the upholstery, the lampshades; you get the picture. Fresh red roses and red candles complete the ensemble. It is a visual stunner, a big success, and the Spradlins are the toast of the avenue.

If you go: Dress up, for cryin' out loud. Dance. Bring a lot of money. It's a pricey place but everything is top shelf and tastefully done. The din of the crowd can sometimes frustrate the musicians so show your appreciation and clap. Loudly. You can tell folks back home that Picasso, Chagall, Chevalier, and Chaplin used to party here—never mind that the building was 5,000 miles away then.

SATURN BAR

Offbeat lounge and culture-vulture hideout
Who goes there: Mad poets, off-duty cabbies and Lucky Dog salesmen, famous actors, guys who actually were at Woodstock

3067 St. Claude Avenue, 949-7532   Downtown/St. Bernard Zone 5

Cover: None	Specials: None
Minimum: None	Food available: Prepackaged snacks
Mixed drinks: $2.50 and up	Disabled access: None
Wine: $1.50 and up	Hours: Every day, 4 p.m.–12 or
Beer: $1 and up	1 a.m.
Dress: Anything goes	

What goes on: Okay, it's kind of down-and-out at times, smoky and booze soaked, a little bit of a *Barfly* thing going on here, but the Saturn is a true New Orleans classic, a tavern that casts no judgement on its patrons, no matter their stripe. It's a hard-drinking hangout for folks who don't want to be bothered with anything loud or trendy, and that includes a number of Hollywood A-list bad boys who hang out in dark corners when they're in town—Sean Penn, Nicholas Cage, Sam Shepard, Dennis Quaid, and John Goodman among them.

Setting & atmosphere: It's a generally dark place lit in small sections by interesting neon sculptures salvaged from an old French Quarter saloon. The main decor comes from the delightfully twisted artistic vision of a local painter named Mike Frolich, who has painted his version of the history of the universe on the walls and ceilings. We are in no position to interpret these bizarre murals; we'll let them speak their own message to you.

If you go: Beware the occasional angry alcoholic intellectual, the sort who can polish off the *New York Times* Sunday crossword puzzle in 18 minutes but hasn't managed to hold down a steady job since graduating cum laude in economics from Tulane back when LBJ was President. They like to argue about anything, and unless you've got a strong command of LSU football rosters, circa 1955 through 1972, as well as a more-than-passing knowledge of Louisiana's Byzantine political structure and personalities (the difference between Huey and Earl Long, for instance), then steer clear of these types. Also, the Saturn is a bit on the edge, geographically. St. Claude Avenue is a wide and well-lit roadway, but it's fairly run-down and borders the proverbial wrong side of the tracks. Plus, the side streets are a little sketchy. Be aware. (By the way, Earl was the one who dated stripper Blaze Starr; Huey was assassinated in the state capital in 1934.)

THE SHOWCASE

Silky smooth blues, jazz, and soul club
Who goes there: 30–60, music lovers, buppies, working folks from the neighborhood

1915 N. Broad Avenue, 945-5612   Mid-City/Gentilly Zone 6

Cover: $5 weekends
Minimum: None
Mixed drinks: $3.50–6
Wine: $3
Beer: $2.25
Dress: Collars, suits, fedoras, and rhinestones
Specials: Weekday happy hour, 5–6 or 7 p.m., drinks two-for-one
Food available: Kitchen under construction
Disabled access: Adequate
Hours: Opens 5 p.m. daily. Music starts at 7:30 Tuesday, Wednesday, and Thursday; Sunday at 9; and Saturday at 10. Friday night is Deejay Night, with golden oldies and classics beginning in early evening. No music on Mondays.

What goes on: This is a formerly unknown neighborhood juke joint that has transformed into a vital player on the live-jazz and blues scene over the past few years, offering a steady and reliable fare of contemporary jazz and blues to mature folks who've grown weary of the monotonous bass solos, meandering trumpet licks, and loud volume of some modern ensembles. Local favorites Marva Wright, Walter Payton—trumpet phenom Nicholas's father—chanteuse Sharon Martin, and pianist Davell Crawford regularly enchant listeners here, laying down cool, mellow riffs for a mostly local and loyal crowd.

Setting & atmosphere: Neighborhood soul with a piano-shaped bar, red vinyl seat covers, and red runner lights flashing in time to the music. Little tables are huddled about, suggesting a time when there were dozens of clubs like this around town, only to be run off by crime and evolving tastes in urban music. This is a survivor.

If you go: You'll know you're there when you come upon dozens of cars parked in corners, on sidewalks, and on the neutral ground (median). It's away from downtown and not near any other landmarks you're likely to visit during your stay, so we recommend taking a cab.

SNUG HARBOR

Jazz club

Who goes there: Hipsters, buppies, mellow fellows, and anyone named Marsalis

626 Frenchmen Street, 949-0696	Downtown/St. Bernard Zone 5

Cover: Varies, usually $8–20
Minimum: One drink per set
Mixed drinks: $4 and up
Wine: $4
Beer: $3.50 and up
Dress: Classy but comfortable
Food available: A separate dining room full of meat and seafood entrees, salads and soups, and such. Killer burgers.
Disabled access: Yes
Hours: Daily, 5 p.m.–about 2 a.m. Shows at 9 p.m. and 11 p.m.

What goes on: Marsalis, Connick, Batiste, Neville, Payton—this is where the great names of modern New Orleans jazz gather and grow. Snug is the link between the city's past and present musical forms, the serious contemporary jazz club in town, low-down and cool. It's a sit-down joint, not much for hootin' and hollerin', but more prone to an evening of Scotch-sipping, finger-snapping solos, and such. It's where the next toast of New York is playing tonight in New Orleans. You can say you saw them when.

Setting & atmosphere: Very cozy, befitting the name. The outer bar is dark, cool, and romantic—an ideal spot for a starter drink. Inside the small, two-tiered music hall, it is warmly lit and mirrored. Tables are small and tightly packed, and the upstairs has some view-obstructed seats and tables, hence the big mirror on the stage-left wall.

If you go: Parking's tight. It's only two blocks out of the safe side of the Quarter, so walking is fine. There are usually two shows a night, so call and check it out. Arrive early if a big name is on the bill; prime seating can make all the difference. Ellis Marsalis—that's Wynton and Branford's daddy—is one of the city's sublime performers, a Snug regular, and one heck of a lot more fun to watch than his uptight kids.

STORYVILLE DISTRICT

Bourbon Street music mecca
Who goes there: Tourists, conventioneers, and locals who have heard
there's actually some quality music on the city's famous avenue of sin

125 Bourbon Street, 410-1000   French Quarter Zone 1

Cover: None
Minimum: None
Mixed drinks: $5.50 and up
Wine: $5.50 and up
Beer: $4.50 and up

Dress: Casual
Food available: Yes
Disabled access: Yes
Hours: 5 p.m.–whenever the last
    band ends

What goes on: Quint Davis and George Wein, the two founders and producers of the great New Orleans Jazz and Heritage Festival, teamed with
famed restaurateur Ralph Brennan to bring authentic contemporary New
Orleans music and food back to a street better known for bad cover bands,
greasy gumbo, and collegiate karaoke. They poured a ton of money into
the roomy corner building, dividing the place into three different venues—
two for live music, one for hanging out. Then they hired, against all odds
and no doubt at loss-leader rates, some of the city's finest musical talents to
play to crowds who often don't know the difference between jazz and jambalaya. Never mind that—it's the only place you'll hear the likes of the
Dirty Dozen Brass band, piano pounder Henry Butler, or trumpet virtuoso
Nicholas Payton on Bourbon Street.

Setting & atmosphere: It's minimalist cozy in a sort of stripped-down
House of Blues way, with exposed beams and corrugated tin. The entrance
bar feels more like an ice-cream parlor but serves some memorable dishes.
It's reserved for eating, drinking, and hanging out. There are two micro-
music clubs inside Storyville, one a bordello-red saloon for low-down and
smoky sets of music by solo acts and combos, the other a broad music hall
where divas like soul singer Marva Wright can fill the house with the shear
force of her voice and personality.

If you go: The daily newspaper will give you the music line up. There's no
cover and you can come and go at your leisure and soak up some of the
great jazz, blues, and gospel sounds of the city. But be prepared for amateurs: some who are around you may neither know nor care about such
things—they just think it's cool to be in New Orleans no matter who's
blowing the horn. Also, the food is pretty darn good, contradicting another
local adage that you don't eat on Bourbon Street. The shrimp and smothered duck po'boys will save your soul.

TIPITINA'S

New Orleans' quintessential music club
Who goes there: Frat boys and debs, mods and rockers, aging hippies, and people who actually saw Professor Longhair play

501 Napoleon Avenue, 895-8477   Uptown above Napoleon Zone 4

Cover: Varies from occasional free weeknight shows to about $15 for big names
Minimum: None
Mixed drinks: $3.50 and up
Wine: $3 and up
Beer: $2.75 and up
Dress: Khakis, old Jazz Fest

T-shirts, tie-dyes, and suits
Food available: Burgers, red beans and rice, cheese fries
Disabled access: Yes
Hours: Sunday, 5–10 p.m.; Monday–Thursday, 5 p.m.–2 a.m.; Friday and Saturday, 5 p.m.–3 a.m.; bar opens at 9 p.m.

What goes on: Tip's is the heart and soul and somewhat faded glory of the city's musical renaissance of the 1970s, when Fess, James Booker, Dr. John, and the Neville Brothers got everybody hip to the city's non–Dixieland musical heritage. Although the House of Blues has definitely altered Tip's ability to book big-name talent, Tip's is still the place to go for New Orleans R&B, rock, and the occasional big name from the college circuit. The Sunday-afternoon fais-do-do (Cajun dance) with Bruce Daigrepont is a New Orleans institution—good, sweaty family fun.

Tipitina's has a second location, in the French Quarter (233 N. Peters; 895-8477), around the corner from the House of Blues. It's not just a commercial effort to grab a portion of the French Quarter market, but a bold and roomy music hall presenting funk, blues, zydeco, and jazz shows seven nights a week. James Andrews, the young trumpet-lion known as "Satchmo of the Ghetto," is a regular, as is jazz-standards-crooner Harry Connick Sr., the city's district attorney and the father of a very famous piano player.

Setting & atmosphere: Wide-open spaces and the checkerboard floor give it an old dance-hall feel. There are stools down the two side bars, and that's about it for seating. Pressure from the House of Blues finally forced Tip's to put up a new coat of paint, fix up the rest rooms, get new refrigeration, and increase the cool-air circulation, so the place is darn near comfortable these days. For big shows, the balcony upstairs offers a respite from the crowd.

If you go: Prepare for the occasional lapses in service. Move slowly and take in the amazing history of the club's past performers via posters plastered all over the walls. Check out the Professor Longhair memorial across the street. And, if you go to the Sunday fais-do-do, you may want to bring a second, dry shirt to wear home. It can be a barn burner.

WHISKEY BLUE

What the Fashion Café was probably meant to be
Who goes there: 25–50, Armani fashion victims, players, paralegals and guys with really expensive watches

333 Poydras Street, 525-9444   Central Business District Zone 2

Cover: None	Food Available: None
Minimum: None	Specials: None
Mixed Drinks: $5 and up	Disabled access: Yes
Wine: $6 and up	Hours: Saturday–Tuesday, 4 p.m.–2
Beer: $4 and up	a.m.; Wednesday–Sunday, 4
Dress: No shorts, hats, or logo shirts	p.m.–4 a.m.

What goes on: The most glaring example of the bi-coastalization of New Orleans nightlife is Whiskey Blue—the city's slow cultural homogenization. In other words, there is absolutely nothing local about the joint, except the staff. Whiskey Blue is one of the links in the chain of nightclubs owned by entrepreneur Rande Gerber, better known as Mr. Cindy Crawford. His bars are generally exclusive, expensive, and sexy. This is all three. It's somewhat of a celebrity hangout, due primarily to its location in the lobby of the very tony W Hotel. That said, don't expect the owner's wife; she's never been seen in the joint.

Setting & atmosphere: The décor is predominantly black, broken up by patches of a very appealing electric ice blue. It's L.A. chic: Too small to dance, too loud to talk. Perfect, in others words, for a singles hangout. Outside the door is the lobby of the hotel, and the W chain's trademark funky padded-chaise lounges and carpeted backgammon tables are more suitable environs in which to catch up with old friends or pursue conversation with a new one.

If you go: Be beautiful. When Whiskey Blue opened, talent scouts were sent to the city's modeling agencies and most fashionable nightspots to recruit bartenders and cocktail waitresses. The women wear revealing black dresses and the guys wear tight black turtle necks and after a couple of beers, they can make you feel pretty miserable about yourself.

Part Nine

Exercise and Recreation

A few years ago, it would have seemed silly to put a chapter on exercise in a vacation guide—particularly a guide to a city as famed for self-indulgence as New Orleans. But most of us at the *Unofficial Guides* are into some form of aerobic exercise, if only as a matter of self-preservation: it reduces stress, helps offset those expense-account and diet–holiday meals (no, it's not true that food eaten on vacation has no calories), and even ameliorates some of the effects of jet lag. Even more remarkably, we have discovered that jogging, biking, and just plain walking are among the nicest ways to experience a city on its own turf, so to speak, and we're happy to see that more and more travelers feel as we do.

However, remember what we said in the beginning about the climate of New Orleans—hot and humid, cool and damp. In the summer months, it's really a good idea to schedule exercise early in the day or in the first cool of the evening; those late-afternoon showers can make a nice difference. (On the other hand, insects prefer the cooler hours, too, so pack some bug spray. Better yet, double up and get sunscreen with repellent built in.) It's rarely too cold for a run even in January, but again it may be damp, so pack a weather-resistant layer as well as a first-aid kit: we go nowhere without sports-style adhesive strips, ibuprofen or some other analgesic, petroleum jelly, and a small tube of antiseptic. Blisters can ruin the most perfect vacation. We know.

WALKING

Considering how strongly we've urged you to walk at least the French Quarter, you may have already guessed that we find not agony but ecstasy in the feet. And in addition to the neighborhood walks, New Orleans has several picturesque options, starting with the roughly two miles of **Riverwalk** from Esplanade Avenue to the Spanish Plaza, which takes you past

Jackson Square, the various cruise ships, and a wonderful assortment of vendors and relaxing natives. (Keep an ear out; this is also popular among rollerbladers.) If you take the St. Charles Avenue Streetcar to where St. Charles ends, you'll discover the tracks take a sharp right turn onto Carrollton Avenue; that's because the Mississippi River takes a hard right as well, and you can get off and walk the levee there, too, before exploring the shops and cafes of the **Riverbend** neighborhood.

City Park covers 1,500 acres, twice the size of New York's sweeping Central Park, and you can wander pretty much as long as you like. If you like those walking trails with built-in exercise stations equipped with chin-up bars and stretching posts and the like, go to **Audubon Park;** part of the macadam bike trail over by the duck pond has 18 mild challenges.

RUNNING AND JOGGING

Again, the riverfront area is a common draw for runners who deal in limited distance, and the long, lovely stretch of **St. Charles Avenue** down through the Garden District is a great possibility. You could run as far as you like and then ride the streetcar back—the annual Crescent City 10K starts in Jackson Square and ends at the zoo—or even go half-marathon distance by running to Audubon Park, circling the two-mile path around the golf course, and returning.

Along with its pleasure paths, City Park has two 400-meter polyurethane tracks built for the 1992 Olympic trials and 1993 NCAA championships, one inside **Tad Gormley Stadium** (483-9496) and one outside (call the park at 482-4888). At the **Chalmette Battlefield** there is a dirt track that is ideal for runners of the contemplative sort; although the car gate is locked at dusk, there is a smaller pedestrian gate next to the national cemetery that will give you access. And if you're used to running with a club, contact the **New Orleans Track Club** (482-6682) or **Southern Runner Productions** (899-3333) for event schedules.

BIKING

We already mentioned that it's easy to rent a bike or even a two-seater in the French Quarter. **Laid Back Tours** provides recumbent bikes for $25 a day and will arrange a "Bike & Blues" tour with guide, if you like; call (800) 786-1274 or go to www.laidbacktours.com for information. **Bicycle Michael's** on Frenchman Street (945-9505) has a 25-mile map for serious bikers that goes out Esplanade Avenue to City Park, around the lake, through mid-city to Audubon Park and the university area, and back along St. Charles. A new riverfront path now extends all the way from Jefferson Parish through Orleans Parish and St. Charles as well. And that two-mile track in Audubon Park is very popular with rollerbladers and bikers, particularly on weekends. You can also contact the **Crescent City Cyclists** (276-2601) for group-ride information.

TENNIS

There are public courts in both **City Park** (483-9383)—which has 39 lighted synthetic–surface courts (making it the largest public facility in the South), USPTA instructors, and even racquet rentals—and in **Audubon Park** at the Magazine Street end (895-1042), which has 10 clay courts and is nice but not lighted. Both charge fees and accept reservations, but they are not required.

There are 11 courts, 3 outdoors, at the **Rivercenter Racquet and Health Club,** which is in the Hilton Riverside at 2 Poydras Street (556-3742), but even hotel guests have to pay the $8 club fee, and court time is hard to get. On the other hand, it has a stringing service and a match-a-partner service as well, so if you can make arrangements in advance, it's a good place to go. The club also has squash and racquetball courts. The **YMCA** on St. Charles at Lee Circle also has racquetball courts (568-9622).

GOLF

Like much of the South, this is popular golf territory, and as usual, you can start at the City Park, where **Bayou Oaks** club (483-9396) is (again) the largest municipal facility in the South. It offers four 18-hole courses, PGA teaching pros, and a huge, 100-tee, double-decker driving range open until 10 p.m. Greens fees are $10–$14; $19 with a cart. **Audubon Park** (865-8260) has only one 18-holer, but it has the advantage of being near the zoo, so you can grab a round while the kids go on safari. Greens fees are $8 weekdays and $12 weekends, with an additional $6 per person riding in the cart. There is also **Joe Bartholomew Course** (288-0928), located in Ponchartrain Park, in the northeast part of the city. It charges a greens fee of $7.75 on weekdays and $11 on weekends, and a $20 cart fee. There are also two public courses just across the river on the West Bank: **Brechtel Park** course (362-4761), which charges $7.75–$10 for greens fees and $16 for carts; and **Bayou Barriere** (394-0662), which combines fees for carts and greens. On weekdays, it's $20 for residents and $29 for nonresidents; on weekends, it's $30 for residents and $40 for nonresidents. The PGA-sanctioned Compact Classic is played in early April at **English Turn** (pro shop, 391-8018), which is on a curve of the Mississippi River, a pretty drive down St. Bernard Highway.

GYMS AND HEALTH CLUBS

The **YMCA** at Lee Circle (568-9622) has a relatively expansive half-mile track, large pool, machines, sauna-steam-whirlpool, and aerobics. The cost is $8 for outsiders and free to Y hotel guests with a valid hotel key.

The **Downtown Fitness Center** in the Canal Place complex has aerobics, treadmills, bikes, stair machines, free weights and leveraged machines, saunas, and even personal trainers. You can get a daily pass for $12 and a three-day pass for $30 (525-2956).

In addition, the **Rivercenter Club** at the Hilton has massage therapists, a whole list of name-brand machines, salon treatments, and even a tanning bed. The somewhat smaller but equally shiny club at **Le Meridien Hotel** (owned by the same company as the Downtown Fitness Center) on Canal Street (525-6500) is also open to outsiders ($12 for one day, $30 for three days, and $45 for 5 days). Here the hotel guests can use the club for free.

OTHER RECREATIONAL ACTIVITIES

If you want to swim and are not staying in a hotel with a pool (which only a few in the French Quarter or Garden District have), check with the Y or the health and fitness clubs. There is a public swimming pool at **Audubon Park** as well.

If you like a little outdoor entertainment, but don't go for regimented exercise, you have a couple of other choices. You can ride at a few stables including, of course, **City Park** (483-9398), which has only a ring, but offers 1-hour group lessons and 30-minute individual lessons in English-style riding. Audubon Park's **Cascade Stables** (891-2246), allows riders to go out into the park a bit.

City Park also offers **canoes** and **paddleboats**; docks for a little light **catfish and bass fishing** (you have to get a license at the boat dock behind the park casino, which is the only so-called casino in town without a deck of cards to its name; **soccer** fields; **baseball** diamonds; and a **batting cage** at the four-field softball center.

If you want to take up rollerblading or just rent a pair of blades, head to **Blade Action** (6108 Magazine Street near Audubon Park, 486-8889).

And if you're interested in serious fishing and hunting a little farther outside the city, perhaps for your second New Orleans visit, there are dozens of guides and charters. There are two famous names, or at least faces, in the fishing biz. One is former TV weatherman Nash Roberts, of **Fishhunter Guide Service,** which will not only supply you with everything you need but come and get you at the hotel (call (800) 887-1385, or 837-0703). The other is TV sportfishing-series character Phil Robichaux of **Captain Phil's Saltwater Guide Services** (348-3264), whose charters leave from the Lafitte Marina near the Barataria unit of the Jean Lafitte National Historic Park and Preserve, about an hour's drive from the French Quarter. You can probably get several other names and numbers out of promotional brochures or by calling marinas and fishing stores, but we suggest you contact the New Orleans Visitors Bureau for a list of reliable guides. Remember, you *do* need a permit from the **Department of Wildlife and Fisheries**

(568-5636). Permits are available from most sporting goods stores, marinas, and guide companies. Three-day licenses cost $55, and full-season licenses are $110. You will need to bring your driver's license.

SPECTATOR SPORTS

New Orleans is not a great football town—which may mean that it's a *great* football town for tourists. Although in most cities with NFL franchises, tickets are sold out well in advance and have to be scalped at the scene, the **New Orleans Saints** (731-1700) do not sell out and there are regularly seats available. The Saints play in the legendary (and newly spiffed-up) Superdome, so you can also call TicketMaster at 522-5555 for information. **Tulane University** also plays its Saturday home games at the Superdome, and every other year, there's a rousing, old-fashioned, rah-rah LSU–Tulane grudge match there; call the Dome offices at 587-3810 or 587-3822 for schedules and ticket information. You can also inquire about ticket availability for the **Sugar Bowl** collegiate duel, but you'll need to do so well in advance of the match.

There are times when New Orleans is a super football town, and that is during the years when the **Super Bowl** is played there. It's a long shot, but you can try to get in on the ticket lottery not by besieging the Superdome itself but by sending a certified letter to the National Football League offices at 410 Park Avenue, New York, NY 10022.

The **New Orleans Brass** hockey team (522-7825) has moved into the spanking-new Sports Arena behind the Superdome. The new facility holds 17,500 fans for ice hockey and 18,500 for basketball.

New Orleans does better in baseball with the **New Orleans Zephyrs** (the Houston Astros AAA affiliate). Zephyr Stadium in Metairie, which opened for the 1997 season, cost $23 million and seats 12,000 in the height of retro-stadium style. For game schedules and ticket information, call the Zephyrs's office at 734-5155.

Zephyr Stadium is also home to the **New Orleans Storm** (734-5155), a minor-league soccer team, which plays from April through September.

New Orleans also does well by the blue-blooded sport of horse racing (as you might expect from such a royalist colony). The **Fair Grounds** (944-5515) near City Park hosts thoroughbred racing from Thanksgiving to mid-April, when it gives way to the Jazz and Heritage Festival.

Part Ten

Shopping in New Orleans

Probably the only reason visitors to New Orleans spend any less time shopping than they do eating and drinking is that the stores close earlier—and even at that, you'll find a surprising number of merchants open until 8 or even 10 p.m. After all, trade and conspicuous consumption are at the heart of New Orleans history. In the mid-eighteenth century, it was the third-busiest port in the United States and had the highest per capita income of any city in the country, according to some figures.

So you can easily shop until you drop. Stores and galleries are abundant in the Vieux Carré, making for spectacular window shopping, and that can be the danger as well. Just as there is a tendency to keep eating because you can smell all that food around you, there's a tendency to keep falling in love with jewelry and posters and rings and masks. (And remember, alcohol loosens your inhibitions, including the financial ones.) If you have a budget, or if you are looking for something particular, it's best to know in advance where you want to go, or you might get sidetracked.

Also, if you think of shopping by "type"—high-end antiques or specialty stores, upscale supermalls or souvenir troves—you can head to the neighborhood with the most options. If you have a couple of days to spare, then you can range a little farther, but even then, if you don't have a background in antiques, a knowledgeable companion, or a friend who lives in town, you're probably not going to stumble onto a hidden treasure.

Among the neighborhoods with good browsing are the most famous shopping strip in New Orleans, Royal Street; the entire riverfront strip from the Farmers Market to the Convention Center; and Magazine Street, uptown from Canal over to Audubon Park. You might also enjoy the somewhat more relaxed **Riverbend District** in Carrollton, which you can stroll as part of the St. Charles streetcar tour (see Part Eleven: "Sight-Seeing and Tours").

Incidentally, sales tax in New Orleans is 9%, so if what you're buying is large, you might consider having it shipped to you; the handling charge may well be less than the tax. If you are visiting from another country, you can take advantage of Louisiana's Tax-Free Shopping, although this will mean carrying your passport with you instead of putting it in the hotel vault. Here's how it works: If the store posts an LTFS sticker (or ask at the counter), show the passport and ask for the special refund voucher. You'll still pay the tax, but when you get to the airport, stop by the LTFS counter and show them your receipts and refund slips. Up to $100 will be refunded in cash (minus a service charge), up to $500 by check; anything over $500 will be mailed to your home.

THE FRENCH QUARTER

As Bourbon Street is to nightlife, so **Royal Street** is to antiques—and if it's not there, it's probably on Chartres. That's an exaggeration, of course, but the Royal antiques row goes back several generations, on both the selling and buying sides. Royal Street makes for the most riveting window-shopping in the city: cases of earrings, necklaces, cufflinks, and enamels; chandeliers and candelabra; gold leaf, crystal, and silver; china dolls; silver-headed walking sticks; and sterling cigarette cases, all glittering with the mystique of Creole culture. Some of these stores advertise all over the country (which is a consideration that cuts both ways—*somebody* has to pay for all that publicity); still others capitalize on Royal Street's reputation to embellish both the value and the actual cost of their goods.

Many hotels and visitors' centers carry a brochure produced by the Royal Street Guild that lists members (or call the guild at 524-1260), but the choices are almost overwhelming, so visitors should start with these reputable dealers: One of the oldest names in the antiques game here is **Keil's** (325 Royal Street, 522-4552), founded before the turn of the century and still among the best choices for French and English art and furnishings, chandeliers, and decorative arts. It remains a family concern, and other stores in the clan's hands are **Royal Antiques** (307–309 Royal Street, 524-7033), its annex around the corner (715 Bienville Street), and **Moss Antiques** (411 Royal Street, 522-3981). Another good spot is the **French Antique Shop** (225 Royal Street, 524-9861). Its collection of bronzes, chandeliers, and Baccarat crystal loom out of the dark to draw you in. **Peter Patout** specializes in French and American antiques and decorative arts (920 Royal Street, 522-0582).

For Asian art and antiquities, contact **Diane Genre,** a member of the International Association of Appraisers and a specialist in Japanese woodblock prints, temple carvings, lacquer work, and extraordinary Japanese and Chinese textiles, including such gold- and silver-embroidered dragons as would bring your fantasies to life. She has closed her retail store but is working out of an apartment showroom overlooking Royal; call for an appointment (595-8945).

If you're interested in fine estate jewelry, Deco, Nouveau, or just retro, check into **Gerald D. Katz Antiques, Inc.** (505 Royal Street, 524-5050) or consult Nancy Kittay, who runs her jewelry business, specializing in Victorian and Early American pieces, from inside **Waldhorn & Adler** (343 Royal Street, 581-6379).

This used to be the financial heart of the Vieux Carré, and several of the old financial institutions are into their second lives as antiques stores. The three-floor Waldhorn building, for example, served as the Bank of the United States in 1800, and the former Manheim Galleries building at Royal and Conti Streets was designed in 1818 by Benjamin Latrobe as the Louisiana State Bank.

For the hostess with the mostest, nothing could be more fun than a lesson in preparing an absinthe cocktail—the sharp-tipped, perforated absinthe spoons range from $65–125—from Patrick Dunne, proprietor of **Lucullus** (610 Chartres, 528-9620). Lucius Licinius Lucullus was a famous Roman epicure, and Dunne's shop stocks cookware, silver, and culinary objets d'art dating to the seventeenth century.

The old **M.S. Rau** store has taken to offering one-day "specials," a la the Manhattan merchants, on such items as walking sticks, music boxes, and decanters; pick the right day, and you might pick a prize (630 Royal Street, 523-5660).

Really serious collectors should be aware of the seasonal and special sales at the **New Orleans Auction Galleries** located upstairs at 801 Magazine Street (call 566-1849), although it's a few blocks outside the French Quarter.

Kurt E. Schon, Ltd. (510 St. Louis, 524-5462) has what he advertises as the largest inventory of nineteenth-century European paintings in this country, particularly featuring works by Impressionist, Post-Impressionist, French Salon, and Royal Academy artists, and the price tags are as breathtaking as the collection. (If your budget only goes up to $100,000 or so, don't even attempt the six floors of private showrooms, open by appointment only.) If you love the styles, but can't quite afford the Schon prices, try the **Vincent Mann Gallery** (713 Bienville Street, 523-2342), which specializes in the second rank, but high second rank, of predominantly French Post-Impressionists.

Books, Records, and Prints

Not surprisingly, a literary town like New Orleans is rich in bookstores, particularly those specializing in out-of-print titles, first editions, and rare publications. **Faulkner House Books** is in the building overlooking St.

Anthony's garden, where William Faulkner lived while writing *Soldier's Pay* and various short stories set in New Orleans. It naturally features first editions of his works and other titles important to Southern literature (624 Pirate's Alley, 524-2940). The house where Tennessee Williams wrote *A Streetcar Named Desire*, coincidentally, is right through Exchange Alley, in the next block, at 632 St. Peter Street.

Other good bookshops in the Quarter, especially for those who love to linger among the shelves, include **Beckham's** (228 Decatur Street, 522-9875) and its sibling **Librarie** (823 Chartres Street, 525-4837); the scholarly **Crescent City Books** (204 Chartres Street, 524-4997); **Arcadian Books and Art Prints** (714 Orleans Street, 523-4138); and **Dauphine Street Books** (410 Dauphine Street, 529-2333).

Faubourg Marigny Bookstore, on Frenchman Street at Chartres (943-9875), specializes in gay, lesbian, and feminist literature. Most of these stores belong to an association of antiquarian and second-hand booksellers, and any one of them can give you a list and a simple map of the others.

In the same way, a musical town like this is a great place to dig up old recordings. For jazz (mostly re-recorded and available on cassette or CD), stop by the shop at the Old U.S. Mint on Esplanade.

New converts to the regional sounds of zydeco, Cajun, blues, swamp pop, and gospel sounds may also want to flip through the goods at **Louisiana Music Factory** (210 Decatur Street, 586-1094).

If you're interested in photographs, either vintage or contemporary, **A Gallery of Fine Photography** (322 Royal Street, 568-1313) carries works by such artists as Berenice Abbott, Eadweard Muybridge, Edward Weston, Yousuf Karsh, Edward Steichen, Henri Cartier-Bresson, Diane Arbus, Ansel Adams, and Helmut Newton. For fine mezzotints and other vintage prints, try the **Stone and Press Galleries** (238 Chartres Street, 561-8555). For animation art and limited-edition prints from Jerry Garcia or Ron Wood, visit **America's Gallery** (522 Royal Street, 586-0801).

Stamp collector extraordinaire **Raymond H. Weill** sold his entire collection to a London firm ten years ago for a staggering $14 million, and has been restocking ever since (407 Royal Street, 581-7373).

For maps, fine-art prints, architectural drawings, star charts, medical diagrams, and official documents—layers and layers of them—try the **Centuries Antique Prints and Maps** (517A St. Louis Street, 568-9491).

Other French Quarter Collectibles

Once you get into New Orleans music, you'll want to join the parade. So for a really unusual souvenir, consider a "second-line" umbrella—the ones you see waving behind the band in those parades—or a fine plantation-worthy parasol. **Anne B. Lane** is the Umbrella Lady (1107 Decatur Street, 523-7791), whose fashionable wares can often be seen on the balcony overlooking the street, if she herself is not waving them in an impromptu kick-line.

Weapons and ammunitions—flintlocks, pistols, muzzle loaders, swords, bayonets, sabers, shot, and even cannonballs—are the signature stock at the fourth-generation **James H. Cohen & Sons** (437 Royal Street, 522-3305). The entrance is guarded—perhaps a little cruelly—by a wooden Indian.

For those who prefer their warfare a little less realistic, **Le Petit Soldier Shop** (528 Royal Street—or as they continue to put it, 528 Rue Royale, 523-7741) carries not only vintage lead and more modern toy soldiers of the familiar Civil War and Napoleonic eras, but figures of Sherlock Holmes and Watson, "Kagemusha"-style samurai, Roman emperors, Winston Churchill, and even Hitler, along with service decorations and pilots' wings. For dolls, check out **Boyers Antiques & Doll** shop (241 Chartres Street, 522-4513). For dollhouse furniture and miniatures, stop by **Boyers Miniature Shop** (330 Chartres Street, 522-4513), the **Black Butterfly** (727 Royal Street, 524-6464), or the **Ginja Jar Too** (611 Royal Street, 523-7614).

The most fanciful and zoological furniture—alligator fainting couches, zebra side tables, heron-necked CD towers—can be found at **The Private Collection** (1116 Decatur Street, 593-9526) and **Tropical Reflections** (51 French Market, (800) 264-6117). Great-looking pens are found for $4 or $5 apiece at the **MMC Enterprises** stand inside the French Market, or call Charles Chen at 433-2838.

What would a trip to the voodoo capital of the country be without a little mysticism? For charms, potions, mojo dolls, and the most atmospheric palm or tarot readings, head to the **New Orleans Historic Voodoo Museum** (724 Dumaine Street, 523-7685), which is more theater than museum; or visit **Marie Laveau's House of Voodoo** (739 Bourbon Street, 581-3751). If you prefer to walk on the sunnier side, the **Bottom of the Cup Tearooms** stock crystals, wrought-iron stands and heavy crystal balls, and scores of tarot decks reproduced from various countries and centuries (732 Royal Street, 523-1204 and 616 Conti Street, 524-1997).

Another New Orleans must is pralines, those brown sugar–pecan sweets. While there are several fine and old confectionaries, the **Old Town Praline Shop** (627 Royal Street, 525-1413) has even more than its candy to recommend it—hometown ladies behind the counter and a lovely courtyard in the back, one of the few still open to visitors and a welcome respite from the shopping grind. French Opera diva Adelina Patti, who set Creole hearts aflame during the 1860 season, used the house as her residence, and photos of her triumphal tour dot the walls.

To check your e-mail over your morning coffee, start at **Royal Blend**

Tea & Coffee (621 Royal Street) and then head upstairs to **Royal Access Internet Cafe** (525-0401).

For neo-Creos who can't live without their morning stogie, there's **Cafe Havana** (842 Royal Street, 569-9006 or (800) 860-2988) or **The Epitome** (631 Royal Street, (800) 444-3741 or 523-2844). The cigars aren't truly Cuban, of course, but they are sufficiently showy.

Although it's now in the Pontalba complex next to the 1850 House, **Bourbon French Perfume** (525 St. Anne Street, 522-4480) used to be on the street it's named for—back in 1843, when it opened. You can either get French scents like those preferred by Creole society (see the super economy-sized bottles in the Hermann-Grima House, for fun) or have one blended for you.

There are masks and Mardi Gras paraphernalia all over, but unless you just want a mass-produced version, head for the **Little Shop of Fantasy** (523 Dumaine Street, 529-4243), which stocks all handmade masks and costumes by about two dozen local artists. This is also where you can get those Victorian stovepipes and ubiquitous *Cat in the Hat* toppers, if you must. Not far away are the elaborate and fantastic leather disguises of **Masquerade Fantasy** (1233 Decatur Street, 593-9269).

If your boss is the sort of guy who has everything, here are a few leather items that might save you the annual Christmas-list blues: hanging suit bags for $335; golf bags, tooled or smooth, for $495; roll-on suitcases for $265, even cellular phone carriers of various sizes. The smartest idea yet is a leather duffel weekender that folds flat into itself so you can pack it inside another suitcase for souvenirs. All, as well as belts, shoes, totes, and purses, are at **Leather Creations** (837 Decatur Street, 527-0033).

Finally, for those interested in restoring old homes, it's worth heading over to **Architectural Antiques** (4531 North Rampart Street, 942-7000) to look over the mantelpieces, corbels, and columns. **Sigle's Antiques and Metalcraft** is stocked with balcony iron and ornamental hangings and brackets (935 Royal Street, 522-7647). **Bevolo Gas and Electric Lights** has been turning out lamps, including the gas-look fixtures around Jackson Square, for half a century (521 Conti Street, 522-9485).

(For more architectural and salvage spots, see the description of the Warehouse/Arts District below.)

MAGAZINE STREET

In recent years, with rising rents and stiffer competition, many antiques dealers have either moved off the main drag or out of the French Quarter altogether. A number of stores and galleries have opened on **Magazine Street** in the Uptown/University area, and the Magazine Street merchants have been promoting their association with brochures and maps—which brings up a sticky point: there are a great number of interesting stores along Magazine Street, to be sure, but whether it actually makes sense for visitors to the city, especially those staying only a few days, to venture over there is another issue.

For one thing, despite the promotional brochures raving about "six miles of antique shops, art galleries, restaurants, and specialty shops in Historic Uptown New Orleans," the road is still primarily residential; there is a block or two with a lot of stores, and then it may be several blocks before another cluster. If you don't have a car, it's difficult to see more than a few stores at a time. The confusion is increased by the fact that Magazine Street begins in the new Warehouse/Arts District near the Convention Center, so that some visitors believe they can walk to the antiques strip, whereas it's quite a hike to the real clusters.

Second, alongside many of the nicer stores are still lower-scale salvage shops, more like flea market or "granny's-attic" affairs. So if you don't already know something about antiques, and if you aren't willing to spend a couple of hours sorting through showrooms and comparing prices, you may be disappointed.

One possibility is to hire a professional antiquing companion, such as **Macon Riddle** of Let's Go Antiquing, who's made a career of designing half- or full-day shopping tours geared to your interests. For $50 an hour, minimum three hours, you get her expert advice, too; call 899-3027. Another possibility is to drive about 45 minutes to Ponchatoula, on the other side of Lake Pontchartrain, which has more than 30 antiques shops at non-Royal prices.

If you do want to go to Magazine, here are a few clusters of specialty shops of particular interest, so you can make at least some sort of park-and-walk visit or walk over from the streetcar without exhausting yourself. Or consult with the Regional Transit Authority about bus routes and VisiTour passes, as described in "Getting Around New Orleans."

Start off at the corner of St. Andrew Street with **Jim Smiley's Fine Vintage Clothing** (2001 Magazine Street, 528-9449), the sort of place that knows the difference between vintage and merely used. Smiley's runs the gamut from haute couture dresses to 1940s suits, serious antique wedding gowns and bodices, silk step-ins, and even bloomers—and has some riotous hats to boot.

Next stop is **Bush Antiques,** which has an amazing assortment of ecclesiastical remnants, so to speak: gilded high altars; heavy bishops' chairs; old chapel statuary, including the Virgin Mary and various saints; iron crucifixes from cemeteries; stained glass; and even vestments (2109–2111 Magazine

Street, 581-3518). If you're attracted to the vividly painted bayou folk art of the sort that adorns the House of Blues, be sure to step through to the courtyard for a look at the "studio" there.

Across the street are **Hands** (2042 Magazine Street, 522-2590), where owner Rachel Dalessandro specializes in pre-Columbian art and artifacts as old as 3,000 years (some astonishingly affordable); and **Gerry White Glass** (2036 Magazine Street, 522-3544), the showroom/studio of a man whose custom architectural glass, etched and carved, ranges from tables to standing screens. (The panels in the window, etched to look like venetian blinds, won him his wife.)

The sleazy-chic name of the **House of Lounge** just about says it all, from lingerie to furniture (2044 Magazine Street, 671-8300). A few blocks farther is **George Herget Books,** which is one of the most important rare and secondhand bookstores outside the French Quarter, housing an estimated 20,000 volumes (3109 Magazine Street, 891-5595). Right next door is **Magazine Arcade Antiques** (3017 Magazine Street, 895-5451), stocking thousands of music boxes, home furnishings, high-end bric-a-brac, porcelain, and cloisonné; and a mix of American, European, and Asian antiques. And if you've got the money, honey, they've got the time: **Kohlmaier and Kohlmaier** (1018 Harmony Street, just off the 3200 block of Magazine Street, 895-6394) specializes in standing and cabinet clocks, mantel clocks, and personal timepieces.

Another few blocks out is a cluster for decorators with an eye for decorative accessories and ethnic and folk arts. Jewelry designers **Mignon Fager** (3801 Magazine Street, 891-6789) and **Anne Pratt** (3937 Magazine Street, 891-6532) are local artists developing national reputations. And **Neal Auction Co.** at 4038 Magazine Street (899-5329) specializes in estate jewelry as well as art. Pottery fans will be drawn to the studio showroom of **Charles Bohn** at Shadyside Pottery (3823 Magazine Street, 897-1710). Bohn served his apprenticeship in Japan but also loves classical Greco-Roman styles. And, if you dare, see the beautifully finished pieces by furniture designer **Mario Villa** (3908 Magazine Street, 895-8731); it was Villa who made the sconces for the Contemporary Arts Center, which gives you an idea how highly his peers regard his work. **Cole Pratt Gallery** (3800 Magazine Street, 891-6789) handles several local artists' works.

For collectors of African art, the **Davis Gallery** (904 Louisiana Avenue, 895-5206) is a must-see: household items, baskets, personal items, cookware, and masks from Central and West Africa—all actually used, not mass manufactured—are displayed in a museum-quality setting. The nearby **Private Connection** does a similar good turn for Indonesian artifacts—

shadow puppets, "flying" temple figurines, batik fabrics, and jewelry—along with colonial-era antiques (3927 Magazine Street, 899-4944).

Lucullus, the culinary antique store, has a branch at 3922 Magazine Street (894-0500). **Jacqueline Vance Rugs** (3944 Magazine Street, 891-3304) specializes in both antique and contemporary Kilims and dhurries. And if you've become one of the retro tea–party crowd, visit **Jon Antiques** (4605 Magazine Street, 899-4482), which specializes in smaller, more portable, but elegant items such as eighteenth- and nineteenth-century porcelains, tea caddies, and fireplace screens.

Finally, hop to **Beaucoup Books** for a full range of Southern fiction (5414 Magazine Street, 895-2663); **Angele Parlange** for home accessories (5419 Magazine Street, 897-6511); **Scriptura** for handmade papers (5423 Magazine Street, 897-1555); and **Pied Nu** for gourmet edibles (5521 Magazine Street, 899-4118).

THE WAREHOUSE DISTRICT

Another neighborhood emerging as a shopping center is the old Warehouse/Arts District, a loosely defined area roughly squared off by the convention center, Lafayette Street to Lafayette Square, St. Charles Avenue between Lafayette and Lee Circle, and Howard Avenue from Lee Circle back to the convention center. A number of former mills, machinery suppliers, and storehouses have been gutted and refurbished as art spaces and condominiums, although there are still pockets of industry all over. Taking most of its impetus from the 1984 World's Fair (which was a *succès d'estime* if not an economic one), this neighborhood is an intriguing combination of retail and residential. It is home to Emeril's Restaurant (and chef Emeril Lagasse himself), the Contemporary Arts Center, the D-Day Museum, the Ogden Museum of Southern Art (still under construction), and the new Louisiana Children's Museum, as well as the Civil War Museum and such historic landmarks as St. Patrick's Cathedral. (See the profiles in "New Orleans Attractions.")

The main strip, nicknamed **Gallery Row,** is along Julia Street between St. Charles and the convention center. Since art is definitely a matter of taste, you'll just have to wander around the galleries and check them out. You can get to the Warehouse District from the French Quarter by riding the Riverfront Streetcar to the Julia Street stop; and if you're not tired afterwards, you can wind up at St. Charles and take that streetcar for a spin out to the Garden District.

Some of the best-known galleries in this district include **Marguerite Oestreicher** (720 Julia Street, 581-9253), who has the sculpture from the estate of Milton Avery, among others; **Simonne Stern** (518 Julia Street,

529-1118), who was one of the first, and remains one of the premier, deal-ers in contemporary regional art; **Wyndy Morehead** (603 Julia Street, 568-9754); **Lemieux Galleries** (332 Julia Street, 522-9888); **Stella Jones** (201 St. Charles, 568-9050); **Heriard-Cimino** (440 Julia Street, 525-7300); **d.o.c.s.** (709 Camp Street, 524-3936); **Arthur Roger** (432 Julia Street, 522-1999); and the **New Orleans Auction Galleries** (801 Magazine Street at Julia, 566-1849), which innovatively employs only women auctioneers.

This is also a great neighborhood in which to find one-of-a-kind hand-made furniture. **Necessities** handles several different designers (832 Bay-onne Street, 581-2333). **Christopher Maier** makes King Tut-inspired thrones; gilded and enameled bureaus; rope-seated, lion's paw-footed chairs; even an armoir with the sun's rays stretching to the floor (329 Julia Street, 586-9079). And **YaYa—Young Artists, Young Aspirations—**is a nonprofit showcase for inner-city youths with artistic talent (628B Baronne Street, 529-3306).

Aside from the art galleries and studios, there are a couple of particu-larly noteworthy addresses. The **New Orleans School of GlassWorks & Gallery** (727 Magazine Street just off Julia, 529-7277) is the largest con-temporary glass-arts studio in the South, and it offers glass-blowing classes to the public—not only six-week courses, but two-day, intensive introduc-tions to the art and even private tutoring. Exhibitions go on constantly, and the studio shares space with fine bookmakers and print- and paper-makers, who also offer exhibitions and workshops. This is a first-class fam-ily attraction as well as an art gallery.

"This Old House" has nothing on **Architectural Salvage and Col-lectibles** at 3983 Tchoupitoulas; **Crescent City Architecturals** is another treasure trove for home renovators (3101 Tchoupitoulas Street, 891-0500). And farther uptown in the Garden District, **Armadillo South** reclaims iron gates, mantlepieces, transoms, doors, and other architectural elements from private homes and—judging from some of the more elabo-rate bar fixtures and lamps—a few "public houses" (4801 Washington Avenue, 486-1150). And although it may be a little fine for beginners, good amateur and even professional musicians should make a special trip to **International Vintage Guitars** (1011 Magazine Street, 524-4557), which has used and vintage Martin, Rickenbacher, Fender, and Gibson instruments, along with accessories, amplifiers, etc.

MALLS OF THE AMERICAS

New Orleans has developed an almost continuous line of those prepack-aged, upscale-label shopping malls stretching along the waterfront from Jackson Square to the convention center, or commercially speaking, from the French Market to the Riverwalk Marketplace. This baby-boomer boomtown also houses that most notorious of souvenir franchises, the Hard Rock Cafe (and was home to the now-defunct Planet Hollywood); across Decatur Street is the Crescent City Brewpub. The whole area is bookended by two other theme-sales centers: the Jimmy Buffett shop, filled with Parrothead paraphernalia, at the corner of Decatur and Ursuline, and the House of Blues souvenir store on Decatur past Bienville.

This Great Wall o' Malls winds in and out among the various riverside promenades, cruise-ship landings, and the Aquarium of the Americas, and in good weather the kite flyers and Rollerbladers wind in and out of tourists hefting huge shopping bags and wielding baby strollers. This can be somewhat wearing, whether or not you're actually purchasing anything, so it's best to stop periodically and admire the river, or get a 15-minute neck massage or a hair wrap.

Starting at the east end of the French Quarter and stretching along North Peters Street to the Café du Monde at Jackson Square is the **French Market,** which legend says was a trading post for Native Americans long before the Europeans arrived. Nowadays the complex comprises a half-dozen nicely restored pink stucco buildings housing everything from high-priced souvenirs to jazz bars to orange-juice stands. The building closest to Barracks Street is the **Old Farmers Market**—or, rather, what is now called the Old Farmers Market. The crates of live poultry, rabbits, turtle, and squid that locals used to buy right off the dock have pretty much been replaced by stands of pepper sauce and braided ropes of garlic being sold at inflated prices to credulous tourists as "Cajun hot garlic."

The next stretch of the market, which spills out into the street on weekends, is the **Community Flea Market,** a grab bag of tie-dyed dresses, carved masks, old chairs, and mass-produced "stained glass" that for most people provides all the cheap souvenirs their officemates can stand. Inside these buildings are scores of vendors offering voodoo dolls, T-shirts, earrings, cheap ties (including Jimi Hendrix patterns and copies of Nicole Miller designs for $5), rock posters, sunglasses, blackface pecan-shell magnets, reproduction grocery labels, fabric pins, mobcaps, novelty ballpoint pens (including some that resemble syringes), rubber-band guns, and sports caps. Hot-sauce and Cajun-spice fans can find stalls like the **N'awlins Cajun & Creole Spices** (1101 North Peters Street, 566-2325 or (800) 237-2325) selling hundreds of gumbo mixes and seasonings bearing both old names (Zatarain's, McIlhenny) and new celebrity imprints (Paul Prudhomme's and Emeril's). You can even have your name inscribed on a grain of rice for $8.

As you work your way toward Jackson Square, you'll find some clothing boutiques, indoor-outdoor bars (there are usually at least two jazz trios playing at any given time), and gift shops with pralines and pepper sauce and cutesy statuettes of Louis Armstrong. (Note that the similarly styled building a little behind the French Market at about St. Philip Street is the Jean Lafitte National Park Visitors Center; see "Sight-Seeing and Tours.") Beyond the legendary **Café du Monde,** where you can buy chicory coffee and beignet mix right from the source, the commercial strip briefly gives way to Washington Artillery Park and the wooden Moonwalk promenade along the river. Of course, down along the Square, the sidewalks will be full of mule carriages, caricaturists, and clowns; and Artillery Park will probably have some street theater or music going on, but that's just for fun.

Then the shopping picks up again at the old **Jackson Brewery,** one-time house of Jax beer (as it's familiarly known), now with a river-view branch of Pat O'Brien's at the top; and the **Marketplace,** home of the **Hard Rock Cafe.** The Marketplace is big-time retail media: it also boasts **Tower Records & Video** and **Bookstar.**

There is another pretty stretch—Waldenburg Park—which meanders over to the Aquarium of the Americas; just west of the Aquarium, the Spanish Plaza segues into the huge **Riverwalk Marketplace** complex, an upscale Rouse development of 200 boutiques and eateries that connects to the Hilton Hotel and the **Flamingo** floating casino. Most of these stores seem to come as a package deal now, and even in duplicate: the **Disney Store** and **Warner Bros., the Gap** and **Banana Republic, Sharper Image** and **Brookstone, Eddie Bauer** and **Abercrombie & Fitch, Victoria's Secret** and . . . well, you get the idea. For something a little less predictable, look into the shop of **Yvonne LaFleur,** who not only carries upscale fashions but custom-designed hats, cocktail dresses, evening gowns, and even wedding dresses. From the river, you can see where the facade of Riverwalk was torn away by the runaway barge—it looks a little like an intentional architectural model, actually—but you'd never know from strolling through the glossy mall inside that anything had ever happened.

At the foot of Canal Street, across the streetcar tracks from the Aquarium, is **Canal Place,** a new, lushly appointed and label-conscious mall that blazons the logos of its **Gucci, Saks,** and **Brooks Brothers** tenants. Be sure to browse through **RHINO,** which is an acronym for "Right Here in New Orleans," describing where the store's crafts were made. It's a nonprofit shop, and the clothing and art are extremely attractive. Canal Place is also the home of jewelry designer **Mignon Faget,** whose creations in silver, 14-karat gold, and bronze d'or for both men and women are highly prized.

There is another upscale mall called the **New Orleans Centre** (1400

Poydras Street, by the Superdome) that houses both **Lord & Taylor** and **Macy's,** but there isn't much reason to make a trip unless you want to tour the stadium and eat in the food court there.

Part Eleven

Sight-Seeing and Tours

The nice thing about sight-seeing is that you can choose your own pace, looking closely at what intrigues you, and pushing right on past what stirs not a flicker of interest. New Orleans is particularly well suited to walking tours, and that's what we recommend. So the latter portion of this chapter is given over to introductory walks around the most important (at least, to visitors) neighborhoods, with a little background flavor and a few landmarks for orientation. We've also suggested ways to customize your visit according to your own interests, by zeroing in on just the military sites, the other-worldly media, etc. The "inside stuff"—museums, historic houses, and so on—are described in more detail in the next part, on "New Orleans Attractions," which also includes some general walking-tour tips.

But as we said before, we know that not everybody prefers do-it-yourself tours. Some people find it distracting to read directions and anecdotes while walking, and others use packaged tours as a way of getting a mental map of the area. So first we'll run through some of the guided tours available. (These are surely not all of them: tourism is a boom industry in New Orleans, and you'll see flyers for new tours every month. If you want to take a guided tour, check through the material at the information desks and visitors' centers or even in your hotel lobby; you may find a discount coupon.)

In New Orleans, you can tour by land or sea, mule carriage or coach. You can see historic spots or "haunts," literary sites or cemeteries, battlefields or bayous. And you can pay nothing or, well, something.

The last thing to consider is that New Orleans is not a one-size-fits-all town. Walking is wonderful if you're young and fit, but if your party includes children or seniors, make sure to pace yourself. Build in a timely stop in a park; split the touring day into shifts, so that those with less stamina can head back to the hotel for a rest while the others continue. Or lay out the schedule on the democratic scheme—that is, plan to visit the attractions everyone wants to see first, the could-be-missed ones later, and the only-for-fanatics excursions last. That way, whoever wants to drop out can.

If each member of the party has his own must-sees, then set a particular hour to split up and a clearly understood place to regroup—General Jackson's statue, for example. If you're worried about a teenager getting wound up in whatever museum or exhibit he's into and losing track of the time, schedule this separate tour session just before lunch; there are few things that can override a kid's stomach alarm. Finally, because the food and beverage lures are everywhere, better carry a supply of snacks in plastic bags.

Guided Sight-Seeing

WALKING TOURS

Members of the nonprofit **Friends of the Cabildo** lead two-hour walks that focus on the more important historic exteriors and some of the state's museum-system exhibits (see more detail on the Louisiana State Museums below and in "New Orleans Attractions"). Admission is called a "donation," and the quality of the work done on the museums in recent years gives resonance to the word; besides, it costs only $10 for adults and $8 for those over 65 or between 13 and 20 (free for children). You can either buy tickets in advance at the Museum Store on St. Ann Street in Jackson Square (523-3939) or just arrive with the funds in hand. Tours begin daily at 10 a.m. and 1:30 p.m., except Mondays (1:30 p.m. only) and holidays.

Rangers from the **Jean Lafitte National Historical Park**—i.e., the Vieux Carré—also lead tours from their new visitors center at 419 Decatur Street (589-2636). There are two each day, one at 10:30 a.m., which lasts about 90 minutes and covers about a mile of the French Quarter; and a 3:30 p.m. walk, the subject of which varies. These tours are limited to 30 people, so each person must pick up a (free) pass before the walk begins.

One of the most interesting tours is **Le Monde Créole,** which explores the intertwined lives of the white and black, free and slave societies within the two sides (and four generations) of the family that owned the Laura Plantation (see the description in "Plantation Tours and Excursions," below). The family also owned seven townhouses in the Quarter, some of which the Tour can access; tours are also available in French. Walks are offered at 10:30 a.m. and 2:30 p.m. Monday through Saturday, 10 a.m. and 2:30 p.m. Sundays; reservations are required (568-1801).

BUS TOURS AND TROLLEYS

Gray Line Tours (call (800) 535-7786, or 587-0861) offers a variety of packages, including walking tours of the French Quarter and Garden District, plantation tours, and a combination tour with lunch aboard the steamboat *Natchez*. The bus tour covers the whole city, but you don't get out and really see anything; the main advantages are that a large group can arrange a tour in advance, and the buses make pick-ups from the major hotels.

Tours by Isabelle (391-3544, for reservations (877) 665-8689) uses minivans, so space is obviously more limited; call as far in advance as possible. The three-hour tours, starting at 9 a.m. and 2 p.m. daily, are among the most comprehensive, covering the French Quarter, the cemeteries, City Park, the Lakefront, Bayou St. John, the Garden District and university neighborhood, and even the Superdome; tours cost $38 per person. For specifics about the available tours, consult www.toursbyisabelle.com.

New Orleans Tours (592-0560) can arrange walking tours, cruises, nightlife jaunts, swamp tours, and combos.

CARRIAGE TOURS

These are becoming common in many cities around the country (and elsewhere—imagine Florence by open buggy), and they're the sort of thing that grabs at your nostalgic heartstrings every once in a while. The French Quarter, especially at night, lends itself to such time travel. A relatively quick two-mile route does help orient you a little, and children will definitely enjoy this.

Most of the carriages just line up along Decatur Street around Jackson Square; the cost ranges from about $10 to $50, depending on the length of the ride. There are a few things to note about such tours, however: Local color definitely doesn't stop at the bridle ribbons. The quality—the factual accuracy, not necessarily the entertainment quotient—varies tremendously, which is one reason there is a movement afoot to license carriage drivers as entertainers rather than as tour guides. And most of the horses are really mules, which doesn't really affect the ride but might affect your view of the ride's authenticity. (Some seem more aromatic than horses, but that may be imagination.) On the other hand, there are drivers usually until midnight, so you can fit this into your schedule at almost any time.

If you want a more elaborate (more expensive) personal tour, contact **Good Old Days Buggies** (523-0804); they will pick you up at your hotel or even at some of the major restaurants.

SPECIAL-INTEREST TOURS

Le'Ob's Tours (288-3478) offers a look at New Orleans that focuses on special connections to African-American culture and its contribution to the city. **Hidden Treasures Tours** (529-4507), which range through both the Upper and Lower Garden District, emphasize women's history, including monuments and authors' homes. They will also take you inside a

Garden District home and through one of the fabled New Orleans cemeteries. One nice aspect of these tours is that they'll pick you up from your hotel. Advance reservations are required, and tickets are $20 per person.

The "faculty" of **Bienville Tours** (945-6789) will lead you on tours geared to a variety of special interests, including black history, women's contributions, and gay cultural history. University of New Orleans professor Kenneth Holditch, of **Heritage Tours,** will lead you through a tour of literary-interest sites and homes (by appointment, 949-9805). **Gay Heritage** tours are irregular (in both senses of the word) but great, if you can get one. They are generally offered on weekends, leaving from Alternatives at 907 Bourbon Street, and promise to dish the gossip on Tennessee Williams, Truman Capote, Claw Shaw, and even Lillian Hellman. Call 945-6789. And in fact, if you read the French Quarter self-guided walking tour we've laid out below, you'll find quite a few of the literary spots listed.

Finally, music lovers should call **Cradle of Jazz** tours to get the score on New Orleans's earliest masters (282-3583).

Walking on the Dark Side

Haunted tours, voodoo tours, and cemetery tours are all the rage in New Orleans, and you can go at practically any hour (and with guides in full capes and pointy-toothed glory, if you want). They cover essentially the same ground, so to a great extent, you just pick your style.

On the straight side is **Save Our Cemeteries** (525-3377), a nonprofit group whose proceeds go toward the restoration of these "cities of the dead." SOC offers a serious and informative tour of St. Louis No. 1 every Sunday at 10 a.m., leaving from Royal Blend Coffee and Tea Room at 621 Royal Street, and leads tours of Lafayette Cemetery in the Garden District every Monday, Wednesday, Friday, and Saturday at 10:30 a.m.

The longest-running haunted tours are probably those offered by the **New Orleans Historic Voodoo Museum** at 724 Rue Dumaine (523-7685 or www.voodoomuseum.com, or e-mail voodoo@voodoomuseum.com). Their cemetery tour, not surprisingly, focuses on Marie Laveau's still-revered tomb and allows you to participate in a wishing ritual, but also explains why the "cities of the dead" are all above ground and shows off various personalities' resting places. The 90-minute tours begin at 10:30 a.m. and 1 p.m. daily (Sundays 10:30 a.m. only) and cost $15 apiece. Also offered is a "Singing Bones" tour (Sundays and Mondays at 4:30 p.m. for $14 per person), which explores voodoo's relationship with traditional New Orleans music. (Subtract 20% from all Voodoo Museum tour prices for groups of 10 or more and 30% for teenagers or AARP members.) Arrive 20 minutes early, and you can tour the museum for free as well.

The voodoo walking tour visits the great voodoo priestess's tomb, and covers haunted houses, Congo Square—emphasizing its history as a voodoo-ritual meeting ground rather than its musical roots—and a Catholic church with a voodoo saint among its statues. This two-and-a-half-hour tour costs $19 per person and begins Monday through Saturday at 1 p.m. and Sunday at 10:30 a.m.

And its "original" voodoo tour, the "Tour of the Undead" route, includes a visit to a voodoo temple, a live witch, and witchcraft and voodoo shops, and each participant gets a gris-gris bag to wear for protection throughout the two-hour tour ($16).

Robert Florence, who has written books on the New Orleans way of death, leads one voodoo and cemetery tour that also includes a temple visit and explores St. Louis No.1; he also leads groups through Lafayette Cemetery and other Garden District sites. The cemetery tour leaves from Cafe Beignet at 334-B Royal Street every day at 10 a.m. and Monday through Saturday at 1 p.m. Prices are $15 for adults, $13 for students and seniors; the tour is free for children younger than 12. Reservations are not required, but come 10 minutes early. For more information, call Historic New Orleans Walking Tours at 947-2120.

The New Orleans Ghost and Vampire Tours were created by Thomas Duran, who used to lead Jack the Ripper and Sherlock Holmes tours (plus Shakespeare and Dickens tours) in London; the staff also includes an "Anne Rice expert" and a Wiccan priestess. One tour is cemetery oriented, and leaves form C.C.'s Coffeehouse at Royal and St. Philip Monday through Saturday at noon and Sundays at 10:30 a.m. ($15); the Literary Garden District tour leaves from the lobby of the Ponchartrain Hotel (streetcar stop 13) on St. Charles Monday through Saturday at 11 a.m. ($15). Both last about two hours; call 524-0708.

Magic Walking Tours (588-9693) offers a similar barrage of mystery-history—a voodoo tour, a haunted-house roundup, a cemetery tour, a vampire tour, and a ghost hunt, in addition to relatively straight neighborhood walks—but they are generally accurate as such things go (they do not mistake one old mansion with a calm history for its sanguine neighbor, as do some self-anointed tour guides). You don't have to make reservations, but the meeting place for each tour differs, so call ahead. Adult tickets range from $9 to $13; kids come along for free.

New Orleans Spirit Tours also runs a Cemetery and Voodoo Tour that leaves the Royal Blend Coffee & Tea House at 621 Royal daily at 10:30 a.m. and 1:15 p.m. (no Sunday afternoon tour); the Ghost and Vampire Tour meets every night at 8 p.m. in the lobby of the Bourbon Orleans at 717 Orleans. Tours last about two hours ($15); call 314-0806.

The **Haunted History Tours** are by far the most theatrical of the bunch—the Lafitte-cum-Lestat hosts of the vampire tours can't be beat—but they do cover a lot of ground, and in grand Gothic style. (And why not? The owners, believers both, threw themselves a vampire wedding.) The Journey into Darkness vampire tour, which focuses both on real-life sites and cinematic backgrounds, leaves every night at 8:30 p.m. from St. Louis Cathedral near the Jackson Square gates (hey, even Lestat went to church there). The Voodoo-Cemetery tour leaves from Rev. Zombie's Voodoo Shop at 723 St. Peter Street daily at 10 a.m. and Monday through Saturday at 1:15 p.m. The Haunted History Tour, which focuses on reported hauntings and paranormal readings, also leaves from Zombie's at 2 p.m. and 8 p.m. daily. And the Garden District tour, which includes both architectural discourse and the obligatory salute to Anne Rice and Lafayette Cemetery, leaves from the Ramada Plaza Hotel at the corner of St. Charles and Jackson. Again, no reservations are necessary (except for large groups) and participants are asked to come 10 minutes early. All Haunted History Tours are $15, $7 for children 12 and under, and last about two hours. For more information call 861-2727.

If you religiously tour beautiful churches or seek out stained glass, be sure to visit the partially restored **St. Alphonsus Church** in the Irish Channel—the fictional Mayfair family church, and Anne Rice's family's church as well—which has some of the most astonishing stained-glass panels you will ever see, a contemporary but slightly smaller replica of the Black Madonna, and at least one of the graves of Pere Antoine.

SWAMP TOURS

The bayous of Louisiana are among the nation's great natural treasures, filled with herons and ospreys, bald eagles, wild hogs, turtles, nutria and mink, deer, bear, and, of course, alligators. Several companies offer guided boat tours. Among the most popular is **Lil' Cajun Swamp Tours** (call (800) 689-3213 or (504) 689-3213), whose guide, Captain Cyrus Blanchard, is as authentic as his Cajun accent and intimately familiar with the twists and turns of his home. If you can take the tour from the boat launch in Crown Point, it's $17 for adults, $15 for seniors, and $13 for children, but it's probably better to arrange with Blanchard for transportation, even though it kicks in another $14 per adult.

Honey Island Swamp Tours of Slidell (641-1769) offers professional naturalists as guides through this rich area; the cost is $20 for adults, $10 for children under age 12; tours begin at 10:30 a.m. and 1 p.m., but like Lil' Cajun, you'll pay extra for transportation from the city. **Gator Swamp Tours** also operate out of Slidell (call (800) 875-4287 or (504) 484-6100), and go through and even a bit beyond Honey Island Swamp with a short nature walk thrown in. Tours cost $20 for adults, $10 for children and begin at 9 a.m. and 2 p.m., with the usual extra charge for pick-up. If you call Enterprise and tell them this is your destination, they will give you a 10 percent car-rental discount.

Cajun Pride Swamp Tours combines visits to the Manchac bayou and two plantations, either Destrehan and San Francisco (Sunday, Monday, Wednesday and Friday afternoons) or Laura and Oak Alley (Tuesday, Thursday, and Saturday). Combo tours include lunch and cost $85 for adults and $60 for children. Call 467-0758 or (800) 467-0758.

Other swamp tours are offered by Jean Lafitte Swamp Tours (592-0560) and Gray Line (569-1401 or www.graylineneworleans.com). For fishing tours of the bayou, see page 205 in Part Nine: "Exercise and Recreation."

If you prefer the walking-tour approach to wildlife, the Barataria Unit of the Jean Lafitte National Park (589-2330) has trails and boardwalks through three different ecosystem routes: bottomland hardwoods, a cypress swamp, and a freshwater marsh. There are fine exhibits in the visitors center as well; take US 90 south and west of the city to state Highway 45/Barataria Boulevard and continue about seven miles.

Almost directly across Lake Pontchartrain from New Orleans, about 45 miles away on Highway 51, is the Joyce Wildlife Management Area. There, a 1,000-foot boardwalk strikes deep into Manchac Swamp and offers great vistas for bird watching, nature photography, and sketching. It's open sunrise to sunset. Stop by the Tangipahoa Parish visitors center (542-7520) at the Exit 28 ramp from I-55 for a free map and birding and animal guide.

A little farther is the Global Wildlife Center (624-9453) on Highway 40, about 15 miles east of I-55, one of only three preserves for endangered and threatened species of birds and animals in the country. It covers 900 acres and is devoted to safe breeding and free ranging of zebras, giraffes, camels (one hump and two), Wildebeests, llamas, gazelles, impalas, and even kangaroos. Staffers will drive you right up to the animals for a photo op, and since many of the animals have learned to beg for treats, you may get quite a close-up—maybe even a frog. (Admission to the park is free, though guided tours are not.)

RIVER CRUISES

Several boats cruise the nearby Mississippi River, some with meals, some with music, but to put it bluntly, a port is not the most scenic of sites. Huge tankers, rusting wharves, and old smokestacks are not exactly what Mark Twain saw when he fell in love with "Life on the Mississippi."

The steamboat *Cajun Queen* (call (800) 445-4109 or 524-0814), for example, offers a one-hour cruise leaving from in front of the IMAX/Aquarium complex to Chalmette Battlefield, site of the Battle of New Orleans. The boat churns past the old Jackson Barracks (where four commanding generals of the Civil War—P.G.T. Beauregard, Robert E. Lee, U.S. Grant, and George McLellan—all did Army time); the Doullut Houses, twin-glazed, white-brick "Victorian Steamboat Gothic" mansions;

the Greek Revival–cum–French Colonial home of Rene Beauregard, planter son of the general; and Pitot House. But the Doullut and Pitot houses are surrounded by smokestacks in a way that is much more obvious from a distance. The Beauregard House is now the battlefield visitors' center, so you can see it up close (and walk the battlefield itself) and visit the homes, too, if you like. (See "Zone 5" in "New Orleans Attractions" on page 276.) And once you're there, the boat turns around, the haphazard narration ends, and you go back past the old naval cruiser *Cabot,* onetime berth of President Bush, and the wharves to Poydras Street. At $11 ($20 including lunch), we really can't recommend it.

The sister-ship paddle wheeler *Creole Queen,* which offers a jazz dinner cruise at 7 p.m. and a two-and-a-half-hour lunch cruise, covers the same territory but with a little more spunk, for $39 and $22. Call for daily times and availability, or go to the ticket booth by the berth in front of the IMAX.

The *Natchez* (call (800) 233-BOAT or 586-8777), a three-deck sternwheeler that docks behind the Jax Brewery, also offers daytime and jazz dinner cruises with optional buffet (tickets for adults cost about $22.50, not including dinner). Call for schedules.

The compromise cruises, especially for those with children (since a couple of hours can be a long time to have to sit still), are probably the **John James Audubon Aquarium-Zoo cruise** or the free *Canal Street Ferry* across to Algiers (and perhaps Blaine Kern's Mardi Gras World). The *John James Audubon* cruises the seven miles between the Aquarium of the Americas and the Audubon Zoo. It leaves the Aquarium at 10 a.m., noon, and 2 and 4 p.m., and comes back from the zoo at 11 a.m. and 1, 3, and 5 p.m. Ticket prices vary, but you can expect to pay over $10 for an adult one-way fare; there are various combination fares that save you money. Boat/aquarium/zoo passes are $26.50 and $13.25, saving adults $5.50, and so on. In fact, if you buy tickets to all four related attractions—the zoo, the aquarium, IMAX, and a round-trip cruise ticket—you may save $8 or so. For more information call (800) 233-BOAT or 586-8777.

The *Canal Street Ferry* just putters back and forth every day except Christmas to Algiers, touching the foot of Canal Street every half hour from 6 a.m. to 11:30 p.m., with the last trip returning at midnight. (The ferry spends the night in Algiers, which you don't want to do.) If you want to visit Mardi Gras World, you can pick up a free shuttle bus at the Algiers dock.

There are also various overnight trips on the paddle wheelers *Delta Queen, Mississippi Queen,* and their younger sibling, the *American Queen.* The Delta Queen is a true wooden ship, while the two larger ones are steel ribbed, but all have etched glass, bright trim, antebellum-costumed staff, and so on. These are three-day to fortnight-long trips, and obviously take you out of New Orleans, although if you want to see Natchez and Memphis, you might be interested. Call (800) 543-1949 or 586-0631.

Self-Guided Tours
EXPLORING NEW ORLEANS'S DIVERSITY

New Orleans has a pleasant case of multiple-personality syndrome. Even in between the big festivals, you can indulge in self-designed tours spotlighting Mardi Gras, music or literature, Creole society, or history; or you can fill your days (and nights) dabbling in that suddenly pervasive supernatural stuff, hauntings and voodoo and vampire lore. If you're sticking to the family-rated attractions, such as those mentioned in Part Two: "Planning Your Visit to New Orleans," you'll be pleased to see how many of them are indoors, so you won't have to worry about the rainy-day blahs, which always hit kids the hardest.

Of course, not all attractions are encased in cemetery stone or museum glass. One easy thing to do is to check through the local papers for announcements of the week's cultural offerings (this is true for music, garden, church, and home tours, as well as special receptions and taste-of-the-town events, many of which may be held in historic sites or houses of special interest).

The *Times-Picayune* newspaper produces a special section on Fridays called "Lagniappe," which lists the best events—concerts, exhibits, tastings, art openings, even flea markets—of the weekend; this is also where you'll find cultural calendars. And remember that bookstores and coffee shops are traditionally neighborhood "bulletin boards" for such events.

But for a few informal do-it-yourself tour ideas, read on. Most of the sites in bold face are described in more detail in Part Twelve: "New Orleans Attractions" and Part Ten: "Shopping in New Orleans."

Mardi Gras and Music

Hangover-wary veterans of Carnival celebrations, or those who prefer the more sophisticated Mardi Gras parades of earlier decades, can get their fill of the frills by visiting the **Old U.S. Mint** and the free **Germaine Cazenave Wells Mardi Gras Museum** at Arnaud's Restaurant, both in the French Quarter; **Blaine Kern's Mardi Gras World** across the river, where the floats are made; and perhaps the smaller **Mardi Gras Museum** in Rivertown. There are also a few Mardi Gras outfits at the **House of Broel** on St. Charles in the Garden District.

You could also browse through mask and costume shops all over town, notably **MGM Costume Rentals** (1617 St. Charles, 581-3999), which has thousands of outfits from the studio's old storerooms; **Momus Masks** (638 St. Peter, 524-6300); **Masquerade Fantasy** (1233 Decatur, 593-9269); or the **Little Shop of Fantasy** (523 Dumaine, 529-4243).

If you're interested in the history of jazz, surprisingly, there isn't as much as you might expect. Start by calling **Cradle of Jazz** tours to make an appointment with one of their guys on the beat (282-3583). The first museum stop for you is also the **U.S. Mint,** which has a rare collection of early instruments; then browse the bins at area record stores (see Part Ten: "Shopping in New Orleans"). There is no trace of the famed Storyville red-light district, where jazz is generally said to have been born, although there is a re-creation and figures of some famous musicians in the **Musée Conti Wax Museum. Congo Square** in Armstrong Park still hosts some concerts, but it is not a neighborhood to visit without knowledgeable company. At night, however, be sure to check out **Preservation Hall** on St. Peter Street, a sort of living-history music museum.

Cruise Bourbon Street and you can still find a little Dixieland struggling to be heard through the rock-and-roll din. Try the **Famous Door** at Bourbon and Conti Streets, **Maxwell's Cabaret** on Toulouse between Chartres and Royal, the **Mystick Den** in the Royal Sonesta Hotel, or **Lafitte's Blacksmith Shop. Donna's Bar & Grill** on North Rampart presents only brass bands, but very good ones. Sunday jazz brunches are popular all over town (the **Court of Two Sisters** offers a jazz buffet for lunch every day). If you're more into zydeco or Cajun or gumbo music, make sure to check the schedules at the legendary **Tipitina's** on Tchoupitoulas Street and its new French Quarter offshoot, or at its across-the-street neighbor, the **House of Blues** on Decatur. For some foot stomping, go take a free Cajun dance lesson at happy hour at **Alex Patout's** bar on Bourbon Street. For more on jazz and music clubs, see the profiles in Part Eight's nightlife section.

Despite the city's history, literary tours are a little harder when self directed, primarily because only a few of the former writers' haunts are identifiable from the street (but we've pointed some out in the walking tours). Your best bet is to see the listings in the "Special-Interest Tours" section earlier in this part.

History and Culture

American-history buffs have an easy time setting their agendas: the **Cabildo** and **Presbytere** complex on Jackson Square; the **Historic New Orleans Collection; the National D-Day Museum, the Confederate Museum, Jackson Barracks Military Museum,** and **Chalmette Battlefield.**

As for historic houses, there are a number that are maintained as museums and decorated with original or period furnishings. For a quick-time dance through New Orleans history, compare the 1792 **Merieult House** of the New Orleans Historic Collection (a must-see); the West Indies plantation-style **Pitot House,** circa 1800; the **Hermann-Grima House,** which shows the influence of early nineteenth-century American society on traditionally Creole architecture; the **Beauregard-Keyes House,** an 1826 "raised cottage" that in its time sheltered both General P.G.T. Beauregard and novelist Frances Parkinson Keyes; and the 1857 **Gallier House Museum,** home of one of the city's premier architects. There is also the **1850 House,** a restored middle-class residence in the Pontalba Apartments on Jackson Square, and **Longue Vue Gardens.** All these sites are profiled in other chapters, along with a few others that are open for viewing only by appointment. And throughout the book, certain buildings of interest are cited as you may come upon them.

As famous as the Garden District is, few buildings there are actually open to the public—but then, the exteriors are what really distinguish them. We have put together a limited walking tour of the area and a bit of streetcar touring later in the chapter.

If you have time, you should take an excursion to the great plantations west of town, but that requires some extra planning, especially if you want to spend the night in the country, or need professional guidance: see the section on plantation tours below. Similarly, if you're captivated by Cajun culture, you'll want to head a few hours west to Lafayette and its environs, but that almost certainly requires two days. See "Cajun Country Festivals" on page 77.

Don't overlook the **New Orleans Museum of Art** in City Park. On the off chance that you happen to be a fan of the Impressionist painter Degas, note that the **Edgar Degas House** at 2306 Esplanade Avenue, where he may have finished as many as 17 works, has recently been restored as a bed-and-breakfast, but visitors are welcome to look around (821-5009 or www.degashouse.com). In fact, there are several houses in town with Degas connections: the building that now houses Brennan's Restaurant was originally built for his great-grandfather, Don Vincenze Rilleaux, and the Pitot House for his great-grandmother, Maria Rilleaux. The Musson House, at 1331 Third Avenue (call (800) 755-6730) in the Garden District, was built for his uncle, who later built the Degas House; and some sources claim the Waldhorn Galleries building on Royal Street was built for Don Vincenze Rilleaux, too. The offices pictured in Degas' masterpiece, "A Cotton Office in New Orleans," were at 407 Carondelet in Factor's Row. There's a tour in itself.

Anyone interested in black Southern culture should take the subway out to **Tulane University's Amisted Research Center,** the world's largest collection of arts and letters on race history, both in this country and elsewhere. Contemporary black art is the specialty of **La Belle Galerie** (309 Chartres, 529-3080); **YA/YA** (628 Bayonne, 529-3306); **Barrister's Gallery** (1724 O. Haley Boulevard, 525-2767), and the **Stella Jones Gallery** in the Bank One Center (201 St. Charles, 568-9050).

The Great Hereafter

If you love old churches, make sure to see **St. Louis Cathedral** in Jackson Square, **St. Patrick's** in the Warehouse/Arts District, and the remarkable but only partly restored **St. Adolphus** in the Irish Channel; for quirkier saints, visit **Our Lady of Guadalupe** in the Central Business District and the **Chapel of St. Roch's** east of the French Quarter. If you're particularly interested in stained glass, which is the real treasure at St. Adolphus, be sure to contact the **Preservation Resource Center** (923 Tchoupitoulas, 581-7032) to see when their next "Stained Glass in Sacred Places" tour is scheduled. Also, see the Garden District walking tour for directions to the Tiffany Glass at Tulane University.

If, on the other hand, it's cemeteries you love, you can either experience them straight or gussied up with vampire and voodoo lore. You can visit several of the "cities of the dead," the most famous being **St. Louis Cemetery No. 1** (where the tomb of the city's famous voodoo madam Marie Laveau still gets nightly petitions) and **Lafayette Cemetery** in the Garden District (where Anne Rice's creation, Lasher, is "buried" in a cast-iron tomb), but you should never go after dark, and preferably go in a group even during the day. Your best bet is to drive out to **Lake Lawn Metairie Cemetery,** which has all the extravagant tombs you could want to see. You can tour **Gallier House,** but the guides there probably won't mention the sometimes residence there of the Vampire Lestat.

If voodoo queens and vampire lovers are your thing, you can, uh, drink your fill. There are now probably as many "haunted," "voodoo," or "magic" tours of New Orleans as general history ones, though not all are particularly serious; see "Walking on the Dark Side" on page 223 for more information. Or stop into the **New Orleans Voodoo Museum,** or the **Voodoo Spiritual Temple** (828 North Rampart, 522-9627).

NEIGHBORHOOD WALKING TOURS

Okay, this is the fun part, at least as far as we're concerned—putting the "tour" back in the "tourist," so to speak. We've designed three routes for you, one in the French Quarter, one giving the flavor of the Garden District, and a third to help orient you to the newer pleasures of the Warehouse/Arts District and a bit of the Central Business District (CBD) at the same time.

How long they will take you depends on your pace and whether you stick to the sidewalk; you can, of course, stop at any museum or site that interests you. But none is either exhausting or exhaustive (to be frank, we think most walking tours tell you more than you need or want to know). These are just pleasant, informative, and intriguing strolls—a little history, a bit of legend, some literary notes, architectural details, and anecdotes. The French Quarter walk is the longest, of course, but then there are the greatest number of opportunities to sit, get something to eat or drink (remember, alcohol dehydrates), or duck into a store. The Garden District tour is the shortest, but it opens onto several other options, including Audubon Park, the zoo, the Riverbend neighborhood, etc.

The Vieux Carré/French Quarter (Zone 1)

It's nicer to think of the Quarter as the "old block" because there are so many influences at play on the tour: Spanish, German, American, and African-Caribbean, as well as French. Our route is divided into two dou-ble-loop halves, somewhat as though a huge E-3 monogram had been printed over the map with the two middle strokes meeting in front of St. Louis Cathedral. The longer part comes first, so that you can stop midway if you like and have an easier return. (This is also designed to help you get the layout of the Quarter in your head and not worry about going too far astray, because the loops go out and come back within view of the cathedral spire.)

The tour begins in the heart of **Jackson Square,** with a mental salute to the statue of General Andrew Jackson. As pointed out in "A Too-Short History of a Fascinating Place," in Part One, this was originally called Place d'Armes by the French, re-accented to Plaza de Armas by the Spanish, and altered permanently after the glorious victory of 1815. It was also the "inspi-ration," or in-spite-ation, for Lafayette Square in the American sector. The statue was erected to honor the hero of 1815, of course, but the inscription, which reads, "The Union must and shall be preserved," was added by federal forces during the Civil War occupation. (To be fair, it is an accurate expres-sion of Jackson's political sentiments.)

Straight before you is **St. Louis Cathedral,** the oldest cathedral in the United States (and even at that, this is the third church to occupy that space since 1722). Constructed in 1794, it was partially remodeled in the late 1840s. The flagstone piazza just outside the church doors is officially called Place Jean Paul Deux, to commemorate the 1987 visit of Pope John Paul II.

To the left of the cathedral is the **Cabildo,** so named because during the Spanish administration, the governing council, or Cabildo, met here. To the left of that is the **Arsenal,** built in 1803 on the site of what had been a Spanish prison, and now, like the Cabildo, it is part of the Louisiana State Museum complex.

Walk around the corner of the Arsenal onto St. Peter, and then turn right into the short **Cabildo Alley** and left again into **Pirates Alley.** This is one of several places in which Jackson and Jean Lafitte are frequently said to have plotted strategy for the Battle of New Orleans, but unfortunately, the alley wasn't cut through until 1831. Its real name is Ruelle d'Orleans, Sud—Little Orleans Way, South. However, there are two spots of interest here. **Faulkner House Books,** at 624 Pirates Alley, is not only a fine Southern literature bookstore but also the house where Faulkner lived while working on his first novel. It borders **St. Anthony's Garden,** officially named the Cathedral Garden but long considered a memorial to the Capuchin Father Antonio de Sedella (the beloved "Pere Antoine," as the Creoles re-christened him), who arrived in 1779 and served the colony for nearly a half century. (The good father's garden was also, oddly, the most popular dueling ground for young aristocrats.) The monument in the middle of the garden was erected by the government of Napoleon III to honor 30 French marines who died serving as volunteer nurses during one of the great yellow-fever epidemics.

Pirates Alley ends at Royal Street; turn left onto Royal and begin enjoying the old buildings around you. Walk a block and cross St. Peter Street. In the next block, on your right, at 627 Royal Street, is the **Old Town Praline Shop,** on the site of an apartment that once was home to nineteenth-century French opera prodigy Adelina Patti and that still sweetly opens its lovely old courtyard to the public. Just beyond that at 613 Royal is the **Court of Two Sisters,** which a century ago was the dry-goods shop of Emma and Bertha Camors and is now a restaurant and jazz bar with its own fine courtyard and informal aviary.

At the next intersection, turn right onto Toulouse Street. On the left at 710 Toulouse, in what is now the Coghlan Gallery, is the house known as the **Court of Two Lions,** named for the two royal beasts that mount the gate pillars. It was bought in 1819 by Vincent Nolte, whose autobiography inspired the huge, and at one point hugely popular, novel-turned-movie *Anthony Adverse.* Across the street, at 727 Toulouse, in a literary small-world coincidence, is the **Hotel Maison de Ville.** There, in room No. 9, lived and wrote Tennessee Williams.

At the next corner, turn left onto Bourbon Street (you can't miss it!), and after one block turn right again onto St. Louis Street. Halfway up on the left at 820 St. Louis is the **Hermann-Grima Historic House,** one of the finest examples of early American architectural shifts and well worth coming back to tour.

At the corner of Dauphine Street, look catty-corner across to 727 Toulouse and the **Audubon Cottages,** also run by the Hotel Maison de Ville; John James Audubon lived in No. 1 while writing and painting his 1821 masterpiece, *Birds of North America.* In the next block of Dauphine Street (turn left) are some buildings with less illuminated histories: at 415 Dauphine is the Dauphine Orleans, whose lounge, **May Bailey's Place,** used to be a bordello (and they can prove it). And at the corner of Conti Street is the **Déjà Vu** bar, said to be haunted and more reliably said to have housed an 1880s opium den.

At the corner of Conti look right; halfway up the block is the **Musée Conti Wax Museum,** but it's not worth staring at unless you're ready to visit it. If not, keep strolling along Dauphine to Bienville Street and turn left, back toward Bourbon Street. Halfway down on the left is the **Arnaud's** complex, which includes not only the restored old mansion of a restaurant (potted palms and ceiling fans, leaded glass, and mosaic tile), dining rooms filled with krewe memorabilia, and a fine old-fashioned bar, but the **Germaine Wells Mardi Gras Museum** upstairs, where you can view for free the fine collection of Carnival costumes.

When you get to Bourbon Street, turn left one block back to Conti and right again to Royal Street; turn left. Now, remember that Royal Street was once the financial center of town. On the right, at 334 Royal Street, is the **French Quarter Police Station,** housed in the 1826 Bank of Louisiana building (it has also served as the state capitol, among other things). On the left, at 343 Royal Street, is the **Waldhorn Company** antique store, a huge, balconied, and wrought iron–decorated three-story Spanish Colonial edifice built around 1800 as the Bank of the United States. And in the next block, just past Conti Street, is the old **Manheim Galleries,** designed in 1818 by U.S. Capitol architect Benjamin Latrobe as the Louisiana State Bank (look for the "LB" entwined in the forged ironwork on the balcony).

Across the street at 417 Royal is the celebrated **Brennan's Restaurant,** originally built for Edgar Degas's Spanish grandfather. A few years later it was sold and became yet another bank office, the Banque de la Louisiane, gaining its own wrought-iron monogram in the balcony, a "BL." A few years after that it was sold again, this time becoming the private residence of the socially prominent Martin Gordon—Andrew Jackson danced here several times when he returned to the city in 1828—but when Gordon went bankrupt, it was sold yet again, at auction, to Judge Alonzo Morphy (perhaps not coincidentally, he was the son-in-law of the auctioneer). Morphy is interesting for two reasons: in the 1850s, his son Paul became the world chess champion at 21, and before buying the house at 417, he lived in what is now the Beauregard-Keyes House (see below).

At **437 Royal,** in what is now the Cohen rare-coins gallery, was the Masonic Lodge where pharmacist Antoine Peychard served his fellow Masons his special after-dinner drink, poured out into little egg cups. The word for the cups was "coquetier," which some people believe became "cocktail," and Peychard himself became immortalized as a brand of bitters. (His tonic included absinthe and Sazerac-de-Forge cognac, the original Sazerac cocktail.)

The huge white building that takes up the whole **400 block of Royal** on your right was built just after the turn of the century as the civil-courts building. Later it housed the Louisiana Department of Wildlife and Fisheries and its wildlife museum; the U.S. Circuit Court of Appeals for the Fifth Judicial District; and was most recently (having been wrested back from the feds by the state) expensively renovated for the Louisiana Supreme Court. It was also used as the setting for Oliver Stone's "JFK."

Cross St. Louis Street to the TV-station building at **520 Royal** and walk through to the fine four-sided courtyard; take note of the "S" worked into the fan-shaped ironwork at the left corner of the third-floor balcony. In the early nineteenth century, this was built for wine merchant and furniture maker Francois Seignouret, who always used to carve that same initial into his furniture. The straightforward Spanish building at **536 Royal** was constructed just after the second great fire, in 1794; the three-story Maison LeMonnier at **640 Royal,** built in 1811, was considered the city's first "skyscraper." (The fourth story was added in 1876.) Note the initials "YLM," for Dr. Yves LeMonnier, in the wrought iron of the balcony.

Across the street, at 533 Royal is the **Historic New Orleans Collection** and the **Merieult House.** The Collection, which faces onto Royal, often has fine historical exhibits (a small but first-class assortment of Mardi Gras costumes, early propaganda posters promising streets of gold to would-be settlers, etc.) and is open and free. It also houses the finest research archives in the city, open to scholars only. Behind it is the late-eighteenth-century Merieult House, one of only two important structures to survive the great fire of 1794, and a nineteenth-century cottage, which are now open for tours with paid admission. Madame Merieult, née Catherine McNamara, had a head of Irish copper that made her the toast of New Orleans. And when she and her husband visited Paris, Napoleon offered her her own castle in return for parting with her hair, which he wanted to make into a wig to woo the Sultan of Turkey (who himself wanted to woo a reluctant harem lady) into an alliance. The high-spirited Merieult refused, however.

Go another block along Royal Street and stop at the corner of St. Peter Street. The **Royal Cafe** building, one of the most popular postcard and photograph subjects in town, is sometimes called the LaBranche House, and its oak-and-acorn-pattern wrought-iron balconies are in very fine condition. Actually, there are 11 LaBranche row houses altogether, built in the 1830s by a sugar planter, that run from the corner of Royal around the block of St. Peter toward Pirates Alley.

Turn right down St. Peter Street. On the right, at the corner of Chartres Street, is **Le Petit Théâtre du Vieux Carré,** home to the country's oldest continuously operating community theater (dating from a 1916 production in the Pontalba Apartments). The whole building is a sort of theatrical set: built in 1922, it's a faithful reproduction of the eighteenth-century residence of Joseph Xavier de Pontalba, last Spanish governor of New Orleans. The chandeliers and the courtyard fountain are of more recent origin; the wrought-iron balcony rail inside the theater is real, though, made in 1796. Le Petit Théâtre is believed to be haunted by a *Phantom*-like, well, phantom, in the balcony, who has been "photographed"; the now-defunct Society for Paranormal Research claimed to have recorded him several times.

Glance across the corner at the back of the Arsenal, and you will see that we have looped back toward Jackson Square for the first time. Now turn your back again and head out along Chartres Street, which is full of strange and wonderful shops and old facades. After you cross Toulouse, look left; at 514 Toulouse is the **New Orleans Pharmacy Museum,** housed in the 1816 shop (believed to have been designed by architect J.N.B. DePouilly) of apothecary Louis Defilho Jr. A little beyond, at the corner of Chartres and St. Louis Streets is the **Napoleon House,** which may look as though the entire plaster interior were about to collapse but which has probably seen more hard living than even its French Quarter peers and remains a favorite of locals despite the tourists. It owes its name to the loyal sentiments of pirate Jean Lafitte (yes, again), New Orleans mayor Nicholas Girod, and various other Creole leaders who fixed up the 1797 house and offered it to the deposed emperor, who was then languishing on the island of St. Helena. A plot was under way to rescue him when he died in 1821. (The third-floor "Appartement de l'Empereur" has been restored in real style, but can only be rented for private functions.) Make sure you look beyond the aging bar to the ageless courtyard.

If you're a fan of Paul Prudhomme, you can walk one more block and sniff the spicy air outside **K-Paul's Louisiana Kitchen** at 416 Chartres; then turn left at Conti Street and head toward Decatur Street. Turn left again onto Decatur and the "new New Orleans," the big-name franchise promenade, stretches out before you. As you head back toward Jackson Square, you pass the Hard Rock Cafe opposite St. Louis Street, the Crescent City Brewhouse, the Millhouse/Jax Brewery complex with its Hooters, and so on. By the time you make it to the square, and see those silly mules in their hats and ribbons, you'll be delighted to look right and mount the steps up to **Washington Artillery Park** and the **Moonwalk** overlooking the river.

Now settle yourself in for a cup of reviving coffee at the **Café du Monde,** tour the caricaturists or just relax in Jackson Park. This is the end of Loop 2, and intermission time for the tour.

Here beginneth Loop 3, as they used to say. Walk along St. Ann Street from Decatur toward Chartres, looking up at the **Pontalba Apartments.** Halfway up the block, at 525 St. Ann, is the **1850 House,** a restored three-story apartment showing how a middle-class Creole family lived at the time the Baroness Micaela Almonester Pontalba built her still-sought-after apartments. This is another part of the Louisiana State Museum, and tickets can be bought here for all LSM buildings. Right next to it, at 529 St. Ann, is a **Louisiana visitors center,** with scores of brochures, maps, and coupons. Intriguingly, while the state of Louisiana owns the block of apartments along St. Ann, the city of New Orleans owns the opposite block along St. Peter, including No. 540, where in the mid-1920s, Sherwood Anderson wrote *Dark Laughter.*

At the corner of St. Ann and Chartres is the **Presbytere,** the fourth Louisiana State Museum property right on Jackson Square, and the most conventional of the buildings in that it hosts both permanent and rotating exhibits about New Orleans and Louisiana history, maritime culture, society, portraiture, and decorative arts. Its most famous possession is Napoleon's death mask.

Walk past the door of the Presbytere and turn right up the 1830s flag-stone walkway called **Pere Antoine's Alley,** which borders St. Anthony's Garden on the other side. (Like Pirates Alley, its official name is more pedestrian: Ruelle d'Orleans, Nord—Little New Orleans Way, North.) Jog left onto Royal and then right onto Orleans Street to the Bourbon Orleans Hotel on your right. The **Orleans Ballroom,** which has now been restored within the hotel complex, was built by entrepreneur John Davis in 1817 to house theatrical productions and opera—and, although some of the official walking tours don't mention it, it was also the site of the famous Quadroon Balls, where Creole aristocrats formally courted mixed-race beauties for their concubines (see Part One's "A Too-Short History of a Fascinating Place"). It apparently served, as did many public buildings, as a hospital during the Civil War, and in 1881 was acquired by an order of black nuns to serve as an orphanage and school. The order sold the building about 30 years ago to the hotel, and there have been rumored ghost sightings, including one of a Confederate soldier and another of a young woman, about the building.

Turn right at Bourbon Street and there on the corner is **Marie Laveau's House of Voodoo,** one of the more popular spots for tarot readings, charms, and souvenirs. Keep strolling past St. Ann and Dumaine Streets to St. Philip; on the left, at 941 Bourbon, is **Lafitte's Blacksmith Shop,** yet another probably apocryphal site but much loved. The story is that the Lafitte brothers, Jean and Pierre, used the blacksmith shop as a front for their smuggling network, but although there are deeds of ownership on the property dating to the early 1770s, none indicates a smithy. Still, it's architecturally interesting—one of the last bits of post-and-brick construction, which means that the bricks were set inside a wooden frame because the local clay was so soft—and is still a great candlelight jazz bar that draws locals even more than tourists. (It's such an old reliable that a few years ago, three sheriff's deputies were moonlighting behind the bar when a fugitive came in for a drink; they arrested him on the spot.) It was also the favorite watering hole of Tennessee Williams.

Continue down Bourbon two more blocks to Gov. Nicholls Street and turn right. Locate 721 Gov. Nicholls Street and the **Thierry House,** built around 1814 to a design proffered by Benjamin Latrobe when he was only 19 years old. Its neoclassical Greek style inspired the whole Greek Revival that so characterized Creole architecture.

At the end of the block turn the corner right again onto Royal. On the left corner, at 1140 Royal, is what is still known as the **LaLaurie House,** and to tour guides as *the* Haunted House. In 1834, it was the home of Delphine LaLaurie, a sort of Creole Elizabeth Bathory, who hosted many brilliant and elaborate soirées there, which despite their popularity fueled gossip about the pitiable appearance of many of her servants. Several of these slaves committed suicide, or so LaLaurie said. One neighbor reported that LaLaurie had savagely beaten a young black girl, who shortly thereafter "fell" from the roof to her death, but a court merely fined her. But on April 10, 1834, when the house caught fire, neighbors, hearing the screams of slaves, broke in to find them chained in a secret garret, starving and bearing the marks of torture. Rumors spread that Madame LaLaurie herself might have set the fire. The house was stormed, and she and her family barely escaped, making their way to Europe. She never returned, although the house was rebuilt, but her body was smuggled back to New Orleans and secretly buried. Some people swear they have heard the shrieking of slaves and the snapping of whips at night, and it is a very popular late-night tourist stop for ghost hosts. Madame LaLaurie is so famous, in fact, that she is memorialized at the Musée Conti Wax Museum.

The neighboring buildings have a much finer reputation, fortunately. Just alongside at 1132 Royal Street is the **Gallier House Museum,** built in 1857 by James Gallier, Jr., son of the architect of the city hall and a prominent architect himself. He designed the building with many ingenious and then-rare fixtures. The house is administered as a museum by Tulane University.

Continue on Royal, past St. Philip, to 915 Royal, where the wrought-iron fence that gives the **Cornstalk Hotel** its name holds court. It was cast in the 1830s in Philadelphia for Dr. Joseph Biamenti as a present for his homesick Midwesterner wife, and its twin can be seen in the Garden District in front of the house at 1448 Fourth Street.

Across the street at **900, 906,** and **910 Royal** are the three Miltenberger houses, built in 1838 and now housing art galleries. The granddaughter of one Miltenberger was Alice Heine, the Barbara Hutton or Pamela Harriman of her day; she married first the Duc de Richelieu and then moved on to Prince Louis of Monaco.

Turn right onto Dumaine and duck up to the **New Orleans Historic Voodoo Museum** at 724 Dumaine, which is part museum (some pretty grisly), part souvenir shop/fortune-telling temple, and part tour central. Then double back down a block to 632 Dumaine and **Madame John's Legacy,** which is put forth by many historians as the oldest existing building in the lower Mississippi River valley. It was originally built between 1724 and 1726 for Don Manuel Lanzos, the captain of the regiment; but it was either repaired or entirely rebuilt to the same design (hence the debate) after the Good Friday fire of 1788. In either case, it is a fine example of French Colonial architecture of the style called a "raised cottage," with a steeply pitched room and dormers, living quarters high above flood level, half timbering on the back of the rear stairs on the second floor (called "columbage") and storage below. The name comes from "Tite Poulette," a short story by the nineteenth-century writer George Washington Cable, about a beautiful quadroon whose white lover wills her the house on his deathbed. It is now part of the state museum complex.

At the corner of Chartres glance right—there it is, Jackson Square—and then turn left onto Chartres for the final loop. At Ursuline Street, turn the corner just long enough to peek at the **Hotel Villa Convento,** 616 Ursuline Street. It's a respectable guest house now, but legend points to it as the famous House of the Rising Sun bordello. Now go back down Ursuline to Chartres and turn left. Just around the corner at 1113 Chartres is the **Beauregard-Keyes House,** built by wealthy auctioneer Joseph Le Carpentier and his son-in-law Judge Alonzo Morphy (see Brennan's, above). In its time it was home to Confederate hero General P.G.T. Beauregard and novelist Frances Parkinson Keyes. Keyes wrote two novels about previous occupants while living here (perhaps she was haunted); the better known is about General Beauregard and is entitled *Madame Castell's Lodger,* and the second one, entitled *The Chess Player,* is about Paul Morphy.

Across the street on the corner of Ursuline and Chartres is the **Old Ursuline Convent,** the strongest candidate for oldest building in Louisiana. Designed in 1745 and completed in 1752, it is the only structure that we know for sure survived the great fires at the end of the eighteenth century. (The Sisters of St. Ursula themselves arrived in 1727, and lived in the meantime in a building at Bienville and Chartres.) It was not only the first nunnery in the state; it was the first orphanage, the premier school for Creole children, and the first school for black and Indian children as well. Between 1831 and 1834 it housed the state legislature—the ultimate proof of charity.

Continue down Ursuline to Decatur and turn right, back toward Jackson Square. The gold-plated warrior astride her fearless steed is, of course, Joan of Arc, the patron saint of France, and a gift to this still-French city from the French government. (She has been almost as restless as her namesake: this is the statue's third location in about five years.) The **French Market** runs along your left, with the tracks of the Riverfront Streetcar beyond it; shops and restaurants line Decatur on both sides. At St. Philip Street look left and locate the National Park Service office peeking through from North Peters; then keep on, back to the Café du Monde, or stop at any of the little cafes along the way. Even better, stop by the legendary **Tujague's** on Decatur at Madison; the long stand-up bar is a New Orleans tradition. The bar itself, which came from Paris back in 1827, is nearly 300 years old. And it was probably here that O. Henry, if he did borrow the pseudonym from a bartender, first got the idea, because he was a regular.

The Garden District (Zone 3)

Although some guidebooks list scores of homes in the Garden District as historically or architecturally important, they are mainly so to real devotees, especially as virtually all are private residences and can only be glimpsed from the outside. You may well see all you want to see by just staying on the St. Charles Avenue Streetcar on the way to Audubon Park. So we have designed a fairly limited walk-through, one that will give you the flavor of the district and several of the celebrity highlights. If you go in the later morning, you may find a lunch stop at the famous Commander's Palace convenient. If you are enjoying the stroll, you can just keep wandering and admiring the facades. (If the present owners are working in the yard, you might stop and ask if they know much about the history of their homes; most of them are quite knowledgeable.) If you are seriously interested, contact the New Orleans Visitors Bureau about the Spring Fiesta, which starts the Friday after Easter and includes many garden and house tours.

The Garden District is the second-largest historic district in the United States, encompassing 10,700 structures. It is usually said to be bounded by St. Charles Avenue and Magazine Street (on the north and south sides, more or less) and Jackson and Louisiana Avenues on the east and west. But neighboring streets continue to claim relationship, and there is now what is sometimes called a "Lower Garden District"—lower as in Downtown—to the east back toward Lee Circle. Its look is so different from the French Quarter that it almost seems like another country, and in fact it almost was. This was the "American Quarter," the area where the rich, the *nouveau riche,* and the well connected from all over the United States built extravagant mansions to show up their new fellow citizens of the Creole aristocracy.

We suggest you start by taking the St. Charles Streetcar to Jackson Street. At 2220 St. Charles is the **House of Broel,** which is both a dollhouse museum and a full-sized one, as well as a bridal and haute couture salon. It was originally built as a two-story pied-à-terre for a planter and his family, but in the 1890s, tobacco tycoon Simon Hernsheim had the whole building lifted and added a new Victorian first floor. It is open for tours, if you want to stop or circle back (522-2220).

Across the street at the end of the block, on the corner of Philip Street at **2265 St. Charles,** is a house that was designed by James Gallier Jr., for

Lavinia Dabney in the late 1850s, about the time his own home in the Vieux Carré was completed. Gallier designed it as Greek Revival; the Ionic columns and side galleries were added later. Across Philip, at **2336 St. Charles** is, for comparison, a Greek Revival raised cottage designed by his father, James Gallier Sr., at just about the same time.

At the corner of First Street turn left, walk a block to Prytania, and turn the corner to get a view. At 2343 Prytania is the Second Empire–style **Louise S. McGehee School,** also known as the Bradish Johnson House after the wealthy sugar trader for whom it was built in 1872, for a then-astonishing $100,000, probably by New Orleans–born, Paris-trained architect James Freret. It has been a prestigious girls' school since 1929; the carriage house is the gymnasium, and the stables have been turned into a cafeteria. According to an odd legend, none of the girls, or anyone else, has been born, died, or married within its walls.

Across the street from the school at 2340 Prytania is what sometimes is called **Toby's Corner,** built sometime before 1838 for Philadelphian Thomas Toby, and believed to be the oldest house in the Garden District. It is put in the shade in both senses, however, by the huge Spanish moss–draped live oak on the grounds, which is several hundred years old.

Continue down First Street, noting the ornate cast iron in front of the circa 1869 Italianate home at **1331 First Street** and the matching galleries at the remarkably similar house at **1315 First Street;** both were designed by Irish immigrant Samuel Jamison in 1869.

Just past Chestnut Street, on the corner at **1239 First Street,** is the 1857 mansion once known as the Rose-Brevard House—it was built for merchant Albert Brevard, and its elaborate ironwork has a rose pattern—but now far more famous as the residence of novelist Anne Rice and the setting of the best-selling book *The Witching Hour.* The original structure cost only $13,000 (the hexagonal wing was added a few years later); restoring the gates would cost that now. Visitors are allowed in between 1 p.m. and 3 p.m. on Monday only, but the author has been known to make a brief appearance for photos and autographs.

Across the street, at **1236 First Street,** is a gorgeous Greek Revival mansion built as a wedding gift in 1847. Walk another block to Camp Street and look across the corner to the house at **1134 First Street,** built about 1850 for Judge Jacob Payne. It is also the home where one-time U.S. senator and former president of the Confederate States of America Jefferson Davis died in 1889.

Turn right onto Camp Street and walk to Third Street, turning right at the corner. The arched and eaved mansion at **1213 Third Street** was built during the Reconstruction for Irish carpetbagger Archibald Montgomery, president of the Crescent City Railroad. Continue on to the Italianate home at **1331 Third Street,** designed in 1853 by James Gallier Sr., for New

Orleans postmaster Michel Musson, who married Edgar Degas's aunt. (The elaborate cast-iron galleries were added later.)

Across Coliseum at **1415 Third Street** is the Robinson House, one of the Garden District's largest and most attractive homes: its curving front seems especially spacious because both stories are the same height, with identical iron balconies and columns. It was built just before the Civil War by architect Henry Howard for Virginia tobacco trader Walter Robinson, and is thought to have been one of the first homes in New Orleans to have indoor plumbing.

Turn left onto Coliseum Street and walk two blocks to Washington Street. On the corner is **Commander's Palace,** where you can stop for lunch or just cast an admiring glance at the courtyard (or finish the tour and circle back around). This stately old-liner of the Brennan's restaurant fleet has been a restaurant for well over a century, and owes its name not to a naval officer but to owner Emile Commander. It's terribly respectable now—it claims to be the birthplace of oysters Rockefeller, and nobody much has contested it—but back during Prohibition, the second story was a high-stakes, high-society bordello.

Behind the high brick walls of Washington and Coliseum is **Lafayette Cemetery,** named for the American sector it served, then the City of Lafayette. Laid out in 1833, the cemetery was designed for the well-to-do; its wide aisles were intended to carry extravagant funeral processions to elaborate tombs. But it was nearly filled within 20 years by victims of repeated epidemics. The cemetery has many fine examples of the above-ground tombs that are New Orleans trademarks, including the cast-iron tomb Anne Rice uses for the elemental spirit Lasher (the cemetery itself served as a setting for scenes from the movie version of *Interview with the Vampire*). The Jefferson Fire Company No. 22 tomb with its bas-relief firetruck is also here, as are other monuments that might look familiar to fans of the seminal film, *Easy Rider*. (Eternal rest or eternal bliss? In 1980, a Neiman Marcus executive and his bride were married here, on Friday, the 13th of June, wearing full black.) Unfortunately, even this cemetery is no longer safe to wander without company, and in any case the gate may be locked. However, if you are waiting at the Washington Street gate at 10:30 a.m. Monday, Wednesday, or Friday, you can hook onto the Save Our Cemeteries tour; or contact one of the commercial tour groups mentioned above in "Walking on the Dark Side."

Walk along the cemetery wall to Prytania and turn back to the right. (Actually, if you're a literary type, turn left and go to **2900 Prytania,** at Sixth Street; that boardinghouse was where Jazz Age icon F. Scott Fitzgerald lived in 1919–1920.) Glance down Fourth Street to **No. 1448** if you want to see the wrought-iron twin to the fence at the Cornstalk Hotel in the French Quarter. Continue on to **2605 Prytania** at the corner of Third Street: the guest house of this pointy-arched Gothic Revival house, designed by the senior Gallier in 1849, is a perfect miniature of the main house.

Just across Third Street at 2521 Prytania is the former Redemptorist Fathers chapel, **Our Lady of Perpetual Help**—"former" because the Italianate home, built in 1857 for a coffee merchant, had fallen into disrepair and has now been purchased, like several other dilapidated historic buildings in the District, by Anne Rice. Across from that, at 2520 Prytania, is the **Gilmour-Parker home,** a Palladium-fronted house built in 1853 for an English cotton trader named Gilmour and later sold to John Parker, father of a future governor. The building around the corner at **1417 Third Street** used to be its carriage house, but later has been considerably expanded.

The Queen Anne–Greek Revival–style hybrid **Women's Opera Guild House,** at the far end of the block, at 2504 Prytania Street, was designed by James Freret in 1858, except for the octagonal turret, which was added toward the end of the century and holds a music room and bedrooms. It was bequeathed to the Opera Guild by its last inhabitant, Nettie Seebold, and its collection of eighteenth- and nineteenth-century antiques, along with some Guild mementos, can only be viewed Mondays from 1 to 4 p.m. (a small donation is requested).

Turn left onto Second Street, walk back to St. Charles, and turn left again. At 2524 St. Charles, on the corner of Third Street, is what is known both as the Dameron House and more romantically—and far more widely, thanks to the publication of Anne Rice's *Violin*—as the **Claiborne Cottage.** That story has it that the Greek Revival raised cottage was the home of Bernard Xavier Phillipe de Marigny de Mandeville, son of one of the wealthiest and more influential Creoles of old New Orleans society, and his wife Sophie Claiborne, daughter of the diplomat who would become the first American governor of Louisiana. Their match marked the first great union of the two societies of New Orleans, but Marigny, who had inherited so much land and money, gambled so obsessively that he is said to have lost a million dollars—not in modern money, but a million dollars *then*—by the time he was 20. In fact, it may have been Marigny who brought back dicing from England: it became known to the Americans as "Johnny Crapaud's game," something like "the Frog's game," and eventually "craps." (Marigny tried to name Burgundy Street "Craps Street," but it didn't take.) Unfortunately, the more people he taught the game to, the more people he lost to. He still managed to live well, but by the time he died at 83, he was a pauper; the neighborhood of Faubourg Marigny is almost the last reminder of his huge holdings. Meanwhile, the house became a convent, a guest house, a rectory, and a school, and was nearly razed several times under various development schemes. However, in the 1950s, when Anne Rice was a teenager, her parents rented the house for several years, and *Violin* was inspired by her memories of the place. She has, needless to say, now purchased the property.

And here you are back at the streetcar.

The Warehouse/Arts and Central Business District (Zone 2)

This is a somewhat mixed tour, primarily pointing out historical buildings, but with a few arts sites thrown in. It has a rather dramatic finale, especially if you schedule it for the afternoon and wind up around dusk. If you are a more serious student of contemporary art, you should also plan to take a walk up and down Julia Street, from Commerce to St. Charles, where there are many fine galleries and studios.

With the World Trade Center on your left, walk along Convention Center Boulevard toward Lafayette Street. Look left down Poydras Street as you pass to flash a victory "V" back to the statue of **Winston Churchill** (the green is called English Place). Turn right at Lafayette and walk two blocks to South Peters Street and the **Piazza d'Italia.** (Remember the Spanish Plaza by the river? They don't call it the World Trade Center for nothing.) The Piazza d'Italia was designed by Charles Moore, and its fountain (shaped like Italy) and partial arches were supposed to suggest a classical ruin, but the heavy, and in many cases unresolved, construction in the neighborhood has added rather unkindly to the effect.

Continue on Lafayette until it runs into **Lafayette Square,** laid out in 1788 and named for the noble marquis who had joined the American Revolution. On the right is a 1974 sculpture by Clement Meadmore entitled "Out of There," and straight ahead, just inside the park, is the Benjamin Franklin monument created in 1871 by Hiram Powers. The statue in the center of the park of statesman Henry Clay, dedicated in 1860, originally stood at the intersection of St. Charles and Canal, and the place of honor in this park once belonged to a statue of the king of Spain. Clay was moved here in 1901, after serving as a gathering place for repeated anti-integration riots. And at the far side of the square, facing St. Charles Avenue, is the John McDonogh monument, portraying the philanthropist, who in the mid-nineteenth century endowed several public schools, as surrounded by grateful children (although until his will was known, he was considered a cranky old miser with radical ideas about educating slaves).

Turning left onto Camp Street (from Lafayette Street) notice the building on the left between Lafayette and Capedeville. The more or less Italian Renaissance building is now the **U.S. Court of Appeals for the Fifth Circuit,** but was built in 1914 as the post office.

Continue on Camp past Girod Street to **St. Patrick's Church** and its rectory. The high and narrow Gothic Revival building, built in the 1830s and for many years the undisputed high point of the area, was modeled after England's York Minster Cathedral by Irish architects Charles and James Dakin, and meant as a rival and rebuke to the close-minded French communicants of St. Louis Cathedral. (The shorthand for their attitude was, "God speaks only in French," though how He felt about canonical Latin is unclear.) Their revenge was complete in 1851, when St. Louis Cathedral was being rebuilt, because Bishop Antoine Blanc had to be ordained as archbishop in St. Patrick's. The design was completed by James Gallier Sr. (born James Gallagher in Dublin), who was responsible for the high, vaulted interior—the nave is 85 feet high, the tower 185—and ribbed sanctuary ceiling with floral bosses. The stained glass over the altar and the three large murals, painted in 1840 by Leon Pomarede, are very fine. (The one on the left shows St. Patrick baptizing the princesses of Ireland: take that, St. Louis!) The Italianate rectory to the church's left was built by Garden District and plantation architect Henry Howard in 1874. The pews, incidentally, are cypress.

At the end of the block, catty-corner across Julia Street, you can see what's called **Julia Row** or **the Thirteen Sisters,** a block of 13 red brick rowhouses of a type that was extremely popular among upper-class residents of the American sector from about 1825 (these were built in the early 1830s) to about 1885. Notice the fan-light transom windows, attic cornices, and iron balconies. These are among the most important buildings being restored in the Warehouse District, and in fact the offices of the Preservation Resource Center of New Orleans are at 604 Julia. (You might stick your head in and ask about their walking tour maps or architectural brochures, if you'd like to see more.)

Continue along Camp past St. Joseph Street to 900 Camp Street and the **Contemporary Arts Center.** This renovated 40,000-square-foot, turn-of-the-century warehouse is both a "living museum," with studios for practicing artists and rotating exhibits, and a theater, with two stages and sometimes concerts. Even the furniture is art—the glass-wave front desk, the lobby information board, the elevator panels, and the lighting sconces are all creations of fine local artists.

At the other end of the block at 929 Camp Street is the **Confederate Museum,** which has the second-largest collection of Confederate memorabilia (after Richmond's Museum of the Confederacy) in the nation. It is also the oldest museum in the state, designed in 1891 with a cypress hallway, 24-foot ceiling, and fireproof cases for its collection of restored battle flags. The body of Jefferson Davis, who died here in 1889 (see the Garden District tour above), lay in state at the museum before being taken to Richmond, and many of his family effects are here, along with uniforms, weapons, insignia, and photographs.

Turn the corner right onto Howard Avenue and you will see the greatest Confederate of them all, Robert E. Lee, on eternal vigilant guard against invasion from the north in the center of **Lee Circle.** (Talk about revered—he's not just on a pedestal, he's on a 60-foot pedestal.) The memorial was dedicated in 1884, and Jefferson Davis and New Orleans hometown hero P.G.T. Beauregard were still around for the ceremony.

This is becoming an even more important arts district: As you approach Lee Circle you will pass the Howard Memorial Library, an 1888 sandstone extravaganza by Romanesque Revival champion Henry Hobson Richardson that is being renovated as the **Roger Ogden Museum of Southern Art.** And facing the circle to the left of Howard Avenue is the **Lee Circle Center for the Arts.**

On the circle to Lee's back is the **K&B Plaza,** an indoor-outdoor sculpture garden including Isamu Noguchi's granite "Mississippi," commissioned for the plaza, and other pieces by an international group of artists including George Rickey, Frank McGuire, Michael Sandle, and Pedro Friedeberg. (The indoor gallery is open weekdays 8:30 a.m. to 4:30 p.m.)

Swing around Lee Circle to Andrew Higgins Drive; two blocks over, at Magazine street, is the D-Day Museum, easily spotted from here. Continue around the circle, watching out for streetcars, and head back downtown along St. Charles. Many of these buildings have great but sad histories—the three-story brick Greek Revival townhouse at **827 St. Charles** is the only survivor of three—but within a few years, many of them will be prime commercial territory again.

At 545 St. Charles, looking out toward Lafayette Square, is **Gallier Hall,** designed in the late 1840s by the senior James Gallier as City Hall for the Second Municipality (i.e., the American Sector) and one of the most beautiful examples of the Greek Revival style in the city—and many believe in the entire country. The figures on the pediment represent Justice, Liberty, and Commerce (the one toting barges and lifting bales). It is now a private office building with a theater in the basement.

Stay on St. Charles Avenue for several blocks to Common Street; turn left for two blocks and then go right onto Baronne Street. At 132 Baronne is the outlandish Alhambra-Moscovy romantic **Church of the Immaculate Conception,** informally known as the Jesuit Church. The original church, erected in the mid-nineteenth century, had so much wrought and cast iron, some 200 tons of it, that it had nearly collapsed after five years. It was replaced in 1930 by an almost identical structure which still has the old church's cast-iron pews and the bronze-gilt altar, designed by James Freret, which won first prize at the Paris Exposition of 1867. And except for rude intervention of the French Revolution of 1848, the statue of the Virgin Mary would have been installed at the Tuileries.

Go to the corner, turn right onto Canal Street, and head back toward the river. This was for many years "the" shopping area for upper- and middle-class New Orleanians ("I wore white gloves to come here," says one native), and after a dispiriting decline, Canal Street is coming back to life with a raft of brand-name shops and luxury hotels.

Past Decatur, at 423 Canal Street, is the restored Egyptian/Greek Revival **U.S. Customs House,** begun in the 1840s (when the Mississippi was within eyeshot) but not usable until 1889, and not fully completed until 1913. The statuary niches along the Decatur Street side are still unfilled. In the meantime, it housed Confederate prisoners of war during the Union occupation. The huge third-floor Marble Hall, with its 55-foot skylight and 14 marble columns, is breathtaking.

Finally, walk one last block of Canal and turn back onto Convention Center Boulevard. Top off your tour at **Top of the Mart,** a slowly rotating 500-seat bar on the 33rd floor of the World Trade Center building. It takes 90 minutes to make a complete circuit, and the view of New Orleans—from the riverfront around the business districts to the genteel old French Quarter—is especially attractive at night, when the bridges seem hung with Christmas lights and the cathedral spire salutes the sky. It's open until midnight most days and 2 a.m. on Saturdays; however, no one under 21 is admitted, so families will have to go instead to the 31st floor and use those giant telescopes made famous by the Empire State Building.

Plantation Tours and Excursions

It is unlikely that you will have enough time to visit the plantations as part of a business trip, and unless you have figured such an excursion into your family vacation schedule (and are planning to rent a car), you may have to settle for a half-day group tour.

There are some good tour packagers who can bus you to a few of the houses; among them **Tours by Isabelle** (391-3544), which offers a couple of different expeditions including an eight-hour, three-home tour, and **New Orleans Tours, Inc.** (call 592-0560 or (800) 543-6332); **Gray Line Tours** (call 587-0709 or (800) 535-7786) offers a seven-hour tour of Nottoway and Oak Alley, but the lunch is not included in the $45 fee. There are also steamboat tours, but they offer no more than a glimpse of the houses from the water, and so are not very satisfying for the time they require.

However, if you would like to strike out by yourself, we have laid out a few options, including a half-day's drive, a full day's tour, and an overnight route that would be a romantic highlight.

There are a half dozen houses along what is called River Road, and a seventh a bit to the south (plus many smaller houses, churches, etc.). What makes this statement a little misleading, is that some are on one side of the Mississippi, and the rest on the other. In fact, there is no great single "River Road." There is instead a pair of two-lane roads, one on each side of the river—generally Route 44 on the north bank and Route 18 on the south—

called various names as you continue west. Just try to keep a sense of where the river is, and watch for the house signs. It's not as difficult as it may sound—these are, after all, major tourist attractions and are well marked.

Because the tour companies are on tight schedules, they usually take Interstate 10 at least part of the way into plantation territory. However, we suggest you try a slightly more scenic route: Head west out of New Orleans on River Road (also marked as Route 44 or Jefferson Highway) and stay on the north side of the Mississippi River past Destrehan, San Francisco Plantation, Tezcuco Plantation, and Houmas House. Then cross the Sunshine Bridge (Route 70) to the southern bank of the river, taking Route 1 a bit farther west to Nottoway and then heading back east, mostly on Route 18 past Oak Alley and back to the city.

The ideal trip would be overnight, stopping for lunch at Texcuco (or holding out for dinner at Lafitte's Landing) and taking a room at Nottoway Plantation, where you can either have dinner or do the big breakfast thing. You can see Destrehan without leaving town; you could drive an hour or so and spend the night at Oak Alley. Or you could probably see Destrehan, San Francisco, Tezcuco, and Houmas and be back in New Orleans for dinner.

All the plantation homes described here have been immaculately restored and are open for tours. However, if you keep your eyes open, you will see many other fine old homes that are still private residences.

The first and closest is **Destrehan Manor** at 13034 River Road/LA 48, just eight miles west of the airport in Kenner (764-9315). Built in 1787 in the French Colonial style by a free man of color, it was given its wings just after the turn of the nineteenth century and renovated by the next generation into a Greek Revival style. Its Doric columns, double porch, and hipped roof will look very familiar to fans of the film *Interview with the Vampire,* and many of the haunted–New Orleans tours mention sightings and even alleged photos of phantasmic shapes here. Restored in 1970, Destrehan is the oldest intact plantation in the Lower Mississippi Valley. Admission is $8; open daily 9 a.m.–4 p.m.

San Francisco Plantation (535-2341 or (800) 322-1756) on Highway 44 a little beyond Reserve is an old and elaborately Gothic Creole-style home begun in the mid-1850s by a planter named Edmond Marmillion and finished in the most fantastical manner—double galleries, widow's walk, highly decorative mouldings and painting, carved woodwork—by his sons, one of whom remarked at the end of the construction that he was now "sans fruscin," or "without a penny." So the house was first called St. Frusquin, eventually corrupted to San Francisco. Its elaborate, almost paddle-wheeling look inspired the setting of Frances Parkinson Keyes' *Steamboat Gothic.* Admission: $8 adults, $4 ages 12–17, $3 ages 6–11, age 5 and under free; open daily, tours every 20 minutes 9 a.m.–5 p.m.

About 25 miles farther at 3138 Highway 44 is **Tezcuco Plantation** (call

(225) 562-3929), one of the bed-and-breakfast facilities (for $60–$160, you can stay in one of the cottages or in a room in the main house, take a tour, drink some welcoming wine, etc.). It also has a restaurant where you can have breakfast or lunch if you're going on. This was built just before the Civil War, using bricks made on the grounds, local timber, and, of course, slave labor. The owner was a veteran of the Mexican war, and gave the mansion the Aztec word for"resting place." The outbuildings include an African American cultural museum, a life-sized dollhouse, a chapel, and more. Admission: $9 adults, $8 seniors and AAA members, $7 ages 13–17, $4 ages 5–12, age 4 and under free; open 9 a.m.–5 p.m. The name, incidentally, comes from the Aztecs and means "place of quiet rest."

A couple of miles farther along 44/River Road at Highway 942 is **Houmas House** (call (225) 473-7841 or (888) 323-8314). It was named for the Indians who originally owned the land and was for decades the largest sugar plantation in Louisiana. The original house was only four rooms; what looks like the main house now, the two-and-a-half-story Greek Revival mansion with columns around three sides, was added on the front in 1840. Built to the fancy of a South Carolinian, it, too, was a film set, in this case for the Southern Gothic *Hush, Hush Sweet Charlotte* with Bette Davis. The hexagonal houses on either side, called "garconnieres," were used by the bachelor sons of the family (the "boys") or by house guests. Admission: $10 adults, $6 children ages 13–17, $3 ages 6–12, 5 and under free; open 10 a.m.–5 p.m. (closes at 4 p.m. November through January).

Retrace Highway 44 to Highway 70, cross the Sunshine Bridge (so named because a former Louisiana governor, Jimmy Davis, wrote the song "You Are My Sunshine") over the Mississippi River to Donaldsonville, and look right toward Frontage Street. There you'll see a famous restaurant called **Lafitte's Landing** (which burned in late 1998, but has since reopened); it has interest, as you may have guessed from the name. It used to be known as the Old Viala Plantation, and was supposed to have been one of the pirates' bases. In any case, his son and entrepreneurial successor, Jean Pierre Lafitte, married the Viala heiress.

From Lafitte's Landing, turn onto Highway 1/Mississippi River Road and head west again for about 15 miles. Near White Castle is **Nottoway Plantation Inn & Restaurant,** a spectacular and almost unique building which was called "the white castle" and so gave its name to the town. Nottoway, built in 1859 by John Hampden Randolph, is the largest plantation home in the South, a hybrid neoclassical beauty with 64 rooms, 22 enormous columns, and a series of staggered porches and bays. Inside is a spectacular ballroom with hand-carved Corinthian columns, plaster friezes, and crystal chandeliers, and a surprising list of then-rare conveniences such as hot and cold running water and gas lights. As the name suggests, you can have lunch or dinner (and swim in the walled garden that once held roses), or stay overnight with breakfast and a tour tossed into the $125–$250 room rate. Otherwise, the admission is $10, $4 for ages 6–12, ages 5 and under free; open 9 a.m.–5 p.m. with the last tour at 4:30 p.m.; call (225) 545-2730.

(Incidentally, when you get as far as Nottoway Plantation, you are only about another 30 miles from Baton Rouge, around which are other plantations and attractions. If you want to go on, contact the Baton Rouge Convention and Visitors Bureau, P.O. Box 4149, Baton Rouge, LA 70821, or (225) 383-1825, and ask for their tour brochures.)

Here's yet another option: If you have the time, or haven't worn out yet, you could instead go south from Donaldsonville on Highway 308 to **Madewood Plantation** on Bayou Lafourche (call (504) 369-7151), a widely admired 1848 Greek Revival manor whose modern travel-mag style restoration has earned it high ratings from *Travel & Leisure,* etc. Again, you can stay in the main house or the cottages and have dinner in the original dining room and a continental breakfast before moving on. Otherwise, admission is $6 for adults, $4 for children; open 10 a.m.–4 p.m.

If you still want to head back toward New Orleans, take Highway 18 from near the Sunshine Bridge about 15 miles to the east and look for the signs to **Oak Alley** (call (800) 44-ALLEY or (225) 265-2151), another Greek Revival beauty whose long drive between rows of 300-year-old live oaks, which gave it its nickname, has become famous through photographs as an example of antebellum architecture. (The real name was Bon Séjour, or "Pleasant Sojourn.") It was built in 1839, and has as many Doric columns, 28, as the oaks themselves. It also has several outbuildings that have been turned into overnight rooms ($95–125) and a restaurant open for breakfast and lunch if you just want to drive over from New Orleans. Admission is $10 adults, $5 students, $3 ages 6–12, age 5 and under free; open 9 a.m.–5:30 p.m. (closes at 5 p.m. November through February).

A few miles south of Oak Alley on Highway 18 is the beautifully preserved 1805 West Indies-style plantation, **Laura,** where Louisiana's multicultural heritage is even more obvious. Among the tours available are discussions of Creole life, German immigrants, slave history (there are slave cabins among the historic buildings), and the particular role of women landowners. Even more touchingly, it was here that Joel Chandler Harris heard and recorded the adventures of "Compair(sic) Lapin" and transformed them into the tales of "Br'er Rabbit." Tours are also given in French on Tuesdays and Thursdays. Admission is $8 for adults, $4 for children ages 3–17; open daily 9:30 a.m.–4:30 p.m.; call (225) 265-7690.

You can take Highway 18/River Road back to the intersection of Route 90, then take the Huey Long Bridge across the Mississippi back into New Orleans. Or go the other way, southwest, on Highway 18 to Route 641, cross the bridge to I-10 and go back that way.

Part Twelve

New Orleans Attractions

As you can tell from the walking tours and our suggestions in Part Two: "Planning Your Visit" about designing your own special-interest tour, New Orleans is a lot more, and a lot more interesting, than Bourbon Street. Some of the finest attractions, such as City Park and the New Orleans Museum of Art, the Historic New Orleans Collection, the Jackson Barracks Museum, and Longue Vue House and Gardens, are often overlooked as tourists rush to the more obvious sites. So we've tried to evaluate most of the attractions in a way that may help you choose what you want to see depending on who's in the party, what your interests are, and how in-depth you would like to get.

For convenience in cross-referencing, these profiles are grouped by zone and alphabetically. However, keep in mind that some cross-zone transportations—the St. Charles Avenue streetcar, the *John James Audubon,* and the Canal Street ferry—are attractions in themselves.

Incidentally, remember that most museums are closed on state as well as federal holidays, and in New Orleans that also means Mardi Gras and frequently All Saint's Day (November 1) as well as the more familiar dates such as Christmas. Many places have group-ticket rates, so if you are traveling with more than just your immediate family, call ahead and ask about discounts. Also remember that ticket prices have a way of inching up without warning, so carry a little extra with you or call in advance.

ZONE 1: THE FRENCH QUARTER
Aquarium of the Americas/IMAX Theater

Type of Attraction: A state-of-the-art and interactive marine museum with a good mix of science and fun

Location: Along the Mississippi Riverfront at the foot of Canal Street

Admission: Aquarium alone: $13.50 adults, $10 seniors, $6.50 kids ages
2–12. IMAX alone: $7.75 adults, $6.75 seniors, $5 kids age 12 and
under. Combination tickets: $17.25 adults, $14 seniors, $10.50 chil-
dren. Additional discount tickets available for boat/aquarium/zoo packages or boat/zoo/aquarium/IMAX.

Hours: Aquarium: Sunday–Thursday, 9:30 a.m.–6 p.m.; Friday and Saturday, 9:30 a.m.–7 p.m.; IMAX (shows every two hours): Sunday–Thursday, 10 a.m.–6 p.m.; Friday and Saturday, 10 a.m.–8 p.m.

Phone: 861-2537

When to Go: Early, if not to see it before it gets crowded, at least to get
timed tickets for later in the day, when the air conditioning may be
welcome

Special Comments: One of the 1990s generation of marine installations,
very pleasant and user-friendly and a best bet for mixed-age groups

Overall Appeal by Age Group:

Pre-School	Grade School	Teens	Young Adults	Over 30	Senior Citizens
★★½	★★★★	★★★★	★★★★	★★★★	★★★

Author's Rating: Visually and intellectually stimulating, with unusual care
taken to make legends both legible and intelligible. ★★★★

How Much Time to Allow: At least an hour for the aquarium, even if you
have restless children; two hours for IMAX, counting standing in line

Description and Comments   It's hard to go wrong here unless you are so
blasé that you can't get a thrill out of stroking the tough-suede skin of a small
sand shark (one of the most popular queues) or of marveling at the beautiful,
transparent, and snowflake-complex bodies of lacy jellyfish, one of the more
astounding exhibits. The museum houses several large permanent exhibits,
including a multilevel, multispecies Amazon rain forest, a penguin house,
Caribbean reef and Mississippi River environments, and a 400,000-gallon
saltwater mini–Gulf of Mexico with 14-foot glass walls and all the sharks and
stingrays any kid could desire. There is a cafe on the second floor and the
usual concessions at the IMAX. The IMAX rotates at least two movies a day,
mostly on environmental themes (even if they are sometimes the Disney version); a few viewers may find the super-realistic wide-angle photography (and
sometimes 3-D effects) dizzying.

Touring Tips   Wear comfortable shoes with no-slip soles; although the
ramps in and out of various environments are not slick, you may be distracted by all that's going on around you. This is a nice spot to meet in the

afternoon if the party wants to split up during the day, because you can buy timed IMAX tickets in advance. Everything is wheelchair accessible, another fact worth noting in a city as old and often inconvenient as New Orleans.

The Beauregard-Keyes House

Type of Attraction: Restored nineteenth-century "raised cottage" and former residence of Gen. P.G.T. Beauregard and novelist Frances Parkinson Keyes, with personal effects and open gardens

Location: 1113 Chartres Street, between Ursulines and Gov. Nicholls streets

Admission: $5 adults, $4 seniors and students, $2 kids ages 6–12, ages 5 and under free

Hours: Monday–Saturday, 10 a.m.–3 p.m.

Phone: 523-7257

When to Go: Anytime

Overall Appeal by Age Group:

Pre-school	Grade School	Teens	Young Adults	Over 30	Senior Citizens
none	★★	★★★	★★★	★★★	★★★★

Author's Rating: Low-key but lovely and a little sad if you know your history. ★★★

How Much Time to Allow: No more than an hour, including guided tour and stroll around the gardens

Description and Comments   This is a lovely old home, even without its many historical connections (see the self-guided walking tour of the French Quarter on page 232 for more details), built in 1826 in raised-cottage style with a lovely twin staircase, Doric columns, and elegant side gallery. The formal gardens probably date back to the 1830s, when it belonged to the Swiss consul. It was a boardinghouse during the Civil War, and when Confederate general and native son Pierre Gustave Toutant Beauregard returned to the area, his own plantation in ruins, he and several members of his family lodged there for about 18 months. It was almost demolished in the 1920s, but a group of ladies lobbied for its restoration, and in 1944 the novelist Frances Parkinson Keyes (rhymes with "eyes") moved in and began meticulous reconstruction, eventually turning the big house over to a charitable foundation and living in the rear cottage, also part of the tour. Many of the furnishings and personal effects belonged to Beauregard. The gift shop has copies of most of Keyes' books, many of them historical novels dealing with Creole society and the house itself.

Touring Tips Like many New Orleans homes, this is strictly a guided tour, with costumed docents. But now that PBS has made *The Civil War* so lively again, even students may find Beauregard's old study intriguing. The gardens make for a nice respite, as well.

The Cabildo and Arsenal

Type of Attraction: Flagship building of the Louisiana State Museum complex in the city. Entrance to the Arsenal, which only occasionally has exhibits, is through the Cabildo.

Location: On Chartres Street facing Jackson Square

Admission: $5 adults; $4 seniors, students, and active military; free for kids ages 12 and under

Hours: Tuesday–Sunday, 9 a.m.–5 p.m.

Phone: 568-6968

When to Go: Anytime

Special Comments: Be sure to check at the front desk for information on changing exhibits or exhibits in the Arsenal.

Overall Appeal by Age Group:

Pre-school	Grade School	Teens	Young Adults	Over 30	Senior Citizens
none	★★	★★	★★★	★★★	★★★

Author's Rating: Not terribly engaging, and sometimes stiffly explained, but if you skim through, picking up the more intriguing exhibits, particularly some of the more subtle folk-art pieces, mildly entertaining. ★★½

How Much Time to Allow: 30–60 minutes

Description and Comments This is not a very hands-on museum, and compared to the new-generation facilities it can be rather dry; you will probably find yourself skimming through unless you stop to watch videos. But there are a few particular exhibits that may hold even a child's attention, such as the Indian pirogue; weapons and uniforms from the Civil War and the Battle of New Orleans; that apocryphal symbol of slavery, the cotton gin; a lock of Andy Jackson's hair; antique medical tools, including a leech jar; a young child's casket; and Napoleon's death mask, with a dark and surprisingly philosophical visage unfamiliar from the typical portraits. African-Americans and Native Americans may find the exhibits devoted to their contributions a little stiff but well intentioned. The building itself has historical significance: the official transfer of the Louisiana Territory from France to the United States was signed here, and since it also housed the State Supreme Court from 1868 to 1910, it saw the arguing of several famous legal cases, including *Plessy v. Ferguson*.

Touring Tips The Cabildo is wheelchair accessible and even offers wheelchairs for use; visitors with other disabilities should check in at the front counter for assistance.

The 1850 House

Type of Attraction: Mid-nineteenth-century middle-class apartment with period furnishings

Location: In the Pontalba Apartments at 523 St. Ann Street facing Jackson Square

Admission: $4 adults; $3 seniors, students, and active military; free for kids ages 12 and under

Hours: Tuesday–Sunday, 9 a.m.–5 p.m.

Phone: 568-6968

When to Go: Anytime, though this might qualify as rainy-day stuff

Special Comments: One of the most intriguing things about these apartments is that they are still occupied, and there's still a waiting list. Also note the Spring Fiesta Association house at 826 St. Ann; open by appointment only (945-2744, or Fridays 581-1367).

Overall Appeal by Age Group:

Pre-school	Grade School	Teens	Young Adults	Over 30	Senior Citizens
none	★	★	★★	★★	★★

Author's Rating: Just a snapshot of social history, but oddly chilly—less palpably lived-in than the Hermann-Grima or Gallier houses. ★½

How Much Time to Allow: 15–20 minutes

Description and Comments This is a sort of single museum exhibit expanded over several stories, a real-sized dollhouse in a way. If you are not curious about the evolution of American social customs, you may not get much out of it. Some of its antiques, particularly the rococo revival bedroom furniture and the rare complete 75-piece set of Vieux Paris tableware will be very significant to some and merely pretty to others. What is intriguing is the apartment's history: Baroness Micaela Almonester de Pontalba, daughter of the Spanish grandee who rebuilt the Presbytere, Cabildo, and Cathedral after the great fires of the late eighteenth century, wanted both to transform the square from a military-parade ground into a European-style public plaza and to improve the value of her land in the declining old city. She went through several of New Orleans' best architects, including James Gallier Sr. and Henry Howard, and micromanaged the contractors who survived (if you see the portraits of the baroness in the Presbytere, you won't be surprised); but the row houses were ultimately a great success, 16 on each side and all with storefronts on the sidewalk level, just as they are today. Note the entwined "A" and "P" cartouche—for Almonester de Pontalba— in the balcony railing.

The apartments did eventually become fairly run-down, but were restored by massive WPA projects. The State of Louisiana owns the Lower Pontalbas (the side including the 1850 House), and the city owns the Upper Pontalbas.

Touring Tips   This museum is not wheelchair accessible, and the rather steep and narrow stairs may be difficult for older or physically limited visitors. The booklet given to visitors for the self-guided tour offers a great deal of information about the original facilities and decoration.

Gallier House Museum

Type of Attraction: Period-correct restoration of the house designed by prominent architect James Gallier Jr. for his own family

Location: 1118–1132 Royal Street, between Ursulines and Gov. Nicolls streets

Admission: $6 adults, $5 seniors and students, free under age 8; $10 adults and $9 seniors and students for both Gallier and Hermann-Grima houses

Hours: Monday–Saturday, 10 a.m.–4 p.m. (last tour begins at 3:30 p.m.)

Phone: 525-5661

When to Go: Anytime, although unlike most historic houses, it's difficult in the rain because you have to go along the upstairs gallery.

Special Comments: Particularly interesting because Gallier designed so many more elaborate homes in the Garden District for American patrons.

Overall Appeal by Age Group:

Pre-school	Grade School	Teens	Young Adults	Over 30	Senior Citizens
none	★	★	★★	★★★	★★★

Author's Rating: House tours are attractions requiring a fair amount of imagination (or desire for imitation), but Gallier's design is both gracious and clever, crammed full of fine architectural and decorative detailing. ★★★½

How Much Time to Allow: 30–45 minutes

Description and Comments   Administered by Tulane University, this is one of the most meticulously correct restorations in town, partly because Gallier's own designs and notes have been preserved. Though not perhaps as wealthy as many of his patrons, Gallier would certainly qualify as comfortably well-off. His house was very up-to-date in many ways—the chandeliers were gas-burning, the bathroom had hot running water, and the whole house had a sort of primitive air-conditioning system with vents and ice-cooled air—but it is also revealing about customs of the times, with its servants' quarters, dish pantry, summer matting vs. winter carpets, children's sickroom, high brick garden walls, etc. The faux painting of the cypress to resemble pine is also very characteristic. The decorative molding and plaster work, gilded capitals, 12-foot ceilings, marble, and paneling are very fine, and the docents here are extremely knowledgeable about the entire inventory. The work on outbuildings continues. Be sure to admire the carriage in the alley between the two buildings.

Touring Tips   Not wheelchair accessible, but not uncomfortable

Germaine Wells Mardi Gras Museum

Type of Attraction: Costume and jewelry collection

Location: Upstairs at Arnaud's Restaurant at 813 Bienville Street, between
    Bourbon and Dauphine streets

Admission: Free

Hours: Monday–Friday, 11:30 a.m.–2:30 p.m. and 6–10 p.m.;
    Saturday, 6–10 p.m.; Sunday 10 a.m.–2 p.m. and 6–10 p.m. (these are
    the restaurant hours)

Phone: 523-0611

When to Go: Anytime

Overall Appeal by Age Group:

Pre-school	Grade School	Teens	Young Adults	Over 30	Senior Citizens
★	★★	★★	★★★	★★★	★★

Author's Rating: This covers less territory than the Mardi Gras exhibit in
    the Old U.S. Mint, since it's primarily his-and-her gowns, but they
    speak volumes about the lost sophistication of old New Orleans. As a
    fast, free diversion, hard to beat. ★★★

How Much Time to Allow: 20 minutes

Description and Comments   The family of restaurateur Arnaud Cazenave, and particularly his daughter, Germaine Cazenave Wells, were mainstays of the old-society Carnival for decades; Germaine alone reigned as queen of nearly two dozen balls, more than anyone else in history. Her collection of royal outfits and jewelry, many of them astonishingly luxurious and accompanied by pictures of the corresponding ball, has been rescued and placed in glass cases in a pretty but simple wing. When you find the spangled gown she wore as the 1954 Queen of Naiades, tip your hat: she loved the gown so much she was buried in a replica of it. A small case out-side displays some of her almost equally exuberant Easter bonnets.

Touring Tips   The costumes are fragile, so the air conditioning is often up pretty high.

Hermann-Grima House

Type of Attraction: Beautifully restored home from the early Federal period, with unusually extensive outbuildings

Location: 818–820 S. Louis Street between Bourbon and Dauphine streets

Admission: Adults $6, seniors and students $5, free for kids ages 8 and under; $10 adults, $9 seniors and students for combined ticket to Gallier House

Hours: Monday–Saturday, 10 a.m.–4 p.m. (last tour leaves at 3:30 p.m.)

Phone: 525-5661

When to Go: Anytime

Special Comments: Occasionally there are special cooking demonstrations in the rear kitchen; ask at the ticket counter in the carriage house.

Overall Appeal by Age Group:

Pre-school	Grade School	Teens	Young Adults	Over 30	Senior Citizens
none	★	★★	★★★	★★★	★★★

Author's Rating: An unusual house and one that says quite a bit about its owners; more fun when the live demonstrations are scheduled. ★★★

How Much Time to Allow: 45 minutes–1 hour

Description and Comments   This is an unusual home in that it represents the style of the so-called Golden Age of New Orleans, meaning the first great commercial boom under U.S. administrations. Though it's usually hard to get younger people interested in old homes, the peculiarities of this one—the shared bathroom, the outdoor kitchens, the young woman's fur-nishings—make it more accessible than most. The house was built in 1831 for a wealthy merchant named Samuel Hermann. It was constructed in the Federal style, with a central doorway and divided rooms rather than the eighteenth-century side-hall style; the exterior plaster is scored to look like brick, which was very expensive and showy. (Much of the decorative work was produced by the free men of color then flourishing in New Orleans.) The house was sold in 1844 to Judge Felix Grima, whose family remained there for five generations. The period furniture is very fine. The master bedroom actually faces the street and has a pocket-door opening to the middle hall and second bedroom for ventilation. The long garden, out-buildings for cooking and household work, and even the original carriage house (the one used for tickets and souvenirs comes from the house next door) are finely restored.

Touring Tips   Because you can buy timed tickets in advance, you may want to ask the guides if there are any large groups already scheduled for a particular tour. You can also stop by in the morning and get tickets for the time of your choice, pass them out, and meet at the appointed hour. Because you don't get to go upstairs, this is a good choice for those with physical limitations, although there are a few steps; those unable to mount the front steps might ask at the counter if they can be brought through from the courtyard.

Historic New Orleans Collection

Type of Attraction: A complex of free exhibits, a late-eighteenth-century residence and a nineteenth-century residence remodeled for 1940s society

Location: 533 Royal Street between Toulouse and St. Louis streets

Admission: Williams galleries free; Williams residence and Louisiana History Galleries in the Merieult House, $4

Hours: Tuesday–Saturday, 10 a.m.–4:30 p.m.; tours at 10 and 11 a.m. and 2 and 3 p.m.

Phone: 523-4662

When to Go: Anytime, but calling ahead is recommended

Special Comments: One of the most satisfying tours in town, historically and culturally

Overall Appeal by Age Group:

Pre-school	Grade School	Teens	Young Adults	Over 30	Senior Citizens
none	★	★★	★★★★	★★★★	★★★

Author's Rating: If you have limited time and want to get a flavor of the social, cultural, and historical evolution of New Orleans, this is the tour to take. Even if you have lots of time, it's the one. ★★★½

How Much Time to Allow: Up to 2 hours including tours

Description and Comments   This is partly a research center, partly a group of restored architectural gems, and a bit of an art gallery as well. The entrance-level Williams galleries have first-class rotating exhibits on Mardi Gras, renovation, arts and crafts, etc., that are free for the browsing. Behind that is the glorious 1792 Merieult House of romantic legend (see the walking tour of the French Quarter), whose airy rooms now house rare materials from the landmark collection of the late Kemper and Leila Williams, including maps, documents concerning the Louisiana Purchase, wildly inflated propaganda posters, rare photographs, and so on. (The extraordinary bulk of their collection is now housed in its own lovely library, the Williams Research Center, at 410 Chartres.) The nineteenth-century brick cottage at the end of the courtyard was the Williams' residence, which they had renovated to suit their own high standards of comfort and hospitality, and to showcase their collections of fine porcelain, antique furniture, and textiles.

Touring Tips   This is a one-stop whirlwind tour of New Orleans history, and a particularly evocative one, since you literally step off Royal Street into a gracious residence of two centuries' standing. Even the gifts in the shop have some historical appeal. Wheelchair access available; ask at the counter.

Musée Conti Wax Museum

Type of Attraction: Pretty much what it sounds like, a Madame Toussaud's of New Orleans history with a little requisite scary stuff mixed in and some surprising Mardi Gras outfits as a lagniappe

Location: 917 Conti Street, between Dauphine and Burgundy streets

Admission: $6.75 adults, $5.25 seniors and students, $4.75 ages 4–17, free for kids age 3 and under; for groups of 25 or more, you get a free tour guide and $1 off each ticket.

Hours: 10 a.m.–5:30 p.m. Monday–Saturday, 12–5 p.m. Sunday

Phone: 525-2605

When to Go: Anytime, though this makes a very diverting rainy-day stop and a cool one on the hottest afternoons.

Special Comments: The special "haunted dungeon" of more or less horrific stuff is off to one side, so young or susceptible children don't have to see it.

Overall Appeal by Age Group:

Pre-school	Grade School	Teens	Young Adults	Over 30	Senior Citizens
★★	★★★	★★★	★★★	★★½	★★

Author's Rating: This is not the sort of attraction to visit twice (unless you're a kid), but the first time around it has its fun moments. ★★½

How Much Time to Allow: 45 minutes

Description and Comments   Wax museums may be corny, but they have a certain appeal to even the youngest of kids, who are fascinated by their immovability, and to seniors, for whom they represent the attractions of an earlier, more innocent age. These are pretty good as such things go, with German glass eyes, human hair imported from Italy, and figures straight from Paris. Many of the exhibits are purely historical—Andy Jackson and

Jean Lafitte (and the Battle of New Orleans in panorama), and the hilarious vision of the Emperor Napoleon, ensconced in his bathtub, impulsively offering to sell the entire Louisiana Territory—while others are more theatrically gory (Marie Laveau leading a voodoo ritual and lovely Delphine LaLaurie gloating over her chained slaves). A few are downright cheerful—there are wax models of Louis Armstrong, Pete Fountain, Huey Long, and Mardi Gras Indian Chief Montana. Even the long-lost Storyville has its moment in the artificial sun. Dracula, the Wolf Man, Frankenstein, and two dozen or so of their friends are kept off to one side.

Touring Tips   Consider before taking small children; a few will find the peculiar, almost-real quality of these mannequins spooky even before they get to the chamber of horrors. International travelers may be surprised at the variety of translated tours available for rent.

New Orleans Historic Voodoo Museum

Type of Attraction: Part museum, part weird-camp souvenir shop—or to put it simply, part shock, part schlock

Location: 724 Dumaine Street, between Royal and Bourbon streets

Admission: $6 adults, $5 seniors and students (if you sign up for a guided tour, the museum tour is free)

Hours: 10 a.m.–5 p.m.

Phone: 523-7685; www.voodoomuseum.com

When to Go: Anytime

Special Comments: One of the hot spots for psychic readings and gris-gris charms as well as "voodoo tours"

Overall Appeal by Age Group:

Pre-school	Grade School	Teens	Young Adults	Over 30	Senior Citizens
★	★★	★★★	★★★	★★	★★

Author's Rating: This absolutely requires that you get into the spirit of things; think of it as an adventure, rather than as a museum per se. ★★★

How Much Time to Allow: 30 minutes

Description and Comments   If something like the Historic New Orleans Collection is the quintessential above-board museum, this is the height of neo–New Orleans exotica—rather grim and sometimes grisly artifacts, strange bones and potions, a voodoo altar, plenty of Marie Laveau lore, stuffed cats and live snakes, low light, and sometimes local low life as well. If you like atmosphere, you'll love this; in fact, if it weren't so dim and dilapidated, they'd have to curse it.

Touring Tips   Children are generally fascinated by the grotesque, but take your own kids' sensitivities into account. Teens and novice occultists will probably think it very cool, but seniors may find it all a little too grim. The museum staff not only arranges readings and tours, but also occasional "rituals."

New Orleans Pharmacy Museum

Type of Attraction: Restored apothecary with period exhibits, old potions, and pharmaceutical supplies

Location: 514 Chartres Street, between Toulouse and St. Louis streets

Admission: $2, $1 seniors and students, for free ages 12 and under

Hours: Tuesday–Sunday, 10 a.m.–5 p.m.

Phone: 565-8027

When to Go: Anytime; good rain alternative

Overall Appeal by Age Group:

Pre-school	Grade School	Teens	Young Adults	Over 30	Senior Citizens
★	★★	★★	★★	★★	★★★

Author's Rating: This is another of those "atmospheric" venues that has to draw you. The subject may seem somewhat limited, but it's quite intriguing if you're not squeamish. ★★★

How Much Time to Allow: 30 minutes

Description and Comments   This was the pharmacy of the very first apothecary to be licensed in the United States, Louis Dufilho, who was certified in 1816 and opened this store in 1823. It's an impressive piece of restoration, with German mahogany cases, antique handblown canisters and apothecary jars, a leech pot, and such famous patent medicines of the past as Pinkham's pills, the vitamin concoctions of Miss Lydia Pinkham that were supposed to resolve both ladies' vapors and, though not said openly, sexual indifference; and Spanish fly, the male equivalent still hotly sought after today. The black and rose marble soda fountain, made in Italy in 1855, is a nostalgic highlight.

Touring Tips   Bring your sense of humor. This will be of some interest to most ages, since the idea of applying leeches and trepanning skulls to relieve pressure (or possession) has a perverse appeal. The courtyard is a nice place to sit for a few minutes, and with the revival of interest in botanicals and alternative medicine, almost trendy. In a funny way, however, this has more appeal to older visitors who recognize more of the names and may even remember tales of defunct medical techniques.

Old Ursuline Convent/Archbishop Antoine Blanc Memorial

Type of Attraction: A 250-year-old complex incorporating several religious sites, formal gardens and archives

Location: 110 Chartres Street, at the corner of Ursuline Street

Admission: $5 adults, $4 seniors and students, $2 kids ages 9 and up, free ages 8 and under; groups of 20 or more, $3 adults and $1 children

Hours: Tuesday–Friday, 10 a.m.–3 p.m. (tours on the hour, except noon); Saturday and Sunday, tours at 11:15 a.m. and 1 and 2 p.m. only

Phone: 529-3040

When to Go: Anytime

Special Comments: Not a lively, elaborate, or particularly varied site, but oddly atmospheric; obviously appeals more to Catholic visitors

Overall Appeal by Age Group:

Pre-school	Grade School	Teens	Young Adults	Over 30	Senior Citizens
none	none	★	★	★★	★★

Author's Rating: Of more historical and religious than visual appeal; an unusually serene tour. ★★

How Much Time to Allow: 1 hour

Description and Comments   This is the only surviving example of pure French Creole construction, begun in 1745, and most people believe it's the oldest surviving building in New Orleans of any sort; it was saved from the fire of 1788 by Pere Antoine and his bucket brigade. The Sisters were the guiding social hand of the city's young people for centuries, educating not only the children of aristocrats (Micaela de Pontalbas, for example) but blacks, Indians, and orphans as well. They served as religious guides, chaperones (it was they who brought over the "casket girls" as brides to the early settlers), nurses, housekeeping instructors, and welfare workers, braving epidemics and massacres alike. Andrew Jackson sent word to the Sisters to ask them to pray for his forces on the eve of the Battle of New Orleans; they responded by spending the entire night in prayer at the chapel here before a statue of the Virgin Mary, and were still there when the messenger brought word of victory. Jackson came in person to thank them, and to this day a celebratory Mass is said on January 8 at the Ursulines' other chapel, the National Shrine of Our Lady of Prompt Succor at State Street and South Claiborne. The lovely old cypress spiral staircase, antique furniture and relics, medicinal garden, and restored chapel, known variously as Our Lady of Victory Church, St. Mary's Italian Church, and the Archbishop's Chapel, are very pretty—but again, of somewhat limited appeal. Incidentally, in the early years of U.S. government, the convent seemed threatened by anti-Catholic educational reforms; the Mother Superior wrote first to President Jefferson and again to President Madison, asking that the school be allowed to continue, and both wrote back assuringly. The Shrine of Our Lady has not only her petitions, but both presidential responses.

Touring Tips   This is pleasant, but rather a lot of walking for the effect.

The Old U.S. Mint

Type of Attraction: Another part of the Louisiana State Museum complex, an imaginatively reconditioned installation housing two of the city's best-kept secret exhibits

Location: 400 Esplanade Avenue, at Decatur Street

Admission: $5 adults; $4 seniors, students, and active military; free for kids ages 12 and under

Hours: Tuesday–Sunday, 9 a.m.–5 p.m.

Phone: 568-6968

When to Go: Anytime

Special Comments: Because of its music exhibits, the museum sometimes hosts concerts of jazz, big band, spirituals, and early ballroom music; inquire at the desk. Also browse through the music collection in the gift shop.

Overall Appeal by Age Group:

Pre-school	Grade School	Teens	Young Adults	Over 30	Senior Citizens
★★★	★★★★	★★★★	★★★★★	★★★★★	★★★★★

Author's Rating: This is virtually the only exhibit on New Orleans music, and requires perhaps a little personal knowledge for the fullest effect, but even the tone-deaf will be floored by the Mardi Gras rooms.
★★★★★

How Much Time to Allow: 1–2 hours

Description and Comments   The building itself, a huge but not clumsy Greek Revival facade with Ionic details, was designed during Andrew Jackson's administration by William Strickland, the most prominent public architect of the day. Its polished flagstone floors, double staircase, and rear galleries are still pretty impressive (although it has to be admitted that engineer P.G.T. Beauregard had to be called in to perform a little facelift in the 1850s). One side of the second floor holds the jazz collection, which arranges old photographs of Jelly Roll Morton, King Oliver, Sidney Bechet, and Fate Marable's Orchestra alongside early instruments (including Louis Armstrong's first cornet), sheet music, and other memorabilia. Snatches of vintage recordings play overhead, and the often overlooked women of early music are also saluted. (Be sure to notice the copy of the notorious "Blue Book," the social register of Storyville ladies, and the delicate stained-glass panels rescued from a demolished bordello.) The other side of the building houses the Mardi Gras exhibit, an astonishing cornucopia of mocked-up floats and authentic costumes, scepters, crowns, krewe decorations and "honors," hat pins, watches, and Carnival favors. The lavish outfits are made of gold lamé, fake fur, appliquéd satin, beads, feathers, velvets, and silk tassels. Even if your kids can resist the music rooms, they'll be stunned by the chief of the Wild Tchoupitoulas in all his glory, and the picture of Louis Armstrong as King of the Zulu Krewe in 1949. Look also at the paintings depicting the duel between rival club owners (that spelled the beginning of the end of Storyville) and the third-floor hallway mural with many famous faces from the musical past. Down in the basement, where the remnants of the mint equipment can be seen, are a few intriguing exhibits as well, including the carved hearse, built at the turn of the nineteenth century.

Touring Tips   This is good wheelchair access territory, with wide aisles and new bathrooms. And if you like old homes, take the time to wander up and down Esplanade Avenue. Although the neighborhood is in mid-revival, it is likely to be the next Garden District. Take particular note of the house at 704 Esplanade, at Royal Street: the Gauche House (so called for owner John Gauche, not as an editorial comment) was built in 1856 supposedly from a drawing by Albrecht Dürer, including cast-iron balconies, cupids, and all. Also note that you are very near the end of the Riverfront Streetcar line, if you're getting tired or want to get across the Quarter easily.

The Presbytere

Type of Attraction: Of the Louisiana State Museum properties in the French Quarter, the most traditional one, with both permanent and rotating exhibits

Location: 751 Chartres Street, facing Jackson Square

Admission: $5 adults; $4 seniors, students, and active military; free for kids ages 12 and under.

Hours: Tuesday–Sunday, 9 a.m.–5 p.m.

Phone: 568-6968

When to Go: Anytime

Overall Appeal by Age Group:

Pre-school	Grade School	Teens	Young Adults	Over 30	Senior Citizens
none	★	★	★★★	★★★	★★

Author's Rating: Like the Cabildo, you have to follow your nose to what interests you, but the rotating exhibits can be very intriguing. ★★★

How Much Time to Allow: 45 minutes–1½ hours

Description and Comments Architecturally speaking, this is a somewhat mongrel building, though not unattractive—it has been renovated and expanded several times, and most recently its really fine plank floors have been reconditioned to fine advantage. Intended to be used as an ecclesiastical residence, it wound up as a courthouse; the mansard roof and hurricane-demolished cupola were supposed to mirror the Cabildo. The exhibits are a bit haphazard but cheerful mishmash: portraits of influential Creoles, such as Don Almonester and his formidable daughter, Baroness Almonester; fine decorative arts, from an eighteenth-century gold- and silver-embroidered velvet altar cloth and local art glass, to wrought iron from the staircase of the great domed (and doomed) St. Charles Hotel; crosses, cameos, and earrings; hand-tinted Audubon plates; silver table settings; etc. Among the busts are two faces of Beauregard, one young and confident, the other older and wiser.

Touring Tips Although the age rating shows low for children, it does depend somewhat on the subject of the rotating exhibits. Among fairly recent examples, the collection of very elaborate to-scale builders' ship models, haute couture (à la the Metropolitan Museum in New York), or antique maps might interest certain youngsters, and the rather weird *Tales from the Crypt* effect of the bust-lined second-floor arcade gallery might tickle others' fancy.

ZONE 2: THE CENTRAL BUSINESS DISTRICT

We've said several times that you should not venture into St. Louis Cemetery without a tour group or at least several friends. One way to get a glimpse of its setting and historic role is to visit Our Lady of Guadalupe, which was once used as a virtual assembly line for yellow-fever victims. Unfortunately, the other important site in this area, Louis Armstrong Park, can't be recommended as a tourist attraction either, although plans to renovate and secure it in the future may change that. The park is a sort of ghost of Storyville (now vanished under an eyesore of a housing project). It is bordered on one side by Basin Street and includes Congo Square, the legendary tribal gathering spot turned jammin' ground; a bandstand (where off and on, free Sunday concerts are scheduled), a community center, and several historic buildings; a jazz and blues radio station (WWOZ 90.7); and even a performing arts center, not to mention the 12-foot statue of Satchmo himself. The neighborhood is gradually reviving, partly thanks to the sentimental "homecoming" of many musicians, but it is not a good idea to walk here. If you do want to hear and see this historic area, contact Cradle of Jazz Tours (282-3583).

Confederate Museum

Type of Attraction: Traditional but unusually large and somber Civil War museum

Location: 929 Camp Street, at Howard Avenue

Admission: $5, $4 for students and seniors, $2 for kids ages 12 and under

Hours: Monday–Saturday, 10 a.m.–4 p.m.

Phone: 523-4522

When to Go: Anytime

Overall Appeal by Age Group:

Pre-school	Grade School	Teens	Young Adults	Over 30	Senior Citizens
none	★	★★	★★★★	★★★★	★★★★

Author's Rating: Moving and interesting. ★★★

How Much Time to Allow: 1½ hours

Description and Comments "Everybody thinks it's a church, but it's not," says the staffer about this medievally somber shrine to the Glorious Cause, the oldest Civil War museum in the country. Homegrown architect Thomas Sully designed it as a complement to the Romanesque Howard Memorial Library next door (itself becoming a museum, as noted in the walking tour of the Warehouse/Arts District), and it looks every bit the sepulcher—as it surely must have in 1893 when 50,000 mourners came to pay respects to the body of Jefferson Davis. There's no substitute for artifacts in a museum: That ineffable dignity that lingers in objects handled by long-dead humans suffuses the most sophisticated installation, and in such items the museum, also known as Confederate Memorial Hall, is rich indeed. Its collection, the second largest in the country, turns arms and armaments into an eloquent commentary on the social impact of the war on men and women alike. Among the most moving items are the frock coats worn by generals Beauregard and Braxton Bragg, whose physical slightness provides a poignant counterpoint to the magnitude of the conflict; the modest headgear of one Landon Creek, who survived 7 battles and 3 wounds to make it to his 15th birthday; a pair of boots, long interred with its owner and now on eerie, empty display; a child's Zouave-style jacket from Marshall Field's, a high-fashion flirtation with rebellion; and part of Lee's battlefield silver. Among the women honored here are those who resisted the occupation of "Beast" Butler's troops by spitting or recoiling in their presence.

Touring Tips Street parking available

Louisiana Children's Museum

Type of Attraction: State-of-the-art children's activity center

Location: 420 Julia Street, at Constance Avenue

Admission: $6

Hours: Tuesday–Saturday, 9:30 a.m.–4:30 p.m.; Sunday, noon–4:30 p.m.;
   Monday (June–August only), 9:30 a.m.–4:30 p.m.

Phone: 523-1357

When to Go: After lunchtime, when the daytrippers and school groups
   have left

Overall Appeal by Age Group:

Pre-school	Grade School	Teens	Young Adults	Over 30	Senior Citizens
★★★★★	★★★★★	½	½	½	½

Author's Rating: The way early learning is supposed to be—exciting and
   fun. ★★★★

How Much Time to Allow: 1½–2 hours

Description and Comments   In a colorful, noisy converted warehouse, this
science- and math-oriented facility teaches kids the inner workings of
things by letting them simply have a good time. Pulleys, gears, wind
machines, bubble rings, and sound-wave amplifiers are offered, along with
an innovative and kindly minded exhibit introducing kids to the difficul-
ties of handicapped—but not limited—life: they shoot baskets from a
wheelchair, stack blocks wearing thick, clumsy gloves, etc. There are
Sesame Street–style areas, such as the cafe where they can pretend to cook, a
grocery store, a Cajun cottage, and an art gallery. There's a special room for
toddlers, so siblings don't feel tied down.

Touring Tips   Being subjected to constant battering means some of the
hands-on exhibits need maintenance; just move on to the next thing. Food
is limited to vending machines. Street parking available.

Louisiana Superdome

Type of Attraction: Enclosed sports arena also used as a concert and convention venue

Location: 1500 Poydras Street, at LaSalle Street

Admission: $6 adults, $5 seniors and ages 5–10, free for kids age 4 and
   under

Hours: Monday–Friday, 10:30 a.m., noon, and 1:30 p.m.

Phone: 587-3810

When to Go: When something's scheduled.

Special Comments: The New Orleans Centre, a three-story pseudo-neo-Disney Victorian crystal exposition hall inside an office building, connects to the Superdome like the super souvenir/concession wing. The new Sports Arena complex is right behind the Superdome.

Overall Appeal by Age Group:

Pre-school	Grade School	Teens	Young Adults	Over 30	Senior Citizens
none	★½	★½	★	★	none

Author's Rating: Strictly for sports-stats freaks. It may be big, and the numbers the tour guides spout are impressive, but hey—if you've seen one stadium, you've seen 'em all.

How Much Time to Allow: 1 hour

Description and Comments The Superdome is, as you will hear repeatedly, one of the largest buildings in the world, 27 stories high, with no obstructing support posts (admittedly impressive, if rather unnerving) and 13 acres' worth of AstroTurf, here called Mardi Grass. It can seat more than 76,000 people, but if there are only 20 or so of you walking around behind a tour guide, it seems a little . . . dumb. And it seems even worse when there are about 20 busloads of tourists looking around, staring.

Touring Tips Plenty of parking

National D-Day Museum

Type of Attraction: Military museum and veterans' memorial
Location: 945 Magazine Street (entrance on Andrew Higgins Drive)
Admission: $7 adults, $6 seniors and students
Hours: Daily 9 a.m.–5 p.m.
Phone: 527-6012
When to Go: Anytime
Overall Appeal by Age Group:

Pre-school	Grade School	Teens	Young Adults	Over 30	Senior Citizens
★	★★★	★★★	★★★	★★★★	★★★★

Author's Rating: Even-handed presentations; film more effective than exhibits ★★★★★

How Much Time to Allow: 1–2 hours

Description and Comments Housed in an old warehouse that has been effectively opened up into exhibit space that almost suggests barracks and aerodromes, this still-unfinished museum combines the now-familiar "voices" (taped recollections of veterans played as background) with uniforms, weapons, rebuilt barracks bunks, radio and newspaper clips and recruitment and bonds posters into a simple but, especially for those who lived through World War II, moving tribute. The introductory half-hour film, narrated by David McCullough (the new Walter Cronkite of documentaries) is laudably free of bias and respectful; children may find a few scenes of battlefield casualties upsetting, but they'll probably be fascinated by the helmet with the bullet hole, etc. Some of the exhibits are a little hard to follow. As yet only the Normandy invasion is covered; a second wing will focus on the war in the Pacific. The museum gift shop has some rather intriguing items, ranging from the inexpensive soldier paper dolls and repro pin-up posters to action figures and vintage recordings to personalized leather jackets for $550. The nicest gift for a veteran, however, would probably be a memorial brick for the pavilion floor; the $100 fee is tax-deductible. For more information, ext. 221.

Touring Tips   Good wheelchair access, though the exhibits twist and turn a little. There's a cafe/coffeeshop on site.

New Orleans Contemporary Arts Center

Type of Attraction: Multidisciplinary arts and performing arts complex

Location: 900 Camp Street, at St. Joseph Street

Admission: $5 adults, $2 seniors and students; free on Thursdays. Performance ticket prices vary.

Hours: Monday–Saturday, 10 a.m.–5 p.m.; Sunday, 11 a.m.–5 p.m.

Phone: 523-1216

When to Go: After lunchtime on weekdays to avoid school-class groups

Overall Appeal by Age Group:

Pre-school	Grade School	Teens	Young Adults	Over 30	Senior Citizens
½	★★	★★★	★★★★	★★★★	★★★★

Author's Rating: Worth a visit for the high caliber of exhibitions. ★★★★

How Much Time to Allow: 1–1½ hours

Description and Comments   The CAC's gallery spaces total 10,000 square feet and rotate about every six to eight weeks among international as well as national and local artists' exhibits. It also includes spaces for theatrical, musical, and dance performances, as well as some cutting-edge performance art. Call for a schedule of events. That's the up-side. The slight down-side is that this somewhat raw, accessible renovated warehouse can be very loud when groups of school kids come in.

Touring Tips   Street parking available

Our Lady of Guadalupe/Shrine of St. Jude

Type of Attraction: Simple but quirky little chapel built to serve St. Louis Cemetery, but with a couple of not-so-strict saints in charge

Location: 411 North Rampart Street, at Conti Street

Admission: Free (donations welcome)

Hours: 7 a.m.–6 p.m.

Phone: 525-1551

When to Go: Anytime

Special Comments: This is the official chapel of the city's fire and police departments, so don't be surprised by any uniforms.

Overall Appeal by Age Group:

Pre-school	Grade School	Teens	Young Adults	Over 30	Senior Citizens
none	½	½	★½	★½	★★

Author's Rating: An eccentric but lively side trip. ★★½

How Much Time to Allow: 15 minutes; also tours by appointment

Description and Comments   This little chapel, built in 1826 as the Chapel of the Dead and originally opening directly onto the cemetery (there's a street between now), is intriguing for several reasons. First, because in the days of continual epidemic, it operated at tragic speed: Bodies were brought in, a swift service was said, and they were shipped right into the waiting graves. (The victims were brought here instead of St. Louis Cathedral in a vain effort to limit contagion.) The second intriguing aspect, for those who take saintly intercession with a grain of salt, is that the shrine is now dedicated to St. Jude, he of the lost causes, who might be considered a sort of lost cause himself: despite his connections—he may have been the brother of either Jesus or James—he has lost a little status, although the petitions and published notices of thanks continue to flow in. Step to the right into his grotto, and see for yourself how active he is. Third, this is also the shrine of the one and only (as far as anyone knows) St. Expedite, whose statue arrived at the chapel without its papers or even an address. Look to the right just as you enter the chapel. He had no identifying attributes, and no other church in New Orleans claimed to be expecting a new saint, so the only thing written on the packing crate—Expedite!—was carved into the base by the confused workers, who didn't speak much English. Gradually petitioners began taking him at his word. The legend goes that if you have a request, you go out toward St. Louis Cemetery and say five rosaries; if your prayer is answered (it will be within 36 hours, or probably not at all), you return to the chapel and leave him a teaspoon of salt and a slice of pound cake.

ZONE 3: UPTOWN BELOW NAPOLEON (GARDEN DISTRICT)

Unless you have several days, are making a return trip, or have a real shopping "jones," it is unlikely you will spend much time around here. The run of Magazine Street from the Central Business District through Zone 3 to Audubon Park in Zone 4 is often touted as the new antiques center, though it is extremely drawn out; you could get off the St. Charles streetcar and walk about three blocks south (that is, turning left as you face uptown from the French Quarter). If you love stained glass, however, jump off at St. Andrew Street and walk four blocks to Constance for St. Alphonsus.

St. Alphonsus Church

Type of Attraction: Stunning, partially restored chapel with extraordinary stained glass

Location: 2029 Constance Street, at St. Andrew

Admission: None

Hours: Tuesday, Thursday and Saturday, 10 a.m.–2 p.m.

Phone: 524-8116

When to Go: Anytime

Overall Appeal by Age Group:

Pre-school	Grade School	Teens	Young Adults	Over 30	Senior Citizens
none	★★	★★	★★★	★★★	★★★

Author's Rating: Absolutely beautiful. ★★★★★

How Much Time to Allow: 30–45 minutes alone

Description and Comments   It's astonishing to consider by what scrimping and sweating the Irish immigrants of the mid-nineteenth century managed to erect this lovely church. Note the unusual "repertory cast" of faces used in the astonishing stained-glass windows, shamrocks in the floor tiles, and tomb of the popular Redemptorist priest, Father Francis X. Seeles, who is credited with several miracles. This was the home church of Anne Rice and her family, and served as the model for the church the Mayfair sisters attend.

Touring Tips   Contact the Preservation Resource Center (604 Julia Street; 581-7032) to obtain info on their next "Stained Glass in Sacred Places" tour.

Zone 4: Uptown above Napoleon/University

Although they do not qualify as "attractions" in the usual sense, the campuses of both Loyola University and Tulane University make for nice strolling if you happen to be in the neighborhood. They sit virtually side by side at streetcar stops 36 and 37 on St. Charles Avenue across from Audubon Park. (The statue that greets you at the entrance to Loyola, which seems to be running with its arms flung high, has been known on campus for decades as "the touchdown Jesus.") On the Tulane campus is the Amistad Research Center, which has the world's largest collection of documents, letters, diaries, photographs, and even art concerning civil rights and black history; the collection is open to the public 9 a.m.–4:30 p.m. Monday–Saturday, and is housed in the three-story Tilton Hall right at the St. Charles entrance (865-5535). And there are a few Tiffany studio stained-glass windows at Tulane's Rogers Chapel, which is about four blocks off St. Charles on Audubon Place.

If you take the streetcar out to Audubon Park, you may want to notice a few buildings (although there are so many fine fronts that the ride itself qualifies as an attraction). At 3811 St. Charles, between Penniston and General Taylor Streets, is the sweeping double-porch-fronted **Columns hotel,** designed by architect Thomas Sully in 1883 for a wealthy tobacco merchant and used as the setting for, among other movies, *Pretty Baby.* (If you want to jump off and admire the interior, *Esquire* magazine once rated its Victorian Lounge the best bar in the city; look for the "private" room.) At 4010 St. Charles, between General Taylor and Constantinople streets, is the **Queen Anne home** Sully designed for himself. He also designed some three dozen houses along St. Charles, but unfortunately only a few remain. What is now the **New Orleans Public Library** at 5120 St. Charles, between Soniant and Dufossat, is a fine turn-of-the-century house that was home to, among others, aviator Harry Williams and his film star wife Marguerite Clark; the reading rooms still have their ceiling murals and chandeliers. And just past the edge of the park at Walnut Street is the **Park View hotel,** an ornate Victorian that was originally built to accommodate visitors to the 1884 World Cotton Exposition in Audubon Park.

Finally, you may want to spend a few hours wandering the Riverbend neighborhood for a window-shopping variety as nice as the Quarter's but much less touristy. Take the St. Charles streetcar just past the big right turn onto South Carrollton Avenue (or ask for stop 44), and start strolling up and down Maple Street and then a little farther along Carrollton. There are fine artisan shops here, including boutiques from both Mignon Faget and Yvonne LaFleur; cafes and coffee shops; bookstores; and bars. Among local favorites: **Brigtsen's** for a Cajun and Creole dinner (chef Frank Brigtsen is a protégé of Paul Prudhomme) and the **Camellia Grill** for a locally popular version of steak tartare called the Cannibal Special.

Audubon Park

Type of Attraction: Public green and pedestrian retreat with riding stables, conservatory, swimming pool, miniature train, playgrounds, golf course, bandstands, soccer fields, jogging path, etc.

Location: Entrances at 6800–7000 St. Charles Avenue and 6500 Magazine Street

Admission: Free

Hours: 6 a.m.–10 p.m.

Phone: 861-2537

When to Go: Anytime except after dark, no matter what the signs say

Special Comments: One of the reasons to choose to stay in the Garden District instead of the French Quarter; not quite as fine a facility as City Park but very close

Overall Appeal by Age Group:

Pre-school	Grade School	Teens	Young Adults	Over 30	Senior Citizens
★★★	★★★	★★★	★★★★★	★★★★	★★★

Author's Rating: If you're staying in town long enough to seek out exercise and recreation, this is prime; even a jog or hour's reading in one of the shady gazebos can be an essential break for a visiting executive. And, of course, it has something for everyone in a family. ★★★★½

How Much Time to Allow: Varies by activity

Description and Comments   This is the classic ideal of a public green, built on what was originally a sugar plantation (in the very beginning, it belonged to the Sieur de Bienville himself) and which still boasts live oaks from before the city's founding, along with magnolias, lagoons, formal plantings, hothouse flowers (the Heymann Memorial Conservatory), benches, and trails. The 365-acre park was laid out in the 1890s by John Olmstead, son of the architect of New York's Central Park, after the Cotton Exposition of 1884 was held there. Cars are prohibited around the St. Charles end, so you can wander without fear. Across the railroad tracks toward the Mississippi is the less-publicized area called River View, popular for picnics or jogging. For more on the sport and exercise facilities, see "Exercise and Recreation" on page 202.

Touring Tips   Most of the more organized activities and the zoo are at the Magazine Street end of the park. It's a fairly long walk from St. Charles

Avenue if you're only trying to get from here to there, but the zoo operates a shuttle van from St. Charles around to the parking lot.

Audubon Zoo

Type of Attraction: Popular and professionally acclaimed zoological park with naturalistic environments, hands-on exhibits, a tropical bird house, live-animal feedings, etc.

Location: 6500 Magazine Street in Audubon Park

Admission: $9 adults, $5 seniors, and $4.75 kids ages 2–12

Hours: 9:30 a.m.–5 p.m. daily (ticket booths close at 4 p.m.)

Phone: 861-2537

When to Go: Anytime

Overall Appeal by Age Group:

Pre-school	Grade School	Teens	Young Adults	Over 30	Senior Citizens
★★★	★★★★	★★★	★★★½	★★★	★★★

Author's Rating: Extremely well designed and stocked, with huge family appeal. ★★★★

How Much Time to Allow: 2–3 hours

Description and Comments   There are nearly 2,000 animals here, many of them rare or endangered species, in carefully re-created environments such as the 6½-acre Louisiana Swamp, crisscrossed with boardwalks so you can spy on the white alligators. It's only a short stroll to other continents, however: the Asian Domain, with its Indian temple, rhinos, elephants, and a white tiger; the African Savannah; the South American pampas, the primate house . . . well, you get the idea. For kids of the *Jurassic Park* generation, there's good info on dinosaurs, a group of "living dinosaurs," namely Komodo dragons, and so on. And all around, the keepers offer chances to stroke or feed the tamer animals.

Touring Tips   The Cypress Knee Cafe has great food. Remember to consider the package tickets combine which zoo admission with a cruise from the aquarium, etc. However, the number of steps and escalators in the park may make you wish you hadn't brought the stroller; piggy-backing may save some trouble.

St. Elizabeth's Orphanage Museum

Type of Attraction: A historic orphanage that has been extensively renovated as an office, family home, and exhibition hall by author Anne Rice.

Location: 1314 Napoleon Avenue

Admission: $7 adults, $5 children

Hours: Guided tours only, Monday–Friday at 1 p.m.; Saturday and Sunday at 11 a.m., and 1 and 3 p.m.

Phone: 899-6450

When to Go: Anytime

Special Comments: A fantastic glimpse of the interests of an unusual and theatrical mind, and an attraction with unusual age-range appeal

Overall Appeal by Age Group:

Pre-school	Grade School	Teens	Young Adults	Over 30	Senior Citizens
★★★★	★★★★	★★★★	★★★★	★★★★	★★★★

Author's Rating: More curious than compelling, unless you are a true doll aficionado; it's actually the formerly sacred objects and religious icons, and the various items relating to scenes and characters in her books that are most intriguing. ★★★★

How Much Time to Allow: Tours last an hour.

Description and Comments   The greater part of the 800-plus pieces is Rice's astonishing collection of antique dolls—paper, rag, porcelain, ceramic, primitive, sophisticated, and so on. She also has doll houses, including one that is an exact scale copy of her home in San Francisco (the one detailed in *The Witching Hour*); and several full-sized mannequins, four of which are seen playing cards around a table. The onetime chapel, where the Memnoch Ball has often been held, is just one of several such sites that have obvious power for Rice, and there are dozens of old-saint figures and other religious statuary around. (The admissions go to the restoration of other buildings.) Other oddities about the place: Walls full of art by her husband Stan Rice, whose poetry serves as epigrams for her books; the coffin in which she often makes grand public entrances; and some rare or just nostalgic books. Although they are not open to the public, the upper floors contain some living quarters for family members, a gym for employees, and some quite lavish and theatrical guest rooms—like the Sunset Boulevard room, with twin four-poster beds hung in gold lamé and animal print, giant TV, etc.

Touring Tips   Anne Rice's residence, a few blocks away at 1239 First Street, is also open to the public, but only on Mondays from 1 to 3 p.m.

ZONE 5: DOWNTOWN/ST. BERNARD

We remind you again that cemeteries, as distinct a New Orleans feature as they are, can be dangerous places for solitary visitors or even small groups.

However, if you are seriously intrigued by the offbeat, stop by St. Roch Cemetery (945-5961) at Derbigny Street and St. Roch Avenue, modeled on Campo Santo dei Tedeschi near the Vatican in Rome. The story begins with the French-born St. Roch (or Rocco) who, at the beginning of the fourteenth century, gave away all his possessions and turned to nursing victims of the plague, often curing them by making the sign of the cross. When he himself fell ill, he was kept alive by a dog who brought him food (he's the patron saint of dog-lovers); nevertheless, he was so altered that when he went home he was thrown into prison (he's also the patron of prisoners). Visited in his cell by an angel for five years, he finally died there. In Europe, VSR ("Viva Saint Roch") was often carved over doorways to ward off disease.

When yellow fever broke out in 1868, Father Thevis of nearby Holy Trinity Church prayed to St. Roch, promising to build a monument with his own hands if the saint would intercede. The epidemic ended, and Father Thevis built this little chapel, which is now absolutely crammed with prostheses, crutches, glass eyes, and bandages from those who have come here praying for recovery from their injuries. And that's just what's arrived recently; there are hundreds of such offerings in storage.

If you are with a group and call in advance, you may be able to get inside the Doullut Steamboat House on Egania Street near the river (949-1422). It and its neighbor, built just after the turn of the century by Milton Doullut, are two of the most extravagant examples of what is called Victorian Steamboat Gothic architecture, with cypress furbelows, glazed brick, marching columns, great steamboat-style galleries, and glass pilot houses perched on the tops.

Chalmette National Battlefield

Type of Attraction: Scene of the Battle of New Orleans, Jackson's famous victory over the British in 1815

Location: 8608 St. Bernard Highway (Rampart/St. Claude extended)

Admission: Free

Hours: 9 a.m.–5 p.m.

Phone: 281-0510

When to Go: January 7–8 to see the battle re-enactment; otherwise anytime

Special Comments: Although the car gate closes at 5 p.m., there is a pedestrian entry near the cemetery.

Overall Appeal by Age Group:

Pre-school	Grade School	Teens	Young Adults	Over 30	Senior Citizens
none	★★	★★	★★½	★★★	★★★

Author's Rating: Admittedly, battlefields (and military cemeteries) don't appeal to everyone, but if you do find wandering such grounds moving, this is an unusually reassuring and well-marked route—an unalloyed, Hollywood-cheery victory, not a haunting experience like revisiting Antietam, for example. And you can't beat the scenery. ★★★

How Much Time to Allow: 1–2 hours

Description and Comments   The bare bones of this battle, so to speak, are familiar to most Americans, by film and pop-music history, if nothing else. Here, on January 8, 1815, British forces under Lt. Gen. Edward Pakenham, brother-in-law of the great Duke of Wellington, were crushed (and Pakenham killed) by the ragtag coalition of Tennessee volunteers, other Southern regiments hustled down for support, free men of color, and Barataria pirates under the able and often ruthless Andrew Jackson. More than 2,000 British were killed on that last day (there had been skirmishes since before Christmas), but only 13 Americans were lost, all but two of them black. The other ironies are almost as well known: The Treaty of Ghent, ending the war, had been signed on Christmas Eve, making the battle moot; Jackson made several errors in judgment that might easily have thrown the victory the other way; and Jackson, who had unsuccessfully tried to persuade President Jefferson to name him governor of Louisiana, wound up far more famous as a result of the battle—the city threw him a triumphal parade modeled on those of the conquering Caesars—which was in effect the first great stroke of his own presidential campaign. It also marked a great turning point in the city's history, uniting Creoles and Americans (and pirates) against a common threat. The annual re-enactment is highly theatrical, beginning the night before with staged spying on Pakenham and Jackson. Oddly, the adjoining Chalmette National Cemetery dates from the Civil War and holds only two veterans of the Battle of New Orleans; most of the other bodies, some 14,000 of them, are Union soldiers.

Touring Tips   You can just drive past the landmarks, but the visitors center, once the plantation home of Rene Beauregard, son of the general, holds good exhibits that help you understand the battle's waves, a half-hour film, and well-informed rangers. Be sure to walk over to the levee and look onto the Mississippi River.

Jackson Barracks Museum

Type of Attraction: Military museum with antique and modern armaments and aircraft from the Revolutionary War through the 1990s.

Location: 6400 St. Claude Avenue (Rampart Street extended)

Admission: Free

Hours: Monday–Friday, 8 a.m.–4 p.m.; Saturday, 9 a.m.–3 p.m.

Phone: 278-8242

When to Go: Anytime

Overall Appeal by Age Group:

Pre-school	Grade School	Teens	Young Adults	Over 30	Senior Citizens
★	★★★★	★★★	★★★★	★★★★	★★★★

Author's Rating: Fantastic variety of exhibits in this small space, and almost guaranteed to make kids happy. And since even Operation Desert Storm is represented here (by a Phantom jet and a Russian-made tank abandoned in the Gulf War), veterans or students of any war in U.S. history will find something to marvel at. ★★★★

How Much Time to Allow: 1½ hours

Description and Comments   Tanks, artillery, jets, battle flags, decorations, uniforms, maps. . . . This military museum seems to have acquired relics from every skirmish and siege in the nation's history, but without the sometimes-morbid touch of the Confederate Museum. The museum's main building is a powder magazine dating to 1837, but not surprisingly, it had to expand into an annex. The presence of Guardsmen may make this even more realistic for youngsters.

Touring Tips   This is now headquarters for the National Guard, and subject to "internal business," so it wouldn't hurt to call ahead. As you pass the Jackson Barracks next door, you may feel the ghosts even more strongly: The base was built by order of (President) Andy Jackson, and Civil War generals Robert E. Lee, P.G.T. Beauregard, Ulysses S. Grant, and George McLellan were all stationed here as young West Point graduates.

ZONE 6: MID-CITY/GENTILLY

Pitot House

Type of Attraction: Historic, early-nineteenth-century home

Location: 1440 Moss Street

Admission: $5 adults, $3 seniors and children under 12

Hours: Wednesday–Saturday, 10 a.m.–3 p.m.

Phone: 482-0312

When to Go: Anytime

Overall Appeal by Age Group:

Pre-school	Grade School	Teens	Young Adults	Over 30	Senior Citizens
none	½	★	★★½	★★★	★★★

Author's Rating: Evocative and in fine condition. ★★★

How Much Time to Allow: 1–2 hours, depending on your interest

Description and Comments   When it was built in 1799 for Degas' great grandmother (it's named for James Pitot, first mayor of the city, who bought it soon after), this West Indies–style home—encircled by porches, protected by full shutters—was a block away where the Catholic school now stands. It was used in this century as a convent by Mother Francis Xavier Cabrini, the first canonized saint of the United States. It has been beautifully restored to its original condition and furnished with period antiques.

Touring Tips   Under the aegis of the State Landmarks Society, who moved it in the 1960s, this house has been made wheelchair accessible.

ZONE 7: LAKEVIEW/WEST END/BUCKTOWN

If you're headed toward City Park, and you should be, you can visit Lake Lawn Metairie Cemetery on Pontchartrain Boulevard at Metairie Road (486-6331), probably the only safe cemetery for tourists to explore (but don't just wander off by yourself, even here). It's younger than the others, built after the Civil War, and not so crowded, but it houses some of the most elaborate sepulchers around: Moorish, Japanese, Greek, Egyptian, Gothic, you name it. At the foot of the 85-foot obelisk are four statues, because although grieving widower Daniel Moriarty was told there were only three Graces, he insisted there be one at each side, so they've been nicknamed Faith, Hope, Charity and Mrs. Moriarty. You can borrow a general recorded tour at the funeral home, as well as one that locates Civil War veterans and statesmen.

City Park

Type of Attraction: Municipal park with a variety of recreational and cultural attractions

Location: 1 Palm Drive off I-10 (City Park/Metairie exit)

Admission: Park free; museum, botanical gardens, and some recreational centers have fees.

Hours: Sunrise to sunset

Phone: 482-4888

When to Go: Anytime

Overall Appeal by Age Group:

Pre-school	Grade School	Teens	Young Adults	Over 30	Senior Citizens
★★★	★★★★★	★★★	★★★★★	★★★★★	★★★

Author's Rating: An unrivaled family venue, with attractions for kids, jocks, picnickers, nature-lovers, and general romantics. ★★★★★

How Much Time to Allow: 1–4 hours

Description and Comments   This is an extraordinary municipal gift, 1,500 acres from the old Allard Plantation. It was presented to the city by John McDonough, whose statue stands in Lafayette Square, and is home to the largest stand of mature live oaks in the world. City Park has an almost unequaled variety of recreational facilities, golf courses, tennis courts, batting cages, riding stables, lagoons, etc., plus a bandstand (the Beatles played here in 1964), the New Orleans Museum of Art, the Botanical Gardens, and the famous Dueling Oaks beneath which hundreds of formal duels were fought during the nineteenth century. The park also has many simpler attractions, including the Storyland Amusement Park, an old-fashioned but swell children's fairyland where kids can climb over, around, and into the larger-than-life storybook exhibits and hear the out-loud stories straight from the "books'" mouths. *Child* magazine calls this one of the top ten playgrounds in the United States. Next door is Carousel Gardens, known to locals as The Flying Horses, one of the few surviving carved wooden merry-go-rounds in the country. And beyond that are a kid-scaled Ferris wheel, miniature trains, bumper cars, a roller coaster, and so on.

Touring Tips   From Thanksgiving through New Year's, nearly a million tiny lights are strung among the trees, and the Carousel stays lighted and alive into the evening. Long lines of locals make this an annual holiday event. That's Beauregard at the front gate, of course. Also be sure to notice the WPA symbols, chisels, hammers, and so on, worked into the iron of the bridges around the grounds.

Longue Vue House and Gardens

Type of Attraction: Historic home, decorative arts museum, and formal gardens

Location: 7 Bamboo Road off I-10 (Metairie Road exit)

Admission: $10 adults, $6 seniors, $3 students and children

Hours: Monday–Saturday, 10 a.m.–4:30 p.m. (last tour at 4 p.m.); Sunday, 1–5 p.m. (last tour at 4:15 p.m.)

Phone: 488-5488

When to Go: Anytime, but flowering gardens peak in spring.

Special Comments: Check out the web page at www.longuevue.com.

Overall Appeal by Age Group:

Pre-school	Grade School	Teens	Young Adults	Over 30	Senior Citizens
½	★	★★	★★★	★★★★★	★★★★★

Author's Rating: Elegant, interesting, and satisfying. ★★★★★

How Much Time to Allow: 2 hours (1 each for house and gardens)

Description and Comments   The sumptuous Greek Revival home of phil-anthropist Edgar Bloom Stern and Edith Rosenwald Stern, daughter of Sears tycoon Julius Rosenwald, was constructed with the express idea that it would be left as a museum. It was designed by William and Geoffrey Platt, and the gardens were laid out by Ellen Biddle Shipman, who also oversaw much of the interior decoration, which features important antiques, rice-paper wall coverings, needlework, Oriental carpets, and Wedgwood creamware. The house also offers rotating exhibits in its gal-leries. Among the gardens are the Spanish Court (modeled after the gardens of the Alhambra), the Portuguese Canal, the Wild Garden, and the Walled Garden.

Touring Tips   The home is wheelchair accessible and a good choice for older visitors. Tour guide brochures are available in French, German, Ital-ian, Spanish, and Japanese, as well as large print. Educational programs are offered for both children and adults; inquire at the desk.

New Orleans Botanical Gardens

Type of Attraction: Formal gardens and conservatory

Location: Victory Avenue in City Park, across from the tennis center

Admission: $3 adults, $1 children ages 5–12, free for ages 4 and under

Hours: Tuesday–Sunday, 10 a.m.–4:30 p.m.

Phone: 483-9386

When to Go: Anytime; seasonal exhibits

Special Comments: A quiet respite, not as elaborate as Longue Vue Gar-dens, but only a few minutes' stroll from the New Orleans Museum of Art and emotionally well paired with it

Overall Appeal by Age Group:

Pre-school	Grade School	Teens	Young Adults	Over 30	Senior Citizens
★	★★	★★	★★★★	★★★★	★★★★★

Author's Rating: A fine refuge. ★★★★

How Much Time to Allow: 15 minutes–1 hour

Description and Comments   This was the city's first public classical gar-dens, an Art Deco–style WPA creation marrying art and nature. Today its 10 acres house about 2,000 varieties of plants grouped into theme gardens and settings, among them a tropical conservatory, aquatic gardens, an aza-lea and camellia garden, a rose garden, cold frames, and horticultural trails.

Touring Tips The Garden Study Center offers 90-minute educational and how-to programs for about $10; call 483-9427 for a schedule.

New Orleans Museum of Art

Type of Attraction: Wide-ranging fine arts and decorative arts collection

Location: Lelong Avenue and Dueling Oak Drive in City Park

Admission: $6 adults, $5 seniors, $3 children ages 3–17; free admission Thursdays 10 a.m.–noon for Louisiana residents only

Hours: Tuesday–Sunday, 10 a.m.–5 p.m.

Phone: 488-2631

When to Go: Anytime

Special Comments: An all-ages introduction-to-art exhibit called "The Starting Point" is as good as it gets.

Overall Appeal by Age Group:

Pre-school	Grade School	Teens	Young Adults	Over 30	Senior Citizens
★	★★★	★★★	★★★★★	★★★★★	★★★★★

Author's Rating: Art lovers should not miss this. ★★★★★

How Much Time to Allow: 1–3 hours

Description and Comments This neoclassical building, commissioned in 1910 by Jamaican-born New Orleans philanthropist Isaac Delgado to benefit "rich and poor alike," lives up to its mission, housing more than 35,000 works by not only the premier American and European artists— Picasso, Miro, and Degas, whose studio was nearby—but African, Japanese, Chinese, and Native American art as well. Its "Art of the Americas" collection, ranging from pre-Columbian through Spanish Colonial times, is one of the largest, as is its decorative glass works. There are miniatures, furnishings, and regional arts and crafts from the nineteenth century to today—you can find even the trendy Faberge represented. Sketching of these masterworks is welcome, but in dry media only (pencil, charcoal, etc.) and on a single tablet no larger than legal size. One wing is devoted to rotating exhibits. General tours and special exhibition lectures are offered daily; the courtyard cafe serves lunch and afternoon beverages.

Touring Tips Free parking

ZONE 8: NEW ORLEANS EAST

Louisiana Nature Center

Type of Attraction: Nature preserve and planetarium

Location: Joe W. Brown Memorial Park, 11000 Lake Forest Boulevard (off I-10)

Admission: $4.75 adults, $3.75 seniors, $2.50 children

Hours: Tuesday–Friday, 9 a.m.–5 p.m.; Saturday, 10 a.m.–5 p.m.; Sunday, noon–5 p.m.; planetarium laser concerts Friday and Saturday at 9 and 10:30 p.m. and midnight

Phone: 861-2537; planetarium schedule, 246-STAR

When to Go: Anytime

Special Comments: Parts of the trails have wheelchair-accessible boardwalks.

Overall Appeal by Age Group:

Pre-school	Grade School	Teens	Young Adults	Over 30	Senior Citizens
★★	★★★	★★	★★½	★★	★★★

Author's Rating: A rare urban reserve. ★★½

How Much Time to Allow: 1–2 hours

Description and Comments   This may be one of those places you don't get to until the second trip, but it would be worth visiting: an 86-acre forest and wetlands reserve with trails, greenhouses, changing science exhibits in the center, and a hands-on Discovery Loft with fossils, skeletons, etc., plus some live specimens. Local wildlife can be observed either from the trails or from window overlooks at the Wildlife Garden.

Touring Tips   Weekend visitors should inquire about special activities such as canoeing, bird-watching, etc.

ZONE 10: METAIRIE ABOVE CAUSEWAY/KENNER/ JEFFERSON HIGHWAY

If you are staying out near the airport, Destrehan Manor is very close, about eight miles farther west. However, since most people consider the River Road plantations as out-of-town attractions, we have included it with the other plantation homes in "Sight-Seeing and Tours" on pages 247–250.

Rivertown

Type of Attraction: Family amusement/education complex, with a dozen small museums and activity centers along three blocks in suburban Kenner

Location: Welcome center at 405 Williams Boulevard off I-10

Admission: All-complex pass $13 adults, $9 seniors and children ages 12 and under; single venues $3 adults, $2.50 seniors and children ages 12 and under

Hours: Tuesday–Saturday, 9 a.m.–5 p.m.; observatory, Thursday–Saturday, 7:30–10:30 p.m.

Phone: 468-7231 or (800) 473-6789

When to Go: Anytime

Special Comments: Business travelers bringing the family along may find this a good reason to stay in an airport-area hotel.

Overall Appeal by Age Group:

Pre-school	Grade School	Teens	Young Adults	Over 30	Senior Citizens
★★	★★★★★	★★★	★★★★	★★★★	★★★

Author's Rating: A mixed bag, but at least something for everyone. ★★★★

How Much Time to Allow: 2–4 hours

Description and Comments   Families with children can duck the Bourbon Street barrage for at least a half day by heading toward this Victorian village–style complex a half mile from the airport. The Louisiana Toy Train Museum is one of the all-ages attractions, with a half dozen large dioramas crisscrossed with tracks for the vintage Lionel, American Flyer, and other small-gauge collections (most dating to the 1950s). The Mardi Gras Museum conveys the trashy, flashy fever of Carnival at safe and PG-rated distance, with costumes, beads, a simulated costume shop, and lots of live-action video. Probably only the most hardcore football fans, or small children, will find more than a few minutes' entertainment at the New Orleans Saints Hall of Fame, which is primarily a giant locker room of helmets, uniforms, game balls, etc. The Daily Living Science Center, a hands-on if lightweight introduction to car engines, weather, dental hygiene, commercial laundries, and other strange and sundry aspects of everyday life leads into a full-sized NASA space station, complete with weightlessness chamber. It also has a planetarium and an observatory, which is open Thursday through Saturday, 7:30–10:30 p.m. (582-4000). On the other hand, the Louisiana Wildlife Museum and Aquarium is well organized and attractive, with over 700 preserved specimens of indigenous mammals and reptiles and a 15,000-gallon tank holding marine life. Literally in the backyard of the Wildlife Museum is the Cannes Brulee Native American Center of the Gulf South, a living history installation that re-creates a Native American village, complete with live hogs, poultry, rabbits, and crayfish, and staffed by serious and well-spoken native craftsmen and "residents." There is also a 300-seat Repertory Theatre, and the Children's Castle offers puppet shows, magic displays, and storytelling.

Touring Tips   Like many children's museums, this tends to be busier before lunch than after. Walk across to LaSalle's Landing for a good view of the mighty Mississippi.

ZONE 11: WEST BANK

Blaine Kern's Mardi Gras World

Type of Attraction: Year-round factory of flamboyant Mardi Gras floats and costumes

Location: 223 Newton Street, Algiers (across the river from the World Trade Center)

Admission: $13.50 adults, $10 seniors, $6.50 children ages 3–11

Hours: Daily, 9:30 a.m.–4:30 p.m.

Phone: 361-7821

When to Go: Anytime

Special Comments: One of the four major year-round ways to experience Mardi Gras, and a sure-fire kids' favorite, especially combined with the free ferry ride

Overall Appeal by Age Group:

Pre-school	Grade School	Teens	Young Adults	Over 30	Senior Citizens
★★★	★★★	★★★★	★★★★	★★★	★★★

Author's Rating: Impressive and fantastical, if a little static. ★★★

How Much Time to Allow: 1½–2 hours

Description and Comments   Blaine Kern is known as "Mr. Mardi Gras," and for good reason: He made his first float in 1947, at the age of 19; and since then has become probably the busiest float-makers in the world, responsible for not only more than half of the floats and multistory-sized figures for Mardi Gras, which brings in a reported $20 million a year alone, but also for Macy's Thanksgiving Day parade, the Bastille Day celebrations in Cannes, France, and more than 40 other parades around the world. They even make sculptures and props for Disney. The sculpture company was founded right before the 1984 World's Fair in New Orleans to build the giant characters for that event, and now works for amusement parks all over the world. These huge warehouses, more than 500,000 square feet of them, called "dens," are filled with props, celebrity statues, royal regalia, and the artists creating them; you can even dress in costume and have your picture taken alongside one of the characters.

Touring Tips   Take the Canal Street Ferry across and look for the shuttle bus. For older visitors, the architecture of the Algiers neighborhood may hold some interest, but it is not a great area to walk around, especially late in the day.

Part Thirteen

Dining in New Orleans

Food is THE big deal in New Orleans.

Observe the conversations in any restaurant. In other cities, they'd concern sports, politics, or business. In New Orleans, the talk is all about eating. It's entered into with earnestness and knowledge, and occasionally even seriousness.

Although the whole country is food mad these days, the passion in New Orleans wells up through six or seven generations of genes. There was a full-blown regional cuisine here over a century ago, long before America got the gourmet bug.

The best way to enjoy eating in New Orleans is to understand that it's intensely local. Kind of like in Europe. In just the way that French or Italian towns offer their local culinary styles to the near-exclusion of anything else, so too is southeast Louisiana obsessed with Creole and Cajun cooking.

Which brings up a question that will only get you into trouble. "What's the difference between Creole food and Cajun food?" After noting that Creole is city and Cajun is country, just abandon the matter. Creole and Cajun have influenced each other so much in recent years that you find the same menus and flavors throughout southeast Louisiana. It's a vaporous issue—which means, of course, that it gets talked about a lot, usually in restaurants.

Creole and Cajun chefs cook the same raw materials. Which is a big reason why they're both so good. First, this is a land of superb seafood, starting with the Big Four: oysters, shrimp, crabs, and crawfish. Supporting them (or vice-versa) is a large cast of finfish from local waters.

There's nothing quite like the freshness of seafood that came to your plate by way of a beat-up old truck that only had to drive a few miles. There are restaurants in New Orleans where you can eat a fish while watching his relatives swim and jump in the lake right outside the window.

I suppose you're expecting me to define the Creole taste now. Well, I give up. I'm blinkered by having eaten Creole food all my life, which makes me think of it as totally normal. What I can tell you is what I miss in the food I eat when I travel. I find non-Creole American food lacking in salt, pepper, richness, and general intensity of flavor.

One of the explanations for this is the amount of salt, pepper, cream, butter, and other fats in classic Creole cooking. Indeed, an often-cited characteristic of New Orleans recipes is that they have a way of beginning, "First you make a roux." (Roux, a blend of flour and oil, butter, or other fat, cooked to various shades of brown, is the main active ingredient in dishes from gumbo to oysters Rockefeller.) As a result, much of Creole and Cajun cooking in the old style is high in all those things that the food police tell us to stay away from.

But during the past decade there's been a revolution in Creole cooking, spurred by intense competition from the hundreds (this is no exaggeration) of new restaurants that have opened. Diners have come to expect new dishes, ingredients, and flavors, and the younger, higher-profile chefs have been happy to invent them. Most of the new Creole cuisine is much lighter than its predecessors. Even roux is becoming rarer. Occasionally it's even left out of gumbo (a state of affairs that an old-time Creole cook would consider heresy).

The more innovative local chefs are, at this writing, pulling back from the one-big-world-of-taste fusions they spent the 1990s creating. We're seeing a revival of classic local ideas. The dishes don't taste or look like they did 20 years ago—the ingredients, for one thing, are a lot better now. But you can see a lot of familiar old friends under the new guises.

As the 1990s ended, a flood of ethnic restaurants moved onto the scene. Local diners welcomed the diversity, and at last some of the exotic cuisines are getting their due in terms of quality foodstuffs, skilled chefs, and pleasant restaurants. I've included a good assortment of them among the restaurants recommended in this book.

If that last fact causes you to cock an eyebrow and wonder whether our gustatory island will lose its distinctiveness, rest easy. No matter how enthusiastically even the most sophisticated New Orleans diner waxes about some new Vietnamese-Mexican fusion bistro, you can be sure that in his most relaxed moments he's still munching down poor-boy sandwiches, boiled crawfish, jambalaya, and bread pudding. As will all other aficionados of Creole food from near or far. Because we all know that, like all the world's great ethnic cuisines, great Creole and Cajun cooking is only found in the land of its birth.

A FEW THINGS YOU SHOULD KNOW

Because the cuisine of New Orleans is so intimately tied to the indigenous ingredients, it's important to pay attention to the seasons. Although many restaurants serve, say, crawfish year round, crawfish are incomparably better in the peak of their natural cycle. Here's the schedule:

Crawfish: Christmas through the Fourth of July, with the peak of quality in April and May.

Crabs, soft-shell and otherwise: April through October. There's a dip in quality in July, then they get good again. Usually the warmer it is, the better the crabmeat.

Oysters: Good year round, but a little off during the spawn in July and August. (In other words, forget that months-with-an-R myth.) The best months are November and December, especially if a convincing cold front has passed through.

Shrimp: There are several species, so seasons click on and off. The best times are late spring, late summer, and most of the fall. The only poor month for shrimp is March.

Speckled trout: October through January.

Tuna: May through September.

Pompano: July through October.

Creole tomatoes: These meaty, sweet, gigantic, sensual tomatoes have a short season, in April and May, but are worth waiting for. Lately we've seen a second crop of Creoles in the fall.

The calendar is also reliable in predicting when restaurants will be at their best. Absolutely the worst time to eat in New Orleans is during the Mardi Gras season, which extends three weeks before the movable Ash Wednesday (in February or early March). The city's restaurants are stretched thin at that time of year by tourists, conventions, and Mardi Gras balls. What's more, waiters and other restaurant personnel tend to be heavy participants in Carnival hi-jinks and are, shall we say, not at their peaks.

The best times for a serious eater to come to town are the months of October and April. The weather is beautiful for patio dining, the food supplies are at their best, and the conventions aren't overwhelming. Also good are the summer months, especially July and September. The heat and humidity convince tourists and conventions to stay away (despite the fact that there may be no better air-conditioned city on earth), and the restaurants are eager to please you.

Also of note are two superb food festivals. The New Orleans Jazz and Heritage Festival takes place on the last week of April and the first week of May, with an outdoor surfeit of music and indigenous food. Then, in June or July (the date varies from year to year), the New Orleans Wine and Food Experience brings you indoors for an extended weekend of special feasting with the city's best chefs and drinking with the world's best winemakers.

TOURIST PLACES

In the restaurant profiles that make up most of this chapter, you may notice that a few well-known or highly visible restaurants are missing. This is not an oversight. These restaurants, listed below, in my opinion are not as worthwhile as other comparable options.

Andrew Jaeger's House of Seafood   622 Conti 522-4964

The place looks great and the chef/owner talks a good game, but the restaurant is maddeningly inconsistent.

Central Grocery   923 Decatur 523-1620

As this old emporium of imported food allowed its floor space to become more taken over for the vending of muffulettas to tourists, both the store and the muffulettas have declined.

Deanie's Seafood   1713 Lake Ave., Bucktown 831-4141

Deanie's is immensely popular, but what brings that about is the eye-popping size of its indifferent seafood platters.

Jimmy Buffet's Margaritaville Cafe   1104 Decatur 592-2565

A must for parrot heads—but only after eating somewhere else.

Landry's Seafood House   400 N. Peters 558-0038

A regional chain, Landry's has the look of a great old middle-of-nowhere Louisiana roadhouse, but the food is strictly formula and not very good.

Mulate's   201 Julia 522-1492

A mammoth place copied from the original Cajun dance restaurant in Breaux Bridge, Mulate's does indeed have good Cajun music, but the food is only occasionally interesting.

Patout's Cajun Cabin   501 Bourbon 524-4054

They occupy the space where Al Hirt plays when he's in town, with gilded versions of Cajun food. Although it can be quite good, the inconsistency is so extreme as to make the place unrecommendable.

Ralph & Kacoo's   519 Toulouse 522-5226

It started as a fine seafood house upriver and expanded into a chain of very large, somewhat overpriced, and mediocre food factories.

NEW PLACES

Here are a few restaurants that opened too soon before we went to press for a review to be reliable in the long term. I include them for those who like to hit the new places and who don't mind being part of a work in progress.

Cafe Indo   216 N. Carrollton Avenue, Mid-City—Zone 6

It evolved out of the original Lemon Grass Cafe, and occupies that now-spiffy restaurant's old digs. The menu is almost evenly split between Vietnamese and French dishes. This is not as schizophrenic as it might seem, and both parts of the menu are delicious.

56 Degrees   610 Poydras Street, CBD—Zone 2

The name is a reference to the perfect temperature for storing wine. So wine is a theme. So is a fusion between Southeast Asian cooking (the native style of chef/owner Minh Bui) and everything else. All this is served in a tasting menu of some six or seven courses in half of what once was the most striking antique bank lobby in town.

Herbsaint   701 St. Charles Avenue, CBD—Zone 2

The second restaurant of Bayona's chef Susan Spicer, this corner cafe is a little more casual about itself—in every sense of the word. The style is reminiscent of a hip French bistro. The basics are good, but the frills are unpolished.

Indigo   2285 Bayou Road, Mid-City—Zone 6

Indigo is associated with one of the most impressive guest houses along Esplanade Avenue, where there are many such. The kitchen likes to cook both local and American food, and is stridently inventive in doing so. Unusual fish, meats, and vegetables mark the menu. The dining room is separate from the guest house and is handsome and comfortable.

Lillette   3637 Magazine Street, Uptown—Zone 4

Lilette was created by former Gautreau's chef John Harris, a serious talent. The palce is tiny, tiled, with fewer than 40 seats. The menu is a bit eclectic, with French dishes next to the likes of a take on Philly cheese steak. The chef has an excellent palate, however, and the food is interesting.

The Restaurants

OUR FAVORITE NEW ORLEANS RESTAURANTS: EXPLAINING THE RATINGS

We have developed detailed profiles for the best restaurants (in our opinion) in town. Each profile features an easily scanned heading which allows you to check out the restaurant's name, cuisine, star rating, cost, quality rating, and value rating very quickly.

Star Rating   The star rating is an overall rating that encompasses the entire dining experience, including style, service, and ambiance in addition to the taste, presentation, and quality of the food. Five stars is the highest rating possible and connotes the best of everything. Four-star restaurants are exceptional, and three-star restaurants are well above average. Two-star restaurants are good. One star is used to connote an average restaurant that demonstrates an unusual capability in some area of specialization, for example, an otherwise unmemorable place that has great barbecued chicken.

Cost   Below the restaurant's name and the star rating is an expense description that provides a comparative sense of how much a complete meal will cost. A complete meal for our purposes consists of an entree with vegetable or side dish, and choice of soup or salad. Appetizers, desserts, drinks, and tips are excluded.

Inexpensive	$14 and less per person
Moderate	$15–25 per person
Expensive	$26–40 per person
Very Expensive	Over $40 per person

Quality Rating   To the right of the cost rating appear a number and a letter. The number is a quality rating based on a scale of 0–100, with 100 being the highest (best) rating attainable. The quality rating is based expressly on the taste, freshness of ingredients, preparation, presentation, and creativity of food served. There is no consideration of price. If you are a person who wants the best food available, and cost is not an issue, you need look no further than the quality ratings.

Value Rating   If, on the other hand, you are looking for both quality and value, then you should check the value rating, expressed in letters. The value ratings are defined as follows:

A	Exceptional value, a real bargain
B	Good value
C	Fair value, you get exactly what you pay for

D   Somewhat overpriced
F   Significantly overpriced

Location   To the right of the restaurant's address is a designation for geographic zone. This zone description will give you a general idea of where the restaurant is located. For ease of use, we divide New Orleans into 12 geographic zones.

Zone 1	French Quarter
Zone 2	Central Business District
Zone 3	Uptown below Napoleon
Zone 4	Uptown above Napoleon
Zone 5	Downtown/St. Bernard
Zone 6	Mid-City/Gentilly
Zone 7	Lakeview/West End/Bucktown
Zone 8	New Orleans East
Zone 9	Metairie below Causeway
Zone 10	Metairie above Causeway/Kenner/Jefferson Highway
Zone 11	West Bank
Zone 12	North Shore

If you are in the French Quarter and intend to walk or take a cab to dinner, you may want to choose a restaurant from among those located in Zone 1. If you have a car, you might include restaurants from contiguous zones in your consideration. (See pages 10–25 for detailed zone maps.)

OUR PICK OF THE BEST NEW ORLEANS RESTAURANTS

Because restaurants are opening and closing all the time in New Orleans, we have tried to confine our list to establishments—or chefs—with proven track records over a fairly long period of time. Those newer or changed establishments that demonstrate staying power and consistency will be profiled in subsequent editions.

The list is highly selective. Non-inclusion of a particular place does not necessarily indicate that the restaurant is not good, but only that it was not ranked among the best or most consistent in its genre. Detailed profiles of each restaurant follow in alphabetical order at the end of this chapter. Also, we've listed the types of payment accepted at each restaurant, using the following codes:

AE	American Express	DC	Diners Club
CB	Carte Blanche	MC	MasterCard
DS	Discover	V	VISA

The Best New Orleans Restaurants

Restaurant/Type	Star Rating	Price	Quality Rating	Value Rating	Zone
American					
Cuvee	★★★★	Very Exp	87	D	2
Cajun					
K-Paul's Louisiana Kitchen	★★★★	Very Exp	88	D	1
Alex Patout's Louisiana Restaurant	★★★★	Very Exp	86	C	1
Bon Ton Cafe	★★★	Exp	84	B	2
Caribbean					
Martinique	★★★	Exp	85	B	4
Chinese					
China Blossom	★★★★	Mod	86	B	11
Trey Yuen	★★★★	Mod	85	D	12
Creole					
Commander's Palace	★★★★★	Very Exp	97	B	3
Dakota	★★★★★	Very Exp	96	C	12
Emeril's	★★★★★	Very Exp	93	C	2
Gabrielle	★★★★	Very Exp	96	B	6
Brigtsen's	★★★★	Very Exp	94	B	4
Gautreau's	★★★★	Very Exp	93	C	4
Clancy's	★★★★	Exp	92	B	4
Bella Luna	★★★★	Very Exp	92	C	1
Le Parvenu	★★★★	Very Exp	91	C	10
Upperline	★★★★	Exp	90	B	4
Mr. B's	★★★★	Very Exp	90	C	1
Nola	★★★★	Very Exp	89	C	1
Wolfe's of New Orleans	★★★★	Exp	88	B	7
Palace Cafe	★★★★	Exp	88	C	2
Jacques-Imo's	★★★★	Mod	87	B	4
Gallagher's	★★★★	Exp	87	C	12
Dick & Jenny's	★★★★	Exp	87	B	4
Cafe Marigny	★★★★	Exp	87	C	5
Red Room	★★★★	Very Exp	86	D	3
Red Fish Grill	★★★★	Exp	86	B	1
Tujague's	★★★★	Exp	85	C	1

The Best New Orleans Restaurants *(continued)*

Restaurant/Type	Star Rating	Price	Quality Rating	Value Rating	Zone
Creole (continued)					
Mat & Naddie's	★★★	Exp	87	B	4
Mandich	★★★	Mod	86	B	5
Kelsey's	★★★	Exp	86	B	11
201 Restaurant and Bar	★★★	Exp	86	C	1
Court of Two Sisters	★★★	Very Exp	85	C	1
Cafe Sbisa	★★★	Very Exp	85	C	1
Gumbo Shop	★★★	Inexp	84	B	1
Feelings	★★★	Exp	84	B	5
Creole French					
Galatoire's	★★★★	Very Exp	92	C	1
Christian's	★★★★	Very Exp	90	B	6
Delmonico	★★★★	Very Exp	89	D	3
Broussard's	★★★★	Very Exp	89	D	1
Arnaud's	★★★★	Very Exp	89	D	1
Brennan's	★★★★	Very Exp	88	D	1
Antoine's	★★★★	Very Exp	84	D	1
Creole Italian					
Vincent's	★★★★	Mod	88	B	10
Pascal's Manale	★★★★	Exp	86	B	4
Vincent's	★★★	Mod	87	B	4
Mosca's	★★★	Very Exp	86	C	11
Eclectic					
Bayona	★★★★★	Very Exp	98	B	1
Grill Room	★★★★★	Very Exp	97	D	2
Victor's	★★★★★	Very Exp	92	D	1
French					
Peristyle	★★★★★	Very Exp	95	C	1
Artesia	★★★★★	Very Exp	95	C	12
Gerard's Downtown	★★★★	Very Exp	91	C	2
Bistro at Maison de Ville	★★★★	Very Exp	87	C	1
French Bistro					
The French Table	★★★★	Very Exp	92	C	10

The Best New Orleans Restaurants *(continued)*

Restaurant/Type	Star Rating	Price	Quality Rating	Value Rating	Zone
French Bistro (continued)					
La Crepe Nanou	★★★★	Exp	89	A	4
Cafe Degas	★★★	Mod	86	B	6
Fusion					
Pelican Club	★★★★	Very Exp	93	C	1
Marisol	★★★★	Exp	92	B	1
Indian					
India Palace	★★★	Mod	84	C	10
Italian					
Cafe Giovanni	★★★★	Exp	94	B	1
La Riviera	★★★★	Exp	88	C	10
Irene's Cuisine	★★★★	Exp	87	B	1
Japanese					
Sake Cafe	★★★★	Exp	87	B	10
Shogun	★★★★	Mod	85	C	9
Korean					
Genghis Khan	★★★	Mod	85	C	6
Mediterranean					
La Provence	★★★★	Very Exp	89	C	12
Byblos	★★★★	Inexp	86	A	9
Odyssey Grill	★★★	Mod	87	B	9
Neighborhood Cafe					
Mandina's	★★★	Mod	85	A	6
Northern Italian					
Andrea's	★★★★	Very Exp	87	C	9
Bacco	★★★★	Exp	87	C	1
Sandwiches					
Kosher Cajun Deli	★★	Inexp	82	B	10
Mother's	★★	Inexp	81	D	2
Seafood					
Drago's	★★★★	Mod	87	C	10
Uglesich's	★★★★	Mod	86	D	3

The Best New Orleans Restaurants *(continued)*

Restaurant/Type	Star Rating	Price	Quality Rating	Value Rating	Zone
Seafood (continued)					
Bozo's	★★★★	Inexp	85	B	9
Middendorf's	★★★	Mod	85	B	12
Mike Anderson's	★★★	Mod	84	C	1
Bruning's	★★★	Inexp	84	A	7
Restaurant des Familles	★★★	Mod	81	C	11
Barrow's Shady Inn	★★★	Inexp	81	B	4
Southwestern					
Vaqueros	★★★★	Mod	86	C	4
Spanish					
Vega Tapas Cafe	★★★	Mod	87	B	9
Steaks and Chops					
Ruth's Chris Steak House	★★★★	Very Exp	89	D	6
Ruth's Chris Steak House	★★★★	Very Exp	89	D	10
Dickie Brennan's Steakhouse	★★★★	Very Exp	88	C	1
Mike Ditka's	★★★★	Very Exp	88	D	2
Thai					
Basil Leaf	★★★★	Exp	90	C	4
Vietnamese					
Lemon Grass Cafe	★★★★	Exp	89	D	2
Kim Son	★★★★	Inexp	87	A	11

More Recommendations

Best Sunday Brunch

Andrea's   3100 19th Street, Metairie   834-8583

Arnaud's   813 Bienville   523-5433

Artesia   21516 LA 36, Abita Springs   892-1662

Bacco   310 Chartres   522-2426

Begue's (Royal Sonesta Hotel)   300 Bourbon   553-2278

Brennan's   417 Royal   525-9711

Cafe Sbisa   1011 Decatur   522-5565

Cafe Volage   720 Dublin   861-4227

Charley G's   111 Veterans Boulevard, Metairie   837-6408

Commander's Palace   1403 Washington Avenue   899-8221

French Market Bar (Ritz-Carlton Hotel)   921 Canal   524-1331

Grill Room (Windsor Court Hotel)   300 Gravier   522-1992

Mr. B's   201 Royal   523-2078

Mike Ditka's   600 St. Charles Avenue   569-8989

Palace Cafe   605 Canal   523-1661

Veranda (Hotel Inter-Continental)   444 St. Charles Avenue   525-5566

Red Fish Grill   115 Bourbon   598-1200

Best Breakfasts

Abita Cafe   22132 Level, Abita Springs   867-9950

Begue's   300 Bourbon   553-2278

Bluebird Cafe   3625 Prytania   895-7166

Brennan's   417 Royal   525-9711

Cafe Atchafalaya   901 Louisiana Avenue   891-5271

Camellia Grill   626 S. Carrollton Avenue   866-9573

Coffee Pot   714 St. Peter   524-3500

Grill Room   300 Gravier   522-1992

La Madeleine   547 St. Ann   568-9950

Louis XVI   730 Bienville St.   581-7000

Mother's   401 Poydras   523-9656

Judice's   421 E. Gibson Covington   892-0708

Peppermill   3524 Severn Avenue, Metairie   455-2266

Petunia's   817 St. Louis   522-6440

Tally-Ho   400 Chartres   566-7071

Best Hamburgers

Beachcorner Lounge   4905 Canal   488-7357

Bywater Bar-B-Que   3162 Dauphine   944-4445

Camellia Grill   626 S. Carrollton Avenue   866-9573

Clover Grill   900 Bourbon   523-0904

KY's Olde Towne Bicycle Shop   2267 Carey Slidell   641-1911

Lakeview Harbor   911 Harrison Avenue   282-7639

Lee's Hamburgers   904 Veterans Boulevard, Metairie   836-6804

Michael's Mid-City Grill   4139 Canal   486-8200

Port of Call   838 Esplanade   523-0120

Snug Harbor   626 Frenchmen   949-0696

Ye Olde College Inn   3016 S. Carrollton Avenue   866-3683

Restaurants with Most Striking Architecture

Antoine's   713 St. Louis   581-4422

Arnaud's   813 Bienville   523-5433

Bacco   310 Chartres   522-2426

Bella Luna   914 N. Peters   529-1583

Brennan's   417 Royal   525-9711

Broussard's   819 Conti   581-3866

Cafe Sbisa   1011 Decatur   522-5565

Commander's Palace   1403 Washington Avenue   899-8221

Dickie Brennan's Steakhouse   716 Iberville   522-2467

56 Degrees   610 Poydras   212-5656

Grill Room   300 Gravier   522-1992

La Provence   25020 US 190, Lacombe   626-7662

Mike Ditka's   600 St. Charles Avenue   569-8989

Napoleon House   500 Chartres   524-9752

Red Fish Grill   115 Bourbon   598-1200

Red Room   2040 St. Charles Avenue   528-9759

Smith and Wollensky   1009 Poydras   561-0770

Trey Yuen (Mandeville)   600 Causeway Boulevard, Mandeville
626-4476

Tujague's   823 Decatur   525-8676

Best Cafes for Dessert and Coffee

Angelo Brocato   214 N. Carrollton Avenue   486-1465

Cafe du Monde   800 Decatur   525-4544

Coffee Cottage   2559 Metairie Road, Metairie   833-3513

La Madeleine   601 S. Carrollton Avenue   861-8661;
547 St. Ann   568-9950;   3300 Severn   456-1624

La Marquise   625 Chartres   524-0420

Morning Call Coffee Stand   3325 Severn Avenue, Metairie   885-4068

Best Restaurants for Dining with Children

Bozo's   3117 21st Street, Metairie   831-8666

Bull's Corner   1036 W. Airline Highway, Laplace   652-3544

Cavallino's   1500 S. Carrollton Avenue   866-9866

Corky's   4243 Veterans Boulevard, Metairie   887-5000

Creola   2891 US 190, Mandeville   727-4336

Drago's   3232 N. Arnoult Road, Metairie   888-9254

El Patio   3244 Georgia Avenue, Kenner   443-1188

Fury's   724 Martin Behrman Avenue, Metairie   834-5646

La Madeleine   601 S. Carrollton Avenue   861-8661;
547 St. Ann 568-9950;   3300 Severn   456-1624;

Mike Anderson's   215 Bourbon   524-3884;
2712 N. Arnoult   779-6453

New Orleans Hamburger & Seafood Co. 817 Veterans Boulevard, Metairie 837-8580

Peppermill 3524 Severn Avenue, Metairie 455-2266

Semolina 3226 Magazine 895-4260; 5080 Pontchartrain Boulevard 486-5581; Oakwood Mall (197 West Bank Expressway), Gretna 361-8293; 3501 Chateau Boulevard, Kenner 468-1047

West End Cafe 8536 Pontchartrain Boulevard 288-0711

Best Restaurants for Local Color

Antoine's 713 St. Louis 581-4422

Arnaud's 813 Bienville 523-5433

Bella Luna 914 N. Peters 529-1583

Brennan's 417 Royal 525-9711

Broussard's 819 Conti 581-3866

Bruning's West End Park 282-9395

Cafe du Monde 800 Decatur 525-4544

Commander's Palace 1403 Washington Avenue 899-8221

Court of Two Sisters 613 Royal 522-7273

Galatoire's 209 Bourbon 525-2021

Jacques-Imo's 8324 Oak 861-0886

Napoleon House 500 Chartres 524-9752

Pat O'Brien's 718 St. Peter 525-4823

Peristyle 1041 Dumaine 593-9535

Tavern On The Park 900 City Park Avenue 486-3333

Tujague's 823 Decatur 525-8676

Uglesich's 1238 Baronne 523-8571

Best Muffulettas

Anselmo's 3401 N. Hullen, Metairie 889-1212

Central Grocery 923 Decatur 523-1620

Come Back Inn   8016 W. Metairie Avenue, Metairie   467-9316

Johnny's Po-Boys   511 St. Louis   524-8129

Mr. Ed's   1001 Live Oak, Metairie   838-0022

Napoleon House   500 Chartres   524-9752

Ragusa's Sicilian Deli   3363 Severn Avenue, Metairie   454-2723

Best Restaurants with Oyster Bars

Acme Oyster House   724 Iberville   522-5973;   519 E. Boston
898- 0667;   7306 Lakeshore Drive   283-2096

Bozo's   3117 21st Street, Metairie   831-8666

Bruning's   West End Park   282-9395

Casamento's   4330 Magazine   895-9761

Drago's   3232 N. Arnoult Road, Metairie   888-9254

Felix's   739 Iberville   522-4440

Mike Anderson's   215 Bourbon   524-3884;
2712 N. Arnoult   779-6453

Red Fish Grill   115 Bourbon   598-1200

Remoulade   309 Bourbon   523-0377

Uglesich's   1238 Baronne   523-8571

Best Restaurants for Outdoor Dining

Bayona   430 Dauphine   525-4455

Broussard's   819 Conti   581-3866

Cafe Volage   720 Dublin   861-4227

Commander's Palace   1403 Washington Avenue   899-8221

Court of Two Sisters   613 Royal   522-7273

Feelings   2600 Chartres   945-2222

Gabrielle   3201 Esplanade Avenue   948-6233

Louis XVI   730 Bienville   581-7000

Marisol   437 Esplanade Avenue   943-1912

Martinique   5908 Magazine   891-8495

Mat & Naddie's   937 Leonidas   861-9600

Napoleon House   500 Chartres   524-9752

Royal Cafe   706 Royal   528-9086

Best Pizza

Bacco   310 Chartres   522-2426

Bravo   1711 St. Charles Avenue   525-5515

Brick Oven Cafe   2805 Williams Boulevard, Kenner   466-2097

Cafe Buon Giorno   830 Third, Gretna   363-9111

Cafe Italiano   3244 Magazine   891-4040

Cafe Nino   1519 S. Carrollton Avenue   865-9200

Cavallino's   1500 S. Carrollton Avenue   866-9866

Figaro Pizzerie   7900 Maple   866-0100

Italian Pie   417 S. Rampart   522-7552;   5219 Elysian Fields
   288-0888;   3002 Cleary   780-7500;   5650 Jefferson Highway
   734-3333;   3600 Williams Boulevard   469-4999;   1914 E. Judge
   Perez Drive   278-0001

Mark Twain's Pizza Landing   2035 Metairie Road, Metairie
   832-8032

Pizza Man of Covington   1248 Collins Boulevard (US 190),
   Covington   892-9874

201 RESTAURANT AND BAR ★★★

Contemporary/Creole	Expensive	QUALITY
		86

	VALUE
201 Decatur Street; 561-0007	C
French Quarter Zone 1	

Reservations: Accepted
When to go: Dinner
Entree range: $12–24
Payment: All major credit cards
Service rating: ★★★
Friendliness rating: ★★★
Parking: Pay parking lots nearby

Bar: Full service
Wine selection: Good; many by the glass
Dress: Casual
Disabled access: Limited
Customers: A mix of visitors and locals early; later, waiters and bartenders from other Quarter restaurants

Dinner: Sunday–Thursday, 6–11 p.m.; Friday–Saturday, 6 p.m.–midnight

Setting & atmosphere: The one overly spacious room could be cast as the lobby of a bordello in a movie. Big double-hung windows give views onto both Iberville and Decatur streets and their constant pedestrian traffic.

Recommended dishes: Barbecue shrimp; steamed mussels with saffron tomato broth; grilled quail with pears; baked oysters of the day; crab and oyster-stuffed shrimp; pasta with wild mushrooms, asparagus and truffle oil; seared duck breast with mashed sweet potatoes and cherry-port reduction; grilled pork tenderloin with blackberry sauce; poached pears with mascarpone; creme brulee with berries.

Entertainment & amenities: Sometimes they have live music.

Summary & comments: The premises feel more like a bar than a restaurant, and when it fills up it's noisy. But that makes the food here a pleasant surprise. While the presentations are not as polished as they would be in the more expensive places, the kitchen's work is carefully done. One wants for nothing in the way of ingredient quality or creativity. The service staff is very friendly and well informed, even about the ample assortment of wines by the glass. 201 stays open later than most full-service places, serving till midnight on Friday and Saturday.

ALEX PATOUT'S LOUISIANA RESTAURANT ★★★

Contemporary/Cajun	Very Expensive	QUALITY
		86

	VALUE
221 Royal Street; 525-7788	C
French Quarter Zone 1	

Reservations: Recommended

When to go: Anytime

Entree range: $14–22

Payment: All major credit cards

Service rating: ★★★

Friendliness rating: ★★★★

Parking: Validated at Dixie Parking, around corner on Iberville

Bar: Full service

Wine selection: Substantial; emphasis on California

Dress: Jacket recommended but not required

Disabled access: Limited

Customers: Tourists, some locals

Dinner: Sunday–Thursday, 6–10 p.m.; Friday–Saturday, 6–11 p.m.

Setting & atmosphere: The large dining room looks much more formal than it acts. Big comfortable chairs and other handsome furnishings rarely come with Cajun food, but why not?

Recommended dishes: Boudin and andouille sausages; baked oysters; gumbo; grilled fish; crabmeat imperial; crawfish étouffée; roast duck with rice dressing; bread pudding; sweet potato pie.

Summary & comments: Alex Patout has kept a high profile since Cajun food became popular. Some years ago he left his native New Iberia and the rest of his family's restaurants to open this handsome dining room. The cooking is Cajun, but beyond typical. Although the chef never hesitates to add the cream and butter to a dish, they go through all the lengthy cooking processes for which Cajun food is known. This is not a place where they merely throw a piece of fish or meat on the grill and call it a dish. The restaurant is somewhat inconsistent, but when it's hot it can serve quite a meal.

ANDREA'S		★★★★
Northern Italian	Very Expensive	**QUALITY** 87
3100 19th Street; 834-8583 Metairie below Causeway Zone 9		**VALUE** C

Reservations: Recommended

When to go: Anytime

Entree range: $10–28

Payment: All major credit cards

Service rating: ★★★★

Friendliness rating: ★★★★★

Parking: Free lot adjacent

Bar: Full service

Wine selection: Substantial list, mostly Italian and French; a bit overpriced

Dress: Jacket recommended but not required

Disabled access: Full

Customers: Professionals at lunch; daters

Brunch: Sunday, 11 a.m.–4 p.m.

Lunch & dinner: Monday–Thursday, 11 a.m.–10 p.m.; Friday, 11:30 a.m.–11 p.m.; Saturday, 4–11 p.m.; Sunday, 11 a.m.–9 p.m.

Setting & atmosphere: The restaurant feels distinctly suburban, but 15 years of bringing in Italian furnishings has given it personality. Lots of private dining rooms.

Recommended dishes: Antipasto; angel-hair pasta Andrea; mussels or clams marinara; pasta fagioli soup; fresh cheese salad; fish basilico; fish with cream pesto sauces; veal chop Valdostana; duck with green peppercorns; steak with three-pepper sauce; panneed veal Tanet; tiramisu; strawberry cake.

Entertainment & amenities: Strolling accordionist at Sunday brunch.

Summary & comments: Capri native Andrea Apuzzo and his restaurant are a formidable presence on the New Orleans Italian dining scene. It's certainly the most ambitious Italian place—the chef barely stops short of offering to do all things for all people. The quality of the ingredients (especially vegetables and fish) is unimpeachable. But pleasing his customers has caused the chef to compromise his classical Italian recipes, and Andrea's tastes more like a New Orleans restaurant every day. Fortunately, the attitude that they'll bend over backwards for you can solve a lot of that. At its best, Andrea's can still put out a great romantic dinner, and the chef's engaging style charms many. Don't come here on a big holiday: they always overbook.

ANTOINE'S ★★★

Creole/French	Very Expensive	QUALITY
		84
713 St. Louis Street; 581-4422		VALUE
French Quarter Zone 1		D

Reservations: Recommended

When to go: Lunch and early evenings; avoid days before holidays

Entree range: $16–40

Payment: All major credit cards

Service rating: ★★★

Friendliness rating: ★★

Parking: Pay garages nearby

Bar: Full service

Wine selection: Distinguished, broad, and French-dominated; many older vintages

Dress: Jacket required at dinner

Disabled access: Limited

Customers: Tourists; some locals

Lunch: Monday–Saturday, 11:30 a.m.–2 p.m.

Dinner: Monday–Saturday, 6–10 p.m.

Setting & atmosphere: Antoine's rambling, antique premises are fascinating. The wine cellar presents a great visual, and the many dining rooms recall different eras and flavors of the city's social life. The front dining room is charming, but only at lunch; at dinner the bustle of arriving diners dominates the atmosphere. Most locals eat in the red-walled (well, we think it's red—most of the surface is covered by framed memorabilia) annex.

Recommended dishes: Oysters Rockefeller; oysters Foch; escargots Bordelaise; shrimp rémoulade; crawfish cardinale; grilled pompano; soft-shell crabs Colbert; chicken Rochambeau; chicken bonne femme; tournedos marchand de vin; lamb chops Béarnaise; baked Alaska.

Summary & comments: Antoine's is a living museum of New Orleans dining. Founded in 1840, it's the oldest restaurant in America under continuous operation by one family. And it's not for everybody. If you're fascinated by the history of Creole food, you'll be able to put up with the restaurant's many peccadilloes. If history is not your bag, this may not be the place for you. The best time to figure it all out is lunch, which is rarely busy and offers the same menu as at dinner. Antoine's best dishes, once common elsewhere, are now unique to the restaurant. The beef, chicken, and more straightforward seafood dishes provide the best eating here. But you may want to make an entire meal of appetizers, of which there is a large array. The finest food here is served to regulars, so either be one or go with one. That might not even work these days: there's been more waiter turnover than usual lately.

ARNAUD'S		★★★★
Creole/French	Very Expensive	**QUALITY** 89
813 Bienville Street; 523-5433 French Quarter Zone 1		**VALUE** D

Reservations: Recommended	Bar: Full service
When to go: Anytime	Wine selection: Distinguished, internationally balanced; a bit pricey
Entree range: $16–40	
Payment: All major credit cards	Dress: Jacket recommended but not required
Service rating: ★★★★	
Friendliness rating: ★★★★	Disabled access: Full
Parking: Validated free at garage (corner of Dauphine and Iberville)	Customers: Tourists; some locals

Brunch: Sunday, 11 a.m.–3 p.m.

Lunch: Monday–Friday, 11:30 a.m.–2:30 p.m.

Dinner: Sunday–Thursday, 6–10 p.m.; Friday–Saturday, 6–11 p.m.

Setting & atmosphere: Nobody ever gave a moribund old restaurant a better rebirth than did Arnaud's owner Archie Casbarian. Atmospherically, it's an exemplar of the old-style New Orleans Creole dining institution: tiled floors, tin ceilings, beveled-glass windows, and ancient overhead fans.

Recommended dishes: Shrimp Arnaud (rémoulade); oysters Arnaud (five different ways); shrimp Bellaire; smoked pompano; oysters stewed in cream;

trout meunière; pompano David; pompano en croûte; duck Ellen; steak tartare (lunch); veal tournedos Chantal; crème brûlée; bananas Foster; bread pudding; café brûlot.

Entertainment & amenities: A small jazz band plays through dinner in the Richelieu Room for a small cover charge. Strolling jazz trio at Sunday brunch.

Summary & comments: In its first heyday, Arnaud's was the great restaurant of New Orleans, reinventing the way people dined out. It slipped into obscurity in the 1970s, and was brought back to life in 1979. The modern Arnaud's blends dishes created eons ago by Count Arnaud with spiffy new food—all with an unmistakable Creole taste. The only thing missing is a strong local clientele, but that's missing from restaurants all over the French Quarter these days. The wine list's pricing is a bit dear, but the selection is excellent. There is also an exceptional collection of ports, Cognacs, and cigars.

ARTESIA		★★★★
Contemporary French	Very Expensive	**QUALITY** 95
21516 LA 36; 892-1662 North Shore Zone 12		**VALUE** C

Reservations: Required	Bar: Full service
When to go: Avoid Fridays and Saturdays	Wine selection: Excellent, though a bit
Entree range: $17–30	unbalanced on the expensive side
Payment: AE, DC, MC, V	Dress: Jacket recommended but not
Service rating: ★★★	required
Friendliness rating: ★★★★	Disabled access: Full
Parking: Ample parking lot adjacent	Customers: North Shore gourmets

Brunch: Sunday, 11 a.m.–3 p.m.

Lunch: Wednesday–Friday, 11:30 a.m.–2:30 p.m.

Dinner: Wednesday–Sunday, 6–10 p.m.

Setting & atmosphere: Artesia is the restored Long Branch Inn, a 100-year-old resort in Abita Springs to which Orleanians once repaired in summer. The main house is now used for dining both upstairs and downstairs. The tables are spread well apart in a simple, antique space.

Recommended dishes: Alain Assaud's soup de poisson (crab soup with an intense flavor); foie gras three ways (smoked, seared, parfait); Alsatian onion tarte; salad Artesia; grouper with crawfish and crabmeat; roast duck with rosemary honey; roast chicken Grand Mere's style; petite tarte Tatin; double chocolate torte; crème brûlée.

Summary & comments: Artesia is operated by the always-chic Vicky Bayley, but its excellence is based on the personal cuisine of Chef John Besh. He cooks mostly in the contemporary French vein, using big-flavored sauces but not necessarily rich ones. Many of the ingredients come from a small nearby farm the restaurant uses to grow herbs and vegetables. The result is a singularly pure, elegant, yet simple style that is as satisfying as the premises are charming.

BACCO ★★★

Northern Italian	Expensive	QUALITY
		87
		VALUE
		C

310 Chartres Street; 522-2426
French Quarter   Zone I

Reservations: Recommended
When to go: Anytime
Entree range: $12–24
Payment: All major credit cards
Service rating: ★★★★
Friendliness rating: ★★★★★
Parking: Valet (free) in hotel garage
Bar: Full service

Wine selection: Substantial, mostly Italian and Californian; many interesting, offbeat bottles
Dress: Jacket recommended but not required
Disabled access: Full
Customers: Mostly locals; a few tourists

Brunch: Sunday, 11 a.m.–2:30 p.m.

Lunch: Every day, 11:30 a.m.–2:30 p.m.

Dinner: Every day, 6–10 p.m.

Setting & atmosphere: Striking dining spaces, shaped largely from concrete, create a distinctive environment. Particularly interesting is the vaulted rear dining room.

Recommended dishes: Uovo fritto (a fried hard-boiled egg with black truffles); white pizza; grilled eggplant; pasta rags, spinach and chicken; crawfish ravioli; grilled fish; grilled veal T-bone; roasted pork tenderloin; tiramisu; homemade ice creams.

Summary & comments: The original concept of Bacco was that of the Tuscan trattoria, but even though that was a culinary success the place has had to evolve in a Creole direction to stay busy. Service is also unusually good. Lots of food is cooked by burning wood: pizza, meat roasts, poultry, and fish. The wine list is exceptional, particularly for Italian wines. Bacco's month-long white-truffle festival in October is worth scheduling a trip for. The white-truffle dishes appear on a special menu during the event, and they change from year to year.

BARROW'S SHADY INN   ★★★

Seafood	Inexpensive	QUALITY
		81
		VALUE
		B

2714 Mistletoe; 482-9427
Uptown above Napoleon   Zone 4

Reservations: Not accepted	Parking: Free lot adjacent
When to go: Anytime	Bar: Full service
Entree range: $10	Wine selection: A few house wines
Payment: Cash only	Dress: Anything goes
Service rating: ★★	Disabled access: Limited
Friendliness rating: ★★★★	Customers: Neighborhood residents

Lunch: Thursday–Saturday, 11 a.m.–2 p.m.

Dinner: Tuesday–Saturday, 6–10 p.m.

Setting & atmosphere: It looks more like a bar than a restaurant, but more people eat than drink.

Recommended dishes: Fried catfish with potato salad.

Summary & comments: Barrow's, well hidden Uptown since 1943, fries incomparably light catfish that's so good you eat it like popcorn. And that's all they have. The fish has a little touch of pepper in the flavor that makes it unusual. You also get some fine homemade potato salad.

BASIL LEAF   ★★★★

Thai	Expensive	QUALITY
		90
		VALUE
		C

438 S. Carrollton Avenue; 862-9001
Uptown above Napoleon   Zone 4

Reservations: Accepted	Bar: Full service
When to go: Anytime	Wine selection: Much better than in most
Entree range: $9–24	Asian restaurants
Payment: AE, DC, MC, V	Dress: Casual
Service rating: ★★★★	Disabled access: Full
Friendliness rating: ★★★	Customers: Young uptowners
Parking: Curbside	

Lunch: Monday–Friday, 11:30 a.m.–3 p.m.

Dinner: Monday–Saturday, 6–10 p.m.

Setting & atmosphere: A single room decorated simply but tastefully, with lots of windows.

Recommended dishes: Seared-scallop salad; spring roll; sauteed calamari; daily soups; pad Thai; grilled-chicken- or beef-noodle salads; green curry with chicken; soft-shell crabs with sesame.

Summary & comments: After making a hit in an unpromising space in Metairie, the Basil Leaf moved to more accessible, more comely quarters in Carrollton, near the streetcar barn. Here the ambitions of the chef are fully realized, such that the Basil Leaf now serves the best Thai food in the area. Thai food is usually well presented, but this is notably beautiful. The menu deviates from those of all the previous Thai restaurants hereabouts, at least a little. As in other gourmet bistros, the chef sees no reason why he shouldn't create new dishes. Service is also better than what's usually found in local Asian restaurants.

BAYONA		★★★★★

		QUALITY
Eclectic	Very Expensive	98
		VALUE
430 Dauphine Street; 525-4455		B
French Quarter Zone 1		

Reservations: Required	**Bar:** Full service
When to go: Anytime	**Wine selection:** Distinguished; many off-
Entree range: $14–25	beat bottles and by-the-glass selections
Payment: All major credit cards	**Dress:** Jacket recommended but not
Service rating: ★★★★★	required
Friendliness rating: ★★★★	**Disabled access:** Limited
Parking: Validated at garage across	**Customers:** Mostly locals; a few tourists
the street	

Lunch: Monday–Friday, 11:30 a.m.–2:30 p.m.

Dinner: Monday–Thursday, 6–10 p.m.; Friday–Saturday, 6–10:30 p.m.

Setting & atmosphere: All dining rooms other than the main one are quite small, and can sometimes get a bit noisy. In decent weather you may also dine under the banana trees in the courtyard—very pleasant.

Recommended dishes: Grilled shrimp with coriander; sweetbreads any style; roasted-garlic soup; shrimp curry; salmon with choucroute and Gewürztraminer; pork, lamb, or veal chops; quail dish of the day; lemon tart; apple-almond gratin; orange-scented crêpes with gelato.

Summary & comments: The understated personal cuisine of Susan Spicer may underwhelm you during the menu-reading part of the repast. But her brilliant sense of taste and culinary curiosity comes through where it counts—on the plate. This is particularly impressive given the wide range of flavors you encounter here. French, Indian, Mediterranean, New Orleans, Far Eastern. . . she seems to understand the essence of every style. Wine drinking here is rewarding: the list is full of rare and unusual bottles at decent prices.

BELLA LUNA		★★★★
Contemporary Creole	Very Expensive	**QUALITY** 92
914 N. Peters Street; 529-1583 French Quarter Zone 1		**VALUE** C

Reservations: Recommended
When to go: Anytime
Entree range: $14–25
Payment: All major credit cards
Service rating: ★★★★
Friendliness rating: ★★★★
Parking: Validated free for French Market lot, immediately adjacent
Bar: Full service

Wine selection: Distinguished; many interesting bottles and by-the-glass selections
Dress: Jacket recommended but not required
Disabled access: Limited
Customers: Mostly locals; a few tourists; couples

Dinner: Sunday–Thursday, 6–10 p.m.; Friday–Saturday, 6–11 p.m.

Setting & atmosphere: Bella Luna's matchless asset is a view of the Mississippi River—something few New Orleans restaurants have. The long dining room, with its panoramic windows, stretches along the second floor of the French Market.

Recommended dishes: Crab-cakes rémoulade; fettuccine with aged Reggiano; pasta with truffles; caesar salad; shrimp quesadillas; grilled or blackened tuna; veal T-bone; osso buco; grilled pork tenderloin; veal T-bone with herb olive oil; any game special; dessert assortment; fudge brownie cappuccino pie; warm apple tart.

Summary & comments: Take away the great view, and avid diners would still come here for the cooking of chef/proprietor Horst Pfeifer, who unites Italian, Southwestern, and Creole flavors into singular creations. All methods of cooking are explored, but grilling, roasting, and smoking are specialties. The chef ranges wide with his ingredients, too, buying more different species of fish, birds, and chops than chefs in most places. A few blocks away, in the garden of the historic Ursuline Convent, he grows fresh herbs. The consistency of the food is not perfect, and the front door greeting could stand a great deal of warming up, but few places can provide the package of gustatory and atmospheric pleasure that Bella Luna does.

BISTRO AT MAISON DE VILLE ★★★★

		QUALITY
Contemporary French	Very Expensive	87
		VALUE
733 Toulouse Street; 528-9206		C
French Quarter Zone 1		

Reservations: Recommended

When to go: Anytime

Entree range: $16–26

Payment: All major credit cards

Service rating: ★★★★

Friendliness rating: ★★★★

Parking: Several pay lots within two blocks

Bar: Full service; many single-malt Scotches, Cognacs, Armagnacs, etc.

Wine selection: Decent; many offbeat bottles and by-the-glass selections

Dress: Jacket recommended but not required

Disabled access: Limited

Customers: Mostly locals; a few tourists

Brunch: Sunday, 11:30 a.m.–2:30 p.m.

Lunch: Every day, 11:30 a.m.–2:30 p.m.

Dinner: Every day, 6–10 p.m.

Setting & atmosphere: Nice room, but there's not enough space. Tables are uncomfortably small. You might be able to escape by dining in the courtyard, but that's also teeny.

Recommended dishes: Crawfish rémoulade; steamed mussels with warm potato salad or pommes frites; escargots on grilled rosemary flatbread; grilled shrimp with poblano-cheese hominy cakes and pepper jelly; poached pear and mixed green salad with pecans and Roquefort; grilled sea scallops with saffron risotto; sautéed salmon with ravioli of lobster and spinach; grilled double pork chop with apples; pan-seared venison with pumpkin spaetzle; chocolate cake; crème brûlée.

Summary & comments: Claustrophobic but chic, the Bistro (as it's simply called by its regulars) has a history of hiring hot young chefs on their way up. The current chef is Greg Picolo, who has now been on the job longer than several of his predecessors combined. It's a Bistro tradition for the menu to be unpredictable, but there's a certain hard-to-nail-down style that is consistent. Ingredients and techniques tend to the unusual, and a certain Mediterranean aspect seems always to be present. The dining room is orchestrated by the always-accommodating Patrick Hoorebeek, whose stamp is even more pervasive than chef's. He's responsible for the unusually good list of wine and spirits as well as service.

BON TON CAFE   ★★★

Cajun	Expensive	QUALITY
		84
		VALUE
		B

401 Magazine Street; 524-3386
Central Business District   Zone 2

Reservations: Recommended	Bar: Full service
When to go: Anytime	Wine selection: A few house wines
Entree range: $12–18	Dress: Jacket recommended but not
Payment: AE, DC, MC, V	required
Service rating: ★★★	Disabled access: Limited
Friendliness rating: ★★★★	Customers: Mostly locals at lunch; mostly
Parking: Pay lot and curbside (metered)	tourists at dinner

Lunch: Monday–Friday, 11:30 a.m.–2:30 p.m.

Dinner: Monday–Friday, 6–10 p.m.

Setting & atmosphere: One big brick-walled room, its tables covered with checked tablecloths; full of people who look like regulars.

Recommended dishes: Turtle soup; fried catfish fingers; shrimp rémoulade; Cajun Caesar salad; crawfish dinner (crawfish four ways: étouffée, bisque, fried, and omelette); crabmeat au gratin; redfish Bon Ton; oysters or soft-shell crab Alvin; pan-broiled oysters; bayou étouffée; bread pudding.

Summary & comments: The Bon Ton has specialized in crawfish longer than anyone else in New Orleans, and can claim to be the town's oldest Cajun (as opposed to Creole) restaurant. But Cajun cooking is itself regional, and this style comes from the Bayou Lafourche area. It's mild in its pepper levels and a bit old fashioned. You'll see touches you haven't been treated to since the early 1960s. (The service style is definitely from that era.) It's a charming, unaffected place delivering good food and value. But go with the specialties, and don't make it jump through hoops.

BOZO'S   ★★★★

Seafood	Inexpensive	QUALITY
		85
		VALUE
		B

3117 21st Street; 831-8666
Metairie below Causeway   Zone 9

Reservations: Not accepted	Service rating: ★★★
When to go: Anytime except the very	Friendliness rating: ★★★★
busy Fridays	Parking: Free lot adjacent
Entree range: $6–12	Bar: Full service
Payment: MC, V	

Wine selection: A few house wines

Dress: Casual

Disabled access: Full

Customers: Mostly locals; a few tourists

Lunch: Tuesday–Saturday, 11 a.m.–3 p.m.

Dinner: Tuesday–Thursday, 6–10 p.m.; Friday–Saturday, 6–11 p.m.

Setting & atmosphere: Two utilitarian, bright rooms connected by a great oyster bar and an open kitchen.

Recommended dishes: Oysters on the half shell; boiled crawfish or shrimp in season; chicken andouille gumbo; fried oysters; fried catfish; broiled shrimp; stuffed shrimp; stuffed crab; hot sausage poor boy; bread pudding.

Summary & comments: Bozo's demonstrates how great simple fried seafood can be when it's meticulously selected and prepared. The catfish, for example, are small, wild Des Allemandes cats (as opposed to the inferior farm-raised fish). They are fried to order and served while still crackly hot. Each type of seafood is fried separately, which keeps everything from tasting the same. They also have great boiled seafood here, especially crawfish in season. The portions are not piled as high as elsewhere, but the quality is consistently satisfying. The gumbo, raw oysters, and broiled shrimp are the major specialties on a menu full of good food.

BRIGTSEN'S ★★★★

Contemporary Creole	Very Expensive	QUALITY
		94

723 Dante Street; 861-7610	VALUE
Uptown above Napoleon Zone 4	**B**

Reservations: Required

When to go: Early evenings

Entree range: $16–28

Payment: All major credit cards

Service rating: ★★★★

Friendliness rating: ★★★★

Parking: Curbside

Bar: Full service

Wine selection: Modest, but well chosen for the food

Dress: Jacket recommended but not required

Disabled access: Limited

Customers: Mostly locals; a few tourists

Dinner: Tuesday–Saturday, 6–10 p.m.

Setting & atmosphere: It's a 100-year-old cottage with three small rooms. The best tables are in the windows up front. The conviviality among customers keeps the walls from closing in.

Recommended dishes: Grilled rabbit tenderloin; shrimp rémoulade; sesame-encrusted foie gras; soup or gumbo of the day; panneed rabbit; veal specials; fish specials; tournedos of beef; chicken with hot and sweet peppers; banana bread pudding; ice creams; double chocolate cake.

Summary & comments: Unless you have a problem with small dining rooms, you'll find Brigtsen's hospitable and easy to love. Marna Brigtsen acts more like the hostess of a guest house than that of a restaurant. The familiarity and informality are perfect for husband/chef Frank's original but very Creole cooking style. Because the menu changes every day and because the chef loves to experiment, you'll find fish and vegetables here you never heard of before, as well as more familiar eats. The problem will be that too much of it will sound irresistible, and ordering may be traumatic. The wine list is short but right for the food and attractively priced.

BROUSSARD'S ★★★★

Creole French	Very Expensive	QUALITY
		89
819 Conti Street; 581-3866		VALUE
French Quarter Zone 1		D

Reservations: Recommended
When to go: Anytime
Entree range: $17–26
Payment: All major credit cards
Service rating: ★★★
Friendliness rating: ★★★★
Parking: Validated parking across street
Bar: Full service

Wine selection: Decent, with good international balance; a bit overpriced
Dress: Jacket recommended but not required
Disabled access: Full
Customers: Tourists, plus a few adventuresome locals

Dinner: Every day, 6–10 p.m.

Setting & atmosphere: Three plush, old-style dining rooms surround one of the French Quarter's largest courtyards. You can dine out there if you like.

Recommended dishes: Delice ravigote; shrimp-and-crab cheesecake; baked-oyster trio; sweet potato, corn-and-shrimp bisque; poussin Rochambeau; pecan-stuffed salmon; pompano Napoleon; veal filet on braised leeks; wild-game grill; chocolate pava; crêpes Broussard; bananas Foster.

Summary & comments: Broussard's opened in 1920 and is one of the grande dames of Creole cuisines. But it's been through many more changes than Galatoire's, Arnaud's, and other members of its generation. It may be at its all-time best right now. Chef Gunter Preuss—an old hand in continental restaurants here, and the owner—updated the menu to current tastes and ingredients, with a distinct New Orleans flavor. Nevertheless, the missing element is local diners, who have never been actively wooed for some reason.

BRUNING'S ★★★

		QUALITY
Seafood	Inexpensive	84
		VALUE
West End Parkway; 282-9395		A
Lakeview/West End/Bucktown Zone 7		

Reservations: Not accepted
When to go: Anytime, but Fridays are very crowded
Entree range: $8–16
Payment: All major credit cards
Service rating: ★★★
Friendliness rating: ★★★★

Parking: Free lot adjacent
Bar: Full service
Wine selection: A few house wines
Dress: Anything goes
Disabled access: Limited
Customers: Locals; families

Lunch & dinner: Every day, 11:30 a.m.–10 p.m.

Setting & atmosphere: While the old place above the lake's waves is being rebuilt, a smaller but equally scenic building nearby is open. There's a nice view of the lake from the upstairs dining room.

Recommended dishes: Oysters on the half shell; seafood gumbo; boiled crabs, crawfish or shrimp; whole broiled flounder; whole fried trout; fried seafood platter; broiled redfish; stuffed shrimp; fried chicken; bread pudding.

Summary & comments: Possibly the oldest continuously operated fried-seafood house in the world, Bruning's opened in 1859 at West End. Now owned by the sixth generation of the founder's family, its old original building has been out of action since Hurricane Georges in 1999. In the interim quarters, the food didn't change. They cook the archetypical platters of fried seafood and mounds of boiled seafood. The distinctive specialty is a whole flounder—the size that fishermen call "doormats"—fried or broiled. A very casual place for eating, drinking, and reveling in the New Orleans life.

BYBLOS ★★★★

		QUALITY
Middle Eastern	Inexpensive	86
		VALUE
1501 Metairie Road; 834-9773		A
Metairie below Causeway Zone 9		

Reservations: Accepted
When to go: Anytime
Entree range: $8–14
Payment: All major credit cards
Service rating: ★★★
Friendliness rating: ★★★★

Parking: Ample parking lot adjacent
Bar: Full service
Wine selection: A few house wines
Dress: Casual
Disabled access: Full
Customers: Locals

Lunch & dinner: Monday–Saturday, 11:30 a.m.–10 p.m.

Setting & atmosphere: The dining room has a lofty ceiling and a comfortable, uncluttered look.

Recommended dishes: Hummus; baba ghanouj; stuffed kibbeh; falafel; stuffed cabbage rolls; cheese pie; tabbouleh salad; beef shawarma; beef kabob; chicken kabob; kafta kabob; fried kibbeh; kibbeh nayyi; ashta (flaky dessert pastry).

Summary & comments: Byblos (named for an ancient city in Lebanon) is the best Middle Eastern restaurant this area has ever had. The ingredients are first class (i.e., filet mignon is used for the beef kabob), and the cooking is careful and light. Much care is given to plate presentation, but everything comes out hot anyway. The appetizer meza brings forth an assortment of some 15 appetizers for 4 to 6 people—a great way to eat. Byblos is usually populated by Lebanese, Syrians, Israelis, Turks, and others who know how this food is supposed to taste.

CAFE DEGAS ★★★

French Bistro	Moderate	QUALITY
		86
3127 Esplanade Avenue; 945-5635		VALUE
Mid-City/Gentilly　Zone 6		B

Reservations: Accepted	Bar: Full service
When to go: Anytime	Wine selection: Limited, ordinary, and
Entree range: $7–15	French-dominated
Payment: All major credit cards	Dress: Casual
Service rating: ★★★	Disabled access: Limited
Friendliness rating: ★★★★	Customers: Neighborhood residents
Parking: Curbside	

Lunch & dinner: Tuesday–Thursday,11:30 a.m.–10 p.m.; Friday–Saturday, 11:30 a.m.–11 p.m.

Setting & atmosphere: The tables are on a covered deck surrounded by a jungle-like growth of plants, through which we get a view of Esplanade Avenue—very inviting, especially considering the rarity of alfresco dining in New Orleans.

Recommended dishes: Onion-soup gratinée; couscous and vegetable salad; sweetbreads Grenobloise; magret of duck à l'orange; shrimp fettuccine; roasted Cornish hen with rosemary; faux filet mignon Bordelaise; omelettes; crème brûlée; chocolate mousse.

Summary & comments: Cafe Degas (named for the French artist who once lived a few blocks away) used to get by on its open-air charm, but no more. The food gets better with each visit. Like in the French bistros after which the place is pattered, you find simple ingredients cooked simply and in familiar ways—but very well. The service staff is either absurdly over-enthusiastic or missing in action, but it's that kind of place and nobody cares. In fact, when I come here I'm looking to linger.

CAFE GIOVANNI		★★★★

		QUALITY
Contemporary Italian	Expensive	94
		VALUE
117 Decatur Street; 529-2154		B
French Quarter Zone 1		

Reservations: Recommended
When to go: Anytime
Entree range: $14–22
Payment: All major credit cards
Service rating: ★★★★
Friendliness rating: ★★★★
Parking: Valet ($5)

Bar: Full service
Wine selection: Substantial, mostly Italian; many by-the-glass selections
Dress: Jacket recommended but not required
Disabled access: Full
Customers: Mostly locals; a few tourists

Dinner: Sunday–Thursday, 6–10 p.m.; Friday–Saturday, 6–11 p.m.

Setting & atmosphere: Cafe Giovanni is one of the gems on the revived Lower Decatur strip. Its dining spaces straddle two old townhouses and the courtyard between them. The busy, rather noisy main rooms have a striking and uniquely New Orleans look.

Recommended dishes: Oysters Giovanni; grilled portobello mushroom; grilled scallops and shrimp with sake soy sauce; eggplant LoCicero (shrimp and crabmeat); Sicilian wedding soup; crabmeat Siciliana salad; pasta Gambino; cioppino; seared pork loin with crawfish and tasso; filet mignon Tuscany; roast chicken with rosemary and garlic; tiramisu; dessert pastries (change daily).

Entertainment & amenities: Several nights a week, waiters who sing opera (or, more appropriately, singers who wait tables) put on a substantial show. But they sing a little bit every night, and well.

Summary & comments: Chef/owner Duke LoCicero emphasizes both Sicilian and Creole culinary traditions, but doesn't hesitate to employ tastes from anywhere else in the world. All this is rendered with polish, interesting local ingredients, and fresh, original touches. The best strategy is to let the chef feed you an assortment of small portions of the day's specials for about $50.

CAFE MARIGNY ★★★★

Contemporary Creole	Expensive	QUALITY
		87
1913 Royal Street; 945-4472		VALUE
Downtown/St. Bernard Zone 5		C

Reservations: Recommended	Bar: No alcohol
When to go: Anytime	Wine selection: Bring your own wine ($6
Entree range: $10–20	corkage)
Payment: AE, MC, V	Dress: Casual
Service rating: ★★★	Disabled access: Limited
Friendliness rating: ★★★	Customers: Marigny residents; couples
Parking: Curbside	and singles

Breakfast: Saturday–Sunday, 8–10 a.m.

Lunch: Every day, 11:30 a.m.–2:30 p.m.

Dinner: Every day, 6–10 p.m.

Setting & atmosphere: An old grocery store in the bend of Royal Street has been renovated—but not too much—into an L-shaped dining room. Big door-windows allow oneness with the pedestrian traffic outside.

Recommended dishes: Duck-andouille spring rolls; seafood wontons; steamed mussels with tomato and corn; grilled vegetable Napoleon; grilled tuna with artichoke hearts and tomatoes; grilled smoked veal chop; Asian-marinated, grilled pork loin with Asian noodles and vegetables; panneed veal with fettuccine Alfredo.

Summary & comments: Cafe Marigny is an imaginative Creole bistro, more sophisticated than you expect. (Maybe it's that battered concrete floor that fools you.) Even familiar-sounding dishes get ratcheted up with a special ingredient or fine detail. A draw for many customers is that Cafe Marigny doesn't have a liquor license. So don't forget to bring your own bottle of wine.

CAFE SBISA ★★★

Creole	Very Expensive	QUALITY
		85
1011 Decatur Street; 522-5565		VALUE
French Quarter Zone 1		C

Reservations: Recommended	Service rating: ★★★
When to go: Anytime	Friendliness rating: ★★★★
Entree range: $15–23	Parking: Validated free at French Market
Payment: All major credit cards	lot, one block

Bar: Full service

Wine selection: Decent, French-dominated

Dress: Jacket recommended but not required

Disabled access: Limited

Customers: Mostly locals, a few tourists

Brunch: Sunday, 11 a.m.–2:30 p.m.

Dinner: Sunday–Thursday, 6–10:30 p.m.; Friday–Saturday, 6–11 p.m.

Setting & atmosphere: In its third incarnation and second century, this charming two-level parlor of antique wood panels and mirrors recalls a different era, when the French Market across the street was a bustling place of commerce.

Recommended dishes: Shrimp rémoulade; crab cakes with horseradish cream sauce; turtle soup; trout amandine; trout Eugene; barbecue shrimp; duck with green peppercorns; eggs Sardou (brunch); grillades and grits (brunch); pecan pie; chocolate sin cake.

Entertainment & amenities: Jazzy, bluesy live music at Sunday brunch.

Summary & comments: Cafe Sbisa these days concentrates on the traditional classics of Creole cooking, but has no hesitation about dressing them up with new ingredients and styles of cooking. The result never quite achieves brilliance, but the evening is always enjoyable. On Sundays, there's a lively brunch.

CHINA BLOSSOM ★★★★

Chinese	Moderate	QUALITY
		86
		VALUE
		B

1801 Stumpf Boulevard; 361-4598

West Bank Zone 11

Reservations: Accepted

When to go: Anytime

Entree range: $7–15

Parking: Free lot adjacent

Bar: Full service

Wine selection: Limited and ordinary

Payment: All major credit cards

Service rating: ★★★

Friendliness rating: ★★★★

Dress: Casual

Disabled access: Full

Customers: Locals

Lunch: Tuesday–Friday, 11:30 a.m.–2:30 p.m.; Sunday, noon–3 p.m.

Dinner: Tuesday–Sunday, 6–10 p.m.

Setting & atmosphere: It's a storefront in a strip mall and rather spare, but pleasant enough.

Recommended dishes: Spring roll; pot stickers; crawfish and crêpes; hot-and-sour soup; tong-cho shrimp, trout, or oysters; soft-shell crab with crawfish sauce; crab claws with black-bean sauce; Maine lobster with ginger; spicy flaming chicken; wor shu op (crisp half duck); ming steak; beef with oyster sauce; lotus banana.

Summary & comments: China Blossom is the best Chinese restaurant near the center of town (it's across the river, but just). Its menu started out almost identical to that of Trey Yuen, from which most of the staff came. But over the years they've evolved and now have their own style, with a strong specialty in seafood. They buy superb fresh fish and shellfish and cook it with excitement and great sauces. Many of the dishes involve interesting tableside preparations. The dining rooms are understated and comfortable.

CHRISTIAN'S		★★★★
Creole French	Very Expensive	**QUALITY** 90
3835 Iberville Street; 482-4924 Mid-City/Gentilly Zone 6		**VALUE** B

Reservations: Recommended
When to go: Dinner
Entree range: $16–26
Payment: AE, DC, MC, V
Service rating: ★★★★
Friendliness rating: ★★★★
Parking: Ample parking lot adjacent
Bar: Full service

Wine selection: Substantial, equally French and Californian; very attractive prices
Dress: Jacket recommended but not required
Disabled access: Limited
Customers: Mostly locals; a few tourists; couples; gourmets

Lunch: Tuesday–Friday, 11:30 a.m.–2:30 p.m.

Dinner: Tuesday–Saturday, 6–10 p.m.

Setting & atmosphere: The restaurant is housed in a former church, although it was called Christian's (after one of the founders) before it moved there. Cathedral ceilings and tall windows provide spaciousness. Still, some diners may find the deuces (tables for two) along the perimeter a little too close together.

Recommended dishes: Oysters Roland; oysters en brochette; shrimp rémoulade; saffron shrimp; crawfish Carolyn; smoked salmon; smoked soft-shell crab; shrimp-and-crabmeat-stuffed fish; stuffed eggplant; Avery Island duck; trout meunière amandine; filet mignon stuffed with oysters; strip sirloin au poivre; crème caramel; homemade ice creams.

Summary & comments: No gimmick, really. This is a serious, consistent, original restaurant, as well as one of the better values in the gourmet arena. The menu is grounded in the classics of New Orleans restaurant cuisine, more or less in the style of Galatoire's (there's a family connection). But it has always included dishes influenced by country French cooking and some entirely new ideas. The service staff has an easy style, the wines are sold at bargain prices, and the early-evening special menu is almost too inexpensive to be believed.

CLANCY'S	★★★★

Creole	Expensive	QUALITY 92
6100 Annunciation Street; 895-1111 Uptown above Napoleon Zone 4		VALUE B

Reservations: Recommended
When to go: Anytime
Entree range: $13–22
Payment: All major credit cards
Service rating: ★★★★
Friendliness rating: ★★★★
Parking: Curbside
Bar: Full service

Wine selection: Substantial, full of oddities; the owner is an oenophile and buys many short-lot wines; many by-the-glass selections
Dress: Dressy casual
Disabled access: Limited
Customers: Locals; gourmets

Lunch: Tuesday–Friday, 11:30 a.m.–2:30 p.m.

Dinner: Monday–Saturday, 6–10 p.m.

Setting & atmosphere: The long downstairs dining room is convivial and bright. Upstairs tables are in a sort of maze. Many people dine at the bar.

Recommended dishes: Oysters with Brie and spinach; crabmeat ravigote; shrimp rémoulade; house salad; smoked soft-shell crab and crabmeat; smoked shrimp with ginger; seafood pasta specials; veal liver Lyonnaise; veal and lamb chops; smoked duck; filet mignon with port and Stilton; crème caramel.

Summary & comments: Clancy's was one of the original crop of bistros that redefined Creole cooking in the early 1980s. It's matured into an Uptown answer to Galatoire's, with a passionate local following. Its culinary bona fides are solidly enough established that it can lean back on some old, funky, but delicious Creole dishes that most hip places are afraid to serve. Likewise, the service staff can joke around and take certain unusual informalities with the mostly-regular clientele. This is my favorite kind of menu. While the standards are really quite traditional in style, the specials are as adventuresome as any you'll find. Clancy's also has more than a few signatures. It was the first local restaurant to smoke foods in house, and that's still a good part of the menu. Clancy's has a great bar. The collection of Cognacs, Armagnacs, single-malt Scotches, and small-batch bourbons is tremendous. They can even make you a fine cocktail, something that is becoming a lost art.

COMMANDER'S PALACE ★★★★★

		QUALITY
Contemporary Creole	Very Expensive	**97**

	VALUE
1403 Washington Avenue; 899-8221	**B**
Uptown below Napoleon　Zone 3	

Reservations: Required
When to go: Lunch and weekday dinner
Entree range: $18–32
Payment: All major credit cards
Service rating: ★★★★
Friendliness rating: ★★★★★
Parking: Valet (free)
Bar: Full service

Wine selection: Distinguished and inter-
　nationally balanced; many rare wines
　(although not many older ones) from
　France and California
Dress: Jacket required at dinner
Disabled access: Limited
Customers: Half tourists, half socializing
　locals; couples

Brunch: Saturday–Sunday, 11:30 a.m.–2:30 p.m.

Lunch: Every day, 11:30 a.m.–2:30 p.m.

Dinner: Every day, 6–10 p.m.

Setting & atmosphere: The Victorian mansion and adjacent courtyard go back to the middle 1800s and are a part of the fabric of the surrounding Garden District. The upstairs Garden Room is most popular with locals, but the whole restaurant is pleasant.

Recommended dishes: Shrimp rémoulade; smoked-fish cake; caviar club sandwich; turtle soup; lyonnaise fish; sautéed fish with pecans; air-dried duck; veal chop Tchoupitoulas; roasted strip sirloin steak; rack of lamb; bananas Foster; bread pudding soufflé.

Entertainment & amenities: Strolling jazz trio at Sunday brunch.

Summary & comments: Commander's Palace is perennially New Orleans's most popular first-class restaurant. The kitchen is a local energy center, inspired by a succession of chefs whose careers took off here (Paul Prud-homme and Emeril Lagasse, to name two). Commander's menu combines both old and new styles of Creole cooking, using first-class, interesting foodstuffs. This is the flagship of the Brennan family's restaurant empire, and all their tricks are refined to high art here. One of those is value: a four-course dinner can be had for $40, and a lunch for $18. Service can be a bit over-rehearsed—be sure to tell the waiter you're in no hurry. Both the kitchen and service staffs are responsive to special wants.

COURT OF TWO SISTERS ★★★

Creole	Very Expensive	QUALITY
		85

613 Royal Street; 522-7273
French Quarter   Zone 1

	VALUE
	C

Reservations: Recommended
When to go: Dinner
Entree range: $15–23
Payment: All major credit cards
Service rating: ★★★
Friendliness rating: ★★★
Parking: Pay garages nearby

Bar: Full service
Wine selection: Decent, but only a few bottles of more than routine interest
Dress: Jacket recommended but not required
Disabled access: Full
Customers: Tourists

Breakfast & lunch: Every day, 9 a.m.–2 p.m.

Dinner: Every day, 6–10 p.m.

Setting & atmosphere: If you dine in the lovely courtyard when the weather is right and you're in the mood for some Tennessee Williams–style New Orleans atmosphere, the evening will be unforgettable. Pick a sweltering, airless evening or a chilly, drippy night, and it's less charming—as are the interior dining rooms.

Recommended dishes: Baked oysters melange (two each of three different kinds); escargots in mushroom caps; crawfish Louise; seafood gumbo; Caesar salad; shrimp Toulouse; crabmeat St. Peter; trout Amandine; trout Picasso; veal Fein; coq d'Orleans; bread pudding; chocolate mousse; cherries jubilee.

Entertainment & amenities: Strolling jazz trio at brunch daily.

Summary & comments: Local diners who consign this finest of all restaurant courtyards to tourists are missing something good. It is touristy and full of cliches, both in the dining room and the kitchen. Still, the Court at dinner is much better than it's reputed to be. The service staff is accommodating, but make sure they know you're a local both when you make the reservation and meet the waiter. The brunch/lunch buffet they serve here has great jazz but the food is just okay.

CUVEE   ★★★★

Contemporary American	Very Expensive	QUALITY
		87

322 Magazine Street; 587-9001
Central Business District   Zone 2

	VALUE
	D

Reservations: Recommended
When to go: Dinner
Entree range: $18–29
Payment: AE, DC, MC, V
Service rating: ★★★
Friendliness rating: ★★★★
Parking: Valet (free)

Bar: Full service
Wine selection: Distinguished, with wide
    variety from all around the world
Dress: Jacket recommended but not
    required
Disabled access: Full
Customers: Gourmets and wine buffs

Breakfast: Monday–Saturday, 7–10 a.m.

Lunch: Monday–Friday, 11:30 a.m.–2:30 p.m.

Dinner: Monday–Thursday, 6–10 p.m.; Friday–Saturday, 6–11 p.m.

Setting & atmosphere: Wine dominates the decor. Chandeliers, for example, are made out of large-format Champagne bottles. The brick-walled dining room is artfully hard edged, but there are soft corners here and there.

Recommended dishes: The menu changes often. Typical dishes include: Mirliton and shrimp Napoleon; smoked chevre and lamb tortilla; roast poussin on tasso-smothered greens; chive-battered salmon with crawfish-vegetable slaw; sugar cane–smoked duck breast, crisp confit leg, and foie gras; peach tarte tatin; duo of crème brûlées.

Summary & comments: It's currently hip for major restaurants to start with a wine cellar and build a menu around it. This is such a place, as the name implies. ("Cuvee" is a French wine word, most often seen in connection with Champagne, that refers to the art of the blend.) Dinner here is a touch pretentious. They go overboard in the service department; even in a romantic situation, they won't leave you alone. The chef does elaborate presentations using all the "in" foods of the moment, with a predilection for layering them vertically. The flavor palette could use a bit more contrast, something you'll especially notice if you go for the six-course degustation. Individual dishes are beyond reproach on their own merits, however, and the menu changes continually.

DAKOTA ★★★★★

Contemporary Creole	Very Expensive	QUALITY
		96

629 N. US 190 ; 892-3712
North Shore   Zone 12

VALUE
C

Reservations: Recommended
When to go: Weeknights
Entree range: $13–24
Payment: AE, DC, MC, V
Service rating: ★★★★★
Friendliness rating: ★★★★★
Parking: Ample parking lot adjacent
Bar: Full service

Wine selection: Distinguished, with
 emphasis on California; many excellent
 boutique wines; the owner is a wine
 buff in search of discoveries
Dress: Jacket recommended but not
 required
Disabled access: Full
Customers: Locals; couples; gourmets

Lunch: Monday–Friday, 11:30 a.m.–2:30 p.m.

Dinner: Monday–Thursday, 6–10 p.m.; Friday–Saturday, 6–11 p.m.

Setting & atmosphere: The two large dining rooms are spacious almost to the point of echoing. They're furnished in a distinctive modern style, with particularly interesting floral arrangements.

Recommended dishes: Sweet-potato nachos with lamb; seafood beignets with lobster sauce; grilled rabbit tenderloin; smoked chicken gumbo; roasted salmon with fried spinach; stuffed soft-shell crab; honey-and-rosemary roasted chicken; cane-smoked pork tenderloin; mixed grill; rack of lamb; bread pudding; dessert pastries.

Summary & comments: Dakota raised the standard of dining on the North Shore when it opened in 1990. It's still one of the two or three best restaurants there, and not far below that in the larger metro-area ranking. Chef and co-owner Kim Kringlie (he's the Dakota connection) cooks contemporary Creole food in its most intensely flavorful forms, and shows no shyness about using salt, pepper, cream, butter, smoke, or anything else that might make flavors detonate. More exotic styles work their ways into a few dishes. Strong daily specials round out a fascinating array of food. Dakota is rare among North Shore restaurants in having a well-trained service staff and a distinguished wine cellar. Problem: the owners recently opened another major operation (Cuvee) on the South Shore, resulting in some inconsistency at the flagship.

DELMONICO   ★★★★

		QUALITY
Creole French	Very Expensive	**89**
		VALUE
1300 St. Charles Avenue; 525-4937		**D**
Uptown below Napoleon Zone 3		

Reservations: Recommended
When to go: Anytime
Entree range: $20–36
Payment: All major credit cards
Service rating: ★★★★
Friendliness rating: ★★★★★
Parking: Valet (free)
Bar: Full service

Wine selection: Distinguished cellar man-
 aged by a well-informed sommelier
Dress: Jacket recommended but not
 required
Disabled access: Full
Customers: A lot of overflow from
 Emeril's winds up here (read tourists);
 locals dominate at lunchtime

Brunch: Sunday, 11 a.m.–2:30 p.m.

Lunch: Monday–Friday, 11:30 a.m.–2 p.m.

Dinner: Sunday–Thursday, 6–10 p.m.; Friday–Saturday, 6–11 p.m.

Setting & atmosphere: Delmonico was a 100-year-old Creole standard when chef Emeril Lagasse bought the place in 1998. He treated it to an expensive, well-wrought renovation. Now it looks completely new, but its design still suggests a subtle antiquity.

Recommended dishes: Turtle soup; shrimp rémoulade; crab chop ravigote; crawfish vol-au-vent; redfish meunière; oysters Delmonico with crabmeat dressing; fried buster crabs choron; filet mignon with oyster stuffing and fried oysters; Creole cream cheesecake; bananas Foster; coconut cream pie.

Summary & comments: Dishes from decades ago and tableside prepara-tion set Delmonico's culinary theme. The timing was perfect: the last of the old places doing that kind of stuff had just died. But the food didn't find its way until chef David McCelvey—one of chef Emeril Lagasse's top field marshals—came in to rework the package. Since then, the food has been much more appealing and consistent, and can even become brilliant on a given night. Personally, I keep hoping for an elaboration of even more clas-sic haute cuisine. The premises and the general style beg for it. A note to those who may have dined in the old Delmonico: there are a few of the old dishes now, but the restaurant is almost entirely a different place, and it's much, much more expensive.

DICK & JENNY'S ★★★★

		QUALITY
Contemporary Creole	Expensive	87
		VALUE
4501 Tchoupitoulas Street; 894-9880		B
Uptown above Napoleon Zone 4		

Reservations: Not accepted
When to go: Early dinner
Entree range: $14–21
Payment: AE, MC, V
Service rating: ★★
Friendliness rating: ★★★★
Parking: Curbside
Bar: Full service

Wine selection: Modest list matched to
the food
Dress: Casual
Disabled access: Limited
Customers: Clientele tends to the
younger side and others who have time
to wait in line

Dinner: Tuesday–Saturday, 6–10 p.m.

Setting & atmosphere: An eye-catching old corner cafe on the Uptown riverfront, with enough New Orleans raffishness to make it appealing to a younger crowd. You'd want to check it out even if there weren't food inside.

Recommended dishes: Crab cakes; duck-and-brie pain perdu; filet mignon with foie gras; pecan catfish; seafood hot pot.

Summary & comments: Dick is Richard Benz, formerly the chef of the Upperline and a few other very good places. Jenny is his wife, a former floral designer. Both of them had their eyes on this grubby-but-cool old joint for a long time. When the previous tenants folded, they moved in and fixed the place up—but not too much. The whole idea caught on with the younger end of the Uptown gourmet spectrum, and suddenly everybody was hanging around inside and outside waiting for a table. (No reservations.) It's a little uncomfortable, but the prices are lower than average for a place like this.

DICKIE BRENNAN'S STEAKHOUSE ★★★★

		QUALITY
Steaks and Chops	Very Expensive	88
		VALUE
716 Iberville Street; 522-2467		C
French Quarter Zone 1		

Reservations: Recommended
When to go: Anytime
Entree range: $16–32
Payment: All major credit cards
Service rating: ★★★
Friendliness rating: ★★★★
Parking: Validated parking next door
Bar: Full service

Wine selection: Excellent; many selections by the glass
Dress: Jacket
Disabled access: Full
Customers: Professionals at lunch; couples at dinner; some tourists and conventioneers

Lunch: Monday–Friday, 11:30 a.m.–3 p.m.

Dinner: Every day, 6–10 p.m.

Setting & atmosphere: This is the only below-street-level restaurant in New Orleans. Handsome place. Tile floors, banquette seating, and unusual displays of antique weapons in the private dining rooms lend a distinctly New Orleans, masculine look.

Recommended dishes: Baked oyster combination; tomato-and-onion salad with blue cheese and rémoulade; turtle soup; strip steak; porterhouse steak; house filet mignon (with oysters); grilled fish; pontalba potatoes; bananas Foster bread pudding.

Summary & comments: No sooner had the Brennans of Commander's Palace split their restaurant holdings among the members of the third generation than Dick Brennan, Jr. announced he was going to bring to fruition an idea his father had for years: a first-class steakhouse. The beef is USDA prime without exception. (Most steakhouses that claim to serve prime beef actually serve less-than-prime filets.) Each cut is cooked differently: the filet is broiled, the strip is cooked in a hot black-iron skillet, and the ribeye is roasted. The menu is simple, but significantly more original than what we're used to finding in steakhouses.

DRAGO'S		★★★★
Seafood	Moderate	**QUALITY** 87
3232 N. Arnoult Road; 888-9254		**VALUE** C
Metairie above Causeway/Kenner/Jefferson Highway Zone 10		

Reservations: Accepted	**Bar:** Full service
When to go: Anytime	**Wine selection:** House wines, including a
Entree range: $7–16	few from Croatia
Payment: All major credit cards	**Dress:** Casual
Service rating: ★★	**Disabled access:** Full
Friendliness rating: ★★★	**Customers:** Locals; families
Parking: Small parking lot adjacent	

Lunch: Monday–Friday, 11:30 a.m.–2:30 p.m.

Dinner: Monday–Saturday, 6 p.m.–1:30 a.m.

Setting & atmosphere: This old seafood house has exploded into an insanely popular restaurant in recent years. The modernized dining rooms are a little high tech for my taste and more than a little noisy. Best place to eat—the bar.

Recommended dishes: Raw oysters; char-grilled oysters; seafood gumbo; shrimp Ruth; shrimp fondue; salad with feta vinaigrette; grilled, stuffed drumfish Tommy; fried- or broiled-seafood platter; boiled lobster; lunch specials.

Summary & comments: Ambitious as casual seafood restaurants go, Drago's is our premier oyster specialist, both at the raw bar and in the kitchen. The great cooked dish is char-broiled oysters (grilled in the shell, basted with garlic-herb butter). Almost everything else in the way of local seafood is here in some interesting, garlic-laced incarnation. They use basic boiled Maine lobster as a loss-leader specialty; one of these is a 6-to-8-pounder with a bottle of wine for $100. Specials are good, especially when Klara Cvitanovich cooks some Croatian food.

EMERIL'S		★★★★★

		QUALITY
Contemporary Creole	Very Expensive	**93**

	VALUE
800 Tchoupitoulas Street; 528-9393	**C**
Central Business District Zone 2	

Reservations: Required	**Wine selection:** Distinguished, with
When to go: Lunch and early dinner	emphasis on California; many well-
Entree range: $18–32	known but rarely-seen bottles; many
Payment: All major credit cards	by-the-glass selections
Service rating: ★★★★	**Dress:** Dressy casual
Friendliness rating: ★★★	**Disabled access:** Full
Parking: Valet (free)	**Customers:** Mix of tourists and locals;
Bar: Full service	hip, gourmet crowd

Lunch: Monday–Friday, 11:30 a.m.–2:30 p.m.

Dinner: Monday–Saturday, 6–10 p.m.

Setting & atmosphere: In 2000, ten years after opening, Emeril's under-went a major renovation. The old warehouse was softened (noise continues to be a problem, however), and the furnishings moved far into the realm of artful design. Particularly interesting is the arch over the food bar, where those most interested in cooking can watch the action while eating atop barstools.

Recommended dishes: Specials are always the best bets. Barbecue shrimp; smoked-trout dumplings; gumbo of the day; andouille-crusted redfish; panneed quail; "study of duck" (three ways); filet of beef with blue cheese; double-cut pork chop with green mole; banana cream pie; chocolate pecan pie; chocolate Grand Marnier soufflé; cheeses.

Summary & comments: Emeril Lagasse is America's best-known gourmet chef, thanks to his winning personality, his television shows, and his constant release of cookbooks. His media activities and empire of five restaurants (the other two in New Orleans are Nola and Delmonico) take him out of the restaurant. But this is where it all started, and he's never let the place tank. Indeed, regulars who know how to play the place still report spectacular meals. The menu is based on Louisiana flavors. It's also highly ingredient-driven. Emeril's ruling principle is that the menu should obey the vagaries of the fresh-food market. The rarer the food, the better. The result is big taste and high adventure. A great way to sample it is to get the tasting menu, but you should always pay much attention to the specials.

FEELINGS		★★★
Creole	Expensive	**QUALITY** 84
713 St. Louis Street; 581-4422 Downtown/St. Bernard Zone 5		**VALUE** B

Reservations: Recommended	Bar: Full service
When to go: Anytime	Wine selection: Limited and ordinary
Entree range: $10–16	Dress: Casual
Payment: All major credit cards	Disabled access: Limited
Service rating: ★★★	Customers: Mostly neighborhood
Friendliness rating: ★★★★	residents
Parking: Curbside	

Brunch: Sunday, 11 a.m.–2:30 p.m.

Lunch: Friday, 11:30 a.m.–2:30 p.m.

Dinner: Sunday–Thursday, 6–10 p.m.; Friday–Saturday, 6–11 p.m.

Setting & atmosphere: An engaging, unique restaurant in a 200-year-old building in the Bywater section, Feelings has dining rooms in the main house, the slave quarters, on the balcony, and in the covered brick courtyard.

Recommended dishes: Shrimp étouffée spread; oysters en brochette; pâte maison; house salad; red snapper moutarde; trout pecan; soft-shell crabs with avocado butter; shrimp Clemenceau (with garlic, peas, mushrooms and potatoes); chicken Clemenceau; tournedos au poivre; veal Florentine; duck bigarrade (Grand Marnier sauce); peanut-butter pie; French silk (chocolate mousse) pie.

Summary & comments: The menu is mostly Creole, but you won't see this exact style anywhere else. It's a very polite, almost old-fashioned kitchen, but never boring or bland. The five-course table d'hote menu is the way to eat here; the courses are small, but they fill every sector of your appetite. Very popular in the neighborhood, Feelings sometimes has few or no tables available immediately, but the courtyard bar is a great place to wait.

THE FRENCH TABLE ★★★★

French Bistro	Very Expensive	QUALITY
		92

		VALUE
3216 W. Esplanade Avenue; 833-8108		C
Metairie above Causeway/Kenner/Jefferson Highway	Zone 10	

Reservations: Recommended
When to go: Weeknights; lunch
Entree range: $16–24
Payment: AE, DC, MC, V
Service rating: ★★★★
Friendliness rating: ★★★★
Parking: Ample parking lot adjacent;
valet parking at lunch
Bar: Full service
Wine selection: Decent; French-dominated
Dress: Dressy casual
Disabled access: Full
Customers: Locals; couples

Lunch: Monday–Friday, 11:30 a.m.–2:30 p.m.

Dinner: Monday–Thursday, 6–10 p.m.; Friday–Saturday, 6–11 p.m.

Setting & atmosphere: The restaurant is in an anonymous strip mall, which makes its pretty dining rooms that much more charming.

Recommended dishes: Pâte maison; magret of duck; escargots bourguignonne; onion soup gratinée; salade maison; poached fish hollandaise; coq au vin; sweetbreads Grenobloise; veal Crozier; steak au poivre; filet mignon Perigourdine; gratin dauphinoise; floating island; crème caramel; gâteau de pain au whiskey.

Summary & comments: In its first 26 years this was Crozier's, a very personal bistro run by Lyon-born chef Gerard Crozier. He sold it to some long-term customers, who wasted no time expanding the menu, premises, and hours. To the surprise of the regulars, this actually seemed to improve the restaurant. The big change is that some Creole food edged onto the menu, and the near-perfect record of consistency has been compromised a little. Still, the dish Crozier cooked for you a decade ago can still be had almost exactly today. Service and presentations are understated.

GABRIELLE ★★★★

Contemporary Creole	Very Expensive	QUALITY
		96
		VALUE
		B

3201 Esplanade Avenue; 948-6233
Mid-City/Gentilly   Zone 6

Reservations: Required
When to go: Early evenings, weeknights
Entree range: $14–22
Payment: All major credit cards
Service rating: ★★★
Friendliness rating: ★★★
Parking: Curbside
Bar: Full service

Wine selection: Modest; mostly California wines well-chosen to complement the food; many by-the-glass selections; attractive prices
Dress: Dressy casual
Disabled access: Limited
Customers: Locals; couples; gourmets

Lunch: Friday, 11:30 a.m.–2:30 p.m.

Dinner: Tuesday–Thursday, 6–10 p.m.; Friday–Saturday, 6–11 p.m.

Setting & atmosphere: The restaurant is tiny, crowded, and noisy, and even with a recent addition there is never enough room for all the people who want to dine here.

Recommended dishes: Oysters Gabie; sausage mixed grill; grilled rabbit tenderloin; blackened steak; blackened tuna; pork chop any style; roasted duck; fish specials; bread pudding; lemon chess pie; dessert specials.

Summary & comments: Gabrielle is the personal restaurant of Greg and Mary Sonnier, both of whom are chefs. After Mary prepares the evening's desserts, she spends her time running the dining room. From the micro kitchen proceeds a menu of imaginative but distinctly Louisiana-style dishes. The repertoire supplies a slightly different menu every day. Sonnier opened this place after stints at K-Paul's and Brigtsen's, and like those restaurants, it prizes robustness of flavor above niceties of atmosphere and service. The Friday lunch is easygoing and a good introduction. It's also popular among the regulars, so don't figure on just sauntering in.

GALATOIRE'S ★★★★

Creole French	Very Expensive	QUALITY
		92
		VALUE
		C

209 Bourbon Street; 525-2021
French Quarter   Zone 1

Reservations: Not accepted
When to go: Late lunch or early dinner; locals completely take over on Fridays and Sundays

Entree range: $12–26
Payment: All major credit cards
Service rating: ★★★
Friendliness rating: ★★★

Parking: Pay garages nearby

Bar: Full service; drinks are very generously poured and modestly priced

Wine selection: Peculiar list of French
and California wines with the absolute
minimum of identification of maker
and vintage; very attractive prices

Dress: Jacket and tie required at dinner
and all day Sunday

Disabled access: Full

Customers: Both tourists and locals; the
latter tend to be regulars who know all
the other regulars

Lunch & dinner: Tuesday–Sunday, 11:30 a.m.–10 p.m.

Setting & atmosphere: A cornerstone of fine Creole dining throughout
the 1990s, Galatoire's ended the century with a $3 million renovation—the
first thorough one in the restaurant's history. The main dining room downstairs kept its tiled floors, mirrors, motionless ceiling fans, and bright,
naked light bulbs. The second-floor dining room opened for the first time
since the 1940s. A new bar and waiting area all but eliminated the trouble-
some queue on the sidewalk.

Recommended dishes: Shrimp rémoulade; crabmeat maison; canape
Lorenzo; oysters Rockefeller; oysters en brochette; green salad with garlic;
trout meunière or amandine; grilled pompano; poached salmon or drum
hollandaise; shrimp Marguery; crabmeat Yvonne; chicken Clemenceau;
filet or strip steak Bearnaise; lamb, veal, or pork chop; crème caramel;
crêpes maison.

Summary & comments: When the management reconfigured Galatoire's
interior in 1999, they knew better than to make many changes in the
kitchen. The definitive French-Creole menu remained inviolate, as did the
loose, generous operating style of the cooks. Seafood is the main draw, but
everything is cooked deftly. Regular diners can recommend their own
favorite dishes from the catalog-like menu. Here you find the bedrock of
New Orleans's culinary society, being served well-made, simple standards in
Galatoire's old-fashioned, unceremonious way.

GALLAGHER'S ★★★★

Creole	Expensive	QUALITY
		87
1630 N. US 190 (Causeway Boulevard); 892-1444		VALUE
North Shore Zone 12		C

Reservations: Accepted

When to go: Anytime

Entree range: $12–22

Payment: All major credit cards

Service rating: ★★★

Friendliness rating: ★★★★

Parking: Ample parking lot adjacent

Bar: Full service

Wine selection: Decent list, emphasis on
California

Dress: Dressy casual

Disabled access: Limited

Customers: Locals; gourmets; couples

Lunch: Monday–Friday, 11:30 a.m.–2:30 p.m.

Dinner: Monday–Thursday, 6–10 p.m.; Friday–Saturday, 6–11 p.m.

Setting & atmosphere: A collection of smallish rooms, the place has a comfortable intimacy and a very lively bar.

Recommended dishes: Crab cakes; fried baby soft-shell crabs; baby-back ribs; smoked duck and andouille gumbo; charcoal grilled tuna; trout Winner's Circle (in artichokes and lemon cream sauce); grilled quail; smoked duckling; veal St. Tammany (in mushrooms and garlic); chicken Lafayette (in a rich sauce with tasso); different desserts daily.

Summary & comments: Pat Gallagher established his culinary credentials in the 1970s, bounced around here and there for a few years, and finally opened this, his most substantial venue, in 1995. Indeed, Gallagher's is one of the few North Shore restaurants that manages to stay busy all week long. That is all due to the cooking. The emphasis is on grilled foods, seasoned and cooked with excitement. Same goes for the Creole and American basics that complete the comprehensive menu. Two words to remember here: lamb and quail. Together or apart, these are rarely done better than here.

GATREAU'S		★★★★
Contemporary Creole Very Expensive		**QUALITY** 93
1728 Soniat Street; 899-7397		**VALUE** C
Uptown above Napoleon Zone 4		

Reservations: Recommended	Bar: Full service
When to go: Anytime	Wine selection: Modest but well-chosen
Entree range: $18–26	for the food
Payment: All major credit cards	Dress: Jacket recommended but not
Service rating: ★★★★	required
Friendliness rating: ★★★★	Disabled access: Limited
Parking: Valet (free)	Customers: Locals; couples; gourmets

Dinner: Monday–Saturday, 6–10 p.m.

Setting & atmosphere: The small dining room was once an antique pharmacy, from which some relics remain. There's more room upstairs, but the space is not used every night.

Recommended dishes: Crisp duck confit with mustard and sage; seared sea scallops; cold poached lobster with smoked corn; salmon tartare with sesame seaweed salad; cream-of-corn soup with crabmeat; roasted grouper and fennel; roast chicken with wild mushrooms; beef tournedos and artichoke ragout; roasted lamb chops and truffle risotto; crêpes with cherry fig sauce; crème brûlée.

Summary & comments: Deep in an Uptown residential neighborhood, Gautreau's many regulars (they're the only ones who can find the place) have come to expect a certain hard-to-define but polished style of contemporary cooking. The abbreviated menu has one of just about everything, whipped up with light touches of both innovation and Creole flavor. The best dishes tend to be the least exotic—the filet mignon and roast chicken, to name two such. Service has a rather chummy style about it; the servers give frank opinions about everything. It's difficult to get a table here on short notice, and there's no comfortable place to wait.

GENGHIS KHAN		★★★

		QUALITY
Korean	Moderate	85

	VALUE
4053 Tulane Avenue; 482-4044	C
Mid-City/Gentilly Zone 6	

Reservations: Accepted	Parking: Curbside
When to go: Anytime	Bar: Full service
Entree range: $8–14	Wine selection: A few house wines
Payment: AE, MC, V	Dress: Casual
Service rating: ★★★★	Disabled access: Limited
Friendliness rating: ★★★	Customers: Locals

Lunch: Tuesday–Friday, 11:30 a.m.–2 p.m.

Dinner: Sunday and Tuesday–Thursday, 6–10 p.m.; Friday–Saturday, 6–11 p.m.

Setting & atmosphere: A long dining room is dominated by a grand piano and a music stand in the center. There's live classical and show music here almost every night. In the rear on some nights, regular customers play long games of Go while eating noodles.

Recommended dishes: Fried mandu (dumpling); calamari tempura; kim (seaweed wafers) and rice; spinach namul; kimchee; bulgoki; whole, marinated tempura fried fish; shrimp Genghis Khan; chongol hot pot (beef and shrimp in broth); tempura banana split.

Entertainment & amenities: Live classical, opera, and show music nightly, with singers and instrumentalists of great talent.

Summary & comments: For over 25 years, classical violinist Henry Lee has operated a terrific restaurant featuring the food of his homeland, Korea. If you've had Korean food before, be aware that this menu is much adapted to Western tastes, but what comes out is undeniably delicious. Charcoal-grilled, marinated beef is an essential part of the menu; so are cold, very full-flavored concoctions of leafy green vegetables. Some of the food is quite spicy. But the most popular dish here among the regulars is the whole fried fish, ample and greaseless.

GERARD'S DOWNTOWN ★★★★

		QUALITY
Contemporary French	Very Expensive	**91**
		VALUE
500 St. Charles Avenue; 592-0200		**C**
Central Business District Zone 2		

Reservations: Recommended	Bar: Full service
When to go: Dinner	Wine selection: Excellent wine list, with
Entree range: $16–28	many surprises
Payment: All major credit cards	Dress: Jacket recommended but not
Service rating: ★★	required
Friendliness rating: ★★★	Disabled access: Limited
Parking: Valet (free)	Customers: Gourmets and hotel guests

Brunch: Sunday, 11 a.m.–2:30 p.m.

Lunch: Monday–Friday, 11:30 a.m.–2:30 p.m.

Dinner: Monday–Saturday, 6–10 p.m.

Setting & atmosphere: Just off Lafayette Square, it's a pleasant, if not quite stunning, long room with a lot of windows and a cool style.

Recommended dishes: Mussel soup; salmon gravlax; Gerard's baked oysters with pancetta; roast chicken with herbs; herb-and-mustard lamb chops; London broil; salmon baked in pastry; crabmeat and asparagus risotto; theobroma (chocolate soup over cake); crème brûlée.

Summary & comments: Gerard Maras was the chef who brought Mr. B's to its peak. After spending some years farming (a passion for him), he returned to the kitchen in his own new restaurant. The food is a bit of a surprise. Almost everything has the ring of the classical French repertoire. The good news is that we have not seen these dishes in a long time. In many cases Maras deviates from vogue by buying less-than-glamorous foodstuffs (flank steak, for example) and doing what needs to be done to make it delicious. It's all a bit understated by today's standards. But Maras is a chef who knows what he's about, and if you do too, you'll have a very good meal here.

GRILL ROOM ★★★★★

		QUALITY
Eclectic	Very Expensive	**97**

	VALUE
300 Gravier Street (in the Windsor Court Hotel); 522-1992	**D**

Central Business District   Zone 2

Reservations: Required
When to go: Wednesday through Friday
  nights
Entree range: $18–34
Payment: All major credit cards
Service rating: ★★★★★
Friendliness rating: ★★★★★
Parking: Valet (free)
Bar: Full service
Wine selection: One of the town's best

cellars, with a thick book of unusual
bottles from all over the world; the large
stock of older French wines was assem-
bled by buying private collections at
auction
Dress: Jacket recommended but not
  required
Disabled access: Full
Customers: A mix of locals, hotel guests,
  and tourists; gourmets

Breakfast: Every day 7–10 a.m.

Brunch: Sunday, 11:30 a.m.–2:30 p.m.

Lunch: Monday–Saturday, 11:30 a.m.–2:30 p.m.

Dinner: Every day, 6–10 p.m.

Setting & atmosphere: The best and most expensive napery, china, silver-
ware, flowers, foodstuffs, and wines are placed at your disposal by an
extremely amenable service staff. The dining room is modern but furnished
with an impressive collection of art and antiques, most with a British
cachet.

Recommended dishes: Kumamoto oysters with ginger; smoked salmon;
seared foie gras; turtle soup; Windsor Court salad; grilled tuna Rossini;
grilled fish; rack of lamb; dessert soufflés; crème brûlée tart; chocolate
breathless.

Entertainment & amenities: Live chamber music in lounge.

Summary & comments: Grill Room is the restaurant of the Windsor
Court Hotel, which has been called by various authorities the best hotel in
the world. This is a restaurant for an evening of unusual tastes and presentations—and for dining at the highest levels of service and price. The best
way to experience the Grill Room is through the degustation—some eight
courses of the night's best specials. With accompanying wines it tops $100
per person, but the evening will not soon be forgotten. There may be a dish
or two in there that may appeal more to the brain than to the palate, but
what the stylish want is what the stylish get.

GUMBO SHOP   ★★★

Creole	Inexpensive	QUALITY
		84

		VALUE
630 St. Peter Street; 525-1486		**B**
French Quarter Zone 1		

Reservations: Not accepted	Parking: French Market pay lot, one block
When to go: Middle of the afternoon or evening	Bar: Full service
	Wine selection: A few house wines
Entree range: $7–14	Dress: Casual
Payment: All major credit cards	Disabled access: Limited
Service rating: ★★★	Customers: Tourists; some locals
Friendliness rating: ★★★★	

Lunch & dinner: Sunday–Thursday, 11 a.m.–10 p.m.; Friday–Saturday, 11 a.m.–11 p.m.

Setting & atmosphere: The dining room isn't as old as its yellowed murals or antique dressings suggest. But it feels good anyway. There are also a few tables in the carriageway.

Recommended dishes: Shrimp rémoulade; seafood gumbo; jambalaya; red beans and rice; crawfish pie; crawfish étouffée; redfish Florentine; blackened redfish; pecan pie; bread pudding.

Summary & comments: This best-named of all New Orleans restaurants is a great resource. If it's traditional everyday New Orleans eats you want, here they are. Gumbo and the other homestyle Creole specials are very credibly done every day, and the menu can even turn out something fancy with elan. Prices are a lot lower than they could be, given the popularity and great location (less than a block from Jackson Square).

INDIA PALACE   ★★★

Indian	Moderate	QUALITY
		84

		VALUE
3322 N. Turnbull Street; 889-2436		**C**
Metairie above Causeway/Kenner/Jefferson Highway Zone 10		

Reservations: Accepted	Parking: Free lot adjacent
When to go: Anytime	Bar: Full service
Entree range: $8–18	Wine selection: A few house wines
Payment: All major credit cards	Dress: Casual
Service rating: ★★★	Disabled access: Full
Friendliness rating: ★★★★	Customers: Locals

Lunch: Every day, 11:30 a.m.–2:30 p.m.

Dinner: Every day, 6–10 p.m.

Setting & atmosphere: They go easy on the ornate Indian furnishings and wall hangings in this informal and very comfortable restaurant.

Recommended dishes: Samosas (small pastries stuffed with meat or vegetables); tandoori chicken or prawns; the entire range of curries, including the very hot vindaloo curries; saag paneer (homemade cheese in a creamed-spinach sauce); lamb or chicken saagwala (in a sauce similar to that of saag paneer); yogurt-marinated lamb rack; naan (tandoor-baked bread); cream cheese and pistachio pudding; mango sundae.

Summary & comments: The range and goodness of the cooking here are at least as advanced as what you'll find elsewhere. At lunch, of course, there's a buffet. The variety and temperature of the buffet selections are suitable, but the real food is at dinner, when the offerings include everything from tandoori-roasted meats and seafoods to fried foods to curries and other saucy plates. A couple of nights a week, they do the southern Indian crêpe called dosa. Everything is served with appropriate and first-class condiments and sauces. The staff is very helpful, if not always polished.

IRENE'S CUISINE		★★★★
Italian	Expensive	**QUALITY** 87
539 St. Philip Street; 529-8811 French Quarter Zone 1		**VALUE** B

Reservations: Not accepted
When to go: Early evenings
Entree range: $11–19
Payment: AE, DC, MC, V
Service rating: ★★★
Friendliness rating: ★★★
Bar: Full service

Wine selection: Decent; mostly Italian wines
Dress: Casual
Disabled access: Full
Customers: Mostly locals; a few tourists; many Quarterites

Dinner: Sunday–Thursday, 6–10 p.m.; Friday–Saturday, 6–11 p.m.

Setting & atmosphere: The main dining room is in an old paper warehouse and is pleasantly rough. A big part of the experience of dining here involves who you'll socialize with during the almost-inevitable wait for a table.

Recommended dishes: Mussels marinara; oysters Irene (with pancetta and Romano); oysters Vittorio (Italian style, plus artichokes); grilled shrimp and panneed oysters; roasted chicken with rosemary and garlic; veal Sorrentino; roast duck with spinach and mustard; sautéed soft-shell crab and pasta; lamb rack à la Provence; tiramisu; Italian ice creams.

Summary & comments: Irene DiPietro cooks up lusty, robust, generally simple food with a country Italian flavor (meaning lots of fresh herbs, garlic, and olive oil). It's a style you don't run into much around here (Mosca's is about the only other place), which may explain the crowds that usually make it at least a little difficult to get a table. Service operations are overseen by former Sazerac maitre d' Tommy Andrade (a co-owner), but the trattoria-authentic bustle can reach chaos at times. A recent addition has loosened things up a bit, fortunately. This is one of the few restaurants deep in the French Quarter that has a substantial local clientele.

JACQUES-IMO'S   ★★★★

Creole	Moderate	QUALITY
		87

		VALUE
8324 Oak Street; 861-0886		B
Uptown above Napoleon Zone 4		

Reservations: Accepted for parties of five or more	Parking: Curbside
	Bar: Full service
When to go: Tuesdays, Wednesdays, or Thursdays	Wine selection: Modest and matched to the food
Entree range: $9–18	Dress: Casual
Payment: All major credit cards	Disabled access: Limited
Service rating: ★★	Customers: Younger crowd, plus hip visitors with a taste for New Orleans funk
Friendliness rating: ★★★	

Dinner: Tuesday–Saturday, 6–10 p.m.

Setting & atmosphere: Dining spaces include a little room in front, a larger one near the kitchen, and a rear courtyard. All have that slight hint of swamp voodoo Orleanians like.

Recommended dishes: Eggplant with oyster dressing; fried oysters with spicy garlic sauce; fried green tomatoes with shrimp rémoulade; fried chicken; smothered chicken; broiled escolar with shrimp; stuffed pork chop; Cajun bouillabaisse; blackened tuna; panneed rabbit with oyster-tasso pasta; sautéed veal Bienville; banana cream pie; white-chocolate bread pudding.

Summary & comments: Jack "Jacques" Leonardi, a former K-Paul's chef, teamed up with legendary soul-food chef Austin Leslie to create a convincing neighborhood Creole cafe. It's so appealing, in fact, that at this writing it's a major phenom, and difficult to penetrate without a long wait. This is easy to explain. The food here is unapologetically lusty, fresh, and local; always interesting, and sometimes amazingly good.

K-PAUL'S LOUISIANA KITCHEN ★★★★

Contemporary Cajun	Very Expensive	QUALITY
		88

		VALUE
416 Chartres Street; 524-7394		D
French Quarter Zone 1		

Reservations: Not accepted downstairs; required upstairs

When to go: Lunch, and during slack tourist and convention periods

Entree range: $22–32

Payment: AE, MC, V

Service rating: ★★★

Friendliness rating: ★★★

Parking: Jackson Brewery pay lot, one block

Bar: Full service

Wine selection: Good; includes many selections by the glass

Dress: Casual

Disabled access: Full

Customers: Mostly tourists at dinner, but there's a good contingent of locals at lunch; gourmets

Lunch: Monday–Saturday, 11:30 a.m.–2:30 p.m.

Dinner: Monday–Saturday, 6–10 p.m.

Setting & atmosphere: The renovation of a few years ago transformed Paul Prudhomme's headquarters both physically and spiritually. In the casual downstairs dining room, small parties still share tables with others, and amenities are still minimal. The new upstairs dining room offers everything local diners held out for: tablecloths, private tables, and even reservations.

Recommended dishes: Chicken-andouille gumbo; Cajun popcorn with sherry sauce; shrimp or crawfish étouffée; stuffed soft-shell crab choron; blackened tuna; fried mirliton and oysters with tasso hollandaise; roast duck with pecan gravy; pan-fried veal with roasted stuffed peppers; blackened beef tenders in debris sauce; sweet potato-pecan pie; bread pudding with lemon sauce; chocolate mocha cake.

Summary & comments: Chef Paul Prudhomme's fame as the archetypal Cajun chef allowed his restaurant to be high-handed for years. But K-Paul's is now much friendlier—even to the point that locals are returning. Whether you sit upstairs or downstairs, you get the unique recipes of Chef Paul, with his consistently impressive ability to make the first-class ingredients explode with flavor, not all of which is Cajun. Also still in place: prices at dinner higher than you think they'll be.

KELSEY'S ★★★

Contemporary Creole	Expensive	QUALITY
		86

3923 Magazine Street; 897-6722
West Bank   Zone 11

	VALUE
	B

Reservations: Recommended
When to go: Anytime
Entree range: $11–23
Payment: All major credit cards
Service rating: ★★★
Friendliness rating: ★★★★
Parking: Free lot across the street,

plus curbside
Bar: Full service
Wine selection: Good; mostly California
   wines
Dress: Casual
Disabled access: None
Customers: Uptowners; couples at night

Lunch: Tuesday–Friday, 11:30 a.m.–2:30 p.m.

Dinner: Tuesday–Sunday, 6–10 p.m.

Setting & atmosphere: The restaurant was built from an antique corner grocery. Now there are two long rooms—one with the bar, the other with dining tables. The atmosphere at all hours is congenial.

Recommended dishes: Eggplant delight (fried, topped with spicy shrimp); shrimp Bombay pie; oysters-and-Brie pie; Creole gumbo; eggplant Kelsey (stuffed with seafood and herbs); grilled fish; barbecued fish; panneed rabbit with pasta; stuffed duck breast; chocolate hazelnut torte; orange poppyseed cheesecake; bread pudding.

Summary & comments: Chef/owner Randy Barlow is one of many chefs who worked with and were influenced by the style of Paul Prudhomme. Barlow still cooks in that intense style, although he's developed many of his own tastes. The big flavors originate in the profligate use of cream, assertive seasoning blends, aromatic vegetables, and tasso—not to mention fresh seafood and vegetables. The menu is epitomized by the eggplant with seafood in cream sauce, a major specialty. But there's a lot of variety here.

KIM SON ★★★★

Vietnamese	Inexpensive	QUALITY
		87

349 Whitney Avenue; 366-2489
West Bank   Zone 11

	VALUE
	A

Reservations: Accepted
When to go: Anytime
Entree range: $6–11

Payment: AE, MC, V
Service rating: ★★
Friendliness rating: ★★★★

Parking: Free lot adjacent
Bar: Full service
Bar: Full service
Wine selection: Limited and ordinary

Dress: Casual
Disabled access: Limited
Customers: Locals; gourmets

Lunch: Monday–Saturday, 11:30 a.m.–2:30 p.m.

Dinner: Every day, 6–10 p.m.

Setting & atmosphere: A large room with the usual Asian kitsch. An alarmingly big fish levitates in a tank. Men must check out an amazing apparatus in the bathroom.

Recommended dishes: Imperial roll; spring roll; Vietnamese hot-and-sour fish soup; charcoal-broiled beef and cold noodles; salt-baked crab; salt-baked scallops; fish cooked in clay pot; steamed whole fish; clay-pot chicken curry with coconut; leaf-bound beef; beef fondued in boiled vinegar; eggplant and bean cake in clay pot.

Summary & comments: Kim Son provides the best introduction you could have to Vietnamese food. The underpriced menu is loaded with great dishes, usually involving the heavy use of fresh herbs and grilled meats—both hallmarks of Vietnamese cooking. It's best to bring a large group, the better to sample the wide range of the menu. Some of the best dishes involve charcoal grilling, claypot braising, and salt baking. The restaurant also offers some unexpectedly wonderful noodle and vegetarian dishes. The staff is very helpful about the more exotic fare. The Chinese food on the menu is not bad, but it's not nearly as good as the Vietnamese dishes.

KOSHER CAJUN DELI ★★

Sandwiches	Inexpensive	QUALITY
		82
3519 Severn Street; 888-2010		VALUE
Metairie above Causeway/Kenner/Jefferson Highway Zone 10		B

Reservations: Not accepted
When to go: Anytime except right before and during Jewish holy days
Entree range: $5–8
Payment: AE, DS, MC, V
Service rating: ★★
Friendliness rating: ★★★★
Parking: Free lot adjacent

Bar: Beer and wine
Wine selection: A few kosher wines, from Israel and elsewhere
Dress: Anything goes
Disabled access: Full
Customers: Observant Jews and Muslims; locals

Lunch & dinner: Monday–Thursday, 11 a.m.–7 p.m.; Friday and Sunday, 11 a.m. –3 p.m.; Saturday, closed

Setting & atmosphere: It's a combination grocery and deli, with tables in a bright, windowed area up front.

Recommended dishes: Chopped liver; lox and bagel; cole slaw; J&N special sandwich; pastrami sandwich on rye; corned beef sandwich on pumpernickel; roast beef on onion roll; turkey and chopped liver with cole slaw on rye; hot dog with sauerkraut; parve cheesecake; strudel; Dr. Brown's sodas.

Summary & comments: Joel and Natalie Brown run one of the only strict kosher restaurants in the area. They recently expanded to attract gentile customers, but all Jewish dietary laws are observed—so don't be put off about not being able to get cheese on your corned-beef sandwich. All the cold cuts are of superb quality, brought in from New York and Chicago. They make the best chopped liver I've had in a restaurant, and a great sandwich from it. Knishes, pickles, and the remainder of the standard deli menu is here, all served generously for eating in or taking home. Also here is a large stock of kosher groceries, including wines.

LA CRÊPE NANOU ★★★★

French Bistro	Expensive	QUALITY
		89
1410 Robert Street; 899-2670		VALUE
Uptown above Napoleon Zone 4		A

Reservations: Not accepted	Bar: Full service
When to go: Early evenings	Wine selection: Substantial and French-
Entree range: $9–20	dominated; many by-the-glass selec-
Payment: AE, MC, V	tions; attractive prices
Service rating: ★★★	Dress: Casual
Friendliness rating: ★★★	Disabled access: Limited
Parking: Curbside Robert Street side of	Customers: Uptowners; Francophiles;
parking lot	Baby Boomers

Dinner: Sunday–Thursday, 6–10 p.m.; Friday–Saturday, 6–11 p.m.

Setting & atmosphere: It looks as if it had been transported here from a Parisian back street. The premises are a collage of mismatched decors and furnishings. Always busy, with a happy crowd of locals waiting for tables.

Recommended dishes: Pâte maison; mussels mariniere; escargots de bourguignonne; onion soup au gratin; salad tropicale; crêpes, especially crab, crawfish, florentine, and Provençal; grilled salmon Béarnaise; roast chicken; grilled quail with mushrooms; filet mignon with green peppercorn sauce; lamb chops with Cognac sauce; sweetbreads with lemon, capers and butter; dessert crêpes, especially Antillaise, Belle Helene, and Calvados; baked Alaska for two.

Summary & comments: Evolved far beyond its origins as a crêpe shop, Nanou is a fix for Francophiles. Understandably popular, meals here usually mean at least a short wait for a table to open; the social scene during the delay is a subspecies of the Uptown cocktail party. The food is stereotypical bistro fare: fresh, very French, inexpensive, and more delicious than you anticipate. Crêpes—both entree and dessert varieties—remain a specialty that no other local restaurant can match in quality or taste.

LA PROVENCE		★★★★

Mediterranean French	Very Expensive	QUALITY 89
25020 US 190; 626-7662 North Shore Zone 12		VALUE C

Reservations: Required
When to go: Sunday afternoon
Entree range: $14–24
Payment: AE, MC, V
Service rating: ★★★
Friendliness rating: ★★★
Parking: Free lot adjacent
Bar: Full service

Wine selection: Distinguished and French-dominated; the policy on corkage is draconian
Dress: Jacket recommended but not required
Disabled access: Full
Customers: Gourmets from all over the area; couples

Lunch & dinner: Sunday, 1–9 p.m.

Dinner: Wednesday–Thursday, 5 p.m.–10 p.m.; Friday–Saturday, 5 p.m. –11 p.m.

Setting & atmosphere: Dining at La Provence is like dining in the countryside of Europe. Still surrounded by forest on the old Mandeville-Slidell highway, it feels rural and sophisticated at the same time.

Recommended dishes: Merguez (lamb sausage); gravlax; baked oysters three ways; escargots bourguignonne; quail gumbo; Greek salad; quenelles of scallops; sautéed thyme-marinated quail; duck à l'orange; rack of lamb; tournedos Bordelaise; sweetbreads braised in port wine; diplomat pudding; dessert cart.

Entertainment & amenities: Pianist in lounge nightly.

Summary & comments: Chef/owner Chris Kerageorgiou has been a delightful character on the dining scene for three decades. He assumes that he knows everybody in the dining room, so even if you're a stranger you'll get a visit and maybe even a hug or an invitation to take a tour of the kitchen. Chris blends the flavors of his French and Greek heritage with Creole touches for some endlessly delicious, original food. While the food is not as consistent as it once was, an amazing thing has happened: the prices have dropped, with a particularly attractive three-course, 15-dollar early-evening special. The somewhat casual service style (again, much like what one finds in the French countryside) is offputting to some diners, but get past it.

LA RIVIERA		★★★★

Italian	Expensive	QUALITY
		88

4506 Shores Drive; 888-6238	VALUE
Metairie above Causeway/Kenner/Jefferson Highway Zone 10	**C**

Reservations: Recommended	Bar: Full service
When to go: Anytime	Wine selection: Substantial list, mostly
Entree range: $9–22	Italian
Payment: All major credit cards	Dress: Jacket recommended but
Service rating: ★★★★	not required
Friendliness rating: ★★★★	Disabled access: Full
Parking: Ample parking lot adjacent	Customers: Locals; couples

Lunch: Tuesday–Friday, 11:30 a.m.–2:30 p.m.

Dinner: Monday–Thursday, 6–10 p.m.; Friday–Saturday, 6–11 p.m.

Setting & atmosphere: The slightly gaudy dining room feels a bit formal—at least until it fills up, when it gets more than a little noisy.

Recommended dishes: Crabmeat ravioli; fried calamari; fettuccine La Riviera; baked oysters Italian style; stuffed mushrooms; broiled trout; seafood-stuffed eggplant; soft-shell crab with crabmeat; spaghetti and meatballs; osso buco; veal pizzaiola; veal piccata; filet mignon with Madeira sauce; spumoni; Amaretto kiss.

Summary & comments: The first successful effort at serving more-or-less classical (as opposed to Creole) Italian food to the New Orleans dining public has run for over a quarter century, and chef Goffredo Fraccaro is still at it. The menu is easy to get into. For example, completely out of place, here is the best plate of meatballs and spaghetti around. But more ambitious dishes abound, particularly in the veal and seafood departments. Nobody does better broiled fish, osso buco, or fried calamari. And Goffredo's signature creation—crabmeat-stuffed ravioli—is such a hit that every Italian restaurant in town now serves it. Outgoing service and well-selected Italian and other wines complete an agreeable lunch or dinner.

LE PARVENU ★★★★

Contemporary Creole	Very Expensive	QUALITY
		91

VALUE C

509 Williams Boulevard; 471-0534
Metairie above Causeway/Kenner/Jefferson Highway   Zone 10

Reservations: Recommended
When to go: Anytime
Entree range: $13–24
Payment: All major credit cards
Service rating: ★★★
Friendliness rating: ★★★
Parking: Small parking lot adjacent; lots of curbside parking nearby

Bar: Full service
Wine selection: Modest list matched to the food
Dress: Jacket recommended but not required
Disabled access: Limited
Customers: Residents from the nearby towns along the river

Lunch: Wednesday–Saturday, 11:30 a.m.–2:30 p.m.

Dinner: Wednesday–Saturday, 6–10 p.m.

Setting & atmosphere: A porch-surrounded cottage in the historic Rivertown part of Kenner, Le Parvenu's dining spaces are small but kept from being claustrophobic by the restaurant's many windows.

Recommended dishes: Crabmeat Patricia; lemon-smoked snapper; mirliton, shrimp and crab bisque; artichoke-and-garlic cheese soup; lobster Le Parvenu; lamb chops with rosemary and mint sauce; filet mignon with shrimp and peppercorns; roast duck with smoked orange sauce; lemon crêpes; crème brûlée.

Summary & comments: The name means "the newcomer." Chef/owner Dennis Hutley never really was that, having cooked in glitzy restaurants for years before he opened this place. Here he shifted from continental to Creole food, but a touch of the old school remains in the polish he applies to every presentation. A good strategy for dining here is the "And Den Sum" four-course, twelve-dish sampler. Service might be a bit too casual, particularly as regards the dress of the waiters.

LEMON GRASS CAFE ★★★★

Vietnamese	Expensive	QUALITY
		89

221 Camp Street (in International House Hotel); 523-1200
Central Business District   Zone 2

VALUE
D

Reservations: Recommended	Parking: Small parking lot adjacent
When to go: Dinner	Bar: Full service
Entree range: $12–22	Wine selection: Good wine list
Payment: All major credit cards	Dress: Casual
Service rating: ★★★	Disabled access: Full
Friendliness rating: ★★★★	Customers: Gourmets and hotel guests

Lunch: Monday–Friday, 11:30 a.m.–2:30 p.m.

Dinner: Every day, 6–10 p.m.

Setting & atmosphere: The premises look like a converted 1950s warehouse, decorated with fanciful window treatments and lots of shiny metal.

Recommended dishes: Spring rolls; pan-seared scallops and eggplant; artichoke salad with crabmeat and shrimp; salt-and-pepper roasted soft-shell crab; happy pancake; wok-smoked salmon steak; tropical Asian curry with shrimp and pasta; roast lacquered duck; grilled double pork chop; pear-almond tart.

Summary & comments: Chef/owner Minh Bui started his career at Commander's Palace and Emeril's. He did well with his own traditional Vietnamese cafe, so he opened this—a much more ambitious restaurant whose menu covers not only Vietnamese dishes but those of other cuisines as well. For example, one day gumbo was the soup of the day, and bouillabaisse was the entree. In between came a straight-ahead Vietnamese spring roll. Service, wine, and amenities are first class, and well above the standard for Asian cafes.

MANDICH ★★★

Creole	Moderate	QUALITY
		86

3200 St. Claude Avenue; 947-9553
Downtown/St. Bernard   Zone 5

VALUE
B

Reservations: Accepted	Service rating: ★★★
When to go: Anytime	Friendliness rating: ★★★★
Entree range: $11–16	Parking: Free lot adjacent
Payment: MC, V	Bar: Full service

Wine selection: A few house wines, arrayed with supermarket-style price tags on the bar for your choosing

Dress: Casual

Disabled access: Limited

Customers: Locals

Lunch: Tuesday–Friday, 11:30 a.m.–2:30 p.m.

Dinner: Friday–Saturday, 5–10 p.m.

Setting & atmosphere: The dining-room design is unchanged since the 1960s, and the look persists even as constant maintenance keeps the place in good repair.

Recommended dishes: Fried calamari; oysters Bordelaise; seafood gumbo; red-bean soup; trout Mandich (broiled with a crisp breading, with lemon butter); crab cakes; oyster platter (four different ways); stuffed shrimp; garlic chicken; sweet-potato duck; panneed veal; filet mignon; cheesecake; bread pudding.

Summary & comments: Mandich is predominantly a lunch place; its original clientele worked in the port, which starts and ends early. That legacy lives on in the food, which is a cut or two better than that of the typical neighborhood restaurant—although you shouldn't entertain any notions of finding anything unconventional. Most of the customers are regulars, but they always welcome unfamiliar faces. Few enough restaurants of this ilk survive these days that a meal here might just be special.

MANDINA'S   ★★★

Neighborhood Cafe	Moderate	QUALITY 85
3800 Canal Street; 482-9179 Mid-City/Gentilly Zone 6		VALUE A

Reservations: Not accepted

When to go: Off-peak lunch and dinner hours to avoid waiting

Entree range: $9–17

Payment: Cash only

Service rating: ★★

Friendliness rating: ★★

Parking: Ample parking lot adjacent

Bar: Full service

Wine selection: A few house wines

Dress: Casual

Disabled access: Limited

Customers: Locals; families; professionals at lunch

Lunch & dinner: Monday–Saturday, 11 a.m.–10 p.m.; Sunday, noon–9 p.m.

Setting & atmosphere: A recent expansion made tables a little easier to come by, but did nothing to change the worn-out, always-bustling original dining rooms. The front room's tables vie for space with customers waiting at the bar. The whole place is furnished with old neon painted signs, beer clocks, and other relics.

Recommended dishes: Shrimp rémoulade; crab fingers in wine sauce; oyster and artichoke soup; fried soft-shell crab; trout Amandine; spaghetti and Italian sausage; daily specials, especially: red beans with Italian sausage (Monday); beef stew (Tuesday); braciolone (Thursday); stuffed crab (Friday); crabmeat au gratin (Sunday); bread pudding.

Summary & comments: Mandina's comes to most Orleanians' minds when they try to conjure up the cherished image of the old-time neighborhood cafe. The best food on any given day will be the homestyle specials. These are almost uniformly good, and when you factor in the prices, the appeal of the place becomes obvious. All portions are titanic, but somehow avoid grossness. You might hesitate to order it, but they have one of the best roast-beef poor boys around here. The service staff has been here a long time and will not be impressed by anything you have to offer. A recent, big improvement: a parking lot.

MARISOL		★★★★
Fusion	Expensive	**QUALITY** 92
437 Esplanade Avenue; 943-1912		**VALUE** B
French Quarter Zone 1		

Reservations: Recommended	**Parking:** Curbside
When to go: Dinner	**Bar:** Full service
Entree range: $17–27	**Wine selection:** Good if abbreviated
Payment: AE, DC, MC, V	**Dress:** Casual
Service rating: ★★★	**Disabled access:** Full
Friendliness rating: ★★★	**Customers:** Local gourmets and tourists

Lunch: Friday, 11:30 a.m.–2:30 p.m.

Dinner: Sunday and Tuesday–Thursday, 6–10 p.m.; Friday–Saturday, 6–11 p.m.

Setting & atmosphere: Marisol has dining areas in both its spacious old building and in the courtyard just outside. Across Esplanade Avenue is the historic Old U.S. Mint.

Recommended dishes: Steamed mussels; raw oysters mignonette; foie-gras specials; crabmeat-and-coconut soup; roasted or steamed fish; tropical float.

Summary & comments: Chef/owner Peter Vazquez works up a highly personal cuisine at Marisol. It begins with a French inspiration, adds a Mediterranean freshness, then departs for every other part of the world. The menu changes daily, but there are some predictable aspects. Mussels, foie gras, seared tuna, and cuts of meat involving bones and slow cooking have been there on my every visit. All of the above have been good enough to be called specialties. Desserts seem to revolve around the availability of fresh fruit. All of this is turned out with an agreeable degree of polish in a charming environment.

MARTINIQUE		★★★
Fusion	Expensive	**QUALITY** 85
5908 Magazine Street; 891-8495		**VALUE** B
Uptown above Napoleon Zone 4		

Reservations: Not accepted	need to walk a block or more
When to go: Early evenings	**Bar:** Beer and wine
Entree range: $12–17	**Wine selection:** Modest, but wines are
Payment: MC, V	well chosen for the food
Service rating: ★★★	**Dress:** Casual
Friendliness rating: ★★	**Disabled access:** Limited
Parking: Curbside (metered); you may	**Customers:** Locals; couples; gourmets

Lunch: Tuesday–Saturday, 11:30 a.m.–2:30 p.m.

Dinner: Tuesday–Sunday, 6–10 p.m.

Setting & atmosphere: It's a small, somewhat spare restaurant in the tradition of a Parisian bistro. A small courtyard helps the crowding from getting out of control.

Recommended dishes: Grilled black-bean cake with bell-pepper coulis; oysters sautéed with lime and cayenne; mussels steamed in Chablis and herbs; salad of lamb sausage and lima beans; chicken stuffed with goat cheese and prosciutto; pork chop grilled with coconut and balsamic vinegar; sesame-seed–crusted salmon with pickled ginger; filet mignon with sautéed pecans and orange zest; scallops Provençale; desserts of the day.

Summary & comments: Hubert Sandot grew up on the Caribbean island for which the restaurant is named. He worked in Europe and elsewhere as a chef. Martinique is his second local bistro. In this one, his rather light style of cooking takes on a Caribbean flavor. It's as good as it is unusual. Service here has never been up to the quality of the food.

MAT & NADDIE'S   ★★★

Contemporary Creole	Expensive	QUALITY
		87

937 Leonidas Street; 861-9600
Uptown above Napoleon   Zone 4

VALUE: B

Reservations: Recommended
When to go: Dinner
Entree range: $12–19
Payment: All major credit cards
Service rating: ★★★
Friendliness rating: ★★★★
Parking: Curbside

Bar: Full service
Wine selection: Modest list that comple-
    ments the food
Dress: Casual
Disabled access: Limited
Customers: Uptowners

Lunch: Tuesday–Friday, 11:30 a.m.–2:30 p.m.

Dinner: Tuesday–Saturday, 6–10 p.m.

Setting & atmosphere: Operations are in an old house on the Uptown riverfront, where the freight trains that pass in the night somehow become romantic. The feeling that you've discovered a hidden gem charms you.

Recommended dishes: Coconut lemon-grass shrimp; oysters Bienville in phyllo; seaweed salad; pan-sautéed salmon; rice-stick noodles with shrimp and ginger; roasted rack of lamb; crème brûlée; chocolate truffle cake.

Summary & comments: The name is a kidspeak version of the founder's kids' names. The restaurant is now in the hands of the former sous chef, who—if anything—has made the food even better. The contemporary Creole dishes stop short of avant garde, but a few fusion elements are incorporated. This is done with enough skill and distinction to make the restaurant an enjoyable, if offbeat, place to eat.

MIDDENDORF'S   ★★★

Seafood	Moderate	QUALITY
		85

Manchac Street; 386-6666
North Shore   Zone 12

VALUE: B

Reservations: Not accepted
When to go: Anytime
Entree range: $8–14
Payment: MC, V
Service rating: ★★★
Friendliness rating: ★★★

Parking: Free lot adjacent
Bar: Full service
Wine selection: A few house wines
Dress: Casual
Disabled access: Full
Customers: Day-trippers; families

Lunch & dinner: Tuesday–Thursday,11 a.m.–9:30 p.m.; Friday–Saturday, 11 a.m.–10 p.m.

Setting & atmosphere: Middendorf's is a big, busy place. When it's really hectic, they open up a complete second restaurant on the other side of the parking lot.

Recommended dishes: Seafood gumbo; barbecue oysters; fried catfish; fried-seafood platters; stuffed crab; bread pudding.

Summary & comments: The area's most famous catfish restaurant is in a tiny, exotic fishing town in the wetlands. Interstate all 40 miles of the way, it's still a long drive—yet lots of Orleanians make it. Middendorf's menu is simple: all the local seafoods in every imaginable platter configuration. The fried catfish comes either in thick fillets or crisp, thin slices. Either way, it's the proverbial golden brown, greaseless, hot, and wonderful. As is all the fried seafood here. Service is a little rushed.

MIKE ANDERSON'S		★★★
Seafood	Moderate	**QUALITY** 84
215 Bourbon Street; 524-3884 French Quarter Zone 1		**VALUE** C

2712 N. Arnoult;
Metairie above Causeway/Kenner/Jefferson   Zone 10

Reservations: Not accepted	**Bar:** Full service
When to go: Anytime	**Wine selection:** A few house wines
Entree range: $12–20	**Dress:** Casual
Payment: All major credit cards	**Disabled access:** Limited
Service rating: ★★	**Customers:** Tourists; some locals; profes-
Friendliness rating: ★★★	sionals at lunch
Parking: Pay garages nearby	

Lunch & dinner: Sunday–Thursday, 11 a.m.–10 p.m.; Friday–Saturday, 11 a.m.–11 p.m. or later

Setting & atmosphere: The original New Orleans–area branch of the seafood-restaurant chain owned by an LSU football hero is one of the busiest restaurants in the French Quarter. The second location, in Metairie, occupies fancier and much larger digs, in a much more accessible location for locals.

Recommended dishes: Oysters on the half shell; three-way alligator; baked oysters four ways; turtle soup; fried-seafood platter; broiled-seafood platter; crawfish, shrimp, or crab dinner; fish stuffed with crab and shrimp; jolie rouge (broiled fish topped with crabmeat).

Summary & comments: Portions greatly exceed appetites here, which explains some of the popularity. However, the stuff is good, too. A major specialty is the seven-way dinner, made with your choice of crawfish, crab, or shrimp. Not all of the seven will be great, but if you eat only the top four you'll still have too much to eat.

MIKE DITKA'S		★★★★

		QUALITY
Steaks and Chops	Very Expensive	**88**
		VALUE
600 St. Charles Avenue; 569-8989		**D**
Central Business District Zone 2		

Reservations: Recommended
When to go: Anytime
Entree range: $14–23
Payment: All major credit cards
Service rating: ★★★
Friendliness rating: ★★★
Parking: Lunch, curbside (metered); dinner, valet ($6)

Bar: Full service
Wine selection: Substantial, emphasis on California; many by-the-glass selections
Dress: Dressy casual
Disabled access: Full
Customers: Hip, social crowd; gourmets; couples; professionals at lunch

Breakfast: Every day, 7–10 a.m.

Brunch: Sunday, 11 a.m.–3 p.m.

Lunch: Every day, 11:30 a.m.–2:30 p.m.

Dinner: Sunday–Thursday, 6–10 p.m.; Friday–Saturday, 6–11 p.m.

Setting & atmosphere: The sports theme you expect is downplayed; most of the pigskin and sweat is in the bar. The main dining rooms are very comfortably appointed, and the restaurant makes for a great date place. Big windows open onto Lafayette Square.

Recommended dishes: Duck spring rolls; seared tuna salad; lobster bisque, cappuccino style; double pork chop; steak Diana; lobster and oyster risotto; grilled fish; pot roast; banana cream pie.

Summary & comments: Mike Ditka spent $2 million rebuilding the old Mike's on the Avenue, then lost his job as head coach of the New Orleans Saints. He went ahead with the restaurant anyway, luring wary diners in with a pair of very handsome, masculine rooms and a French chef. So this is not merely a restrike of Ditka's original Chicago place. Christian Karcher cooks imaginative and refined food. But that country-French style works well with thick pork chops and steaks, as well as homely food like pot roast with mashed potatoes. The service is attentive and entertaining, the wine list is interesting, the drinks are well made, and the cigars and the sports scene in the bar (separate from the dining room) complete the manly image without going overboard.

MOSCA'S		★★★

Creole Italian	Very Expensive	QUALITY
		86

4137 US 90; 436-9942		VALUE
West Bank Zone 11		**C**

Reservations: Accepted but rarely honored
When to go: Weeknights; closed the month of August

Friendliness rating: ★★
Parking: Ample parking lot adjacent
Bar: Full service
Wine selection: Almost entirely Italian; several Amarones

Entree range: $16–22
Payment: Cash only
Service rating: ★★

Dress: Casual
Disabled access: None
Customers: Mostly locals (many of them regular customers); a few tourists; families of adults

Dinner: Tuesday–Saturday, 5–10 p.m.

Setting & atmosphere: A two-room shack, stark and noisy. The location is daunting: way on the highway out of town, surrounded by marshland. It does not look inviting from the outside, but ignore that.

Recommended dishes: Crab salad; chef's bean soup; oysters Italian style; shrimp Italian style; chicken grandee; roast chicken; roast quail or squab; Italian sausage; filet mignon; pineapple fluff.

Summary & comments: Mosca's has hardly changed, except in price, since it opened in the 1940s. Finally, here is all the olive oil, garlic, and rosemary you always wanted, scattered around roasted chickens, sausage, shrimp, and oysters. All this is delivered with a startling lack of ceremony—big platters of food accompanied by stacks of plates and utensils for you to distribute among yourselves. Come with at least four people to enjoy best; six is even better. The dining rooms are still almost always full, and the staff still turns a deaf ear to your complaints about the wait for a table or anything else.

MOTHER'S ★★

Sandwiches	Inexpensive	QUALITY
		81
		VALUE
401 Poydras Street; 523-9656		D
Central Business District Zone 2		

Reservations: Not accepted

When to go: Anytime except around noon and during large conventions

Entree range: $6–14

Payment: Cash only

Service rating: ★★

Friendliness rating: ★★★

Parking: Curbside pay lot nearby

Bar: Beer

Wine selection: A few house wines

Dress: Anything goes

Disabled access: None

Customers: Tourists; some locals; professionals at lunch

Open: Every day 6 a.m.–10 p.m.

Setting & atmosphere: A cramped, concrete-floored dining room with a line of customers snaking through it.

Recommended dishes: Breakfast special; Mae's omelette; pancakes; ham poor boy; Ferdi (ham and roast beef debris); turkey poor boy; fried-seafood poor boys; red beans and rice; gumbo of the day; jambalaya; corned beef and cabbage; bread pudding; brownies; muffins.

Summary & comments: The world's most famous vendor of poor-boy sandwiches, Mother's is also among the city's busiest restaurants on a volume-per-square-foot basis. There's almost always a line. While standing in it, you may have cooks break through with their buckets of hot gravy or beans or whatever from the kitchen (which, for some reason, is not behind the cafeteria-like serving line). Everything is cooked on site—exceptional for a poor-boy shop. Portions on the plate specials are absurdly large, and the food tends to the heavy side. Lunch and supper are the main meals, but breakfast is terrific, too. Don't come here when there's a large convention in town, or when you have less than $15 cash in your pocket.

MR. B'S ★★★★

Contemporary Creole	Very Expensive	QUALITY
		90
		VALUE
201 Royal Street; 523-2078		C
French Quarter Zone 1		

Reservations: Accepted

When to go: Early evenings

Entree range: $13–22

Payment: All major credit cards

Service rating: ★★★★★

Friendliness rating: ★★★★★

Parking: Validated (free) at Dixie Parking, behind restaurant on Iberville Street

Bar: Full service

Wine selection: Substantial, almost
entirely West Coast

Dress: Dressy casual

Disabled access: Limited

Customers: Mostly locals; some tourists;
gourmets; couples

Brunch: Sunday, 11 a.m.–3 p.m.

Lunch: Monday–Saturday, 11:30 a.m.–2:30 p.m.

Dinner: Every day, 6–10:30 p.m.

Setting & atmosphere: It's one big, somewhat dark, moderately noisy room with a semi-open kitchen. It's so engaging a scene that the place is usually filled up to the bar, where you might well wait for a table. (The reservation system leaves lots of space for walk-ins.)

Recommended dishes: Shrimp-and-pork spring rolls; skillet shrimp with garlic Crab-tini (crabmeat rémoulade in a martini glass); gumbo ya-ya; pasta jambalaya; hickory-grilled fish; barbecue shrimp; hickory-roasted chicken with garlic glaze; seafood-and-pasta specials; bread pudding; Mr. B's chocolate cake; profiteroles and chocolate sauce.

Entertainment & amenities: Pianist at dinner nightly and at Sunday brunch.

Summary & comments: In 1979 the Brennans turned the New Orleans dining scene around by opening this, the archetype of the casual, contemporary Creole bistro. It was so widely imitated that restaurants like Mr. B's now dominate the scene, where innovative and excellent Creole dishes made from top-rung fresh ingredients are served informally. Hickory-grilled fish, now common, was pioneered here; so was pasta as a non-Italian main theme. The service staff and the wine list are both better than they need to be.

NOLA		★★★★
Contemporary Creole	Very Expensive	**QUALITY** 89
534 St. Louis Street; 522-6652		**VALUE** C
French Quarter Zone 1		

Reservations: Recommended

When to go: Anytime

Entree range: $12–28

Payment: All major credit cards

Service rating: ★★★★

Friendliness rating: ★★★★

Parking: Validated at Omni Royal Orleans
Hotel

Bar: Full service

Wine selection: Substantial, with emphasis on California; many by-the-glass
selections

Dress: Dressy casual

Disabled access: Full

Customers: A mix of tourists and locals,
with a hip, young tilt

Lunch: Monday–Saturday, 11:30 a.m.–2:30 p.m.

Dinner: Sunday–Thursday, 6–10 p.m.; Friday–Saturday, 6 p.m.–midnight

Setting & atmosphere: The building is old, but they did it up in a swell, high-tech way. The whole place is a sort of modern sculpture.

Recommended dishes: Pizzas; crab cake with chili aïoli; shrimp pasta with warm rémoulade; Vietnamese-style seafood salad; cedar plank–roasted fish; double-cut pork chop; New York strip steak; slow-roasted duck; coconut bread pudding; lemon chess pie; chicory coffee crème brûlée.

Summary & comments: The second restaurant of local chef superstar Emeril Lagasse, Nola duplicates Emeril's in its use of extremely well-selected fresh ingredients in innovative ways, while honoring a distinctly Louisiana flavor. Since Emeril reached superstar status, Nola has drawn a large crowd of tourists looking for a glimpse of him. They probably won't get it here, but the wait staff is happy to tell the visitors all about him. The open kitchen sports a wood-burning oven and grill. Full advantage is taken of that resource. The chefs like to use planks of wood to roast and serve various fish and meats upon; this is a major specialty. The other menu entrees are either interesting twists of local standards or totally innovative concoctions—all about equally good. The first-class pastry department makes an exceptional assortment of desserts. Locals love this place, because it's not as expensive or as hard to negotiate as Emeril's other two New Orleans restaurants.

ODYSSEY GRILL		★★★
Mediterranean	Moderate	**QUALITY** 87
2037 Metairie Road ; 834-5775		**VALUE** B
Metairie below Causeway Zone 9		

Reservations: Accepted	Bar: Full service
When to go: Anytime	Wine selection: Decent; several Greek
Entree range: $8–16	wines among the Californians
Payment: AE, DC, MC, V	Dress: Casual
Service rating: ★★★	Disabled access: Limited
Friendliness rating: ★★★★	Customers: Neighborhood residents and
Parking: Small parking lot adjacent	members of the local Greek community

Breakfast & lunch: Saturday–Sunday, 8 a.m.–2:30 p.m.

Lunch: Tuesday–Friday, 11:30 a.m.–2:30 p.m.

Dinner: Tuesday–Sunday, 6–10 p.m.

Setting & atmosphere: The two dining rooms, dominated by a brilliant, calming blue, are so uniquely designed and constructed that you may walk out with an interior-decorating idea.

Recommended dishes: Saganaki (fried, flamed cheese); fried calamari with tsatsiki; hummus; spanakopita; Greek salad; Mediterranean lamb salad; pan bagnat (grilled vegetable sandwich); grilled tuna sandwich with romesco sauce; moussaka; grilled quail with Gorgonzola stuffing; whole grilled fish; grilled veal scaloppine; fish baked in phyllo; couscous with seven vegetables, chicken, lamb, and sausage; galaktoboureko (Greek custard); yogurt cheese with honey and walnuts.

Summary & comments: Rosita Skias is interested in all the cuisines found along the shores of the Mediterranean, and she serves dishes from just about all of them here. Greek, Italian, and Provençal dishes form the bulk of the menu, but you will also find some from Spain, Turkey, and Morocco. All these cuisines have enough elements in common that they come together well, and the chef does so much research that there's a high degree of authenticity. Daily and monthly specials are of particular interest. The grill is used full time, on everything from fish to meat chops to vegetables.

PALACE CAFE ★★★★

Contemporary Creole	Expensive	QUALITY
		88

	VALUE
605 Canal Street; 523-1661	**C**
Central Business District Zone 2	

Reservations: Recommended	**Bar:** Full service
When to go: Anytime	**Wine selection:** Substantial list, almost
Entree range: $11–19	entirely from the West Coast
Payment: All major credit cards	**Dress:** Dressy casual
Service rating: ★★★★	**Disabled access:** Full
Friendliness rating: ★★★★★	**Customers:** A mix of locals and tourists;
Parking: Validated (free) at Holiday Inn	professionals at lunch; families
and Marriott garages	

Brunch: Saturday–Sunday, 11:30 a.m.–2:30 p.m.

Lunch: Monday–Friday, 11:30 a.m.–2:30 p.m.

Dinner: Every day, 6–10 p.m.

Setting & atmosphere: The Palace Cafe occupies most of the historic old Werlein Building, with big windows opening onto Canal Street and its new streetcar tracks. There is no better restaurant for watching Mardi Gras. When the place is full, the tile floors and large windows make it one noisy expanse.

Recommended dishes: Crabmeat cheesecake with pecan crust; corn-fried oysters with artichokes; oyster pan roast with rosemary cream; shrimp rémoulade; turtle soup; blue cheese salad; andouille-crusted fish; catfish pecan; roast duck with field-pea ragout; veal chop with rock-shrimp risotto; Palace potato pie; white-chocolate bread pudding; bananas Foster.

Entertainment & amenities: Unusually good player piano rolls all the time. Live blues supports the Sunday brunch.

Summary & comments: The PC started out as a casual branch of Commander's Palace. When the younger generation of Brennan's reshuffled its ownership, Dickie Brennan took over and made it his headquarters. The food is polished Creole, and in some ways it's reminiscent of what Commander's Palace was doing ten years ago. That was a great style, and it's perfect for this location. In just a few years they've created a few widely copied dishes here—most notably white-chocolate bread pudding. Service appears to be casual, but suddenly they roll up a gueridon and start flaming or carving something.

PASCAL'S MANALE ★★★★

Creole Italian	Expensive	QUALITY
		86
1838 Napoleon Avenue; 895-4877		VALUE
Uptown above Napoleon Zone 4		B

Reservations: Recommended	Bar: Full service
When to go: Anytime	Wine selection: Not what it should be;
Entree range: $10–20	mostly ordinary Italian wines
Payment: All major credit cards	Dress: Casual
Service rating: ★★★	Disabled access: Limited
Friendliness rating: ★★★	Customers: A mix of uptown locals and
Parking: Ample parking lot adjacent	tourists

Lunch & dinner: Monday–Friday, 11:30 a.m.–10 p.m.

Dinner: Every day, 6–10 p.m.

Setting & atmosphere: Manale's feels like neighborhood cafe, with a certain scruffiness that's surprising considering its fame as a venerable local eatery.

Recommended dishes: Raw oysters; oysters Bienville; oysters Rockefeller; stuffed mushrooms; crab-and-oyster pan roast; shrimp-and-crabmeat rémoulade; turtle soup; New Orleans barbecue shrimp; broiled fish with crabmeat and hollandaise; veal Puccini; filet mignon; double pork chop with peppercorns; spaghetti Collins; bread pudding; chocolate mousse.

Summary & comments: New Orleans's oldest Italian restaurant serves the epitome of Creole-Italian cuisine—a hybrid so well blended now that it resembles no known cooking in Italy. The famous dish is barbecue shrimp. Completely misnamed, these gigantic shrimp are neither grilled nor smoked, nor is there a barbecue sauce. They are unforgettably good, though, in a distinctive pepper-butter sauce. Manale's also does terrific things with oysters, veal, and beef. Avoid red-sauce dishes and you'll eat well. Service is a little too casual.

PELICAN CLUB		★★★★

		QUALITY
Fusion	Very Expensive	93
		VALUE
615 Bienville Street; 523-1504		C
French Quarter Zone 1		

Reservations: Recommended	Bar: Full service
When to go: Anytime	Wine selection: Substantial, internationally
Entree range: $14–25	balanced; many by-the-glass selections
Payment: All major credit cards	Dress: Jacket recommended but not
Service rating: ★★★★	required
Friendliness rating: ★★★	Disabled access: Limited
Parking: Validated (free) at Monteleone	Customers: A mix of locals and tourists;
Hotel garage	couples; gourmets

Dinner: Every day, 6–10 p.m.

Setting & atmosphere: The dining rooms stretch out into a long hall, with enough hard surfaces to make the acoustics uncomfortably lively when the place is full.

Recommended dishes: Scallop-stuffed artichoke; beef-and-shrimp pot stickers; escargots with crawfish and mushrooms; Creole Caesar salad; Thai seafood salad; smoked duck and shrimp gumbo; Louisiana bouillabaisse; grilled fish with ginger-lime glaze; filet mignon with Cabernet mushroom sauce; jambalaya; dessert specials.

Summary & comments: Keeping a low profile on mysterious Exchange Alley, the Pelican Club can wine and dine you with the best of them. Chef/owners Richard Hughes and Chin Ling combine Creole, Italian, Chinese, Southwestern, and various other flavors, with ingredients of impressive pedigree. The result is immensely appealing, perhaps because the food has the taste of familiarity for all its innovation. The dining room can get a bit noisy; many of the regulars know one another. Although one is served well, I've never felt a sense of warm accommodation from the dining-room staff here. But that's not something that will ruin the evening, especially on nights when the kitchen is really on.

PERISTYLE   ★★★★★

Contemporary French	Very Expensive	**QUALITY**
		95
1041 Dumaine Street; 593-9535		**VALUE**
French Quarter Zone 1		**C**

Reservations: Required

When to go: Early evenings

Entree range: $14–21

Payment: All major credit cards

Service rating: ★★★

Friendliness rating: ★★★

Parking: Valet (free)

Bar: Full service

Wine selection: Impressive list—not for its size, but for its variety of styles; very interesting to oenophiles

Dress: Jacket recommended but not required

Disabled access: Limited

Customers: Gourmets; couples; mostly locals

Lunch: Friday, 11:30 a.m.–2 p.m.

Dinner: Tuesday–Saturday, 6–10 p.m.

Setting & atmosphere: This space has been a restaurant for nearly a hundred years. After a disastrous fire in 1999 and the complete rebuilding, the dining rooms were decorated in a modern way, with antique fixtures and two old murals, one of which depicts the namesake structure in City Park.

Recommended dishes: Menu changes frequently. I've seen the following more than once: crabmeat ravigote with beets; grilled sea scallops; seared foie gras; roasted squab.

Summary & comments: Chef/owner Anne Kearney was rising to national prominence when her restaurant closed for nine months due to fire. When Peristyle reopened, it did so with even more popularity than before, and tables are more than a little difficult to obtain. (Try getting in here for the Friday lunch.) The chef's ruling principle is polish: perfect leaves of greens, vivid and simple sauces, beautiful seafood, and stunning but straightforward presentations. The style is clearly French-inspired, but also very American and a little bit New Orleans. The wait staff is a little snooty, but they know what they're doing and can converse intelligently about both the food and wine offerings.

RED FISH GRILL ★★★★

		QUALITY
Contemporary Creole	Expensive	86
		VALUE
		B

115 Bourbon Street; 598-1200
French Quarter   Zone 1

Reservations: Accepted	**Bar:** Full service
When to go: Anytime	**Wine selection:** Good; mostly Californian
Entree range: $14–22	**Dress:** Casual
Payment: AE, DC, MC, V	**Disabled access:** Full
Service rating: ★★★★	**Customers:** A mix of locals and visitors,
Friendliness rating: ★★★★	with a sizable local lunch crowd
Parking: Pay parking lots nearby	

Brunch: Sunday, 11 a.m.–2:30 p.m.

Lunch: Every day, 11:30 a.m.–2:30 p.m.

Dinner: Sunday–Thursday, 6–10 p.m.; Friday–Saturday, 6–11 p.m.

Setting & atmosphere: What once was a corner of the old D.H. Holmes department store looks like it was hit by a bomb, then painted over. Walls, floors, and tabletops are fancifully decorated by artist Luis Colmenares in a way that almost suggests a slick chain restaurant, but this is the one and only.

Recommended dishes: Pecan-crusted shrimp; shrimp rémoulade with fried green tomatoes; oysters three ways; red-bean soup; salmon poached in red wine, cherries, and saffron; crabmeat-stuffed shrimp; hickory-grilled fish with shallot-and-herb vinaigrette.

Entertainment & amenities: Ralph Brennan also owns the adjacent and directly connected Storyville District, where live jazz plays every night.

Summary & comments: The decoration as well as the name suggest that seafood is the specialty. But this casual place has ambitions well above those of the standard fried-fish place. The owner is Ralph Brennan, who started Mr. B's and Bacco before dreaming up the Red Fish. The main item is grilled fish, although there's more a choice of preparations than of species. But the strongest course is appetizers, where you find imaginative treatments of all the familiar local shellfish. The rest of the menu is decidedly New Orleans in taste, and is accessible to the uninitiated visitor without coming across as touristy.

RED ROOM		★★★★
Contemporary Creole	Very Expensive	QUALITY 86
2040 St. Charles Avenue; 528-9759		VALUE
Uptown below Napoleon Zone 3		D

Reservations: Recommended

When to go: Dinner; call to find out when your style of music is featured

Entree range: $18–32

Payment: All major credit cards

Service rating: ★★★★

Friendliness rating: ★★★★

Parking: Valet (free)

Bar: Full service

Wine selection: Excellent; tended to by a well-versed sommelier

Dress: Jacket recommended but not required

Disabled access: Full

Customers: Early in the evening, sophisticated diners; later, a more casual crowd comes in for the music and dancing

Dinner: Wednesday–Sunday, 6–11 p.m.; open later some nights

Setting & atmosphere: The circular premises, lifted off the ground in a fanciful steel superstructure, were built using remnants of the restaurant that used to be in the Eiffel Tower in Paris. It's somewhat like a second-story greenhouse.

Recommended dishes: Menu changes frequently; some examples from past selections are tuna pastrami; foie gras du jour; arugula salad with blue cheese; nut-crusted sweetbreads; smoked salmon Napoleon; whole speckled trout; orange-chocolate mousse; red velvet cake.

Entertainment & amenities: The music varies from night to night and includes everything from Big Band and Latin jazz to blues and Western swing. Starting at around 9:30 every night, the place transforms from a dining room with live musicians to a dance club with a few dining stragglers.

Summary & comments: This is the only restaurant locally where you can have a fine dinner and then listen or dance to first-class live music. The food is quirky, contemporary Creole, and there is a tendency for the chefs to make statements with unusual ingredients and presentations. It's served with a great deal of style, and competes with the food in the better gourmet bistros in its tastiness.

RESTAURANT DES FAMILLES ★★★

Seafood	Moderate	QUALITY
		81

	VALUE
LA Highway 45 at LA Highway 3134; 689-7834	C
West Bank Zone 11	

Reservations: Accepted
When to go: Anytime
Entree range: $11–17
Payment: AE, DS, MC, V
Service rating: ★★★
Friendliness rating: ★★★★
Parking: Free lot adjacent

Bar: Full service
Wine selection: Decent and internation-
   ally well balanced
Dress: Casual
Disabled access: Full
Customers: Locals; families; couples

Lunch & dinner: Tuesday–Thursday, 11:30 a.m.–9 p.m.; Friday, 11:30 a.m.–10 p.m.; Saturday, noon–10 p.m.; Sunday, noon–8 p.m.

Setting & atmosphere: Down the highway to Lafitte (one of the ends of the earth), this handsome seafood restaurant has a distinctive setting. Large windows give out onto the lazy Bayou des Familles, as primordial a scene as an alligator ever crawled.

Recommended dishes: Crabmeat Remick; oysters Lafitte; fried-seafood platter; fried soft-shell crabs.

Entertainment & amenities: Live Cajun fiddlers and other musicians are here most nights.

Summary & comments: Local seafood dishes make up most of the menu, which is more ambitious than that of the standard seafood joint. Fried and grilled entrees are good enough; the more involved items, particularly those involving pasta, are less successful. To be avoided is any dish that smacks of home cooking (i.e., the shrimp meatballs). There's enough good food here to make the trip (about 20 minutes from downtown) worthwhile, especially when combined with a visit to neighboring Jean Lafitte National Park.

RUTH'S CHRIS STEAK HOUSE ★★★★

Steak and Chop	Very Expensive	QUALITY
		89

	VALUE
	D

711 N. Broad Street; 486-0810
Mid-City/Gentilly   Zone 6

3633 Veterans Blvd.; 888-3600
Metairie Above Causeway/Kenner/Jefferson   Zone 10

Reservations: Accepted
When to go: Anytime
Entree range: $16–26
Payment: All major credit cards
Service rating: ★★★★
Friendliness rating: ★★★★
Parking: Valet (free)
Bar: Full service

Wine selection: Substantial list, heavily tilted toward reds, but nothing extraordinary (which is just as well, because they don't handle wine well here)
Dress: Dressy casual
Disabled access: Full
Customers: Politicians; media figures; professionals; couples at dinner

Lunch & dinner: Sunday–Friday, 11:30 a.m.–11:30 p.m.; Saturday, 4–11:30 p.m.

Setting & atmosphere: The Ruth's Chris chain started in New Orleans, but the two local outlets have been largely homogenized into the standard chain look. The dining room has a masculine, clubby feel, with well-padded tables either out in the middle of things or secluded, as may suit customers' needs.

Recommended dishes: Shrimp rémoulade; stuffed mushrooms; salad with Creole French dressing; filet mignon; New York strip; porterhouse for two; lamb chops; veal chops; pork chop (lunch only); boiled lobster; lyonnaise potatoes; French fries; baked potato; bread pudding; cheesecakes.

Summary & comments: During the current resurgence of interest in top-notch beef, Ruth's Chris rides higher than ever. Long the dominant steak-house in New Orleans, it's also now a major player nationally. What you get is a top-grade, fresh, dry-aged steak from rigorously selective sources, brought to something like the temperature you ordered in a superheated broiler. It is rendered sinful and irresistibly aromatic by the addition of bubbling butter, the traditional New Orleans abetment to steak. Also here are big lobsters, great lamb and veal chops, and thick flanks of salmon. Side dishes are prosaic but prepared well. Service is effective but unceremonious. Regulars favor one location or the other, but both locations are equally good.

SAKE CAFE ★★★★

		QUALITY
Japanese	Expensive	87
		VALUE
		B

4201 Veterans Boulevard (Independence Mall); 779-7253

Metairie above Causeway/Kenner/Jefferson Highway   Zone 10

Reservations: Accepted

When to go: Anytime

Entree range: $8–17

Payment: All major credit cards

Service rating: ★★★

Friendliness rating: ★★★

Parking: Ample parking lot adjacent

Bar: Full service

Wine selection: Good

Dress: Casual

Disabled access: Full

Customers: Suburban Gen-X-ers and
  other sushi buffs

Lunch: Every day, 11:30 a.m.–2:30 p.m.

Dinner: Every day, 6–10 p.m.

Setting & atmosphere: The Sake Cafe is hidden in a corner of a strip mall otherwise populated by the likes of Houston's and Chili's. So its good looks come as a surprise. It is the handsomest Japanese restaurant we've seen in our town so far, with a cool sophistication.

Recommended dishes: Seaweed salad; salmon-skin salad; shu-mai; oshitashi (steamed spinach with bonito flakes); sushi and sashimi; negimaki (grilled beef rolls); bento box dinners.

Summary & comments: The environment signals the most ambitious kind of dining, and the kitchen is up to the task. The uncommonly large menu moves in arenas of Japanese cooking few other places trouble with. The intrinsic merit of the sushi is evident, and this extends throughout the menu. The staff works more along the lines of Western service and is forthcoming and knowledgeable. And, as you might imagine, the sake selection is pretty good—the wine collection, too.

SHOGUN ★★★★

Japanese	Moderate	QUALITY
		85

2325 Veterans Boulevard; 833-7477
Metairie below Causeway   Zone 9

	VALUE
	C

Reservations: Not accepted	Bar: Full service
When to go: Anytime	Wine selection: A few house wines
Entree range: $8–20	Dress: Casual
Payment: All major credit cards	Disabled access: Full
Service rating: ★★★	Customers: Locals; singles; families at the
Friendliness rating: ★★★	teppan-yaki tables
Parking: Ample parking lot adjacent	

Lunch: Sunday–Thursday, 11:30 a.m.–2:30 p.m.

Lunch & dinner: Friday–Saturday, 11:30 a.m.–10 p.m.

Dinner: Sunday–Thursday, 6–10 p.m.

Setting & atmosphere: Three restaurants in one: a large sushi bar, an area of Benihana-style teppan-yaki tables, and conventional tables.

Recommended dishes: Baked seafood appetizer; gyoza; red miso soup; sushi and sashimi; teishoku-box dinners; shabu shabu (thinly sliced beef quickly boiled at the table); seafood nabe.

Summary & comments: Shogun was the first successful sushi bar in the area, and remains very busy. The oversized sushi bar has a wider assortment than most others around. Cordoned off in one end of the restaurant are the teppan-yaki tables; Shogun bought these from Benihana when it closed. The showy chef grills steak and shrimp and all that; it's a good show the first time, ordinary thereafter. At the standard tables you can get the entire range of Japanese cookery. The most interesting are the teishoku lunches and the boiled meat or seafood dinners prepared at the table. With advance notice, you can also get a kaiseki, the elaborate many-course formal dinner.

TREY YUEN ★★★★

Chinese	Moderate	QUALITY
		85

600 Causeway Boulevard; 626-4476
North Shore   Zone 12

	VALUE
	D

Reservations: Not accepted	Payment: All major credit cards
When to go: Weeknights	Service rating: ★★★
Entree range: $7–24	Friendliness rating: ★★★★

Parking: Ample parking lot adjacent
Bar: Full service
Wine selection: Decent; emphasis on
California

Dress: Casual
Disabled access: Full
Customers: North Shore locals; families

Lunch: Wednesday–Friday, 11:30 a.m.–2 p.m.

Lunch & dinner: Sunday, 11:30 a.m.–10 p.m.

Dinner: Tuesday–Thursday, 6–10 p.m.; Friday–Saturday, 6–11 p.m.

Setting & atmosphere: A large, airy rotunda suggests a temple from the outside, an effect compounded by the well-kept gardens that surround the restaurant. Busy and a little noisy inside.

Recommended dishes: Spring rolls; pot stickers; hot-and-sour soup; seafood with tong cho sauce; wor shu op; satay squid; shrimp in a cloud; lobster with black-bean sauce; scallops Imperial; presidential chicken; spicy lemon chicken; steak kew; lotus banana; ice cream.

Summary & comments: This striking Chinese palace turned the Asian restaurant scene around when it opened in 1981. The surroundings, service, and food were way above what most of us were used to. That resulted in a degree of popularity that makes dining here occasionally inconvenient. Seafood is a particular strength, but they cook everything else well too. The wines and desserts are far above Chinese-restaurant standards. One wishes that the Wong brothers would up the ante again, but they seem to be comfortable with the way things are. Service is unceremonious and sometimes can bog down when the place is busy—which it often is.

TUJAGUE'S ★★★★

Creole	Expensive	QUALITY
		85
		VALUE
		C

823 Decatur Street; 525-8676
French Quarter   Zone 1

Reservations: Recommended
When to go: Anytime
Entree range: Table d'hote, $20–29
Payment: All major credit cards
Service rating: ★★★
Friendliness rating: ★★★★
Parking: French Market pay lot, one

block away
Bar: Full service
Wine selection: Limited and inexpensive
Dress: Casual
Disabled access: Limited
Customers: Tourists; some locals; quite a
few Quarterites at lunch

Lunch: Every day, 11:30 a.m.–2:30 p.m.

Dinner: Every day, 5–10 p.m.

Setting & atmosphere: An historic restaurant, and it looks it. The unreconstructed, minimal dining room is flanked by a great antique bar. The upstairs dining rooms offer a view of the river.

Recommended dishes: Table d'hote dinner: Shrimp rémoulade; crabmeat-and-spinach soup; boiled brisket of beef; chicken bonne femme; filet mignon; cranberry bread pudding; pecan pie.

Summary & comments: In 1856, Tujague's began as a lunchroom for workers in the French Market and on the nearby docks, serving a table d'hote meal of the day. Today, in Tujague's antique dining rooms is served a very traditional five-course homestyle Creole meal, with five or so choices for the entree. One of the courses is always the restaurant's famous boiled brisket of beef, good enough to inspire a desire for seconds. This is a great place to come on the major holidays; they're open for all of them. There's a substantial local crowd for the inexpensive lunches.

UGLESICH'S   ★★★★

Seafood	Moderate	QUALITY
		86
		VALUE
		D

1238 Baronne Street; 523-8571
Uptown below Napoleon   Zone 3

Reservations: Not accepted	Bar: Beer
When to go: Anytime but the noon hour	Wine selection: None
Entree range: $6–14	Dress: Anything goes
Payment: Cash only	Disabled access: Limited
Service rating: ★★	Customers: A mix of mostly young locals
Friendliness rating: ★★★★	and tourists; lots of local chefs and
Parking: Small parking lot adjacent	other restaurant people

Lunch: Monday–Friday, 11:30 a.m.–4 p.m.

Setting & atmosphere: Uglesich's is a concentrated dose of New Orleans funk—a bit much for some who, after eyeballing the place and its neighborhood, drive on by. There's never an open table when you walk in, but there will be by the time the food comes out.

Recommended dishes: Oysters on the half shell; barbecued oysters; shrimp rémoulade on fried green tomatoes; crawfish bisque; grilled fish plate; fried-oyster poor boy; roast-beef poor boy; French fries; blackboard specials.

Summary & comments: Those who seek out Uglesich's are rewarded with food that some gourmet restaurants would do well to imitate. The oyster poor boy, for example, is made from oysters that are not only fried but shucked to order. Anthony and Gail Uglesich have expanded their range far beyond sandwiches in recent years; you can now get an astounding assortment (considering the rudimentary kitchen) of grilled, sautéed, and fried platters, many highly original. Beware: if they tell you something is spicy, believe them. Those raw oysters at the bar are good, too.

UPPERLINE ★★★★

Contemporary Creole	Expensive	QUALITY
		90

	VALUE
1413 Upperline Street; 891-9822	**B**
Uptown above Napoleon Zone 4	

Reservations: Recommended	**Parking:** Small parking lot adjacent
When to go: Anytime; the Upperline's garlic festival in summer is always interesting	**Bar:** Full service
	Wine selection: Excellent; many delightful surprises
Entree range: $14–25	**Dress:** Casual
Payment: All major credit cards	**Disabled access:** None
Service rating: ★★★★	**Customers:** A mix of locals and tourists; artists, gourmets, and oenophiles
Friendliness rating: ★★★★	

Dinner: Wednesday–Sunday, 5:30 p.m.–10 p.m.

Setting & atmosphere: An old neighborhood restaurant flows into an adjacent cottage to form a string of dining rooms. All are filled with art.

Recommended dishes: Fried green tomatoes with shrimp rémoulade; duck gumbo; watercress, Stilton, and pecan salad; onion-crusted fish with tapenade and mustard and fennel sauce; shrimp curry with jasmine rice; rack of lamb with mint and Madeira; filet mignon with garlic Port sauce; roast duck with ginger peach sauce; garlic-stuffed pork tenderloin; pecan pie; double chocolate amaretto mousse.

Entertainment & amenities: Major folk art collection from local artists inside, as well as on the building facade.

Summary & comments: One of the original Nouvelle-Creole bistros, the Upperline is the product of the endlessly fertile mind of owner JoAnn Clevenger. Eating here is to open oneself to a barrage of her creative statements about art, drama, literature. . . and, yes, food. Her most famous culinary idea is the summer-long garlic menu, but there's almost always a festival of something or other here. Not everything is offbeat: the Upperline's menu is full of classic Creole dishes, including a tasting menu of gumbo, beans and rice, etc. Prices are lower than you'd expect. Never a dull moment here.

VAQUEROS ★★★★

Southwestern	Moderate	QUALITY
		86
4938 Prytania　Street; 891-6441		VALUE
Uptown above Napoleon　Zone 4		C

Reservations: Not accepted
When to go: Anytime
Entree range: $9–19
Payment: All major credit cards
Service rating: ★★
Friendliness rating: ★★★
Parking: Curbside

Bar: Full service
Wine selection: Modest but well-chosen
　for the food; many by-the-glass selec-
　tions
Dress: Casual
Disabled access: Full
Customers: Uptowners; gourmets; daters

Brunch: Sunday, 11 a.m.–3 p.m.

Lunch: Monday–Friday, 11:30 a.m.–2:30 p.m.

Dinner: Sunday–Thursday, 6–10 p.m.; Friday–Saturday, 6–11 p.m.

Setting & atmosphere: In the center of the stucco-and-rough-wood dining room is a station where cooks prepare flour tortillas from scratch; these taste and smell wonderful.

Recommended dishes: Chips and five different salsas; seafood and chicken taquitos; venison black-bean chili; Southwestern Caesar salad; corn-fried rock shrimp salad; cheese or chicken enchiladas; Santa Fe salmon cakes; duck tamales; Southwestern grilled pizza; chicken al carbon with red mole; fajitas; taco galeta (fruit-filled); flan.

Summary & comments: The most ambitious, widest-ranging, and best Southwestern restaurant in these parts, Vaqueros takes a gourmet-restaurant approach to a cuisine that can take full advantage of it. The menu blends classical Mexican dishes with those of the American Southwest in imaginative ways. Game, seafood, and other first-class edibles are rendered with excitement and abetted by deftly made sauces. The consistency record is not perfect, but that cuts both ways: when the kitchen is on, you will eat some unbelievably great food.

VEGA TAPAS CAFE ★★★

Spanish	Moderate	QUALITY
		87
2051 Metairie Road; 836-2007		VALUE
Metairie below Causeway　Zone 9		B

Reservations: Accepted
When to go: Anytime
Entree range: $5–12
Payment: All major credit cards
Service rating: ★★★
Friendliness rating: ★★★★
Parking: Small parking lot adjacent

Bar: Full service
Wine selection: Modest list matched to the food
Dress: Casual
Disabled access: Full
Customers: Younger, more adventure-some gourmets

Dinner: Monday–Saturday, 6–10 p.m.

Setting & atmosphere: One long room is broken up by waiter stations into semi-discrete areas. The lights are dim and the environment seems perfect for a first date.

Recommended dishes: Tuna carpaccio; hummus and eggplant salad; marinated mussels; carp roe dip; peppered steak and couscous; seared scallops; sweetbreads with crimini mushrooms; fried calamari with mustard; grilled lamb chops; sautéed rabbit with peppercorn sauce; braised lamb shank.

Summary & comments: Allison Vega cheffed a number of with-it cafes around town before opening her own place. Although it's billed as a tapas restaurant, Vega's offerings are more substantial than the traditional Spanish one-or-two-bite dishes. Almost everything is the size of a large appetizer or small entree. Still, you'll need three at least to make a meal. There's a fascinating variety of flavors, textures, and ingredients. The menu changes often enough to make this a fun place to explore with some frequency. All the food is fresh, imaginative, and well turned out.

VINCENT'S ★★★

Creole Italian	Moderate	QUALITY 87
		VALUE B

7839 St. Charles Avenue; 866-9313
Uptown above Napoleon   Zone 4

4411 Chastant Street; 885-2984
Metairie above Causeway/Kenner/Jefferson   Zone 10

Reservations: Not accepted
When to go: Anytime
Entree range: $9–19
Payment: All major credit cards
Service rating: ★★
Friendliness rating: ★★★★
Parking: Curbside

Bar: Full service
Wine selection: A few house wines
Dress: Casual
Disabled access: Limited
Customers: Neighborhood residents; college students

Lunch: Uptown, Tuesday–Friday, 11:30 a.m.–2:30 p.m; Metairie, Monday–Friday, 11:30 a.m.–2 p.m.

Dinner: Uptown, Tuesday–Sunday, 6–10 p.m.; Metairie, Monday–Saturday, 6–10 p.m.

Setting & atmosphere: Both Vincent's locations are very casual neighborhood cafes; the Uptown spot was one of those for decades before Vincent took it over. Furnishings are utilitarian.

Recommended dishes: Eggplant sandwich; artichoke Vincent (with crawfish and shrimp); veal meatballs on garlic toast; corn and crab bisque en croûte; veal cannelloni in a crepe; soft-shell crab with tomato-garlic sauce; panneed fish in crab cream sauce; garlic chicken; braciolone; veal Florentine; osso buco; tiramisu; chocolate mousse cake; torroncino ice cream.

Summary & comments: Vincent Catalanotto, a former waiter, discovered he could cook as well as any of the chefs who shouted at him. So he opened this unpretentious side-street cafe and started cooking some of the most impressive food ever sold at prices this low. The style is Creole-Italian, with enough polish that it could be sold in a much more expensive restaurant. Seafood is especially fine, sauced with terrific and original sauces. Salad, vegetable, and dessert courses are less impressive, but hardly grounds for complaint. The service staff is chummy. Problem: getting a table, particularly on weekends, is a tough deal. If you're in the mood for a raunchy but funny joke, ask for Vincent.

WOLFE'S OF NEW ORLEANS ★★★★

Contemporary Creole	Expensive	QUALITY
		88

7224 Pontchartrain Boulevard; 284-6004	VALUE
Lakeview/West End/Bucktown Zone 7	B

Reservations: Recommended	Wine selection: Decent, with emphasis on California; many by-the-glass selections
When to go: Dinner	
Entree range: $16–28	
Payment: AE, MC, V	Dress: Casual
Service rating: ★★★	Disabled access: None
Friendliness rating: ★★★★	Customers: Couples and foursomes of gourmets
Parking: Free lot adjacent	
Bar: Full service	

Lunch: Thursday–Friday, 11:30 a.m.–2:30 p.m.

Dinner: Monday–Saturday, 6–10 p.m.

Setting & atmosphere: The restaurant is an appealing cottage near the West End Marina. The room was opened up, painted in lighter tones, and furnished with handsome contemporary tables and chairs—very comfortable.

Recommended dishes: Gumbo of the day; shrimp-and-celery root rémoulade; crab cakes; baked oysters three ways; sweet-potato crusted duck sausage with foie gras; filet mignon with three-potato gratin; cane syrup roast duck; panco-crusted redfish; lamb or pork chops; white chocolate butter bars.

Summary & comments: Chef Tom Wolfe became well known at Emeril's, where he cooked many a meal for that restaurant's patrons at the food bar. In 2000 he took over the former Midnight Star, brightened it, and started cooking. His style shows the Emeril influence, with big Louisiana flavors served in original ways. Some of the dishes are avant-garde; others are modern reworkings of some funky old stuff. All very deftly prepared, generously served, and priced attractively. Service is also more careful than one ordinarily finds in Creole bistros.

Index

Shopping, 207–19
  French Quarter, 208–12
  Magazine Street, 212–15
  Malls of the Americas, 216–18
  tax-free, 208
  Warehouse District, 215–16
Shrimp, season for, 289
Shrine of St. Jude, 271
Shuttles, to/from airport, 136
Sightseeing. *See also* Tours
  guided, 221–27
  self-guided, 228–47
Slave population, history of, 31–32
Smoking regulations, 57
Soccer, 205, 206
Southern Repertory Theater, 158–59
Southern Runner Productions, 203
Spanish influence, 28–29
Special events calendar, 57–61
Sports
  spectator, 206
  at Superdome, 57, 159, 206, 268–69
Spring Fiesta, 58
Stables, 205
Stamps, collectible, shopping for, 210
State Palace Theater, 158
Steak, restaurants for, 297
Steamboat cruises, 226–27
Storyland Amusement Park, 281
Streetcars, 154–56, 221–22
Strip establishments, 145, 160
Sugar Bowl, 44, 57, 206
Super Bowl, 44, 57, 206
Superdome, 57, 206, 268–69
  music at, 159
Swamp Festival, 61
Swamp tours, 225–26
Swimming, 205
Symphonic music, 158

Tad Gormley Stadium, 203
Taxes
  on lodging, 82
  sales, 208
Taxis, 156
  to/from airport, 136
  crime in, 149
  queues for, 149
  tipping for, 145
Telephones, at airport, 135
Temperatures, seasonal, 45–46
Tennessee Williams New Orleans
    Literary Festival, 45, 59
Tennis, 204
Tezcuco Plantation, 248–49

Theater, 158–59
  for children, 55
Thierry House, 238
Third Street, walking tour of, 241–43
Thirteen Sisters, 245
Tickets. *See also specific attractions*
  bus, 156
  festivals, 57
  Mardi Gras seats, 67
  Memnoch Ball, 75
  museum, 221
  New Orleans Jazz and Heritage
      Festival, 74
  parking, 148
  spectator sports, 206
  train, 138
Tipping, 145
Toby's Corner, 241
Tomato festival, 60
Toole, John Kennedy, 42
Top of the Mart, 247
Tours
  antique shopping, 213
  bus, 221–22
  carriage, 222
  cemetery, 223–25, 230–31
  for children, 55
  church, 225, 230–31
  cultural, 229–30
  French Quarter, 232–40
  Garden District, 240–44
  guided, 221–27
  haunted places, 223–25
  historical, 229–30
  Mardi Gras-related, 228–29
  music-related, 228–29
  nature, 225–26
  plantation, 247–50
  river cruises, 226–27
  self-guided, 228–47
  special interest, 222–25
  swamp, 225–26
  taxi, 156
  trolley, 221–22
  walking. *See* Walking tours
  Warehouse/Arts District, 244–47
Tours by Isabelle, 222, 247
Toy-train museums, 285
Train, arrival by, 138
Transportation
  to/from airport, 136–37
  crime in, 149
  public, 154–56
  to/from Morial Convention Center,
      128–29

If you would like to express your opinion about New Orleans or this guidebook, complete the following survey and mail it to:

> *Unofficial Guide* Reader Survey
> P.O. Box 43673
> Birmingham, AL 35243

Inclusive dates of your visit: _____

Members of your party:

	Person 1	Person 2	Person 3	Person 4	Person 5
Gender:	M F	M F	M F	M F	M F
Age:					

How many times have you been to New Orleans? _____
On your most recent trip, where did you stay? _____

Concerning your accommodations, on a scale of 100 as best and 0 as worst, how would you rate:

The quality of your room? _____ The value of your room? _____
The quietness of your room? _____ Check-in/check-out efficiency? _____
Shuttle service to the parks? _____ Swimming pool facilities? _____

Did you rent a car? _____ From whom? _____

Concerning your rental car, on a scale of 100 as best and 0 as worst, how would you rate:

Pick-up processing efficiency? _____ Return processing efficiency? _____
Condition of the car? _____ Cleanliness of the car? _____
Airport shuttle efficiency? _____

Concerning your dining experiences:

Including fast-food, estimate your meals in restaurants per day? _____
Approximately how much did your party spend on meals per day? _____
Favorite restaurants in New Orleans: _____

_____

Did you buy this guide before leaving? ☐ while on your trip? ☐

How did you hear about this guide? (check all that apply)

Loaned or recommended by a friend ☐ Radio or TV ☐
Newspaper or magazine ☐ Bookstore salesperson ☐
Just picked it out on my own ☐ Library ☐
Internet ☐

What other guidebooks did you use on this trip? _____

_____

_____

_____

On a scale of 100 as best and 0 as worst, how would you rate them?

_____

_____

_____

Using the same scale, how would you rate *The Unofficial Guide(s)?*

_____

Are *Unofficial Guides* readily available at bookstores in your area? _____

Have you used other *Unofficial Guides?* _____

Which one(s)? _____

_____

_____

_____

_____

Comments about your New Orleans trip or *The Unofficial Guide(s):*

_____

_____

_____

_____

_____

_____

_____

_____

_____

_____

_____